CROSS-CULTURAL LITERACY

STUDIES IN EDUCATION AND CULTURE
(VOL. 3)

GARLAND REFERENCE LIBRARY
OF SOCIAL SCIENCE
(VOL. 566)

Studies in Education and Culture
David M. Fetterman, General Editor

CROSS-CULTURAL LITERACY
Ethnographies of Communication in Multiethnic Classrooms

Marietta Saravia-Shore and
Steven F. Arvizu
Editors

GARLAND PUBLISHING, INC. • NEW YORK & LONDON
1992

Library of Congress Cataloging-in-Publication Data

Saravia-Shore, Marietta.
   Cross-cultural literacy : ethnographies of communication in
multiethnic classrooms / Marietta Saravia-Shore and Steven F.
Arvizu.
      p.   cm. — (Garland reference library of social science ; vol.
566. Studies in education and culture ; vol. 3)
      Includes bibliographical references (p.   ) and index.
      ISBN 0-8240-4293-X (alk. paper) ; ISBN 0-8153-0465-X
(alk. paper, pbk.)
      1. Intercultural education—United States. 2. Intercultural
communication—United States, 3. Education, Bilingual—United
States. 4. Educational anthropology—United States. I. Arvizu,
Steven F., 1941– . II. Title. III. Series: Garland reference
library of social science ; v. 566. IV. Series: Garland reference
library of social science. Studies in education and culture ; vol.
3.
LC1009.3.S37   1992
370.19'341—dc20   91-11781
                                                          CIP

Printed on acid-free, 250-year-life paper
Manufactured in the United States of America

SERIES EDITOR'S FOREWORD

This series of scholarly texts, monographs, and reference works is designed to illuminate and expand our understanding of education. The educational activity each volume examines may be formal or informal. It may function in an exotic and distant culture or right here in our own backyard. In each book, education is at once a reflection and a creator of culture.

One of the most important motifs sounding through the series is the authors' efforts to shed light on educational systems from the insider's viewpoint. The various works are typically grounded in a phenomenological conceptual framework. However, they will vary in their manifestation of this common bond. Some authors explicitly adopt anthropological methods and a cultural interpretation of events and circumstances observed in the field. Others adopt a more generic qualitative approach—mixing methods and methodologies. A few adhere to a traditional phenomenological philosophical orientation.

These books are windows into other lives and other cultures. As we view another culture, we see ourselves more clearly. As we view ourselves, we make the familiar strange and see our own distorted images all the more clearly. We hope this immersion and self-reflection will enhance compassion and understanding at home and abroad. An expression of a common human spirit, this series celebrates our diversity.

David M. Fetterman
Stanford University and Sierra Nevada College

CONTENTS

Community Contexts

PREFACE

Marietta Saravia-Shore and Steven F. Arvizu

This book advocates and demonstrates the benefits of an anthropological approach that recognizes the centrality of culture in the educational process. This approach, which we are calling cross-cultural literacy, extends beyond "cultural literacy"—the knowledge and understanding of one's national culture—to encompass knowledge and understanding of other cultures' patterns of interaction, values, institutions, metaphors and symbols as well as cross-cultural communication skills. Cross-cultural literacy enables meaningful communication across cultures within this nation as well as among nations. Cross-cultural literacy thus encompasses one of the national goals agreed to by a consensus of the President and Governors at the historic education summit meeting in 1989: "All students will be knowledgeable about the diverse cultural heritages of this nation and about the world community." [1]

The ethnographic studies of multiethnic classrooms and schools in their community context that make up this volume demonstrate the heuristic value of ethnography (the science and art of cultural description). These studies by sixteen ethnographers were carefully selected from research that spans the past decade and were revised for this volume.

Initially this book was developed to inform practice and policy concerning the education of language minority students and their teachers. Gradually, however, cross-cultural communication is being recognized as necessary for all teachers, as school systems in the United States seek to educate culturally diverse groups of students, including recent immigrants, and prepare all students for a future in which increased international interdependence, trade, and communication will involve greater interaction among people of different cultures.

Today, programs such as foreign language education, bilingual education, and English as a second language which have tended to emphasize language and overlook the cross-cultural, interactional aspects of communicative competence are changing. There is a new interest in a "curriculum of inclusion" to increase student understanding of "the history and culture of the diverse groups that comprise American society today and the history and culture of other peoples throughout the world."[2] Concurrently, global and international education, which have emphasized knowledge about areas of the world through their history, geography, and ecology with minimal attention to cross-cultural communication, are also changing.[3] Spurred by the work of Hall (1959, 1966, 1976), Geertz (1973), and Lakoff and Johnson (1980), and with the goal of contributing to such change, the ethnographies in this volume illustrate the significance of both verbal and non-verbal communication in the classroom.

Approaches to the understanding of different cultural groups have been drawn primarily from the discipline of anthropology. Further perspectives on the development of cross-cultural skills have evolved as members of the ethnolinguistic minority groups traditionally studied by anthropolologists have themselves become anthropologists and contributed to this work. After listening to the voices of various cultural groups within these ethnographies, the reader can come to a comparative perspective on the social and cultural realities of multiethnic classrooms.

This volume is representative of a growing tradition: the application of qualitative inquiry to understanding the educational process. The book was written during a period when the field of educational anthropology interacted with increased frequency with educational reform movements, such as bilingual education. Some of the research studies were first presented at an American Anthropological Association annual meeting in a Council on Anthropology and Education symposium, "Policy Implications of Ethnographic Research in Bilingual Education," organized by Saravia-Shore in December 1980. They are complemented by a selection of related papers from a symposium organized by Arvizu on "Micro and Macro Ethnographic Approaches" for the American Educational Research Association's annual meeting of April 1981. Subsequently, papers relevant to the continuing interest in the theme of the book were selected.

The intended audience for the book is diverse: teachers and potential teachers; administrators and those who influence educational policy, curriculum and staff development, such as members of school boards, school district superintendents, state educational agency staffs and legislators; those concerned with diversity and pluralism, as well as bilingual, cross-cultural, foreign language, and global education; researchers and those students of anthropology and the social sciences interested in applying ethnography to understanding culture and learning in educational settings; and parents interested in humanizing education and seeking educational equity and excellence.

The preparation of this volume was made possible by a grant from the Ford Foundation for the Dissemination of Research and Evaluations of Bilingual Education co-directed by Arvizu and Saravia-Shore. The grant was made to the Council on Anthropology and Education and the Cross Cultural Resource Center at California State University, Sacramento. The editors would like to extend warmest thanks to Marjorie Martus for her interest and her support of the Ford Foundation project.

During the Presidency of George Spindler, the Executive Board of the Council on Anthropology and Education (CAE) endorsed a recommendation by Dr. Spindler and Dr. Courtney Cazden, past President of the CAE, to sponsor this volume as a publication of the Council on Anthropology and Education. Their endorsement has been affirmed by the current CAE President, Dr. David Fetterman. Members of the CAE have historically been concerned with culture and learning, as evidenced by their sponsorship of symposia, by their publications in the *CAE Quarterly*, and by resolutions that they have passed over the past decade, which are included in the first chapter.

Endnotes

1. National Education Goals from the National Governors' Association, February 25, 1990.
2. Thomas Sobol, New York State Commissioner of Education, memo of February 22, 1990 re "A Curriculum of Inclusion." New York State Education Department, Albany, New York.
3. Association for Supervision and Curriculum Development, 1990, *Global Education: From Thought to Action*, The 1991 ASCD Yearbook edited by Kenneth Tye.

References

Geertz, Clifford
　　1973　The Interpretation of Cultures. New York: Basic Books.
Hall, Edward T.
　　1959　The Silent Language. Garden City, New York: Doubleday.
　　1966　The Hidden Dimension. Garden City: Doubleday.
　　1976　Beyond Culture. Garden City: Anchor Press.
Lakoff, George, and Mark Johnson.
　　1980　Metaphors We Live By. Chicago: University of Chicago Press.

Cross-Cultural Literacy: An Anthropological Approach to Dealing with Diversity

*Marietta Saravia-Shore and
Steven F. Arvizu*[1]

This chapter introduces and defines terms significant to an anthropological approach to cross-cultural literacy while advocating ethnography as a principal means to understand and interpret educational issues. A framework is provided for the ethnographies introduced below, so that the reader can move from specific studies to general discussions of educational reform. The chapter also discusses critical issues of current educational policy and future applications, such as shifting the dialogue in U.S. education from a focus on "cultural literacy" to cross-cultural literacy.

Definitions

Diversity is a term that has many meanings depending on one's background, experience, concerns, and conceptual framework. In the context of this chapter diversity means recognition of the variation among people related to their cultural heritages, racial and ethnic identities, and gender and class experiences. Diversity then becomes a key concept that organizes our discussion of all that separates and bonds us as people. We advocate a comparative and holistic view: that diversity be grounded in understanding human differences as well as universals, and that such an understanding be translated into behavior which supports respect for and among people and their many forms of

interacting. We suggest that an anthropological approach
has general value and applicability to an accurate analysis
of current educational problems and interpretations of the
social realities of multiethnic classrooms. Having been
educated within the discipline of anthropology at Columbia
and Stanford, two universities with long traditions in
anthropology and established programs of Anthropology
and Education, the co-editors emphasize that culture is
"part of the dynamics of all teaching/learning situations."
Therefore, we propose that cross-cultural literacy, an
anthropological approach to dealing with diversity, be more
widely applied in schools and teacher education for the
analysis of educational issues and the design of more
responsive and humane educational futures. We argue that
a more pluralistic cultural strategy will improve our ability
to adapt and relate to one another in a respectful and
fulfilling manner.

Anthropology has long been recognized as the science
of the study of peoples and cultures. The more common
branches of anthropology have explored human diversity
throughout the world and through time. These branches
include archaeology, physical anthropology, cultural
anthropology, and linguistics. In the discovery and
application of many sources of knowledge, anthropology
has systematically compared and explained the differences
and commonalities among people in cultural groups. In
addition, as anthropologists have applied their tools to
problem solving, fields of study have emerged that represent
major bodies of literature and activity around which
anthropologists struggle to improve the human condition.
Among the fields of cultural and applied anthropology are
medical anthropology, psychological anthropology, symbolic
anthropology, political anthropology, and educational
anthropology. The thread that binds all students of
anthropology together in their study and applications is
a commitment to an anthropological approach which
includes the following characteristics:

1. a mode of inquiry for an understanding of
   culture and an explanation of the underlying
   cultural dynamics of human action and
   interaction;

2. a comparative perspective that enables the investigator to understand one group in the context of the total universe of human groups;
3. a holistic orientation that studies a particular phenomenon by placing it in its total context so that interconnected influences and behaviors are more completely understood;
4. the use of the notion of cultural relativity as a means of understanding, rather than prejudging, a group;
5. a propensity for long-term and continuing contact with the people studied, requiring ethnographic fieldwork. The hallmark of anthropology is ethnography, cultural description and analysis.

To explore what cross-cultural literacy entails we turn to the resolutions of the Council on Anthropology and Education (CAE) of the American Anthropological Association. They are succinct summaries of anthropologists' suggestions to educators concerning the significance of becoming aware of and taking into account their own cultural expectations, perspective, and interaction patterns and those of their students. The resolutions also state clearly the editors' approach and concern for respecting and attending to cultural and linguistic differences in educating students of diverse ethnolinguistic backgrounds and ensuring that members of the community participate in decision-making concerning the education of their children.

One of the resolutions provides an "operational definition" of culture and a cross-cultural approach to education and therefore is presented first. The resolution, developed by Dr. Steven Arvizu and Dr. Margaret Gibson, co-chairs of the Joint CAE/Society for Applied Anthropology Policy Committee on Culture and Bilingual Education, was passed by the Council on Anthropology and Education at the annual meeting of the American Anthropological Association in 1978 and thus reflects the consensus of that body of anthropologists.

Resolution for Action on Culture

Be It Resolved:

That the Council on Anthropology and Education, as a professional association, acknowledge that:

1. Culture is intimately related to language and the development of basic communication, computation and social skills,

2. Culture is an important part of the dynamics of the teaching-learning process in all classrooms, both bilingual and monolingual,

3. Culture affects the organization of learning and pedagogical practice, evaluative procedures and rules of schools, as well as instructional activities and curriculum,

4. Attention to the cultural dimensions of education has widespread potential utility in resolving performance dysfunctions and interpersonal and group conflicts in schools and society,

5. Culture is more than the heritage of a people through dance, food, holidays, and history. Culture is more than a component of bilingual education programs. It is a dynamic, creative, and continuous process that includes behaviors, values, and substance shared by people that guides them in their struggle for survival and gives meaning to their lives. As a vital process it needs to be understood by more people in the United States, a multiple society which has many interacting cultural groups,

6. Public institutions, such as schools, should facilitate the cross-cultural learning of their clients as basic tools for effective citizenry, and economic, political and psychological existence,

7. It is the responsibility of all educational agencies—federal, state and local—to give attention to culture in their programs,

8. All those involved in the educational process—policy makers, program officials,

school personnel, and students—are cultural beings, both products of and producers of culture, influenced in decision making by their cultural background and orientation. Therefore, it is imperative that all personnel responsible for educational decisions be conscious of the cultural factors which shape their actions and also, that they analyze the social/cultural impact of their actions with regard to the realization of quality education and equity of educational opportunity for all students.

Los Angeles   December 1978

CAE concern for cross-cultural education can be traced back to an earlier resolution which was initiated in 1974 by the Council on Anthropology and Education's Committee on Spanish Speaking Concerns, chaired by Dr. Arvizu. The Committee was comprised of bilingual educators from the United States, as well as from indigenous communities in Latin America. After intense debate, CAE members wholeheartedly supported the resolution below at the annual business meeting held in affiliation with the American Anthropological Association.

Mexico City Resolution

1. Whereas, anthropology as a discipline supports the notion of respect for cultural differences, and
2. Whereas, it has been acknowledged and established through symposia sponsored by the Council on Anthropology and Education at the 1974 annual meeting that bilingualism and biculturalism are worldwide phenomena, and
3. Whereas, a number of participants in sessions at this meeting, voicing concerns of their respective communities, have identified the following principles as essential to resolving contemporary problems involving bilingual-bicultural education:

Therefore, be it resolved that the CAE go on record supporting the following resolutions:

1. That every individual has the right to education and the right to receive services in his native language;

2. That the programs developed in education, health and social services in bilingual-bicultural situations be carried forward with the due respect, knowledge, and understanding, not only of the culture of the larger society, but also of the culture and language of the local community;

3. That the community being served participate in the planning, decision-making, implementation and evaluation of bilingual-bicultural programs and services and that the individuals and/or organizations charged with their implementation be accountable to that community.

        Mexico City   December 1974

The cross-cultural aproach, which is the foundation for cross-cultural literacy, was defined further in 1981, when the CAE approved another resolution submitted by the Joint CAE/Society for Applied Anthropology Committee on Culture and Bilingual Education. That resolution, excerpted below, was drafted by the co-editors of this volume and thus makes explicit the approach and assumptions within which this book was developed.

Cross-Cultural Approach Resolution

Whereas legislation presently includes references to "use of cultural and community resources" and "understanding and using the cultural background of the student,"
Therefore, be it resolved that the Council on Anthropology and Education of the American Anthropological Association go on record to support the use of a cross-cultural approach in addressing the concept of culture in the re-

authorization legislation. [for Title VII, ESEA, the Bilingual Education Act]

The cross-cultural approach has the following key components:

1. teaching American culture to assist newcomers to learn about and integrate into U.S. life;

2. facilitating the teaching/learning process by recognizing and integrating the cultural background of the student in programs that are linguistically and culturally compatible and enriching;

3. teaching about the multiple cultural communities within the American cultural heritage to stimulate understanding and social cohesiveness within and between groups;

4. linking school staff with culturally and linguistically different parents as mutual resources for cultural expectations and patterns of behavior;

5. preparing students for the future with communicative and cross-cultural competencies necessary for an ecologically and economically interdependent world.

Los Angeles   December 1981

The approach to education outlined above develops cross-cultural literacy. In school settings, cross-cultural literacy means that staff and students learn to see people, problems, issues, and solutions from various cultural orientations; to respect the human rights and ways of life of individuals and groups, and to interact meaningfully with people of different cultures. For example, a cross-cultural approach can facilitate the acquisition of knowledge about American culture by newly arrived refugee families and assistance in adapting their cultural heritage to new environments. Cross-cultural literacy is essential in moving from reactive to proactive behavior.

In viewing schools and communities as major arenas for cultural transmission and interaction, it is important to maintain a balance between the positive aspects of pride in, understanding of, and respect for one's own way of life and an understanding and respect for the way of life of others. A cross-cultural perspective transcends cultural nationalism—commitment to the interests and independence of one cultural group above others—or biculturalism, which is a commitment to or proficiency in two cultural systems or groups. A cross-cultural approach is also more specific than multiculturalism—commitment to or proficiency in many cultural systems or groups— since it is grounded in an anthropological approach.

An anthropological, cross-cultural approach treats phenomena in their cultural context(s) in a systematic, holistic manner. An event or behavior makes sense when it can be seen in relation to its larger cultural context. A cross-cultural approach provides teachers with methods and tools to learn cultural competencies such as becoming aware of, observing, eliciting, and understanding the values and expectations of parents and students, as well as the resulting culturally-based patterns of interaction between adults and children or among children, termed participant structures. These culturally expected modes of interaction can be discovered by teachers using such ethnographic methods as participant observation, that is, systematic observation while participating in a situation, or through discussion with members of the home culture of the student. Once identified and understood, these culturally compatible participant structures can be integrated into the educational setting to facilitate students' learning, as exemplified in Jordan's chapter concerning Hawaiian students. Students socialized to expect cooperative interaction in their home can benefit from learning organized in groups for collaborative inquiry and problem solving in math, writing for one another in pairs at a computer, or doing cross-age tutoring.

Integration of students' cultural patterns into classroom life conveys knowledge of alternatives within American culture and thus broadens every student's repertoire of available approaches to problem identification and problem solving. Such an approach also increases students' ability to cope with change and to interact with others. These skills of cross-cultural literacy are needed by all students in our changing world.

Further, teachers who learn to use a cross-cultural approach provide supportive learning environments for ethnolinguistic minority group students as well as majority group students. By recognizing the skills which students bring with them from their homes as a foundation upon which to build, teachers can enhance each student's sense of security, self-respect, and belonging. Teacher behavior that demonstrates respect for the value systems of parents from diverse cultures also avoids the alienation between generations which resulted from earlier patterns of immigrant education. That education emphasized assimilation at any cost, including the loss of native language, cultural heritage, and family ties.

By contrast, education within a multilingual, cross-cultural framework develops the language skills of ethnolinguistic minority students in their cultural context, thus promoting intergenerational communication and respect for parents and grandparents as people and cultural resources. Rather than suffering language loss, students develop literacy in two languages and cross-cultural skills, thus realizing the long-term goals of bilingualism and cross-cultural literacy. Several of the ethnographic studies in this volume (Jordan et al., Moll et al., Carrasco et al.) provide case studies of the cross-cultural approach in action, documenting the facilitation of learning that results when this approach is competently implemented.

Finally, ethnography, the science and art of cultural description, analysis, and interpretation, has been practiced in many forms. Traditionallly, ethnographies have required extensive, comprehensive, long-term field work for the qualitative description and interpretation of total cultural communities to other peoples of the world. Some of the more common techniques used in ethnography are participant observation, in-depth interviews, network and event analysis, life history, and ethnographic filming. These methods are further discussed and illustrated in the book, particularly in chapters by Arvizu et al., Trueba and Wright, and Pung Guthrie.

The Need For and Benefits of Ethnography

Educational ethnography has emerged over the past several decades to depict and analyze the culture of schools, the social organization of classrooms, and the interrelationship between communities and schools. Ethnographic evaluation is a more specific form of ethnography that gathers data on the process of implementation and management of educational programs and makes assessments both of impact and of a formative nature to assist in educational decision making. The heuristic value of ethnographic evaluation of educational programs is discussed further in the chapter by Saravia-Shore.

Didactic ethnography represents the use of field work for informal learning by students as they explore new environments and groups of different backgrounds. In didactic ethnography, the goal is self-directed learning with the use of techniques for systematically observing and recording behavior during social events, group processes, rituals, ceremonies, and other diverse forms of human interaction. Didactic ethnography has great potential for assisting a student from one cultural background to learn about students and people of other cultural backgrounds through a safe and supervised form of discovery. Thus, it is a rich method for learning about the world in a general social studies curriculum and liberal arts sequence.

Ethnography can bring greater understanding to the sociocultural context of education through macro and micro-ethnographic studies such as those represented in this book. Macroethnography studies larger social systems and structures to provide the broader sociocultural, political, and economic context in which to view educational problems. Microethnography focuses more specifically on smaller, more particular units of analysis such as classroom interactions, student-to-student relationships, counselor-to-student "gatekeeping," or segments of learning acts, as in the work of McDermott (1976) and Mehan's (1979) *Learning Lessons*. The methodologies and some of the insights derived from various microethnographies of the classroom are discussed more fully in the chapter by Trueba and Wright.

The value of ethnographic research is increased by a number of significant factors. First, such research emphasizes particular description, recognizing diversity within education. While there are standards common to the conduct of ethnographic research, there is also considerable variety in approach, as illustrated by the examples in this volume. Second, ethnographic research, although labor intensive and difficult to do well, yields long-term qualitative analysis of crucial educational problems. Third, ethnography is the most appropriate strategy for research that needs to take into account the sociocultural processes and intergroup relations which provide a contextual background to understanding bilingual, cross-cultural education, the effective schools movement, racial, gender and national origin equity programs, and programs developing compatibility between schools and communities.

Spindler (1955, 1963, 1982, 1987) has for several decades advocated the use of ethnography to understand the process of cultural transmission in schools in relation to the community being served. Gumperz and Hymes (1964) challenged anthropologists to begin an "ethnography of communication" in order to develop sociocultural understanding of the social rules of language usage in different contexts and speech communities, such as the research reported in the chapters by Zentella and Volk. Fishman (1974) has emphasized that bilingual education could only be understood by going beyond language teaching per se to language use and learning in social contexts. Paulston (1977) stressed the role of a language's social status and of the socioeconomic status of the ethnolinguistic groups who are speakers of each language as crucial contextual factors to be considered in research on language and cultural maintenance and loss. Ogbu's (1974) classic ethnographic study clearly argued for understanding the community, societal, and structural contexts of education for minority student populations. Ferguson (1977) summarized the importance of sociocultural context by stating, "we must acknowledge that social, political, psychological, economic and other factors must surely outweigh the purely linguistic factors in any analysis of bilingual education." Cummins' (1987, 1988) analysis also pointed to the crucial role of the political context of bilingual education, and Saravia-Shore (1986) documented the unfolding of that political context in an ethnohistorical analysis of the implementation of federal programs for language minority students such as those funded under the Bilingual Education Act. There have been few ethnographic research studies that document the sociocultural and sociopolitical contexts of the implementation of bilingual programs. The chapters by Arvizu et al., Guskin, and Pung Guthrie in this volume make accessible a selection of studies which do address such contextual issues.

Why Cross-Cultural Literacy?

Cross-cultural literacy is a response to E.D. Hirsch's (1987) call for *Cultural Literacy*[2] Cross-cultural literacy extends cultural literacy, which, from an anthropological perspective is quite limited and misleading. Hirsch's conception of national cultural literacy has provoked interest and raised questions and concerns among educators, anthropologists, and the general public. The primary concern addressed here is the limited concept of culture, and of national culture with the omission of the historical contributions of the many ethnic communities in the United States.

Given the author's claim to use an anthropological perspective in his treatise, one expected to see those traditionally recognized characteristics of an anthropological approach, as discussed above, which include the notion of cultural relativity and the recognition that there are many worthwhile ways of life in our world, each to be respected in its own context and none, *ipso facto*, determined to be superior to the rest. However, reading *Cultural Literacy* left one feeling that anthropology had been selectively exploited. The concept of culture is treated simplistically as though it were a content list, a la "Trivial Pursuit."

True, language can symbolically store the knowledge of a culture and shape perception, values, and behavior, and transmission affects continuity or change for the people involved. Language, however, is only one mode of cultural transmission; patterns of interaction and visual symbol systems are equally significant. From socialization and enculturation studies all over the world, it is well established that formal schooling is only one mode of passing cultural information from one generation to another. Institutions such as the family and religion; the arts, museums, advertizing and the media transmit cultural knowledge, values, attitudes, and behavior.

Culture guides people in their thinking, feeling, and acting. It can be thought of as a roadmap in an evolving journey of survival or as a river bed that creates its own form and direction over time due to a variety of influences. As outlined in the definitions provided by the Council on Anthropology and Education resolutions cited earlier, culture comes closer to being an active verb (an evolving process) rather than a static noun (a thing).

Hirsch advocates one language and one tradition in our heritage to achieve a nation constituted of people who can communicate with one another. He oversimplifies when he advocates a "laundry list" of knowledge as a means to mold "a single, national culture," glossing over the multiple traditions of the indigenous peoples of America and its immigrant groups that have contributed to American culture.

A "cultural trait list" can never represent the dynamic, cumulative, and multi-dimensional way of life that is American culture for the diverse people of the United States. It would have been better to use the notion of American cultural heritages, taking into account changing conditions that shape our knowledge, values, and customs over time, rather than treating our society as monolithic, uniform, and fixed in our cultural character and traditions.

The content approach to cultural literacy is reminiscent of Linton's parody, "The One Hundred Per Cent

American," which anthropologists have seen as a humorous illustration of the obvious; that every culture is a synthesis of indigenous invention, building on previous cultures and borrowing from others. One can see parallels between Hirsch and a young Chicano Nationalist when he commented proudly, "Soy puro Mestizo" (I am a pure Mestizo—person of mixed heritages).

How could knowledge about the Eurocentric tradition of U.S. culture be adequate for those interested in our pluralistic heritage? A cross-culturally literate position would argue for more. It would be more appropriate to consider the American cultural heritage as a major river fed by many streams, recognizing changes within and among important traditions over time, in relationship to other traditions.

The United States consists of diverse peoples with varying reasons for being here and with different commitments to maintaining their own cultural traditions and languages as well as differential group access to resources to integrate into U.S. society. In more extreme cases, individual insecurity encourages ethnocentrism and prejudice among our population and individual frustration leads to hostility toward minorities. The basic institutions of our society, including the schools, need to provide clear guidance to our diverse populations so that we are able to communicate and interact with order, mutual respect, and understanding.

Cultural Literacy perpetuates a myth about conflict and unity in relationship to bilingualism and multiculturalism. The surface-level information and examples of conflict regarding other countries around the world are limited and misleading. There are struggles and conflicts throughout our globe, so careful, comparative study of other situations, historical and current, can be helpful in analysis for the future. However, most conflicts are a consequence of variables other than language and culture (apartheid in South Africa, class struggle in Latin America, and war in Northern Ireland and between Iraq and Kuwait) and there are specific examples in which bilingualism and multilingualism facilitate communication and intercultural understanding and bring about cooperation rather than conflict (Switzerland, the Pacific Rim, and parts of the United States). Those with multiple linguistic and cultural proficiencies have clear advantages in the international and domestic marketplace, in diplomatic relations, in strategic defense operations, and in cross-cultural mediation and problem solving.

In addition, a monolingual or monocultural view limits the recognition of the cultural-creating capacity of significant segments of our fellow citizens in our country and throughout the world. It is a misconception that some people create culture worthy of diffusion in our great country and that others do not. All people are capable of creating culture and, as a consequence of living in a democratic society, we are all able to interact and learn from one another. The questions are: What kind of a society and world do we want? What planning and enabling steps will get us there?

We cannot retreat to a one culture-specific knowledge base in a shrinking world with common ecological, medical and survival problems. The international role of the United States would not be served by a content-oriented curriculum that ignores the world economy, and political relationships with others throughout the globe and that has no vision of cross-national, cross-cultural and multilingual competencies.

The National Council for the Social Studies recognizes this in its definition of global education:

> Global education refers to efforts to cultivate in young people a perspective of the world which emphasizes the interconnections among cultures, species and the planet. The purpose of global education is to develop in youth the knowledge, skills, and attitudes needed to live effectively in a world possessing limited natural resources, ethnic diversity, and characterized by cultural pluralism, and increasing interdependence. (NCSS 1981).

Education is an arena where there is competition among ideas and constant search for knowledge. In developing a cross-cultural, global perspective in our curriculum, we know from ethnographic research and experience that we learn a great deal about what we take for granted in ourselves and our culture when we compare and contrast other cultures to our own. How can we build respect for a common culture in our nation without showing respect for the various peoples of our nation and respect for their heritages and inalienable rights? Our Constitution protects freedom of expression in any language and the pursuit of happiness as well as rights of privacy which include religious and cultural beliefs. One of the bases of our democratic character is that it encourages inquiry, respects minority views, and provides for dynamic change in governance: *E Pluribus Unum* (Out of many, one).

The numbers of diverse peoples in the United States will continue to grow, and they will expect some control over their cultural lives. Changing demographics imply the need for greater understanding of diversity in the United States. Will our future be one of enlightened self-interest in which we recognize that we are all in this together, or will it be one of power struggle and forced assimilation?

Can *Cultural Literacy* and its suggestions for reform be helpful in our consideration of alternative educational futures? Only if they are part of a larger context: cross-cultural literacy. To achieve cross-cultural literacy we must draw upon anthropological literature to broaden and deepen the conceptualizations of curriculum content, the study of schools in relation to communities, the design of staff development and curricula, and the evaluation of programs using ethnographic methods.

There is a need to develop more fully the equity dimension of the educational reform frameworks. This includes understanding diversity, consciously eliminating discrimination, adapting organizational environments, enriching learning environments, and providing mediation and conflict management.

More dialogue is necessary concerning programmatic, structural, and political issues related to educational reform, i.e., the quality and nature of teacher education and personnel development, adequate and equitable resource allocation, curricular innovations, relationships between schools and communities, and opportunity structures across class and ethnic boundaries.

Few anthropologists have been members of teacher education faculties; thus they have not had much influence on schools and schooling. Activities in the ethnic studies and bilingual movements have pioneered in developing innovative alternatives and curriculum approaches to develop cross-culturally literate teachers and students.

The Contributions of This Book

The broad range of competencies encompassed by cross-cultural literacy that are needed by teachers of language minority students are addressed in this book. These ethnographic studies show that proficiencies in the child's language as well as English, that is, communicative competencies, are necessary for such teachers, as are cross-cultural competencies. Several chapters (Carrasco, Jordan, Maldonado-Guzman) illustrate these cross-cultural competencies in the classroom, while Arvizu's chapter documents the necessity for teachers to communicate and interact with linguistically and culturally different parents in the community as well.

The first section of the book consists of ethnographic studies of Cross-Culturally Compatible Schooling. The second section is comprised of macroethnographic studies of the larger political, attitudinal and sociolinguistic Community Contexts of bilingual education programs, and interactions between schools and communities. The third is comprised of microethnographic studies of the joint construction of Classroom Contexts and concludes with a chapter on the implications of these ethnographic studies for policy, curriculum and classroom practice.

Cross-Culturally Compatible Schooling

Cathie Jordan et al.'s chapter illustrates the enhancement of learning that results when ethnographers and teachers learn and understand the cultural expectations and behavior patterns of the home and community, in this case among Hawaiians. Drawing on the work by Susan Philips (1972) with Warm Springs Indians, Jordan et al. applied Philips' concept of participant structures, the expectations and behavior during an interaction, in order to structure culturally appropriate situations, participant structures and patterns of social organization in the classroom for Hawaiian students.

The chapter by Vernay Mitchell is part of a nine-site comparative study of exemplary high schools. She has selected two schools that have high concentrations of African-American students and looked at the role of "fictive kinship" in the social organization of school success among the African-American students.

Bilingual, cross-culturally literate staff are able to work with minority students and parents to build links between school and home. Arvizu's chapter shows how bilingual staff, sensitive to the cultural expectations of parents, can interact in ways which encourage two-way communication, receiving messages from parents as well as giving them. Parents are informants about their cultural expectations; teachers, aware of ethnographic methods, can use them as tools for learning about their students' culture.

A Native American perspective on education is represented in a way that reflects one of their cultural norms: consensus. The chapter "Our Voices, Our Vision: American Indians Speak Out for Educational Excellence" is a departure from an ethnography, but is consonant with one of the purposes of ethnography: to reflect the ideas and worldview of a people in their own words. "Our Voices, Our Vision" embodies suggestions for the education of American Indian youth which resulted from dialogues held in seven regions of the United States by 150 American Indians from 87 tribes in the National Dialogue Project on American Indian Education. Their comprehensive suggestions look forward to future needs while treasuring the spiritual values of their heritage. Their practical suggestions for the incorporation of those traditional values and literature in students' reading materials support the heuristic value of parental and community involvement in determining educational policy.

Community Contexts

The next section of the book consists of macroethnographic studies that portray the dynamics of the community context of educational programs for language minority students. The chapter by Arvizu et al. presents the design and summarizes some of the findings of a two-site ethnographic study of bilingual programs in their community contexts. This Sociocultural Study of a Bilingual Community, an NIE-funded research project, is a comparative inquiry into the interrelationships between two bilingual education programs and the communities they serve in Parlier, California, and Milwaukee, Wisconsin, respectively. Guskin's chapter, a historical and ethnographic description of the neighborhood context of bilingual programs in Milwaukee, provides in greater detail one component of the larger research study. Pung Guthrie's chapter, summarizing her research on a bilingual program in a Chinese commmunity in California, is a vivid illustration of the ethnographic method as applied to the larger context in which a given bilingual classroom is embedded. The significance of hearing what students have to say about the home and school contexts of their schooling experience is demonstrated in the chapter by Saravia-Shore and Martinez, which summarizes and quotes the interviews of Puerto Rican students who dropped out and then returned to an alternative high school.

The importance of understanding language usage in the community is illustrated in two ethnographic studies, one by Zentella, the other by Pedraza and Pousada. The analysis of language use by Pedraza and Pousada is part of a larger research effort by the Centro de Estudios Puertorriquenos of the City University of New York. The larger study, conducted by Pedraza, Poplack, Attinasi, and Pousada (1983) that drew upon research by Labov (1970), and Gumperz and Hymes (1964, 1974), provides sociolinguistic analyses of language use in the school and in the community. Zentella's study documents the range of language usage of bilingual Puerto Ricans on one block in El Barrio.

Classroom Contexts

The third section of the book focuses on ethnographic studies of the development of contexts within specific classrooms with multiethnic students. Trueba and Wright review and assess the contributions of fifteen microethnographic studies, highlighting their rationale and methodology and summarizing some of the results of the research into education in multicultural settings.

The chapter by Luis Moll et al. follows the classroom studies by Mehan (1979), McDermott (1976, 1977), and Erickson (1977) of how contexts are jointly constructed. Moll et al. studied the social organization of two reading lessons, one in Spanish and the other in English, to observe the learning that occurred in the collaboratively constructed interchanges and activities of teachers and students in each language. Students demonstrated certain cognitive and communicative capacities in one language which they were not called upon to demonstrate in the other.

Further metalinguistic skills of bilingual youngsters are reported in Volk's chapter, in which she captured the sensitivity of four-year old bilingual students to sociolinguistic settings. They appropriately used each language with varying sets of fellow students whose language abilities differed.

Two other chapters, one by Pedraza and Pousada and the other by Saravia-Shore, explore the utility of ethnography in language assessment and in the evaluation of programs for language minority students. Saravia-Shore argues for the use of ethnographic methods to address the lack of process evaluation, which would ensure that an educational program's structure and the extent to which it has been implemented are ascertained before its outcomes are evaluated. Pedraza and Pousada's case study illustrates the usefulness of ethnographic techniques in documenting the discrepancies between the results of a standardized language assessment test used for placement and students' actual use of two languages in the different domains of home, street, and school.

The chapter by Carrasco et al. illustrates how Chicano and other Latino teachers facilitate learning with specific participant structures which are motivated by their own attitudes as well as the expectations of their Chicano students.

Maldonado-Guzman quotes teachers of language minority students extensively in his chapter and reflects on teacher differentiation of students and the significance of socioeconomic class and cultural experiences in forming teacher attitudes to standard and non-standard Spanish usage by their students.

In her ethnographic study of an alternative high school in New York City, Maria Torres-Guzman provides two examples of how the ethnographic/participatory research process can uncover teaching/learning situations that empower Latino students and their teachers. An alternative to the use of the text or teacher as the authority in the classroom was observed by the ethnographic team. The teacher organized the teaching/learning sequence so that students' experiences were elicited first and became the focus of discussion before going to the text, thus enabling the students to approach the text critically and relate their experiences to a broader context. Another learning experience, framed as a collective investigation of a community problem, provided opportunities for students to learn science as well as how the political system worked and how they could gain access to being heard and, as an informed group, make a difference. As in the first chapter by Jordan et al., students are empowered by being allowed to participate in negotiating with their peers the development of the learning environment.

The ethnographers who contributed to the volume all share the assumption that cultural and social contexts shape the teaching/learning process and home/school relationships. These applied researchers are exploring innovative features of experimental educational programs for the purpose of more broadly impacting educational practices in a wide variety of settings.

Endnotes

1. Dr. Marietta Saravia-Shore is Director of the Cross-Cultural Literacy Center, Institute for Urban and Minority Education, Teachers College, Columbia University, New York City. Dr. Steven F. Arvizu is Dean of Graduate Studies and Research, California State University, Bakersfield, and a scholar of the Tomas Rivera Center, a national institute for policy studies, Claremont, California.

2. The comments in this section are excerpted from "Cultural Literacy: Yours, Mine or Ours?" by Dr. Steven Arvizu at the Annual Conference of the World Affairs Council at Boulder Colorado, in April 1988, from a panel that debated E.D. Hirsch's notion of cultural literacy.

References

Cummins, Jim
    1987   Bilingual Education and Politics. The Education Digest N. Ann Arbor. 53:30–33.

Cummins, J., and Tove Skutnabb-Kangas, eds.
    1988   Minority Education: From Shame to Struggle. Clevedon: Multilingual Matters, Ltd.

Erickson, Frederick
    1977   Some Approaches to Inquiry in School-Community Ethnography. Anthropology and Education Quarterly 8(2).

Ferguson, Charles A.
    1977   Linguistic Theory *In* Bilingual Education: Current Perspectives/Linguistics. Arlington: Center for Applied Linguistics.

Fishman, Joshua A.
    1974   A Sociology of Bilingual Education. Final Report of Research under contract OECO-73-0538, Division of Foreign Studies, Department of HEW, USOE.

Gumperz, John J., and Dell Hymes, eds.
    1972   Directions in Sociolinguistics: The Ethnography of Communication. New York: Holt, Rinehart and Winston.

Hymes, Dell
  1974   Foundations in Sociolinguistics. Philadelphia:
          University of Pennsylvania Press.
Hirsch, E.D., Jr.
  1987   Cultural Literacy: What Every American Needs to
          Know. New York: Vintage Books.
Labov, William
  1970   The Place of Linguistic Research in American Society.
          In Linguistics in the 1970's. Pp. 41–70. Washington,
          D.C.: LSA and Center for Applied Linguistics.
McDermott, Raymond Patrick
  1976   Kids Make Sense: An Ethnographic Account of the
          Interactional Management of Success and Failure in
          One First Grade Classroom. Unpublished doctoral
          dissertation. Stanford University.
McDermott, R.T., and Lois Hood
  1982   Institutionalized Psychology and the Ethnography of
          Schooling. *In* Children In and Out of School. Perry
          Gilmore and Alan Glatthorn, eds. Pp. 232–249.
          Washington, D.C.: Center For Applied Linguistics.
Mehan, Hugh
  1979   Learning Lessons. Cambridge: Harvard University
          Press.
National Council for the Social Studies
  1981   Global Education. NCSS Position Statement.
          Washington, D.C.: National Council for the Social
          Studies.
Ogbu, John
  1974   The Next Generation: An Ethnography of Education
          in an Urban Neighborhood. New York: Academic
          Press.
Paulston, Christina Bratt
  1975   Ethnic Relations and Bilingual Education: Accounting
          for Contradictory Data. *In* Travaux de Recherches
          sur le bilinguisme. Toronto: Ontario Institute for
          Studies in Education (6). May.
  1977   Theoretical Perspectives on Bilingual Education
          Programs. *In* Travaux de Recherches sur le
          bilinguisme. Toronto: Ontario Institute for Studies in
          Education. Pp. 131–170. May.
Pedraza, Pedro, Shana Poplack, John Attinasi, and Alicia Pousada
  1982   Intergenerational Perspectives on Bilingualism: From
          Community to Classroom. Final Report to the National
          Institute of Education. New York: Research

Foundation of the City University of New York, Language Policy Task Force.

Philips, Susan
1972   Participant Structures and Communicative Competence: Warm Springs Children in Community and Classroom. *In* Functions of Language in the Classroom. Courtney Cazden et al., eds. New York: Teachers College Press.

Saravia-Shore, Marietta
1986   National Origin Desegregation and Bilingual Education: The Inversion of Ideology and Practice. Unpublished doctoral dissertation. Columbia University.

Spindler, George Dearborn, ed.
1955   Education and Anthropology. Stanford: Stanford University Press.
1963   Education and Culture, Anthropological Approaches. New York: Holt, Rinehart and Winston.
1982   Doing the Ethnography of Schooling. Educational Anthropology in Action. New York: Holt, Rinehart and Winston.

Spindler, G.D., and Louise Spindler
1987   Interpretive Ethnography of Education: At Home and Abroad. Hillsdale, N.J.: L. Erlbaum Associates.

PART I

Cross-Culturally
Compatible Schooling

"Just Open the Door": Cultural Compatibility and Classroom Rapport

Cathie Jordan, Roland G. Tharp, Lynn Baird-Vogt[1]

Introduction

Effective bilingual education is, of necessity, cross-cultural education. Achieving effective cross-cultural education requires attention to issues of cultural form and process and to their translation into classroom practices compatible with both the culture of the children and the culture of the school. This chapter presents an instance in which this kind of mutually compatible translation took place in a classroom for children of Hawaiian ancestry and culture.

Most Hawaiian children speak a non-standard dialect of English known as Hawaiian Creole English or Hawaiian Islands Dialect. They enter school speaking Hawaiian Creole but understanding some Standard English, and they rapidly become more competent in Standard. Their teachers speak Standard English, but most also understand Hawaiian Creole. Classrooms are effectively bi-dialectal. Thus linguistic differences, narrowly defined, are minimal. Yet Hawaiian students still present a case of major academic underachievement; most Hawaiian children, especially those from low-income families have not been effectively educated in the State's public schools (Kamehameha Schools 1983; Thompson and Hannahs 1979).

What can be learned from this circumstance? While it is clearly necessary to attend to differences in linguistic code per se, the absence of dramatic differences does not ensure good academic achievement. It is vital also to attend to more subtle aspects of communicative interaction, both verbal and non-verbal. That is, one must attend to the overall culture of the children and to its interaction with the culture of the school. Doing so can yield positive results, as happened for Hawaiian children through the Kamehameha Elementary Education Program (KEEP) of the Center for Development of Early Education. KEEP is a privately funded educational research and development effort, the goals of which have been to discover and then to disseminate methods to better educate Hawaiian children in public school settings. In its laboratory school and in its field test and pilot export operations in the public schools, the program produced consistent national norm level achievement for primary grade, lower socioeconomic status Hawaiian children. For nineteen first- to third-grade classrooms with children from this population in which the Kamehameha Elementary Education Program was implemented by fully trained KEEP teachers from one to three years, combined mean scores on the Gates-McGinitie and Metropolitan tests of reading achievement were the fifty-third percentile for KEEP classes, and the thirty-second percentile for control classes. (For a more detailed report of program evaluation data on laboratory, field test, and pilot export classrooms, see Klein 1981; Jordan and Tharp 1984).

The traditional solution to minority academic underachievement has been to attempt to change the child or the home to conform to school expectations. KEEP has used a different strategy. It has attempted to modify the school context in ways that would enable it to elicit and build on those abilities which the children already possess and which they exhibit in non-school settings. Thus, KEEP has used features of Hawaiian culture as one guide in choosing the educational practices best suited to Hawaiian children (Jordan 1981; 1985). In the example of this process which follows, the mismatch between what takes place in traditional classrooms and what happens in the Hawaiian home settings was dramatic and easily observable.[2]

Hawaiian Children at Home

In school, Hawaiian children, especially those from low-income backgrounds, are often perceived as lazy, irresponsible, and unable to interact cooperatively with teachers or classmates. This is in sharp contrast to patterns that can be observed in the homes of the very same children. Hawaiian children, starting when they are very young, make major contributions to the work of their households. They take initiative, and they accept responsibility. The tasks for which they are responsible are not busy-work; they are the vital functions necessary to keep a large household running, such as laundry, housecleaning, cooking, yard work, car repair, caring for younger siblings, and, for adolescents, especially males, earning cash. Their contributions to the life of the household are made by working as part of a group of children, usually siblings. The members of the sibling group share responsibility and work cooperatively to complete the household work assigned to them. The same child will not necessarily always do exactly the same tasks, although for the group of children, the responsibilities are ongoing. The sibling group organizes its own work routines and operates with only indirect adult supervision. Often the oldest sibling or the oldest girl will act as a kind of teenage "top sergeant" of the group and oversee work organization and completion.

A small child first becomes involved in this working group of siblings as the charge of an older sibling, since the sibling group also provides a great deal of the child care. In a process of graduated participation, young children gradually increase their responsibility with age and competence. The two- or three-year-old may do some small pieces of a larger task, perhaps fetching diapers and powder while older sister diapers baby brother. By the time she is eight or nine, she will be very competent, not only in changing diapers but in all routine aspects of baby care. Most of a child's learning is through observation and imitation, especially of older siblings but also of adults. This was a traditional mode of learning in Hawaiian culture and seems to have persisted in the family as well as in certain other contexts, such as learning to play musical instruments and even learning certain kinds of job skills. As part of this same pattern, children judge for themselves when they are ready to take on larger or more complex portions of a task, although older siblings are there to redirect efforts or give aid if a smaller child overaspires.

Learning and working take place in the context of strong values of helping, cooperation, and contributing to the family. Everyone works to ensure that family needs are met and that all members are provided for. These values and patterns are related to the concept of 'ohana. The 'ohana is the cooperating kin group which shares work and resources. Members of the 'ohana rely on each other—for help, for work, for whatever is needed. In turn, each 'ohana member freely gives whatever he or she can. A household or a group of siblings is a reflection of 'ohana on a small scale.

In the sibling group, in the family, in the 'ohana, affective ties are built through helping each other and working together. Helping is one of the chief ways to create and reinforce affective ties and also to symbolize their presence. For children in particular, helping is probably the main way of signaling a context of good relations, shared interest, and friendly feeling between adult and child; and Hawaiian children love to help adults. Among peers, helping or cooperating on some task is one of the most important ways of building and symbolizing the friendship ties, which along with the family, are the most important aspects of Hawaiian child life (Gallimore, Boggs, and Jordan 1974; Howard 1974).

The responsibilities of Hawaiian children are not thought to be burdens. They are an expected part of contributing to the life of the family—that life that surrounds and incorporates the lives of its individual members and which provides the major source of emotional, social, and material support. It provides these elements not just from the resources of two parents but by the combined efforts and investment of all members, from youngest to oldest. Hawaiian young people are an important, vital part of their families. They are not waiting to become significant individuals in some vague future;

they already have a meaningful, responsible place in their world. This produces qualities of responsibility, initiative, and cooperativeness among the children. Surely these are assets upon which the school can draw.

In the Classroom

In classrooms, Hawaiian children are often perceived by teachers as lazy, uninvolved, and disinterested in school. A cultural perspective suggests that this is because ordinary classrooms neither elicit nor allow the children's repertoires of participation. The classroom is teacher oriented, teacher controlled, teacher dominated. The teacher sets rules, makes assignments, and regulates the classroom's resources. Children are subjected to the classroom; they are not responsible for it. When a Hawaiian mother wants the kitchen cleaned she indicates this, and the children organize to do the cleaning. When the teacher wants the classroom cleaned, the children stand aside for the custodian—or at most, compete for the privilege of dusting erasers. It is no accident that while Hawaiian family life is notable for its solidarity and loyalty, Hawaiian children are "lazy, uninvolved, and disinterested" in school.

It need not be so. The authors (anthropologist, psychologist, and teacher) were involved in the development of an adapted classroom feature which made these aspects of the natal culture and the school culture more compatible for Hawaiian children. Other cultural adaptations in the KEEP program have been described previously (e.g., Jordan and Tharp 1979; Jordan 1984; Tharp et al. 1984); this one was initiated by Vogt in a first-grade rural public school classroom where she was field testing the KEEP reading program, and is designed specifically to enhance motivation, to increase participation, and to create a more humane learning environment. The technique consists simply of the teacher behaving, in selected ways, more like a Hawaiian mother—specifically, by withdrawing from detailed supervision, presuming that children will act responsibly. A remarkable increase in classroom warmth accompanies this profoundly simple device of allowing the children to work:

> The station wagon comes up the long
> driveway, and by the time the teacher has parked
> under the banyan, seven or eight children are
> dashing across the lot to meet her. There are
> more helpers than things to do, so the children
> distribute the small parcels. Some carry and some
> walk beside, chatting and holding her hand.
>
> When they enter the classroom, it is still
> dark, rather like an empty theater. Chairs are
> stacked on bare tables. When the door opens,
> sunlight and children pour in. It is twenty
> minutes before the first bell. Outside we hear the
> sounds of playgrounds everywhere—marbles and
> tag and quarrels and songs; inside, these eight
> children and the teacher are going quietly about
> their work. One is taking the chairs off the tables,
> another raising the shades, another opening the
> windows. The teacher is at her table, absorbed
> in organizing the twelve learning-center
> assignments for the day. Each center must be
> set up anew each morning, requiring a variety
> of assignment sheets and materials. As she
> finishes a stack and sets it aside, a child takes
> it. He counts and reads the papers, then goes
> off to set up what's needed—two paste jars, a
> table covered with newspaper, five worksheets.
> Another boy wanders in, looks around, and begins
> to wash off a smudged table. The teacher almost
> never tells children what to do; she merely puts
> out the work, and some child deals with it. This
> whole process is almost entirely silent. The
> children move freely in and out of the classroom.
> They are never dragooned or even asked to come
> in early or to work. Six or so participate every
> morning, but almost all of them participate on
> some days, depending on when they get to school
> and whether the permanent floating marble game
> captures them. Two older girls are straightening
> up the lockers; they are somebody's cousins from
> third grade, just here to help out.
>
> The clock shows five minutes until "first-

bell"—the time when children are supposed to be in their classrooms. Seventeen are already in this one. Two girls plop down cross-legged in the middle of the floor, so the workers have to step around them. Somebody is still sweeping, but more children begin to sit down. The teacher looks around. A boy dashes out the door, and returns momentarily with three puffing companions. They collapse directly into the circle forming on the floor. The teacher comes round to the front of her table, sits on the edge, and talks with the front-row girls. (A few minutes ago the bell rang, and other children, lined up outside other classrooms, marched dutifully to their seats. In this room the bell was ignored; a different set of signals orders this class.)

Most of the children are now in the cross-legged circle, though a few scamper quietly to finish the last of the set-up. The children know the punctuation of the class-day; the teacher's silence and tranquil expression signal something coming: the quiet-time, the transition period when the teacher chats with them and meets each child's eyes.

The little talk blends seamlessly into the morning lesson. Somewhere in here, school has begun.

Although the emotional impact of this program is best shown by its videotape and film documentation,[3] several aspects can be abstracted and usefully discussed here. The overarching intention of this adapted feature is to make the child's home life and school life more similar in those ways which will increase the child's investment, pride, and participation in the classroom. Not all aspects of the natal culture would do so, but because in their home working patterns Hawaiian children manifest those traits that teachers consider both necessary and absent in the school setting, chore routines and interactions seem particularly suited for classroom adaptation.

Participation through active contribution of effort is a primary solidarity mechanism of Hawaiian family life. The children have these participation routines firmly in their repertoires and need only "permission" or "eliciting conditions" to become (almost instantaneously) contributing members of the classroom culture. These eliciting conditions are complex in analysis and simple in execution: The teacher must, like the Hawaiian parent, (1) minimize verbal directions, (2) minimize close supervision, and (3) allow the peer-group to organize, select, and "assign" specific tasks.

The effects of these simple steps are also complex. The decrease in formality increases the personal relationships between teacher and child and blurs the sharp demarcation between ordinary life and school life. It is no accident that in such a classroom it is difficult to see any precise moment at which "school" begins. The child's participation in creating the learning environment itself provides an excellent learning opportunity. For example, a visitor once asked a child about the worksheets she was distributing to a work center. "These are digraphs," she said. "I not on digraphs yet." And the work that the children contribute is valuable in its own terms; teachers have reported that the help is as good as that of any adult aide. Of course this system requires that the teacher respect and trust the children. But it also develops that respect and trust, because it allows the teacher to see the children operating at their best—motivated, participating, and exercising initiative and inventiveness. One day after the floor was splattered with finger-paint, Vogt found a child mopping; she had no idea where the child even found a mop. This incident may help to illustrate why every instance of this system which we have seen has increased the teacher's admiration and affection for the children, and vice versa.

Process of Adaptation

How can a teacher create the kind of classroom we have just described—one that is responsive to the learning style, helping skills, and sense of responsibility that Hawaiian children bring with them to school?

From the teacher's point of view, the components of the process are:

1. The classroom door must be opened. The teacher allows the students access to the room from the moment of their arrival. This seems simple but is profoundly different from a system in which children line up outside a closed door waiting for a bell to order them in.

2. The teacher models a routine. Modeling—allowing children to observe the teacher's own performance of the required tasks—is important, because the verbal statement of abstract rules and long strings of instructions is not characteristic of the natal culture. Often, however, the modeling includes a verbal component which explicates the whys and wherefores of her actions; that is, the teacher may "talk to herself," when and if words are necessary to provide special emphasis; for example, in explaining how to care for the delicate wires of tape-player headsets. But she "tells herself" (aloud) rather than giving specific instruction directed to a specific child.

3. The teacher retires from the task as soon as the children take over. The children judge their own readiness to take over more complex parts of a job; and this judgment is reliable.

4. The teacher lets leadership emerge from the class. Teachers expect to assign tasks, but effective leadership doesn't always lie where she expects it. The effective work leaders are often surprises to the teacher.

5. The teacher does not interfere when the children are negotiating with one another. The teacher's own cultural values, e.g., "fair play," will not always prevail, but teachers can upset the functioning social system by insisting on their own perceptions.

In consulting with teachers of Hawaiian children, each of these five "simple" rules is often met with resistance. This resistance stems from long-standing expectations about the role of the teacher and about the school institution itself.

Consider the first rule. Opening the door seems so simple, but both the school rules and the teachers' feelings have to be considered. At one of the schools where we consult, aides are in charge of students on the playground until the bell rings each day. These aides are responsible for the safety and good conduct of the students before school. For a teacher to allow the children access to the classroom meant that the responsibility for students had to be shared, a situation involving complicated role renegotiations.

Opening the door also requires a rethinking of when and how school actually starts. The teacher has to allow the children to wander and explore the room and still be able to bring everyone together when she needs to begin formal instruction. She has to have a system for bringing in children who may choose to stay outside. She must adopt an element of informality with the students during this free time and still be able to shift into an authoritative role when needed.

Rules 3 and 4 involve the teacher learning to feel that it is alright to refrain from assigning chores and from interfering as students negotiate about who will do what. Often it seems to violate the very nature of the teacher role not to control every move and regulate every minute of time. However, for the teacher who does give up such authoritarianism, pleasant surprises are in store. For example, a teacher reported that she was clipping assignments together and handing them to different students when John scooted over to the shelf of handwriting paper. Just as he arrived, "tough" Kalani moved in and bumped him away. The teacher saw it from the corner of her eye and held her breath (recalling other times when Kalani and John had come to blows over less), but she chose not to interfere. To her surprise, John waited and Kalani counted out the appropriate number of papers, handed them to John, and John took them to the spelling center. The teacher is now convinced that had she interfered, (1) she would have told Kalani to "go," that "John was there first," (2) that in doing so, she would have made the wrong choice for these two, and (3) that the mistake would have returned to haunt her later in the day when Kalani took up the matter with John. Happily, the two boys were satisfied with the shared job, and both went from there to cooperating on straightening the library shelf. It takes only a few such observations for a caring teacher to drop any remaining defenses and completely "open the door" into the classroom.

However, the speed with which the process of opening up the classroom is implemented must be adapted to each teacher. One teacher who tried it, a Hawaiian woman, was able to use the idea within a few days by simply setting a clear place for each item that needed to be set up and taken down. She had absolute trust in the children and simply opened the doors. A mother of Hawaiian children herself, all she required was permission from the school to behave naturally.

Another teacher, a Caucasian, took a slower track. As she felt the children learned the routine, she allowed a few at a time to enter the room early, then gradually opened it up to more. At first, she took only volunteers who would make commitments ahead of time, but later she let students come in on impulse. Similarly, she began by allowing only "workers" in the room, but later she let students drift in and out and work or relax as they chose.

A third teacher, Japanese, constructed a system where the students were free to help with the daily set-up or not, as they chose, but were assigned as teams of five with rotating "turns" for the clean-up. Even in the clean-up, however, she maintained a policy of non-directiveness and non-interference while the children carried out the work. She was comfortable with a different level of structure while still attending to the basic concepts which made the innovation culturally compatible.

An important issue that had to be confronted when providing consulting to teachers who were trying out this feature was the way teachers see their role as the head of the classrom. It is often seen as threatening to give up completely controlling all activity within the classroom. Any teacher who has had difficulty maintaining student attention while teaching may understandably be especially fearful of letting activity be unstructured in those few last moments before the entry bell rings.

Finally, although teachers can be helped to institute each step of the process for this innovation, "opening the door" is also a state of mind. Culturally sensitive innovations, in order to be successful, involve trust and respect for the children. Fortunately, this innovation itself contributes to that trust and respect, which, once it is well established helps to give both children and teacher a mutually supportive new classroom.

Summary and Conclusions

The "Open Door" feature we have discussed in this chapter is a highly visible example of the translation of cultural data into educational practice. It takes into account the value Hawaiian children place on helping and their well-developed skills in learning by observing a model as well as the fact that they are accustomed to organizing group work efforts independent of adults. It builds on the fact that "helping" is an effective way of both establishing and signaling good relations between teacher and students and among students in the classroom. Opening the Door is a way of making the classroom belong to teachers and students together.

In conclusion, we should make two points. There are a number of ways of building rapport in classrooms, and certainly a subset of these could be successful with Hawaiian students. There is also certainly more than one way to give children some sense of investment in the classroom, thereby setting school tasks in a meaningful context. The Open Door feature is not the only way that these purposes can be accomplished. However, it is essential to good education that they be served in some way; and for Hawaiian children the strategy described here is an especially felicitous one because it builds directly on strong values and well-established behaviors and skills. This means that the goals of rapport and investment can be achieved with relatively little effort by teachers, except for the mental effort of "letting go" of direct control of all classroom events. As a bonus, it produces a classroom which is pleasing to be in and beautiful to behold.

The second point is that the promotion of trust and regard among class members and between students and teacher, which is so well served in the Hawaiian case by the Open Door adaptation, is a necessary part of making minority education programs effective, but it is not, by itself, sufficient to do so. In the field test classroom where the Open Door feature was developed, scores on standardized tests of reading achievement were above national norm level. But in this classroom, as in other KEEP classrooms, this kind of device existed within the context of a total program involving a number of other essential components (Tharp 1981; Tharp et al. 1984). All the components are necessary to produce the good learning that the children deserve and the teachers desire.

Implications for Policy in Bilingual, Cross-Cultural Education

The "culturally compatible education" model illustrated here has several implications for educational policy and teacher training in bilingual, cross-cultural education.

1. The most profitable approach to minority education is not one of remediation but one based on the assumption that children of all linguistic and cultural backgrounds already possess skills and behaviors that can be utilized in learning what the school has to teach. The task then becomes the modification of school environments so that they elicit these behaviors and skills.

2. To do this, it is not sufficient to take into account only linguistic code or the highly visible public features of the children's natal culture. More subtle aspects of culture and communicative interaction must also receive attention. This means that efforts to develop effective education programs for minority children should include provision for generating or accessing knowledge of the culture of the population to be served, especially of the interactional and sociolinguistic contexts in which minority children exhibit skills and behaviors that can serve academic goals.

3. Knowledge garnered from cultural research can best be put to use not by attempting to change the home culture

nor, on the other hand, by efforts to reproduce that culture in the classroom. Rather it should serve as a guide in choosing, from the full range of educational practices, those best suited to a particular population. This translation of ethnography into educational practice requires cooperation among ethnographers, educational researchers and educational practitioners. Educational research and development programs need to provide for both cultural research and culture-education translation in order to produce effective and truly cross-cultural education.

Endnotes

1. Dr. Cathie Jordan is the Chair of the Culture and Learning Department of the Kamehameha Center for Development of Early Education, Hawaii. Dr. Roland G. Tharp was Principal Investigator of KEEP for 18 years and is now Director of the Center for Studies of Multicultural Higher Education, University of Hawaii. Lynn Baird-Vogt, is a teacher with the Kamehameha Early Education Program.

2. The Center is now providing in-service training in KEEP methods to approximately 130 teachers serving some 3000 students in eight public and one private school. Results vary widely by classroom and school but overall do not yet match results from laboratory, field test, and pilot operations. While this fact is seen as in part indicating a need for further program development, it is felt to relate mainly to issues of dissemination and training, which are now a focus of research. For a detailed report of evaluation data on dissemination classrooms, see Klein 1988.

3. The authors acknowledge that there is great variation among classrooms and among Hawaiian children and families, so that there is in reality no such thing as a "typical" classroom or Hawaiian family (e.g., see Weisner, Gallimore, and Jordan 1988; D'Amato 1986.) We will use these shorthand terms for the sake of convenience and brevity, and because we believe that there is something real represented in the contrast between home

and school settings and the differences in behavior of many Hawaiian youngsters in response to them.

    4. Available at cost from the Media Department, Kamehameha Center for Development of Early Education, Kekelaokalani Bldg., Kapalama Heights, Honolulu, HI 96817.

References

D'Amato, John
    1986   "We Cool, Tha's Why": A Study of Personhood and Place in a Class of Hawaiian Second Graders. Unpublished doctoral dissertation. University of Hawaii.

Gallimore, Ronald, Joan Whitehorn Boggs, and Cathie Jordan
    1974   Culture, Behavior, and Education: A Study of Hawaiian-Americans. Beverly Hills: Sage Publications.

Howard, Alan
    1974   Ain't No Big Thing: Coping Strategies in a Hawaiian-American Community. Honolulu: University of Hawaii Press.

Jacob, Evelyn, and Cathie Jordan
    1987   Explaining the School Performance of Minority Students (Theme Issue). Anthropology and Education Quarterly 18(4).

Jordan, Cathie
    1981   The Selection of Culturally Compatible Classroom Practices. Educational Perspectives 20(1):16–19.

    1984   Cultural Compatibility and the Education of Ethnic Minority Children: Implications for Mainland Educators. Educational Research Quarterly 8(4):59–71.

    1985   Translating Culture: From Ethnographic Information to Educational Program. Anthropology and Education Quarterly 16(2):105–123.

Jordan, Cathie, and Roland G. Tharp
    1979   Culture and Education. *In* Perspectives in Cross-Cultural Psychology. Anthony Marcella, Roland G. Tharp, and Thomas Cibrowski, eds. New York: Academic Press.

Jordan, Cathie, and Roland G. Tharp
    1984   Level of Analysis and the Specification of Sources of Academic Underachievement for Minority Cultural Groups: Evidence from the Hawaiian Case. (Working Paper) Honolulu: Kamehmeha Schools, Center for the Development of Early Education. (Revised version of a paper presented at the Annual Meeting of the American Anthropological Association, November 1983.)

Kamehameha Schools
    1983   Native Hawaiian Educational Assessment Project. Honolulu: Office of Program Evaluation and Planning, Kamehameha Schools.
            Program Evaluation of the Kamehameha Elementary Education Program's Reading Curriculum in Hawaii's Public Schools: The Cohort Analysis. Honolulu: Kamehameha Schools/Bernice Pauahi Bishop Estate.

Klein, Thomas W.
    1981   Results of the Reading Program. Educational Perspectives 20(1):8-10.

Thompson, Thomas S., and Neil Hannahs
    1979   Testimony on Behalf of the Native Hawaiian Education Act, Before a Joint Committee on Elementary, Secondary and Vocational Education and Post-Secondary Education of the United States House of Representatives, November 14. (Text available from Kamehameha Schools, Honolulu)

Tharp, Roland G.
    1981   The Direct Instruction of Comprehension. Educational Perspectives 20(1):5-7.

Tharp, Roland G., et al.
    1984   Product and Process in Applied Developmental Research: Education and the Children of a Minority. In Advances in Developmental Psychology. M.E. Lamb, L.Brown, and B. Rogoff, eds. Pp. 91-141. Hillsdale, N.J.: Lawrence Erlbaum Associates.

Vogt, Lynn A., Cathie Jordan and Roland G. Tharp
    1987   Explaining School Failure, Producing School Success: Two Cases. Anthropology and Education Quarterly 18(4):276-286.

Weisner, Thomas S., Ronald Gallimore, and Cathie Jordan
    1988   Unpackaging Cultural Effects on Classroom Learning: Native Hawaiian Peer Assistance and Child-Generated Activity. Anthropology and Education Quarterly 19(4):327-353 Dec.

African-American Students in Exemplary Urban High Schools: The Interaction of School Practices and Student Actions

Vernay Mitchell[1]

Introduction

Despite the enormous problems facing public schools today, a number of high schools that are doing a good job of educating at-risk, inner city youngsters and preparing them for various post graduation roles. As part of a research project which was conducted to explore the present state of career-oriented high schools,[2] I have had the opportunity to observe the operation of some of these schools. This chapter is a new analysis of a small set of those data emphasizing the experiences of African-American students.

In this chapter I use data from two of the schools in the larger study to explore several factors in the successful preparation of at-risk African-American students. The data from observations and interviews have been disaggregated from the totality and show that in both schools African-American students have a record of success. The disaggregation of these data help to illuminate those organizational characteristics and common practices which aid these students in their endeavors.

Site visits to the schools took place during the 1987–1988 and 1988–89 academic years. The schools presented in this chapter were visited for two weeks each. Ethnographic concepts and techniques were used to examine the daily life in the buildings, interview teachers and administrators, observe classes, and talk with students.

After a descriptive overview was obtained, the focus was narrowed to concentrate on the interactions between student action and school practices which might help us understand why at-risk students were, for the most part, doing well academically and were aspiring to enter college at a time when applications and enrollment of minorities are declining, especially for African-American students.

The focus is on the students as actors in the scenario of schooling because it is recognized that students are not passive participants in what institutions do. While I understand and acknowledge that one must look at institutional and societal causes, it is also true that at various junctures in the process students make decisions, follow scenarios, acquiesce and resist. These behaviors influence the outcomes of the educational process.

The Larger Study

In the larger study nine high schools in or near large urban areas were identified as exemplary by the following three criteria:

1. The school was rated highly by school district personnel.
2. More students want to attend the school than can be accepted.
3. The school as a whole is reported to have above average success in motivating students to stay in school.

Although each of the nine schools did not represent the complete embodiment of this set of preferred characteristics, each had a sufficiency to be regarded as distinctive. All of them educate students for specific occupational fields as well as for college entrance.

The research documented key factors which govern the operation of the schools. Information was provided about service delivery and policy. The goal was to stimulate ideas and encourage further development of exemplary career-related/college preparatory education.

The research yielded nine factors which may be associated with the success of the schools. Each school has many, if not all, of the following characteristics:

1. a safe and orderly environment conducive to teaching and learning
2. a businesslike attitude on the part of students and teachers which creates an atmosphere of constructive energy in the school
3. a warm and caring school climate
4. an admissions process that makes students feel special—based upon student interest in the career specialty or set of subjects, not solely upon student test scores
5. a dual mission—to prepare students for an occupation and for college
6. high expectations for all students to succeed accompanied by attempts to minimize grouping of students by ability
7. a curriculum organized around an industry or a discrete set of subjects
8. the integration of theory and practice in the courses of instruction
9. strong linkages with business and industry and sometimes with local institutions of higher education.

Once these practices and aspects of school organization emerged, it became important to explore their effect on minority students. While there is a plethora of studies concerned with minority students for whom schools have not been successful, few studies are conducted with students who are successful in spite of their high risk status and with the schools in which they are successful. What is it about these schools and the interactions in these schools that enable these students to be successful?

At-Risk African-American Students

A review of factors which are generally listed to define at-risk students yields the following:

1. limited English proficiency
2. high chronological age for the grade
3. history of retention
4. truancy or sporadic attendance patterns
5. low Grade Point Index (GPI)
6. inner city location
7. single parent family
8. low income

Although one at-risk student may not have all of these characteristics, when two or more of them are attributed to one individual, generally it identifies him or her as being at risk. For African-American and Hispanic students the probability of being at risk is higher than for others. When the effects of low socioeconomic status are combined with suspensions and other punitive measures used by schools, African-American and Hispanic students tend to be retained in the same grade disproportionately to their numbers. Many of these students are seen by their teachers as low achieving troublesome students; in this regard minority males are particularly at risk.

A review of postsecondary paths for these "at-risk" students reveals that on the employment front the ". . . likelihood of parents serving as role models for their children for specific careers varies with social status" (Thomas 1986:178). Upper-class students do aspire to their parents' careers, whereas lower-class students are discouraged from doing so. However, ". . . always parents are key influences of adolescents' occupational preferences" (Thomas 1986: 178).

Since jobs which do not require college preparation usually are filled through informal networks of information such as walk-in applications and word-of-mouth referrals (Braddock and McPartland 1987), at-risk students may suffer from the barrier called social network segregation. Many African-Americans are not members of the information networks which lead to job information. Other research results demonstrate how Blacks in segregated schools only have access to segregated networks and thus wind up in racially segregated employment, whereas those from desegregated schools are significantly more likely to be employed as adults in desegregated places of work (Braddock, Crain, and McPartland 1984).

Collaborations between schools or school districts and businesses, unions, universities, hospitals and community organizations are growing more common. They have improved school facilities and brought in new programs for students and/or teachers. These have led to an increased number of job placements for at-risk students, but they do not effect structural change or revitalize schools in fundamental ways so that the transition from student to worker will be transformed.

Willie (1987) suggests there are many different ways to attain educational and professional success. One movement to increase success rates is the campaign for educational excellence. This often disenfranchises minority students who have only recently begun participating in the White-dominated system. Since African-Americans have to be better educated than Whites in order to achieve equality in many professions, they are falling short in the competition with better prepared White students for college admissions and financial aid as well as employment (Nettles 1988). Lack of preparation for college is one of the reasons for declining enrollments among minority students (Welch, Hodges, and Warden 1989); the decline in the amount of federal student loans available is another. Thus the question remains, why and how do some at risk African-American students succeed?

A framework for understanding the situation of African-American students in these schools has been suggested by Fordham and Ogbu (1986). They use the notion of "fictive kinship" to explain the manner in which high school students operate. According to this framework, the students feel a sense of collective identity which is manifested in certain activities, behaviors, and symbols. This results in a kinship bond not determined by blood or marriage—a relationship of "fictive kinship."

This fictive kinship system creates a sense of "brotherhood" and "sisterhood" uniting all African-Americans. It is learned during the socialization process in preschool years and continues to be relevant even as the individual encounters formal institutions such as

schools. The extent to which the system of fictive kinship
is permitted or prohibited to operate in formal institutions
affects students' experiences and outcomes. In other words
in educational environments African-American students
may learn better and achieve more when they have the
opportunity to operate within the type of kinship system
which has nurtured them in their lives outside of school.

The Schools

The two schools described here are in the Chicago
Public School System. Aberdeen and Cookman are
pseudonyms. Aberdeen is a magnet school which accepts
applicants from throughout the city. Cookman is one of
nine vocational high schools in Chicago. At the time of the
study the dropout rate in the Chicago Public Schools was
one of the highest in the nation. For the class of 1985
the official figure was 44.9%. Blacks make up over 50%
of the school enrollment.

Aberdeen Magnet High School, Chicago, Illinois

Social Organization of the School. The atmosphere of
Aberdeen Magnet School is pleasant because the staff and
students make it so. A group of photographs displayed on
the school walls make obvious the pride they have in the
school. The walls are free of graffiti and efforts are made
to keep the floors free of debris. The crowded conditions
under which the school must operate are noticeable in
that there is little empty space within the interior of the
school. The emptiness of the main corridors fills to the
brink as the bells ring and students and teachers surge
out of classroom doors.

Physical education is taught in a classroom where
desks and chairs are moved aside. In many instances,
equipment must be moved from place to place. For example,
the library, which seats 44 people, must be used to store
large audio-visual equipment thus blocking a wall of
bookshelves. If students or teachers need books from that

side of the library, the equipment must be rolled to one side where it blocks other shelves. Portable classrooms are being used to accommodate the student body of 467 students.

At times, the small size of the school helps to calm individual and group situations which, in larger schools, may lead to disruption and sometimes violence. Thus even though the school seems to have less of a security presence than others (no uniformed officers, no checking of visitors' identification), there is closer monitoring and a shorter response time when attempts are made to eliminate disruptive incidents.

This aspect of the school organization works not only for security purposes, but it also fosters positive ties between students and teachers and allows for more freedom of movement. Because the school is small and because the same people see each other so often within this small space, teachers get to know more students, including those who are not specifically assigned to them.

There is a warm interpersonal climate in the school between teachers and students and among faculty and administrators. One teacher described the interaction this way:

> Each student usually has a favorite teacher. When that teacher perceives this, he/she takes the student under his or her wing. The teacher fosters the relationship by talking to the student informally as the chance arises. The teacher also keeps in contact with the parents. If difficulties arise with academic work or behavior, that teacher speaks to and for the student.

Other teachers are aware of these mentoring pairings; thus they know which staff member to contact if there are questions about a certain student.

Herein is one instance where the framework of a fictive kinship structure is applicable. Students in this school form linkages with staff members of their choosing. The choice is not obvious. No special time is set aside for choosing a mentor—there is no written confirmation of this process. It happens, as it does in the African-American community, through a subtle process of bonding. Although the principal and many of the teachers at Aberdeen are not Black, there is an openness and the kind of understanding which allows Black students to evoke some of their own criteria for creating the relationships they need. In choosing mentors many of the African-American students pick African-American teachers and guidance counselors.

When asked the question, "Why did you come to this school?" seniors and juniors at Aberdeen mentioned they were intrigued by the range of career options that were offered, especially in a high school which also prepared students for college entrance.

As they began to experience what the school had to offer and they compared it to the experience of their friends in other high schools, they came to know that the relatively small enrollment and staff make the school more conducive to learning. They understand the value of having close working relationships with teachers, counselors, and administrators. They enjoy feeling empowered to propose new activities for the school. Many of the students have ideas for extracurricular and fundraising events. They are confident they will get faculty support.

The Students. Minority-group students constitute a majority of the student body at Aberdeen (67% African-American and 22% Hispanic). Aberdeen has become the school of preference even for students who do not have a specific career area in mind. They attend to get a good high school education which will help to assure success in college. They appreciate the fact that the school prepares students for careers and for higher education. Several of the freshmen said they have siblings who attend the school. Two freshmen said they have a parent who works in the school system and that the parent recommended the school. This demonstrates the amount of confidence the school has generated within families who know what it has to offer to its students in terms of academic preparation and an appropriate climate for young people to grow personally and socially.

Increasing numbers of applications to Aberdeen are

making the student selection process more arduous. An annual open house is held for eighth graders and their parents. As the completed applications are returned, the faculty and administrators of the school interview and screen the prospective students.

The students selected for enrollment at the school come from all parts of Chicago. They represent a broad range of ability levels. Attendance is a highly weighted criteria for acceptance. Some students who have learning disabilities and some who need help with English as a second language are accepted. A staff position is allotted to each of these areas.

The attendance records of prospective students are an important factor for acceptance since the school is located at an extreme end of the city and students may have far to travel. A lottery system at the high school district offices determines the final list of students who attend the school.

The Curriculum. The students who are accepted attend an orientation during August where they learn more about the curriculum, the physical plant, and the high expectations the faculty will have for them. The 43 staff members at Aberdeen include administrators, faculty, and support staff who represent many Chicago neighborhoods and ethnic groups. An African-American woman who heads the guidance staff organizes the student orientation. It includes field trips, advice about study skills, information about the program of study and career opportunities, and preliminary strategies about college admission. She states, "I have them in my grasp for a week and teach them all they need to know."

Many students complain at first when they hear of the exceptionally long hours they must spend in this high school. Some students attend from 7:05 A.M. to 4:19 P.M. some must travel two hours on public transportation. The lunch period is only 30 minutes. But most students admit they learn more because of the extra hours spent in school. One of the key accomplishments at Aberdeen has been its low dropout rate which is less than 2% compared to 44.9% citywide. The attendance rate, at 90%, is above the citywide average.

All classes are heterogeneously grouped, and the program of study is similar for all students. The few electives which exist are in the junior and senior years. Honors credit can be earned for some classes in which teachers have identified special assignments and activities which take the honors student beyond what is normally expected in the class.

The summer courses and internships are quite popular with students. Several students described the pleasure of spending the summer in internship experiences at universities in Illinois, Michigan, Missouri, and Alabama.

Although there are students of all ability levels in the school, the test scores in reading and math have been consistently higher than the citywide average. Many seniors are accepted in four-year colleges with scholarships by the second month of their senior year in high school.

Students who have difficulty with a course may ask for a peer tutor. The peer-tutoring component of the school offers payment to students for helping other students with a course the tutor has already passed. An attempt is made to find a tutor who had the same teacher for the course. Students who need extra help in math can also obtain a tutor from the Math Club.

This practice of peer tutoring offers another opportunity for nurturing relationships among fictive kin. Students who are achieving well in a subject area help others in an environment which is sensitive to student needs. The behaviors, activities, and symbols used to teach and motivate emerge from the relationship between the pair. African-American students in the roles of tutor and tutee can assert their collective identity and feelings of kinship in this endeavor to improve academic performance. It must be said that Asian and Hispanic students in tutoring relationships with students of their background also have the opportunity to employ behaviors and symbols that are appropriate to their cultural backgrounds.

Cookman Vocational High School, Chicago, Illinois

Social Organization of the School. The tallest building in the world, the Sears Tower, can be seen from the third floor windows of Cookman Vocational school. The building stands out in the panoramic view from the school as a tribute to the various building trades, business areas, technical skills and services which are parts of the curriculum at Cookman.

The school is 21 years old. It sits on a large corner of land in a neighborhood of warehouses and run down multi-unit dwellings on Chicago's West Side.

Many of the teachers who have taught in the school since the 1960's or early 1970's knew the school could be better than it was. They thought it was not challenging enough and not as up to date in equipment, materials, curriculum, and organization as it could have been. Some curriculum areas in the school, such as the repair of small electrical appliances, had outlived their usefulness in a society undergoing rapid technological change. They wondered how students who graduated from that department would obtain and hold satisfying employment. Some of the machinery, such as that in the printing department, did not work at all. But there was no incentive for the faculty to evoke changes. Thus, for the most part, they went along with things the way they were.

After the retirement of the former principal, a White male who had been in the school since it began, several members of the community visited other high schools and explored their administrative structures. They asked questions and shadowed principals in an effort to learn new, more innovative ways to organize and administer a high school. They encouraged a very effective elementary school principal to apply for the job of principal at Cookman.

This African-American male became the principal of Cookman in 1982. The student body was and continues to be 100 percent African-American, 70 percent of whom live at the poverty line. The new principal immediately saw the need for improvements and opportunities to bring

Cookman into the mainstream of contemporary high school functioning with more emphasis on future needs in the various occupational areas and further training past the high school level. The outdated shops were closed and new equipment was obtained for others. Remedial programs were eliminated and the mission and philosophy of the school were changed. True restructuring has taken place.

The climate of the school changed along with the new administration. The formation and activities of street gangs which used to exist in the school have been eliminated through new rules which are strictly adhered to and for which student input was sought. The new principal patrolled the hallways continuously in order to monitor student behavior and to make sure that new rules, such as "no flyers pasted on the walls," and "no student enters a classroom without a pass after the tardy bell has rung," were enforced. A dress code was instituted which banned the wearing of any paraphernalia associated with gangs. A new code of conduct for the lunch room was written by students and staff members.

When responding to questions about the present climate of the school, students often use a comparative frame:

> It's the best school in this [an African-American] neighborhood.
> There is [another school], which is better, but this one is in my neighborhood.
> In the schools my friends go to, there is fighting, gangs and drugs . . . but not here."
> My aunt says it has calmed down since she went here . . . about ten years ago.
> If I had gone to another school I would have dropped out and I'd be hanging on the corner . . . all my friends did.

Observations in the halls and classrooms at Cookman show that the school is very quiet and most of the students are orderly. In cases of students who break rules, teachers, or in more serious cases an assistant principal, deal with the students with an air of "no nonsense tolerated here."

Teachers and administrators cite general observations

and specific actions which show the changes in school climate during the past seven years at Cookman:

> . . . under the new administrator it's like a breath of fresh air.
> The change is dramatic, . . . it was needed.
> Now we participate together, before, everyone was in his own world.
> Graffiti is removed soon after it is created.
> . . . the school profits from the increased publicity and recognition.

The responses from students and teachers about the school climate reflect elements of the fictive kinship system. The students express an interest in remaining in "their neighborhood" for schooling. Although many of them live far away from the school, they consider this Black community "theirs" because of the collective identity among African-Americans. They are proud that "their school" has accomplished such positive changes. The teachers appreciate the advent of staff camaraderie associated with the new leadership of the principal. The social atmosphere now simulates the fictive kinship system of the neighborhood. The neighborhood supported the new administrator for his superior skills and because of the brotherhood they felt with him. That support became an enabling factor in the success of the school.

The Students. There has been a change in the abilities and qualifications of students who are accepted in Cookman, especially since the advent of magnet schools in Chicago. Many of the brightest students prefer magnet schools to vocational schools. Also more students from severely impoverished homes are applying and being accepted at Cookman. The poverty rate in the school is presently 60–70%. The acceptees are generally less prepared and more immature, according to staff members, than they used to be. Many times, once they enter high school, the students test lower on tests of basic skills than they did in elementary school.

Applications for Cookman are sent to elementary schools throughout Chicago. The counselors in the feeder schools are informed of the selection guidelines, and elementary school students and their parents are invited to visit the school. Generally 3,000 applications are received for about 550 seats in the freshman class. The administrators at Cookman who participate in the acceptance process look for the following items: (1) reading scores on a sixth-grade level or higher and (2) a record of good attendance.

The goal of the selection procedure is to select a broad cross-section of students in terms of their skills and abilities. No effort is made to find out the applicants' ethnic backgrounds. The entire student body is African-American, at present, as Cookman continues to be known as a place where a better education can be obtained in an African-American neighborhood. As one student put it, " . . . even though it's a vocational school, you can go to college from here." About 60% of the graduates of Cookman enroll in postsecondary institutions. There is an 85% attendance rate and the dropout rate is only 6%.

Although the number of applications is increasing, the number of enrolled students is decreasing. Many of the applicants do not meet the specified guidelines for acceptance, some who are accepted do not enter, many transfer from the school because they find it is too far from their homes. Also, high pregnancy rates cause Cookman to lose students. The present enrollment is 1,650 students in a school which can hold 2,000 students. The enrollment in 1978–1979 was 1,820. However, more girls are being attracted by the new offerings, especially in the business department. The school is 60% female now.

Much time is spent advocating values which pertain to student roles and responsibilities as Cookman students. One particular motto which is encouraged is: "You are in charge of you," making the students feel more responsible for their learning and their behavior.

For students who are doing poorly the school provides laboratories for reading and math. Chapter I funds allotted to Cookman help to fund these laboratories. Programs and kits made by commercial vendors are not used in them; the teachers make and order individualized materials specifically designed to meet the needs of Cookman students who need extra help.

The Faculty. The faculty at Cookman consists of 92 teachers. One principal and two assistant principals are aided by various coordinators, assistants, teacher aides and specialized staff persons for support services, security, food services, attendance, etc. The staff is 59% White and 41% African-American.

The faculty has supported community outreach which has been expanded at the school. Parent participation is sought and encouraged for the decision-making processes and the day-to-day activities of the school. As events and new policies are publicized and the parents' role in them become known, other parents may want to have the same opportunity and to become involved.

The administration has developed links with local colleges and universities. A program began in 1987–1988 with the University of Illinois at Chicago which brings college students into the school before their student teaching experience. They observe and aid teachers at Cookman and gain some of the skills and maturity which will be necessary for their student teaching assignments. Likewise, Cookman gains from the experience as teachers act as role models for the college students and are stimulated by the students' actions and ideas. The students spend at least 20 hours in the school and the participating teachers receive tuition waivers for courses at the University of Illinois.

All of the staff members interviewed mentioned that the strength of the principal is his ability to form networks in the community and with the central administration in Chicago in ways which bring positive publicity and recognition to the school. His strengths have resulted in a definite change in climate and ethos for Cookman Vocational High School. He has helped the school to simulate the fictive kinship system of the community.

Conclusion

At a time when schools have been overrun with panaceas and school improvement programs, there is much resistance to new initiatives and programs which will only add to the already enormous burden which schools face.

These findings suggest that in these two schools African-American teachers, counselors, principals, and other school staff intercede in the careers of at risk students in ways that are more appropriate than those advocated by previous school change models. African-American counselors act as mentors and develop the "fictive kinship" relationships with these students which allow the students to exercise more positive decision making and to develop their choices more productively. The counselors and other staff become linkers to the vast networks which make job hunts successful. Thus the professional who is generally involved with assessment of students becomes an advocate for them (Cummins 1986). These fictive kin motivate students to perform while they are still in high school. They allow the students to rise above negative expectations from teachers and other significant persons in the students' lives that often lead to low student performance (Howe and Edelman 1985). These results contrast with others where high school guidance has been shown to be inadequate and students do not regard counselors as good sources of academic advice (Boyer 1983).

The African-Americans in various roles from the principal to counselors and teachers make the students in these two schools feel empowered. Students participate; they develop the ability, confidence, and motivation to succeed. The social organization of these schools responds to the call for school restructuring that includes redefining the way school personnel interact with students and the way schools interact with families and communities. Student empowerment comes from affirmation of their culture in the school and participation of the community in the schools. For the African-American students in these schools the faculty and staff are seen as part of an extended family. There are role models at various levels of instruction, of staff and at the peer level as they participate in tutoring.

African-American counselors and paraprofessionals as well as teachers, administrators, and tutors link the various systems of meaning which the students encounter in their communities and in the world at large. The African-American counselor who "has the students in her grasp," the African-American teachers chosen by the students as mentors at Aberdeen, the African-American principal at Cookman who brought a new ethos to the school, and the African-American assistant principal who sets high expectations in a climate of "no nonsense" all serve not only as role models but also as culture brokers.

Faculty and staff members who are not African-American have a significant catalytic role in this process. They understand that the developmental needs of this population include good academic preparation as well as social-emotional support that is appropriate to the cultural background of the students. White teachers and administrators in these two schools work with an open-minded posture as the African-American model of fictive kinship is being applied. They endorse that structure explicitly and implicitly. Also they are important representatives of various other subcultures that the students will encounter in the world at large.

Endnotes

1. Vernay Mitchell, Research Associate, International Center for Collaboration and Conflict Resolution, Teachers College, Columbia University.

2. Some of the material in this chapter was taken from the 1989 report, Exemplary Urban Career-Oriented Secondary School Programs co-authored by Vernay Mitchell, Ellen S. Russell, and Charles S. Benson. The research was funded by the National Center for Research in Vocational Education at the University of California, Berkeley.

References

Boyer, E.
  1983   High School: A Report on Secondary Education in
          America. New York: Harper and Row.
Braddock, J.H., R.L. Crain, and J.M. McPartland
  1984   A Long-Term View of School Desegregation: Some
          Recent Studies of Graduates as Adults. Phi Delta
          Kappan. 66:259–264.
Braddock, J.H., and J.M. McPartland
  1987   How Minorities Continue to be Excluded from Equal
          Employment Opportunities: Research on Labor
          Market and Institutional Barriers. Journal of Social
          Issues. 43:15–39.
Cummins, Jim
  1986   Empowering Minority Students: A Framework for
          Intervention. Harvard Education Review 56(1):18–36.
Fordham, S., and J. Ogbu
  1986   Black Students' School Success: Coping with the
          "Burden of 'Acting White'" The Urban Review
          18(3):176–206.
Howe, Harold, and Marion Wright Edelman
  1985   Barriers to Excellence: Our Children at Risk. Boston:
          National Coalition of Advocates for Students.
Mitchell, V., E. Russell, and C. Benson
  1989   Exemplary Urban Career-Oriented Secondary School
          Programs. Berkeley: National Center for Research in
          Vocational Education.
Nettles, Michael T., ed.
  1988   Toward Black Undergraduate Student Equality in
          American Higher Education. Westport, Conn.:
          Greenwood Press.
Thomas, Veronica G.
  1986   Career Aspirations, Parental Support, and Work
          Values Among Black Female Adolescents. Journal of
          Multicultural Counseling and Development. 14:177–
          85.
Welch, O.M., C.Hodges, and K. Warden
  1989   Developing the Scholar's Ethos in Minority High
          School Students: The Link to Academic Achievement.
          Urban Education 24(1):59–76.
Willie, Charles Vert
  1987   Effective Education: A Minority Perspective. Westport,
          Conn.: Greenwood Press.

Home-School Linkages: A Cross-Cultural Approach to Parent Participation

Steven F. Arvizu[1]

Introduction

Voluntarism is an invaluable resource for schools of the future facing reform and the challenges of diversity. Schools and programs seeking greater effectiveness must build bridges between the school and community and strengthen home-school linkages. As demonstrated by many studies as well as experience with program directors, evaluators, and researchers, parent participation is an important variable in the success of innovative programs and projects.[2] Ann Henderson (1987) summarized fifty studies on the relationship between parent involvement and student achievement by concluding, ". . . the evidence is beyond dispute: parent involvement improves student achievement. When parents are involved, children do better in school and they go to better schools." Lindner (1987), however, raises the issue of diversity in parent participation by stating, "Programs to involve parents must take into account the diversity of families, schools and communities and their varying needs. Different types of schools, families and communities require different strategies for involving parents." Cross-cultural strategies for achieving parent participation have not explicitly been explored in the research literature, but there is some implicit evidence from innovative program and project efforts to suggest bilingual and cross-cultural strategies do work in some diverse environments.

In order to establish an overall conceptual framework
for exploring parent participation this paper discusses: (1)
some of the relevant literature from bilingual, migrant,
early childhood, and parenting education (2) a cross-cultural
philosophy of parent participation; (3) conceptual and
theoretical models; (4) major areas and roles, and (5)
questions and challenges for the future.

Background Literature

Of the many resources available to bilingual, cross-
cultural programs, the parent community probably has
the most potential for contributing to their success. Title
VII and many other federal- and state-supported programs
mandate parent participation as one of the activities
required for the development and implementation of
programs. Discretionary and formula-funded projects often
experiment with features and activities involving parents,
the results of which are seldom reported through the
research literature. The following are some examples of
citations from reports, unpublished theses, articles, and
conference presentations which illustrate the value of home-
school linkages.

Matute-Bianchi's (1979) analysis of bureaucratic
conditions argues for more meaningful parent-community
involvement in bilingual programs. Arvizu and Alonzo (1969)
studied successful bilingual programs and found parental
involvement to be an important innovative feature of
programs, especially in achieving cultural relevance in
instruction plans. McConnell (1977) reports that active
parental participation in bilingual program management
decisions, hiring of teaching staff, and program evaluation
resulted in meeting or exceeding program achievement
goals. Carrasquillo and Carrasquillo (1979) describe how
bilingual parents can help teachers reinforce learning
through culturally relevant learning activities and through
supporting learning in different language settings. Berry-
Caban (1983) describes the positive impact of training for
Hispanic parents and bilingual programs in Milwaukee,

Wisconsin. Goldenberg's (1987) case studies indicate Hispanic parents' ability to transcend low-income conditions in facilitating their children's language skill development. Bermudez and Padron (1987) found that successful programs train teachers in improving home-school partnerships through curriculum development relevant to minority community issues. In addition, Gandara (1980) studied high achievers with advanced college degrees and found that parents influenced work ethic and school work, proficiencies in biculturalism, and adaptability as well as attention to role models and mentors (1980). Arvizu et al. (1982) found by contrasting two exemplary programs that successful bilingual programs fully utilize parent, community, and cultural resources while less successful programs underutilize parents.

Early childhood and family projects have similarly expressed the importance of parent participation in programs in minority environments. Slaughter (1975) found skilled parents, as agents of socialization, influenced achievement in early intervention activity. Buriel's (1980) study of locus of control revealed parent and teacher contributions to child socialization and learning. Parental involvement in migrant bilingual/bicultural day care also resulted in positive program impact (De Avila 1976). Successful Head Start projects have used bilingual parent education and training to support parents as the primary educators of their children and to increase parent involvement in program activities (Hutchison 1986). Laosa's (1980) study of Latino mothers teaching their own five-year-old children revealed that teaching strategies in the home influence the development of cognitive styles of learning. Amodeo (1982) found that parents can have a strategic influence on the evaluation and assessment of giftedness as well as in programming through direct participation in the classroom or by indirectly interacting with the school and teachers.

Cross-Cultural Philosophy

The author, former director of the Cross Cultural Resource Center (CCRC) at California State University at Sacramento, herein adopts an anthropological approach to problem-solving based on that discipline's traditions of cultural knowledge, comparison, holism, and its field techniques. Such a cross-cultural and comparative perspective is a necessary philosophical and pedagogical base for success in bilingual education programs. It fosters an understanding of people, problems, solutions, and issues from various cultural orientations as well as respect for the human rights and ways of life of individuals and groups. It makes possible a connection among individuals and groups and transcends specific cultures in both study and action. For example, a social studies teacher, employing a cross-cultural perspective, is able to teach a global perspective through presenting materials on the cultural background of students in the classroom as well as other areas of the world and relate them to general American cultural customs.

While schools and communities must be recognized as major arenas for cultural transmission and interaction, it is also important that the people belonging to them maintain a balance of the positive aspects of pride in, understanding of, and respect for their own way of life as well as an understanding and a respect for the ways of life of others. A cross-cultural perspective goes beyond a belief in cultural nationalism (i.e., commitment to the interests and independence of one cultural group above others), or even biculturalism (commitment to or competencies in two cultural systems or groups), or multiculturalism (commitment to or competencies in many cultural systems or groups). It necessarily approaches phenomena in their cultural context(s), treating them in a systematic and scientific manner. The insight made possible through such systematic comparison helps to clarify the cultural complexities within and between groups. It is not an easy matter to develop a cross-cultural perspective and related skills among students, parents, and school personnel. However, it is possible to do so through the use of the more successful social science tools and techniques used to train such personnel as anthropological fieldworkers, Peace Corps volunteers, and diplomats in their respective fields.

Since 1966 this author has advocated cross-cultural training for personnel in bilingual education. It is important that programs attempt to institute anthropological concepts and techniques to develop a cross-cultural and comparative perspective for use in dealing with the cultural aspects of teaching and learning. Conceptual tools and methodologies from anthropology may also be useful in developing conceptual clarity about home-school linkages and parent participation, and in investigating these relations empirically. Additional conceptual tools can be derived from important relevant bodies of theory and various case studies and models of parent participation.[3]

Conceptual and Theoretical Models

The literature concerning parent participation provides examples of many different approaches that vary according to the ways in which home-school relations are conceptualized, structured, and practiced in different communities. The following three theoretical frameworks of equilibrium, conflict, and eclecticism each has its own respective assumptions and relative strengths and weaknesses for analyzing different models of parental involvement.[4]

Equilibrium Approach

An equilibrium theoretical framework values consensus and the maintenance of balance among opposing or divergent influences or elements. Such a framework assumes that, although it needs some reforms, the existing system is basically worth preserving. It also gives primary concern to harmonious relations among various parts of the system (Paulston 1976). Reform and incremental adjustments within the existing system are mediated in an orderly and systematic manner, and changes are smooth and cumulative.

An approach to parent participation based upon the equilibrium theory will attempt to build harmony and order between the school and the home in the processes and methods employed. Arrangements will routinely and methodically regulate the interactions and contributions of different groups to program goals and activities. The strength of this approach is that it does not require major structural changes in relationships. Thus, it is less threatening to the established order. Its major weaknesses are that only changes that can be integrated within the existing system are allowed, and that changes occur slowly over a long period of time.

Example: The PLACER System. The PLACER System (Krear 1979) uses a modified Delphi technique for systematically obtaining input and participation from a wide variety of opposing groups in order to arrive at a consensus for decision making. It was developed and tested with the parent participation component of the Valley Intercultural Program, a bilingual consortium project operating within seven different school districts and various communities in the greater Sacramento area. The system uses interrelated processes to facilitate the collection and comparison of quantified, documented information from community, educators, and decision makers. The enumeration and order of educational and life goals elicited from many different segments of a community are compared through Venn diagramming (a way of identifying mutually accepted areas of overlap), to arrive at an orderly consensus of goals, objectives, and policy decisions.

The first part of the technique integrates community contributions by systematically eliciting educational data. The second part systematically translates educational data into methods. The third part involves evaluation and weighing of goals. In using this technique, the bilingual staff maximizes harmony and support for the reconciled goals, objectives, and policies as realized in the operations of the bilingual program. Ideally, then, the community, the school personnel, and the policy-making board are orchestrated into a position supportive of the program.

Conflict Approach

A conflict theoretical framework places emphasis on struggle for change, especially as applied by the less powerful, in the relationships between opposing or divergent influences or elements. This approach emphasizes the inherent instability of social systems and views conflict as a commonly occurring consequence of interaction. Change is assumed to be a natural result of contact and conflict. Another assumption upon which this framework is based is that the existing system basically does not work and that large-scale and/or radical changes leading to major restructuring are needed. Attention is devoted to the development of alternative systems. The goal of the conflict approach is major and rapid change. Non-conformity, diversity of ideas, and dialogue are considered important to the struggle for rearrangement of relations.

An approach to parent participation based upon conflict theory attempts to stimulate contact between home and school and change in the processes and methods employed by the system.

The interactions and inputs of different groups into program goals and activities are mediated in such a manner as to foment contrast and to highlight needed changes.

Example: The United Bronx Parents. The United Bronx Parents was a group organized in New York City to protect the participants' children from the harmful effects of the school system. A major overall strategy of the group was to organize so as to acquire greater power in dealing with schools that were dysfunctional and hostile to these children. The issues that brought the parents together convinced them that the schools were organized to serve the school system, not their children. They assumed that the schools required major changes. Their strategy for participating in achieving such changes included learning how to fight the system. In her book, *How to Change the Schools*, Ellen Lurie describes, in case-study detail, how this group worked. The United Bronx Parents' strategies included the following areas of concentration, each with action check lists:

1. How to make a school visit;
2. Reviewing the curriculum;
3. Staffing (hiring, supervising, firing);
4. Reporting (parent-teacher conferences);
5. Cumulative record cards;
6. Student suspension and rights;
7. Public hearings;
8. Parents' rights; and
9. Organizing against the system.

Eclectic Approach

An eclectic theoretical framework emphasizes choice and selection of what seems best from varied sources.[5] A basic assumption of this approach is that flexibility in implementing alternative strategies is pragmatically useful for realizing goals. An eclectic approach to parent participation sometimes prescribes an attempt to function harmoniously within the existing system; at other times, an attempt to change the system through organized conflict. In this approach, the parental community typically makes a choice among various and diverse options.

Two examples of eclectic models for parent participation follow. The first describes the role played by parents in the St. Lambert experiment in Montreal, Canada; the second, parents' roles in Crystal City, Texas.

Example: The St. Lambert Experiment. The St. Lambert experiment was an effort towards bilingual education made in Quebec, Canada, initiated by a parents' group. The English-speaking parents involved were "agents of change" within the public school system. They were able to introduce, and gain acceptance of, an innovative change in their children's school—a bilingual program that emphasized second language immersion, in French. The methods they used to create change and realize success were quite eclectic, reflecting both conflict and cooperation with the status quo (school board members, administrators, and teachers).

The parents laid their groundwork by organizing, requesting a program from the school board, building a mass-media campaign, and exercising pressure through local political action to get an experimental class accepted. The parents' follow-up work included playing a supportive role by forming a study group as a watchdog. The group's final strategy was to help institutionalize the program. They accomplished this by electing members to the school board and by becoming organizers and advocates of bilingual education in other communities. The parents participated in affecting the school program by combining support and cooperation with critical scrutiny and political action. From 1963 to the present they have, after careful consideration, selected those strategies most appropriate for accomplishing their particular goals at particular times.

Example: Crystal City, Texas. Crystal City is a rural town in south Texas, historically controlled by a minority of Anglos. However, it has undergone marked transformation as the result of an organized takeover of city government and schools by Chicanos, who make up approximately 85% of the population (Shockley 1973). The interesting aspect of the "Chicano Revolution" in Crystal City is that issues involving school problems accelerated change—first through a conflict approach, later through an equilibrium approach. Although there were pre-conditions that stimulated the Chicanos to organize (Foley 1976), it was a walkout by students protesting school inequities that mobilized their parents to organize and confront the existing system. Working within the electoral system, the Chicanos elected a majority of their representatives to the City Council and the School Board. Once control was achieved, this group created major and radical changes in the schools, such as banning testing, forcing a large turnover in school personnel, and lowering the median age of teachers by approximately ten years (Melendez 1971). After major changes were accomplished, it was considered important to minimize disorientation and to reassemble, in an orderly manner, the operation of schools.

Before the takeover, Crystal City had a dropout rate of 80%. Subsequently, the proportion of Mexican-Americans on the faculty and in administration increased, and the dropout rate for Chicano children declined. In order to eliminate discrimination and to pursue goals of self-determination, the Chicano voters eventually created an alternative system, *La Raza Unida Party*, rather than working through the existing two political parties. This new political party was constructed upon family and friendship networks and manifested confidence, pride, and a feeling of community. The contact between Anglos and Chicanos in Crystal City had to involve conflict initially in order for Chicanos to eliminate their political and cultural subordination. After restructuring and change, the Chicanos could afford to employ a strategy re-establishing equilibrium.

Major Areas and Roles

The profuse literature concerning parent participation ranges considerably in the topics and issues addressed and varies in quality of treatment. Bibliographies, some of which are annotated, do exist and are available through the usual library, National Network, and National Clearinghouse sources.[6] The major areas usually addressed are: (1) basic information; (2) parents as teachers in the home and community; (3) parents as helpers/teachers in schools; (4) parents and advisory committees; (5) parents and monitoring, evaluation and research; and (6) parents as cultural political brokers.

Basic Information

Information is essential for effective parent participation. Parents who are somewhat active, but not informed, are vulnerable to manipulation or misdirection in their efforts. Parents who are well informed tend to be more active as well as more effective in their activities. Information confers considerable power, as evident in the efforts of those in power to control access to it, as well as the success of parents seeking change who have utilized it to organize themselves. By becoming personally informed about their children's school, parents may gain an insider's view of these institutions and how they operate. Ellen Lurie's book, *How to Change the Schools*, is one guide to becoming informed. At the very least, parents should have access to documents and information concerning: (a) children's and parents' rights; (b) an educational rationale for parental involvement; (c) pertinent laws, guidelines, and district policies as a complement to the specifics of program proposals, budgets, and evaluation reports; and (d) information on particular issues. Some of the materials provided in training legislation contain such information, Title VII, ESEA, guidelines and state legislation as well as resources available through state education departments, parent advocacy groups, and professional associations such as the National Association for Bilingual Education.

Teachers in the Home

As indicated elsewhere in CCRC data and in the writings of Arvizu, Jordan, Carrasco, and Hernández-Chavez, parents in all cultures are transmitters of knowledge and, as a natural consequence of child rearing, are teachers and facilitators of learning. Prior to entering the public school setting, the basic interaction between the children and their environment is mediated by their parents, other adults, and other children. Anthropologists refer to this process of teaching the young what they need to survive in their family and cultural community as "enculturation." In most cases, the parents of students are the "original" teachers and remain a knowledgeable source of insights into the children's particular learning styles, motivations, and attributes. Some writers are beginning to describe how teachers can use parents as a resource for out-of-school follow-ups of school activities.[7] Although helping their children with homework is an important function, one hopes that parents will be seen in the future as guides to learning in deeper and more comprehensive ways.

Helpers/Teachers in the School

Much of recent literature concerning parent participation deals with parents' assistance in schools as volunteers and community aides. The CCRC sequence on culture[8] suggests specific techniques enabling parents to pursue "teaching" roles in schools such as providing "insider" information on culture and on life history technique. The relationship between school and home must be mediated by personnel who are able to facilitate the participation of parents as helpers and teachers in school as well as the complementary participation of teachers as helpers in the community.

Advisory Committee

This is a critical area, because it serves as a clue to the structure of home-school relations. A number of theses and dissertations have focused on parent advisory committees and their effectiveness (e.g., Ramiro Reyes 1972). Various districts and agencies have created manuals for the operation of such groups. However, the literature in this area addresses more than the mechanics of constructing and operating a committee; it also gives attention to policy, decision-making, representation, and evaluation. The composition of an advisory committee; and its operation relative to parental input as it influences a program reveal the depth of its commitment to parent participation. Its participants should have a sense of how their committee functions in comparison to advisory committees in other settings.

Evaluation and Research

Although some literature—that of the Latino Institute in Chicago,[9] for example—gives attention to parents as participants in program monitoring and evaluation, attention is seldom given to the possibility of including parents as participants in the research process. Some programs do attempt to develop research and inquiry skills among parents, allowing them to critique research done on themselves and other parents and children and enabling them to create research priorities for their respective programs. For example, not enough is known about the significance of particular kinds of parent participation in the learning of children. Parents are not generally informed on the inadequacies and limitations of testing instruments nor on their rights in protecting their children from abuse as human subjects involved in research. A well-informed and active person interested in parent participation will not neglect this vital area.

Cultural and Political Brokers

This area addressed innovation, power, and change in schools and communities. Parents and teachers are not only transmitters of cultural knowledge; they are also active political beings who can innovate, mediate, and solve cultural problems. A broker is a go-between, a person who links different entities or mediates opposing forces. Accepting such a role implies that a person has reflected on what exists and what should exist, and is committed to bringing the two into relationship. For parents and teachers to become effective cultural and political brokers, it is imperative that they become proficient at building linkages and bridges between the home and school. The role or roles that a parent or teacher assumes should be informed by a comparative understanding of the various roles that are possible and a careful consideration of strategy and impact. Good training does not leave the formulation of such strategies to chance but attempts to develop various alternatives from which the participant can choose. Ultimate *choice* and *action* are the responsibility of individuals and their respective groups and communities.

Questions and Challenges

Parent participation may effect major changes in the relationship between the school and the home community and the impact of this relationship on students. It also runs the risk of becoming routinized and institutionalized into traditional insignificant forms. The degree of impact that parent participation will make upon bilingual education depends greatly on the quantity of resources and the quality of effort devoted to it. This author's position is that high minimum standards must be set for implementing parent involvement, and critical thinking and conceptual clarity must be brought to bear on the creation of a strong parental component.

It is suggested that integration of the cultural domain of teaching and learning with those components of programs involving parents and community would work to strengthen each. It is difficult to implement adequate cross-cultural instruction without an adequate plan for parent participation. Where a program has developed such home-school linkages, it is probable that cultural resources from the surrounding community are being utilized. It is also suggested that parent participation should not be treated merely as that which is permitted by narrow interpretations of what presently exists. For bilingual education to succeed as an innovative experimental movement, it is important that its clients—i.e., students and parents—participate actively with school personnel in creating and testing innovative approaches.

This presentation of comparative models of such approaches has focused on the kinds of training that may be needed for effective parental involvement to occur. The task of making schools more responsive to various language and cultural groups requires a wide repertoire of strategies, skills, and approaches as well as the conceptual and theoretical tools necessary for developing clarity of direction and for minimizing contradiction and waste of resources. The literature concerning parent participation herein examined does not yet point clearly to any direction or plan of action. But perhaps continuing to ask basic questions can challenge each of us to strive for excellence in parent participation as we strive for excellence in other aspects of the teaching/learning process. Acting on the assumption that asking the right questions is a key to arriving at adequate solutions, the following questions are offered for consideration:

1. What training is necessary for school personnel to help them understand the world of the home, and to help them become effective cultural brokers in home-school relations?

2. What kind of training is important for parents to help them understand the world of the school and to help them become effective cultural brokers in home-school relations?
3. How can we develop quality and clarity of direction in parent participation components?
4. What does "parent participation" mean in different communities?
5. How is it related to the learning of students?
6. What rules or codes of conduct at work in the various communities served by the school does one need to know in order to build home-school linkages?
7. Do certain approaches to parent participation work better than others?
8. What are the responsibilities of parents? Teachers? Administrators? Students?
9. What are the various roles in building home-school linkages? For oneself? For others?
10. What are the ideals for home-school linkages and parent participation in bilingual education programs?
11. What is the reality with regard to parent participation in bilingual programs? Are there disparities between the ideals and realities?

The ongoing process of finding answers to these and other similar questions will help shape the future potential of bilingual and cross-cultural education and other innovative padagogical movements.

Endnotes

1. Dr. Steven F. Arvizu, California State University, Bakersfield.
2. Discussions with many project directors, evaluators, and researchers about priorities for research have noted a consistent

reference to the importance of parent participation. Further research in this area is highly recommended by CCRC.

3. Further explanations of these suggestions can be found in the publication, *"Demystifying the Concept of Culture,"* available from the Cross Cultural Resource Center, California State University at Sacramento, 6000 Jay St., Sacramento, CA 95819.

4. The basic ideas involving equilibrium and conflict theories have been presented by many social scientists, but Roland G. Paulston, in *Conflicting Theories of Social and Educational Change: A Typological Review*, presents a comprehensive and contrastive explanation, some of which is used here.

5. Eclecticism comes from a tradition in anthropology of drawing upon many disciplines. As used here, it is consistent with CCRC ideas of constructive marginality, cultural brokerage, and "code switching."

6. For listings of centers and for information from the Clearinghouse call the toll-free number 1-800-336-4560.

7. See *The Catalog of NIE Education Products*, 1975, for examples.

8. The series of monographs on culture is available from the Cross Cultural Resource Center (address in footnote 3).

9. Materials on the Latino Institute are available directly from their office in Chicago. Additional information has been made available through presentations at various conferences by members of the staff and by Jay and Steve Schensul, consulting anthropologists. For further information contact CCRC, Sacramento, California.

References

Amodeo, Luiza, et al.
    1982   Parental Involvement in the Identification of Gifted Mexican American Children. Paper presented at the Council for Exceptional Children National Conference, Phoenix, Arizona. October.

Arvizu, Steven, et al.
    1982   Bilingual Education Community Study Project. Final Report. National Institute of Education.

Arvizu, Steven F., and Manuel Alonzo
    1969   A Procedural Manual for Implementing Successful

Bilingual Programs. M.A. thesis. California State University Sacramento, California.

Arvizu, Steven F., and Warren Snyder with Paul T. Espinosa
  1978   Conceptual and Theoretical Tools for Demystifying Culture. Monograph I. Sacramento, Calif.: Cross Cultural Resource Center.

Bermudez, Andrea, and Yolanda Padron
  1987   Integrating Parental Education into Teacher Training Programs: A Workable Model for Minority Parents. Journal of Educational Equity and Leadership 7(3):235–244.

Berry-Caban, Cristobal
  1983   Parent-Community Involvement: The Effects of Training in a Public School Bilingual Education Program. Small Group Behavior 14(3):359–368.

Bissell, J.S.
  1983   Program Impact Evaulation: Introduction for Managers of Title VII Projects. Washington, D.C.: Southwest Regional Educational Laboratory.

Buriel, Raymond
  1980   The Relation of Anglo and Mexican American Children's Locus of Control Beliefs to Parents' and Teachers' Socialization Practices. Paper presented at the Western Psychological Association, Honolulu, Hawaii, May.

California State Department of Education
  1978   Community Participation in Determining School Effectiveness. Sacramento, California.

Carrasquillo, Angela, and Ceferino Carrasquillo
  1979   Bilingual Parents Can Help You Teach Reading and Language Arts in English. Journal for the National Association for Bilingual Education. Winter:83–91.

Carrillo, R.A.
  1973   An In-depth Survey of the Attitudes and Desires of Parents in a School Community to Determine the Nature of a Bilingual/Bicultural Program. Unpublished doctoral dissertation. University of New Mexico.

Catalog of NIE Products
  1975   Washington, D.C.: Superintendent of Documents, U.S. Government Printing Office.

Cohen, Bernard
  1983   Parental Involvement in Program Evaluation. Bilingual Journal. Winter.

DeAvila, Marcia Freedman
  1976   A Model Parental Involvement Program for Bilingual/
          Bicultural Developmental Day Care. Unpublished
          Master's thesis. Washington State University:
Edelman, Marian Wright
  1987   Families in Peril: An Agenda for Social Change.
          Cambridge, Mass.: Harvard University Press.
Gandara, Patricia
  1980   Chicano Scholars: Against All Odds. Santa Monica,
          Calif.: Rand Corporation.
Goldenberg, Claude
  1987   Low-Income Hispanic Parents' Contributions to Their
          First-Grade Children's Word-Recognition Skills.
          Anthropology and Education Quarterly 18(3):149–179.
  1984   Low Income Hispanic Parent's Contributions to the
          Reading Achievement of Their First Grade Children.
          Paper presented at Evaluation Research Society, San
          Francisco, California. October.
Henderson, Anne
  1987   The Evidence Continues to Grow: Parent Involvement
          Improves Student Achievement. Columbia, Maryland:
          National Committee for Citizens in Education.
Hutchison, Mary Ann
  1986   Strengthening Head Start Families: Reducing High
          Risk Through Mental Health Prevention/Intervention,
          Final Report. San Fernando, Calif.: Latin American
          Civic Association Head Start.
Isais, Raoul
  1978   A Minority Perspective on a Cultural Approach to
          Parent Participation in Bilingual Cross Cultural
          Education. Sacramento, Calif.: Cross Cultural
          Resource Center.
Konig, Alice
  1984   Parent Involvement in Early Childhood Education.
          Washington, D.C.: National Association for the
          Education of Young Children.
Krear, Morris L.
  1972   The PLACER System: A Three Part Accountability
          Model, Placer County, Office of Education, Auburn,
          California.
Laosa, Luis
  1980   Maternal Teaching Strategies and Cognitive Styles in
          Chicano Families. Journal of Educational Psychology
          72(1):45–54.

Lazos, Hector
    1982   Los Padres Como Maestros de los Ninos: Los Padres
            Como Recursos Para los Maestros. Dallas, Texas:
            Evaluation, Dissemination and Assessment Center.
Lindner, Barbara
    1987   Parental Involvement in Education: The ECS Survey
            of State Initiatives for Youth at Risk. Denver, Colo.:
            Education Commission of the States. November.
Lurie, Ellen
    1970   How to Change the Schools. New York: Random
            House.
Matute-Bianchi, Maria Eugenia
    1979   The Federal Mandate for Bilingual Education: Some
            Implications for Parent and Community Participation.
            Paper presented at the Ethnoperspectives Forum on
            Bilingual Education, Ypsilanti, Michigan. June.
McConnell, Beverly
    1977   Bilingual Mini Schools Tutoring Project. Final
            Evaluation Report. Washington Intermediate School
            District 171, Wenatchee, Washington.
Melendez, Ambrosio
    1971   Crystal City: A Case Study in Educational Innovation.
            Unpublished M.A. thesis. Mexican American
            Education Project. Sacramento, California.
Melikoff, Olga
    1972   Parents as Change Agents in Education: The St.
            Lambert Experiment. *In* Bilingual Education of
            Children. Lambert and Tucker, eds.
National Committee for Citizens in Education
    1982   Parent Participation—Student Achievement: The
            Evidence Grows.
Ochoa, A.M.
    1974   Parental Participation in Bilingual Education: Working
            with the Bilingual Community. National
            Clearinghouse for Bilingual Education.
Office of Bilingual Education and Minority Language Affairs
    1983   Building Capacity and Commitment in Bilingual
            Education: A Practical Guide for Educators.
            Washington, D.C.: U.S. Department of Education.
Ogletree, E.J., and M.P. Walker
    1975   Parental Participation in Bilingual Education: A Study
            of Attitudes of Puerto Rican Parents Toward Bilingual
            Education. Chicago, Ill.: ERIC Document ED 198 634.
Parsons, Kathryn
    1987   Family Support and Education Programs in the

Schools. Harvard Family Research Project, Harvard University. September.

Paulston, Roland G.
    1976   Conflicting Theories of Social and Educational Change: A Typological Review. UCIS University of Pittsburgh, Pa.

Reyes, Ramiro
    1972   The Role of School District Advisory Committees in the Educational Decision Making Process of ESEA Title I Programs for Disadvantaged Children in California. Unpublished dissertation. Michigan State University, Lansing, Michigan

Rich, Dorothy
    1985   The Forgotten Factor in School Success: The Family, A Policymaker's Guide. Washington, D.C.: The Home and School Institute, Inc.

Shockley, John
    1973   Crystal City: Los Cinco Mexicanos. In Chicano: The Evolution of a People. Minneapolis, Minn.: Winston Press.

Slaughter, Helen
    1975   Effect of Parent Involvement in an Early Intervention Program upon Environmental Process Variables Related to Achievement. Paper presented at American Educational Research Association, Washington, D.C. March.

Thomas, J.
    1976   Attitudes of Mexican American Parents Toward Bilingual Education. Unpublished dissertation. University of Michigan.

Troike, R.C.
    1978   Research Evidence for the Effectiveness of Bilingual Education. Roslyn, Va.: National Clearinghouse for Bilingual Education.

U.S. Commission on Civil Rights
    1975   A Better Chance to Learn: Bilingual/Bicultural Education. Washington, D.C. Clearinghouse Publication.

Our Voices, Our Vision: American Indians Speak Out For Educational Excellence

National Dialogue Project on American Indian Education

> Several of our young People were formerly brought up at the Colleges of the Northern Provinces: they were instructed in all your Sciences; but when they came back to us, they were bad Runners, ignorant of every means of living in the woods . . . neither fit for Hunters, Warriors, nor Counsellors, they were totally good for nothing (Chiefs of the Six Nations at Lancaster, Pennsylvania, 1744).

Preface

Much has been written about school reform in America, but very little attention has been given to American Indian students. What little attention has been given to Indian communities has, for the most part, met with failure or limited success because the approval of tribal leaders and parents was not secured and Indian cultural values and agendas were not taken into consideration.

Following through on a recommendation of an earlier Native American Symposium, a series of dialogues on Native American education was initiated in 1987, sponsored jointly by the College Board's Educational EQuality Project (EQ) and the American Indian Sciences and Engineering Society (AISES). Through these dialogues, AISES and the College Board undertook to learn what educational changes

American Indians want for American Indian youth. Enabled by funding from the Charles Stewart Mott Foundation and a number of other contributors, AISES proceeded to conduct seven regional dialogues with grass-roots members of Indian communities. This report represents the outcomes of these meetings and the concensus of 150 Indian leaders, school administrators, teachers, parents, and students from 87 tribes. Every major geographic region in the nation was represented.

It is clear from this report that Indian people want their children to value their culture and traditions, but they also want their children to have basic academic competencies and subject-matter knowledge when they emerge from the educational pipeline. Among the critical issues for American Indians is how to reconcile Indian spiritual values and formal education.

It is our hope that this report will serve as a springboard for the development of policy changes and new program initiatives that are more effective in Indian communities and that it will be an impetus for ongoing dialogue with Indian communities in their quest for educational excellence.

Educational EQuality Project, The College Board, American Indian Science and Engineering Society (AISES)

Introduction

American Indians have many educational needs that differ from those of mainstream society. Many Indians feel that the assimilation objectives of American education are detrimental to the social, economic, and political wellbeing of their communities. These concerns prompted the National Dialogue Project on American Indian Education. Some 150 American Indian students, parents, tribal leaders, and educators, representing numerous urban areas and nearly 87 tribes, discussed these issues in 1987 and 1988 at seven regional dialogues sponsored jointly by the American

Indian Science and Engineering Society and the College Board's Educational EQuality Project. The message emanating from Indians through these dialogues is clear. Indians want direct control over educational institutions serving their children, curriculum reform to make cultural retention an important factor in their education, and tribal community empowerment to strengthen the partnership between communities and educational systems.

Dialogue participants cited historical and contemporary issues that make education reform imperative. Historically, white Americans invaded Indian country, established colonial institutions, and subjugated most sovereign Indian nations to federal domination. Under duress, tribes ceded most of their landholdings and lost their economic self-sufficiency through forced changes in lifestyles. Federal policy makers implemented a coercive assimilation policy aimed at destroying tribal culture. Architects of assimilation targeted Indian children for radical resocialization as a means of destroying tribal life. Traditionally, parents, clan members, and religious leaders taught children tribal values, religious precepts, political ideology, and other skills to live a well-balanced life. Under white authority, Indian children frequently suffered a torrent of abuse. Government officials sent children to distant boarding schools where they were punished for speaking their own language, taught to believe that their Indian ways were evil, and inculcated with values antithetical to tribal life.

In the 1950's, when the federal government sought to cancel its trust obligation to Indian tribes, federal budget cuts shifted emphasis from boarding schools to local public schools. Although most Indian students thereafter lived at home and attended local schools, the aim of state administered education remained essentially the same: assimilation. Non-Indian educators frequently lacked the sensitivity to deal with Indian students in a productive manner. As public opinion became more tolerant of cultural pluralism during the 1960's, Congress authorized funds for Indian education and cultural retention programs. Numerous tribes and communities took advantage of the opportunity by contracting with Bureau of Indian Affairs

(BIA) schools, establishing local school boards, and setting up alternative schools. With this control, Indians began to develop culturally based curricula. Federal budget cuts during the late 1970's and 1980's, however, eliminated or weakened many of these self-determination initiatives in education.

Social, economic, and political problems facing Indian communities today are largely attributed to the disruptive impact of westward American expansion and federal Indian policy. Interracial contact has weakened but not destroyed Indian culture. Pressure to assimilate, interaction with non-Indians, outward migration, and education have impacted tribal communities unevenly. While many Indians have attempted to integrate into the mainstream, others have done so selectively or not at all. While fluency in tribal language has declined in some tribes, it remains firmly entrenched in others. Lifestyle spirituality continues to underpin tribal life.

The legacy of inconsistent and historically conflicting public policies toward Indian people is evident in tribal communities. Teenage pregnancies in many communities exceed national levels. Alcoholism and substance abuse are at epidemic levels in Indian country. Soaring unemployment on reservations makes migration to cities an attractive alternative to poverty for many young families. According to the 1980 census, over half of the nation's 1.4 million Indians live in urban areas. Other problems plaguing Indian people include negative self-concepts and suicide.

Schools administered by non-Indians are often not addressing these issues. Moreover, they fail to educate a large portion of the Indian community. In 1980 the Indian drop-out rate was 45%. According to a 1988 BIA status report, 90% of all Indians attend public schools; the remainder attend BIA and private schools. Family illiteracy keeps Indian youth from mastering basic educational skills. The mainstream orientation of school curricula disorients many Indian students rooted in traditional culture. Because most teachers are non-Indian, school districts do not provide Indian students with positive role models, nor have they developed effective teaching strategies based upon the learning styles of Indian children.

Despite this abysmal record, dialogue participants wanted the American model of education reformed so as to be relevant to Indian concerns. They endorsed EQ's six Basic Academic Competencies (described in Academic Preparation for College, College Entrance Examination Board, 1983) as vital skills needed for success in higher education and employment, but they expressed the need for tribal communities to set their own educational agenda, based upon local needs and concerns.

Drawing upon their impressive knowledge of Indian culture, history, and contemporary status, the participants presented positive formulations for revitalizing Indian life. They affirmed that Indians, whether in reservation or urban settings, must act to remedy many of the social, economic, and political ills plaguing their communities. They wanted curricula to include Indian languages, world views, culture, concepts, values, and perspectives. They articulated the need for schools to offer course work designed to reinforce parental and community teachings. They asserted that children instilled with traditional tribal values could live successfully in the modern world.

The dialogue participants saw little hope of resolving problems affecting their communities without substantial change in the educational status quo. They insisted upon the need for sweeping changes in education. With nearly 50% of the Indian population under the age of nineteen, they saw change as essential.

> Going to school and getting an education are two different things and they do not always happen at the same time. (Dr. Rosa M. Hill, Mohawk, 1930).

Integrating Indian Culture into Basic Academic Competencies and Subjects

Making education relevant to tribal community needs is possible. Dialogue participants agreed that schools must begin to integrate Indian culture into the Basic Academic

Competencies as well as subject-matter areas and to develop appropriate bilingual/bicultural course offerings. They saw close interaction between Indian communities and local schools as a prerequisite to success for Indian students. Indian parents and community leaders must work cooperatively with local educators by sharing their knowledge of tribal culture, philosophy, and history. This approach would provide Indian students with positive reinforcement that the educational process is important for tribal communities.

The following areas of Basic Academic Competencies and subjects should be reoriented to include Indian content and perspectives whenever possible.

English and Language Arts

English is vital to communication in most American settings. Dialogue participants critically analyzed institutional mechanisms that are the official conduit for communication. They suggested culturally appropriate ways in which American Indian students can master English skills effectively. To this end, dialogue participants endorsed the concept of building on basic skills by encouraging schools to create settings where Indian students can speak, read, and write about their own cultural experiences. Participants strongly endorsed using American Indian creation stories in literature and in poetry as a means of building reading and literature appreciation. American Indian poets and authors can be drawn upon to deepen literacy as well as to enhance self-esteem.

Mathematics

Mathematics is a critical academic discipline for the Indian community to master. Schools should stress a strong mathematics program, including algebra, geometry, functions, and calculus, from kindergarten to the college level. If Indian youth are going to have math-based careers, early preparation is imperative. Basic algebra should be a high school graduation requirement for all Indian children. The mathematics curriculum should include practical applications to "real world" situations and should prepare students for standardized tests. Success in mathematics will enhance the academic self-esteem of Indian students and prepare them for a technological society.

"Most students leave school without sufficient preparation in mathematics to cope with either on-the-job demands for problem-solving or with college requirements for mathematic literacy" (National Resource Council, 1989). Many career opportunities are denied because Indian students are not prepared for the jobs of tomorrow.

Dialogue participants discussed the ancient tradition of mathematical genius among indigenous peoples. Their contributions to mathematics and science, such as the medicine wheel and the Aztec calendar, should be incorporated into the historical dimension of modern curriculum offerings. If properly prepared for leadership in math-based fields, American Indians can once again contribute significantly to the technological, economic, and social advancement of native peoples as well as to the society at large.

Science

Biology, chemistry, physics, and other science courses can be made culturally relevant for tribal youth by integrating Indian concepts of natural phenomena, astronomy, medicine, and mythology into the curriculum. For example, teaching the Mother Earth tradition, the notion that all things on earth are sacred and interrelated, would heighten students' awareness of conservation and the interdependence of nature. In light of such dangers as the greenhouse effect, the depletion of the ozone layer, and the ruthless exploitation of the earth's resources, this spiritual message of living in harmony with nature has cross-cultural significance.

Social Studies

Social studies courses frequently sideline, stereotype, and debase Indian culture. Dialogue participants agreed that textbooks, such as those for history and anthropology, commonly present either romantic or negative images of Indians. This propaganda has etched into the American mind that Indians represent human savagery, while Anglos symbolize superiority. On the other hand, the curriculum pays scant attention to contemporary Indian issues, such as tribal sovereignty, economic development, and culture. This leaves students with the impression that tribal cultures vanished after nineteenth century wars or survive only peripherally in the modern world. Consequently, many Indians and non-Indians alike have internalized distorted views of tribal life. Dialogue participants noted that there should be little wonder why so many Indians develop negative self-images.

Participants presented ways in which Indian people can take the distortions, propaganda, and falsehoods out of the classroom. By reeducating non-Indian teachers and writing their own histories, Indians can provide a more truthful interpretation of human interaction. Education materials need to stress Indians' social, economic, and political contributions to the world. This, with the integration of Indian perspectives, knowledge, and philosophies, would remove some sources of bias in classroom learning.

American Indian Languages

Indians want to ensure the survival of their respective tribal languages. Dialogue participants emphasized that language retention is a key to cultural survival. However, many pointed with alarm to the decline of native languages in numerous Indian communities. They wanted schools to help reverse this trend by offering courses at all levels in local tribal languages and in bilingual/bicultural education. Indian students should have the option of studying their native languages to fulfill academic requirements.

Fine Arts

Fine arts, including the visual and performing arts, are an integral part of Indian life. Indian culture allows individuals to express themselves artistically in a number of ways. Yet schools have suppressed Indian creativity in favor of mainstream preferences. Dialogue participants asserted that schools must allow Indian students the option of applying their creativity within the context of tribal traditions. This means that educators must develop expressive classes in art, music, dance, and drama that focus on historical and contemporary Indian culture.

Physical Education and Health

Physical and intellectual development go hand in hand in traditional Indian culture. Schools must integrate Indian recreational activities into curricula to keep tribal youth fit. They must teach Indian students how to prepare traditional foods in wholesome and nutritional ways. Teaching health in accord with tribal values will help eliminate many medical problems facing Indian populations, such as diabetes, obesity, and high blood pressure.

Computer Competency

In a technological society, it is critical that American Indian students understand the use of computers. Many employment opportunities in the future will require computer-based skills. Dialogue participants noted that competency with computers could improve instruction in native content—a blending of modern technology and ancient tradition. For example, a greater understanding and appreciation of American Indian symbolic images for communication could be stimulated by using electronic and computer theory in the development of computer languages and operating systems.

Call to Action

Indian children must be prepared to function effectively in two worlds. They need bridges between traditional values, languages, and spirituality and modern science and technology. With this in mind, dialogue participants issued a call to action. They recognized that future generations must live successfully in both Indian and non-Indian worlds.

Indian wisdom is the accumulated knowledge and tradition of Indian people. Dialogue participants recognized that knowledge and tradition vary among Indian nations and people. However, they also recognized a common world view and collective experience that sustains Indians as a unique people in American society.

American Indian languages, songs, art, and other cultural attributes transcend present-day society. This land is where Indian ancestors are buried, where the faces of the unborn are awaited, and where Indian people are at home.

The call to action recognized that cultural strength will preserve the future of Indian wisdom and will provide Indians with strength to meet the challenges of the modern world. With these thoughts in mind, dialogue participants identified nine major categories of concern. These categories are not presented in isolation, but in interrelation, as they all have impact on education. These categories are: Indian communities, tribes, parents, schools, students, testing, legislation, colleges and universities, and research and publishing.

Indian Communities

Indian community action, dialogue participants agreed, must spearhead drives for educational change. Tribal members must elect tribal officials willing to adopt education codes that mandate the incorporation of tribal language and culture into the curricula of local schools. These codes must clearly define ceremonial-spiritual rights for legitimate or excusable student absence.

Community groups must develop strategies for gaining access to school boards, teachers, and elected officials. They need to develop a system of accountability to assess school performance in meeting local needs. In the process, board members, local administrators, teachers, student policies, and curricula must be periodically evaluated. Communities need to work closely with schools and develop a program of teacher (re)education. Tribal groups should establish culturally based programs for combating alcohol and substance abuse, health problems, teenage pregnancy, and other problems confronting their youth. Urban Indians can use Indian center, churches, and organizations as collective strength for facilitating similar change.

> Many Indians who have succeeded in mainstream society have retained their culture and values. Some of them work in the white world but return to the reservation for religious ceremonies. Others received an education and returned home to live and work among their own people (Richard Johnny-John, Seneca A Faith Keeper of the Long House, 1988).

Tribes

Tribal governments, dialogue participants noted, have the power to become active partners with Indian parents and school districts in educational reform and community initiatives. In doing so, tribes must pass resolutions setting education as a priority. They must develop education codes for all local schools mandating the integration of basic curriculum with tribal values, language, intellectual concepts, and spirituality.

Tribal councils must assist students by establishing scholarship and summer-work projects. They should also encourage college students to return home after graduation. Dialogue participants also stated that tribal leaders should serve as positive role models for students by leading drug- and alcohol-free lives. They also pointed out that tribal councils must link tribal drug and alcohol abuse programs with local schools as a means of combating social problems.

Parents

Dialogue participants held that parents must assume a pivotal role in education. Parents must instill pride and self-esteem within Indian children. They must pass on values and beliefs that give children an Indian orientation toward academic and professional life. Finally, parents are important language and cultural resources in Indian communities.

Local initiatives should empower parents to influence school decisions. They should sit on school boards, organize parent-teacher associations, review curriculum, provide cultural training for teachers, and review textbooks. These activities would help school instruction present accurate interpretations of Indian history and culture.

Parents should launch community education programs designed to strengthen local education initiatives. These include programs for family literacy in English, for tribal education codes, and for community-school coordination. Finally, parents should assume ultimate leadership in cultural retention through home-bound language and cultural programs.

Schools

Dialogue participants stressed the central role that schools play in the lives of Indian children and communities. However, most schools have been unreceptive to tribal concerns and needs.

Dialogue participants articulated ways in which schools can establish linkages with tribal communities. First, schools must promote Indian identity by implementing a holistic curriculum, including language, history, and culture courses. Second, schools need to attract top-quality teachers and administrators, especially Indians who could serve as role models. Third, schools should encourage Indians to become more active in decision-making processes. In this regard, Indian parents should seek positions on school boards, and students must have a say in school affairs. Fourth, school and classroom environments should stress historical and contemporary Indian themes. For example, teachers could display pictures of Indian leaders, scientists, and spiritual leaders as a motivational strategy to encourage Indian students to succeed. Fifth, schools should investigate alternatives to standardized testing or create local methods of testing as a means of assessing Indian students' full intelligence and potential.

Students

American Indian students, the bearers of Indian tradition, must play an active role in merging tribal culture with education. Dialogue participants agreed that rigorous intellectual training will foster individual and tribal development. Education provides the student with knowledge of self and the world. Moreover, education provides the student with analytical and problem-solving skills. Consequently, the student should exploit available educational opportunities for individual and tribal betterment. Standards of high academic expectations and achievement must replace former ones of mediocrity and remediation. All academic and psychological barriers between the student and success, including alcohol and substance dependency, must be identified and eliminated.

> Search for the truth. Indian values teach the holistic approach to the use of technology for mankind's good (Al Qoyawayma, Hopi, 1984).

Education should include traditional spiritual, cultural, and linguistic orientation. Toward this end, the performance arts should be explored and applied. Open and honest communication among student, parent, and teacher will best safeguard against individual alienation. With regard to academic preparation, the Indian and non-Indian must be treated equally. However, Indian culture must be viewed and used as a strength in providing students with this preparation.

Fear of computers and technology must be overcome if students are to grow into productive adults. Computers should be used within the classroom to instill traditional Indian ideas and values while cultivating academic competencies and subject-matter knowledge.

Native language acquisition is crucial for functioning within a multicultural world. Indian students should be allowed to study their native tongues instead of foreign European languages. This language training should start in preschool and continue throughout the educational process.

Informed students will know that American history, literature, art, philosophy, and religion are not restricted to the Anglo-American heritage. America is a country of ethnic and cultural diversity, and American Indians have rich cultures that need to be more widely appreciated. Indian students should be encouraged to bring their culture into the classroom when germane to the issues discussed.

Testing

Dialogue participants acknowledged that success on standardized tests is an important measure for students, particularly those who are college bound. However, standardized tests can reflect serious cultural bias. As a consequence, results will not measure intelligence among Indian students. For American Indian people, standardized testing sometimes serves as an impediment to college. Often testing has been more a measure of acculturation than of the probability of college success. Thus, standardized testing for American Indian students needs to be considered in an appropriate context, used as one indicator along with others in college admissions.

Testing agencies should ensure that standardized tests are used and interpreted appropriately. They should encourage counselors and teachers to put more effort into preparing students for standardized tests and to communicate the merits and limitations of tests to students.

Legislation

Before culturally based education can become a reality, federal and state legislators must set a harmonious tone for change by enacting supportive legislation. Historically, local school districts have rejected reform initiatives in Indian education. Dialogue participants stated that legislative action—mandating revisions in teacher training, in teacher certification programs, in curriculum, and in standardized test questions—would help break down this resistance.

These legal actions would change education in several ways. First, school compliance with laws requiring teacher training and certification programs in cross-cultural education, with emphasis on Indian culture, would necessitate the hiring of culturally sensitive teachers.

Second, school implementation of bilingual and bicultural education would serve two fundamental purposes. It would help preserve tribal language and culture. It would also bridge the gap between Indian communities and school systems by bringing more tribal members into the educational process as cultural and language specialists.

Third, schools would give native languages the same respect as European languages. Native speakers would have the opportunity to learn in their native language when that language is the student's first, thereby learning English as a second language. Conversely, Indian students should have the opportunity to learn their native tongue as a second language, when English is their first. Bilingualism goes hand in hand with biculturalism.

Finally, culturally appropriate standardized tests would raise Indian test scores. Standardized tests should not reflect acculturation more than intellectual development or potential. But too often tests discourage rather than encourage Indian students. If standardized tests are not made culturally appropriate, schools should use other measurements of scholastic achievement for Native American students. Alternative measurement methods need to be devised and implemented.

Colleges and Universities

Dialogue participants insisted that institutions of higher learning must become key partners in Indian education reform initiatives. They noted that scholarly writings and course offerings profoundly impact American education. Information disseminated through universal sources, whether factual, biased, or distorted, ends up in textbooks, documentary films, and classroom instruction.

Universities must change their curricula to reflect a multicultural society. They must develop courses that address Indian issues from Indian perspectives. They must invigorate teacher training programs by including classes focusing on Indian education and cultural issues. In the process, academia should establish linkages with Indian tribes and communities in order to ensure accuracy.

Dialogue participants noted that comparatively few Indians (10 %) who enter college ever earn degrees. This statistic can be improved by providing Indian college students with career and culturally based psychological counseling, relevant coursework (such as tribal political and economic development), and Indian mentorship. University diversification, especially the recruiting of Indian students, faculty, administrators, and staff, would make the campus experience more rewarding and personal for Indian students. Racially mixed faculties would set the stage for drastic revisions in the curriculum, ending the non-Indian domination of higher learning. As a retention strategy, counsellors must urge students to take advantage of scholarship and fellowship opportunities.

Research and Publishing

Just as the exploitation of American Indian land and resources is of value to corporate America, research and publishing on American Indian topics is valuable to non-Indian scholars. As a result of racism, greed, and distorted perceptions of native realities, Indian culture as an economic commodity has been exploited by the dominant society with considerable damage to Indian people. Tribal people need to safeguard the borders of their cultural domains against research and publishing incursions.

Community-based research in Indian communities needs to be conducted in conjunction with the endorsement by tribal authorities for the purpose of ensuring that the finished product has value to Indian people and is educationally beneficial. Tribally sanctioned research on obesity, substance abuse, and alcoholism must be conducted to identify the nature and scope of these problems and to develop culturally acceptable therapy.

Scholarly research on Indian history and culture must take into account Indian perspectives. Published and unpublished manuscripts germane to Indians, as well as tribal history projects, could provide writers with a wealth of untapped information about historical and cultural processes not found in primary and secondary source materials. This methodology will help scholars avoid perpetuating stereotypes of Indians based on mythology, misconceptions, and romanticism. American Indian scholars need to become involved in producing research rather than serving as subjects and consumers of research. Measures such as these will ultimately introduce more accurate depictions of Indian experiences and lifestyles into the classroom.

Recommendations

Dialogue participants affirmed a holistic approach to education. Elementary, secondary, and university programs for Indian students should be guided by the spirituality that is immanent in tribal communities. Education cannot be treated as an institution separate from communities. It is part of us, just as the sun, moon, stars, rain, snow, and wind affect us as we walk on Mother Earth.

The recommendations address key elements for holistic integration. This will lead to cooperation from tribal leaders and elders, improve self-image and analytical skills among Indian children, and ensure that accurate cultural portrayals are integrated in the teaching of academic competencies and subject areas. Ultimately, the recommendations are offered in the interest of self-respect and partnership—self-respect for educators and Indians alike—so that a partnership of cultural equality can be fostered.

Consensus among dialogue participants resulted in a call for concerted action in seven principal areas that require intensive treatment:

1. Inaccuracies and biased historical textbook accounts of American Indians inhibit native educational progress and mandate action in generating a correct version of American Indian history.

2. Progress of Indian students through the educational system has been thwarted by

repressive factors that make it imperative for all programs and individuals dealing with American Indian education to accelerate their commitment in order to improve the self-image of American Indian students.

3. In order to ensure understanding among educators regarding uniformity of approach to the education of American Indian students, it is essential that Indian communities develop and provide in-service training to teachers, administrators, and school personnel through community training of educators.

4. The cultural and philosophical uniqueness of American Indian world views requires an emphasis on the development of cultural curricula based on American Indian holistic educational concepts.

5. American Indian educational processes can benefit greatly by organizing parents to exert direct influence on educational policies, program development, and practices through positive parental involvement in schools.

6. The dialogue participants strongly encouraged parents to initiate minidialogues in their communities involving other parents, students, local school representatives, and Indian community leaders. Such minidialogues would focus on local educational needs and issues concerning Indian children and would provide additional opportunities for parents and community members to become more actively involved in local policy and programs regarding the education of their children.

7. Dialogue participants recommend that BIA and tribal scholarship support be considered sovereignty awards similar to academic excellence awards. Participants recommended that eligibility for such college-scholarship support be exempted from the criteria of financial need alone.

> Our religion is the traditions of our ancestors—
> the dreams of our old men, given them in the
> solemn hours of the night by the great spirit;
> and the visions of our sachems, and it is written
> in the hearts of our people (Seattle, Chief,
> Suquamish and Duwamish Tribes, 1853).

Endnotes

1. Dedication

This report is dedicated to all American Indian people who have preserved their identity and culture. Like their ancestors before them, Indians want their values, spiritualism, and way of life passed on in perpetuity.

The National Dialogue Project on American Indian Education is dedicated to the memory of Michael N. Taylor. Taylor, an Oglala Sioux, participated in Indian affairs for 35 years. Throughout his life, Michael inspired people and worked tirelessly toward achieving a dream. He envisioned a day when Indian people would gain control over educational systems serving their children. He viewed education as a process of empowerment by which Indians could improve their lives.

Taylor influenced the momentum, tone, and content of the National Dialogue Project during its conceptual stages. He died on January 5, 1988, shortly after the second regional dialogue convened. Though he is no longer with us, his vision continually guides the effort. As we take the torch from Michael's spirit, we will pass it on to others, always remembering our ancestors.

2. Acknowledgments

The American Indian Science and Engineering Society (AISES), the College Board's Educational EQuality Project (EQ), and National Dialogue Project staff thank everyone involved with the National Dialogue Project on American Indian Education. Without support from many individuals, foundations, corporations, and organizations, the voices of some 150 Indian students, parents, tribal leaders, and educators contained within this report may not have been recorded.

AISES provided project staff; EQ provided the initial impetus. The College Board and the Charles Stewart Mott Foundation provided the majority of the financial support. Supplemental funding came from the Southern Education Foundation, Pacific Bell, the Association on American Indian Affairs, Inc., and the Eastman Kodak Company. The Zuni Public School district (Zuni Pueblo, New Mexico), the Association on American Indian Affairs, Stanford University, the University of New Mexico, and the University of Colorado at Boulder donated meeting space and personnel.

Hayes Lewis, William Gollnick, Dean Azule, Helen Peterson, Anne Medicine, George Abrams, Carmaleta Monteith, and Annette Jaimes served as Regional Dialogue Directors. They deserve special recognition for their dedicated effort. Working under financial and time constraints, they assembled a knowledgeable and professional core of participants from their respective geographical regions.

The assistance of AISES secretarial staff, student organizations, and individuals aided the project effort. Of these, Beverly Singer, Navajo/Zia, the Educational Program Officer of the Association on American Indian Affairs, deserves special recognition for her loyalty. She inspired those struggling to improve Indian education. Stanford University hosted a traditional sweat-lodge that was led by Arvol Looking Horse, Cheyenne River Sioux, that was a profound moment in molding Indian spiritual tradition and formal education.

This report was developed by the American Indian Science and Engineering Society (AISES) and written in conjunction with the staff at the American Indian Studies Center at UCLA, which included James Riding In, Pawnee; John Red Horse, Cherokee; and Jeremy Rockman, Winnebago. Lenore Stiffarm, Gros Ventre, served as principal investigator. Lenore Stiffarm, James Riding In, and Troy Johnson served as Dialogue recorders. Cecil Leighton, Rosebud Sioux, provided editorial assistance. Sue Ware, Modoc, provided outstanding administrative coordination throughout the project.

From beginning to end, the National Dialogue Project was guided by the collaboration of Norbert Hill, Jr., Executive Director of AISES and James Herbert, Executive Director for Academic Affairs, the College Board.

3. The Dialogue Format

This report documents the findings and recommendations of American Indian professionals and tribal members who possess first-hand knowledge of educational, social, political, and economic issues facing their communities. Twenty invited participants and others who covered their own expenses, including Indian students, parents, tribal leaders, and educators, expressed their views during each of seven dialogues. This report will be used to develop education reform initiatives in school systems serving American Indian students and communities.

During 1987 and 1988, some 150 American Indians, representing over 87 Indian tribes and communities and Alaskan natives, convened in seven American cities and reservations:

> Northwest Coast/Alaska; Portland, Oregon
> Cosponsor: Northwest Laboratory
> California/Great Basin; Palo Alto, California
> Cosponsor: Stanford University
> Northeast Woodlands; Rochester, New York
> Cosponsor: Kodak Corporation
> Midwest/Great Lakes; Oneida Reservation, Oneida, Wisconsin
> Cosponsor: Oneida Tribe of Wisconsin
> Desert/Southwest; Albuquerque, New Mexico
> Cosponsors: Zuni Public School District and the University of New Mexico
> Gulf/Southeast; New Orleans, Louisiana
> Cosponsor: Southern Education Foundation
> Great Plains; Denver, Colorado
> Cosponsor: University of Colorado at Boulder

The National Dialogue Project has laid the groundwork for broad educational reform in elementary and secondary schools serving American Indians by fostering community involvement in educational reform efforts, encouraging local initiatives that respect tribal values and agendas, influencing legislation and national programs that impact the education of Indian youth, and encouraging positive partnerships between Indian communities and educational leaders.

Dialogue participants divided into four groups and used their expertise as well as personal experiences to respond to one of the following concerns:

1. Identifying proper academic preparation for the modern world (using Academic Preparation for College, College Entrance Examination Board, 1983, as a reference point);
2. Identifying modern applications of traditional Indian educational techniques and understanding the critical place of cultural issues;
3. Academic motivation of Indian Students in K–12 for future college success—overcoming fear, barriers to learning, and alienation;

4. How to mobilize community support and participation in the improvement of academic preparation and student performance.

Each group spent a full day and a half discussing its respective area of concern. The four groups assembled in two plenary sessions where a spokesperson for each group presented its findings. Staff of the American Indian Studies Center of the University of California, Los Angeles (UCLA), drafted reports of the proceedings and disseminated copies to dialogue participants for comments.

All regional directors, the project coordinator, and other key project personnel met during December 1988 in Boulder, Colorado, to discuss the dialogue findings and to shape the final report.

Copies of the report will be disseminated to state and federal legislators, education policy makers, college and university administrators, clergy, educators, tribal leaders, and others who influence grass roots American Indian education.

4. Dialogue Participants

Northwest Area Dialogue Participants:

Regional Director, Dean Azule, Pima

Ronalda Cadiente, Tlingit * Debra V. Smith * Luella J. Azule, Yakima/Umatilla * Norrine Smokey-Smith, Washo * Mike Darcy, Siletz * Arlen Washines, Yakima * Jacob Bighorn, Sioux * Kathleen D. Gordon, Umatilla * Deloria Bighorn, Choctaw/Sioux * Darlene "Doll" Watt, Spokane * Willard Bill, Suquamish * Joseph Diego Cantil, Tlingit * Phyllis Covington, Colville * Tom Ball, Klamath * Brad Darcy, Siletz * Twila J. Souers, Sioux * Robin Butterfield, Chippewa/Winnebago * Darryl Brown, Tlingit

California Great Basin Dialogue Participants:

Regional Director, Anne Medicine, Oneida/Seneca/Mohawk

Andy Andreoli, Hupa * Murial Byerly Antoine, Sioux * Dr. William Demmert, Tlingit * Dr. Delores Huff Cherokee * Dr. Jack Forbes, Lanape * Diane Espina, Yakima * Dr. John Red Horse, Cherokee * Michael Joseph Raymond, Northern Cheyenne * Dr. Dave Risling, Hupa * Gregg Sarris, Pima * Dr. Lenore Stiffarm, Gros Ventre * Wes Williams, Nevada Paiute * Isidora Gali, Pit River Paiute * Ed Johnson, Paiute * Ben Aleck, Paiute * Mary Belgarde, Isleta * Carlos Cordero, Maya * Bobby Wright, Chippewa-Cree * Arvol Looking Horse, Cheyenne River Sioux

Great Plains Dialogue Participants:

Regional Director, Annette Jaimes, Juaneño (Calif. Mission)/Yaqui

Dave Archambault, Sioux * Mr. Eddie Box, Sr., Southern Ute * Sally Carufel Williams, Chippewa/Santee Sioux * Karen Chockrell,

Cherokee * Barbara Conness, Cherokee * Robert Daugherty, Cherokee * Debra Echo-Hawk, Pawnee * Gloria Grant-Means, Omaha/Navajo * Carol Gipp, Standing Rock Sioux * Theresa Halsey, Hunkpapa Sioux * Jan Jacobs, Osage * Lisa Harjo, Choctaw * Patrick Lee, Oglala Sioux * Vivian Locust, Cheyenne/ Ogala Sioux * Russell Means, Oglala Sioux * Dr. James Shanley, Sioux * Janine Pease-Windy Boy, Crow * Twila Martin, Turtle Mountain Chippewa * Dr. Grayson Noley, Choctaw * Pandy Plume, Ogala Sioux * B.J. Warclub, Yankton Sioux * Darryl Alcott, Ogala Sioux

Desert Southwest Dialogue Participants:
Regional Director, Hayes A. Lewis, Zuni
Phyllis Anton, Tono O'dham * Julie Abeyta, San Juan/Santa Domingo * Gerald Anton, Salt River/Pima/Maricopa * Sharlene Begay, Navajo * Angela Barker, Navajo * Andrew Becenti, Navajo * Robert Bennett, Oneida * Margaret Eriacho, Zuni * Wilfred Eriacho, Zuni * Joy Hanley, Navajo * Darlene Herrera, Chippewa/ Cochiti. June Leach, Oneida/Mohawk * Joe Montana, Jicarilla * Mary Palanco, Jicarilla Apache * Regis Pecos, Cochiti * Levi Pesata, Jicarilla Apache * JoAnne Ragnese, Laguna * Joseph Suina, Cochiti * Joe Shunkamola, Kiowa/Osage * Beverly Singer, Navajo/Zia * Richard Torralba, Comanche * Verna Williamson, Isleta * Michael Wolf, Zuni * Ruby Wolf, Zuni * Ted Jojola, Isleta * Rena Oyengue-Salazar, San Juan * Dr. John Philips

Gulf/Southeastern Dialogue Participants:
Regional Director, Carmeleta L. Monteith, Eastern Cherokee
Suzanne Benally, Navajo * Nancy Billie, Seminole * Marie Osceola Branch, Miccosukee * Larry Burgess, Chitamacha * Jeannette Campos, Ute Pueblo * Wilma Godwin, Lumbee * Ernest Grant, Eastern Cherokee * Alton Leblanc, Chitamacha * Paula Maney, Eastern Cherokee * Alice Nunez, Seminole * Remy Ordoyne, Choctaw * Ernest Sickey, Coushatta * Roseanna Sneed, Eastern Cherokee * Roger Trimnall, Catawba * Eddie Tullis, Creek * Kirby Verret, Houma * Gregory Wahnee, Comanche * John Wahnee, Comanche * Kim Willis

Great Lakes Dialogue Participants:
Regional Director, Bill Gollnick, Oneida
Storm Carroll, Sauk and Fox * Susan Chicks, Stockbridge-Munsee * Ernest Clark, Colville * Dr. John Derby, Sisseton-Wahpeton * Genevieve Gollnick, Oneida * Gordon Henry, White Earth Chippewa * Joan Jourdan, Winnebago * Debra Klien, Oneida of the Thames * Helene Lincoln, Winnebago * Ruth Meyers, Grand Portage Chippewa * Dr. Robert Powless, Oneida * Alfred Pyatskowit, Menominee * Mary Alice Tsosie, Navajo * Robert Van Alstine, Sault Ste Marie Chippewa * Betty Walker, Creek-Seminole

* Jerome War Cloud, Cherokee * Pat Wesaw, Mohawk * Donald
Wiesen, Fond du Lac Chippewa
Northeast Dialogue Participants:
Regional Director, George Abrams, Seneca
Kenneth Attocknie, Comanche-Caddo * Michele Dean-Stock,
Seneca * Martha Krype de Montana, Pottawatomie * Betty Haskins,
Western Cherokee * Natalie A. Hemlock, Munsee-Seneca * Richard
Johnny-John, Seneca * Mark Lindall, Narragansett * Marlene
Martin, Mohawk * Daisy P. Moore, Wampanoag * Brian Myles,
Mohegan * Katherine Nahwooksy, Comanche * Doris Norman,
Mohawk * Bruce Oakes, Caughnawaga Mohawk. Jim Sam,
Oklahoma Choctaw * John Tiger, Delaware * Geri Toyakoyah,
Kiowa * James Riding In, Pawnee * Judith Wills, Onondaga

   5. The interpretations and conclusions contained in this
publication do not necessarily represent the views of the Charles
Stewart Mott Foundation, the Southern Education Foundation,
Pacific Bell, the Association on American Indian Affairs, Inc.,
Eastman Kodak Company, their trustees, or officers, or of the
College Board. Any nonprofit organization or institution is
encouraged to reproduce this [chapter] in its entirety in quantity
sufficient for its own use but not for sale, provided that the
copyright notice be retained exactly as it appears below.

   Copyright © 1989 by College Entrance Examination Board.
All rights reserved, College Board, the EQ logo, and the acorn
logo are registered trademarks of the College Entrance
Examination Board. Educational EQuality Project and EQuality
are trademarks owned by the College Entrance Examination
Board.

   6. Copies of this report are available from the College Board,
Box 886, New York, NY 10101-0886, or from the American Indian
Science and Engineering Society (AISES), 1085 14th Street, Suite
1506, Boulder, CO 80302.

PART II

Community Contexts

Bilingual Education in Community Contexts: A Two-Site Comparative Research Design

Steven F. Arvizu
Eduardo Hernández-Chavez
Judith Guskin
Concepción Valadez[1]

Introduction

This chapter presents a portion of the research from the Bilingual Education Community Study Project, one of three studies funded by contract with the National Institute of Education to conduct research on Bilingual Effects of Community and Schools, which examined exemplary bilingual education programming in Latino settings, while the other two studied bilingual education in Asian and Native American communities.[2] A team of researchers and support staff from the Cross Cultural Resource Center, California State University at Sacramento, including Steven F. Arvizu and Eduardo Hernández-Chavez, participated as Principal Investigators, and Judith T. Guskin and Concepción Valadez were Co-Investigators. The other studies were conducted by ARC Associates in the Bay Area and Dine Biolta Associates in New Mexico.[3] This two-site community study investigated exemplary bilingual education programs in Latino community contexts in Milwaukee, Wisconsin, and Parlier, California. While the major emphasis of this paper is on the two-site design, it also summarizes findings and concludes with a brief discussion of implications for future research in bilingual settings. A more complete discussion of the research project is contained in the five-volume Final Report.

The Bilingual Education Community Study Project performed three major tasks. It (1) identified and selected exemplary bilingual programs for study, (2) conducted sociolinguistic studies of the schools and communities, and (3) conducted ethnographic studies of the schools and communities. By descriptive and qualitative research, the Study viewed the sociolinguistic and cultural contexts of learning in bilingual settings.

Background

The education of Latino students and other minority language learners in the U.S. has historically been grossly inadequate and in need of improvement as evidenced by lower educational achievement levels, higher attrition rates, inequitable fiscal support for educational opportunity, and a generally deteriorated educational condition.[4]

The educational situation of Latino students has not improved over the past several decades, a fact that affects the status and participation of the group in American society (Brown et al. 1980). Research studies and reports have consistently shown the adverse effects of lack of educational achievement and of exclusion of Latino students from equitable practices and processes (Pifer 1979; Duran 1983; Arvizu 1985; Olsen 1988).

Bilingual education programs were created in part as an experimental response to the educational neglect of Latinos (Segura and Carter 1979) and as a consequence of litigation, community pressures, and federal and state legislation. Even though bilingual programs have existed with federal support for decades, the research available on bilingual education is inconsistent in quality (Zappert and Cruz 1977), inconclusive in its findings (Troike 1980; Harrington 1980), and quite controversial and contradictory in impact (AIR 1976; Epstein 1977; Trueba and Arvizu 1979).

Most of this research has not given qualitative explanations of the internal dynamics of programs nor focused on the particular school and community contexts, or the environmental and historical conditions at work in the research settings.

A few studies have described exemplary bilingual programs using sociolinguistic and ethnographic research approaches. For example, The *Next Generation*, an early work of John Ogbu (1974), began as a study of a bilingual program in Stockton, California. Richard Warren (1980) conducted an ethnographic study of a mature bilingual program in Southern California that primarily served Spanish-speaking learners. Carrasco et al. (1979) have studied bilingual program classroom interactions in Chicago, Puerto Rico, and Mexico. Pedro Pedraza (1980) has conducted ethnographic studies of bilinguals through the Centro de Estudios Puertorriqueños in New York, and Luis Moll (1980) has studied bilingual programs in San Diego, California. In addition, Doug Foley's (1977) historical work in South Texas ethnographically described the transition of people from *peones* to *politicos* with attention to education.

Recent demographic data show that the Latino population is growing at significantly high rates. Due to factors of lower median age, higher fertility rate, and continued immigration from Mexico, Puerto Rico, and other Spanish-speaking countries, it is anticipated that the need for research on language use in socio-cultural contexts will increase (Estrada 1978). Community studies provide invaluable insight into the processes of mobility and migration, social and political organization, and the leadership dynamics of important national issues such as immigration policy for Mexicans, Puerto Rican statehood, and national language policy. In addition, the educational conditions of Latinos and other language minority students have created a need to know which innovative practices of programs are effective and why.

This Research Project follows the above tradition as a consequence of pursuing similar questions in different settings, using similar research methods and techniques, and facing similar problems involving access, controversy, source, amount of support, and ethical issues of audience, reciprocity, and accountability.

Major Tasks

The Bilingual Education Community Study Project was conceptualized to carry out three main tasks in describing and explaining the historical and political implementation of bilingual education in Latino community contexts. The first of three tasks, the identification of an exemplary program to study, was completed at the initial conceptual state of the research and is described below, together with the two-site comparison design, the process and criteria used, and the rationale for pre-selection of sites.

The Study Project studies social and educational change in two Latino communities. The stories of this original research evolve slowly and are narrated throughout the five volumes of the Final Report. The intent of the Project was to conduct descriptive research on exemplary bilingual education programs in Latino settings with specific attention to sociolinguistic, cultural, and educational characteristics of the communities and schools. The ultimate purpose of the research was to describe the dynamics and development of bilingual education programs as interfaces between schools and communities and from qualitative research to interpret and analyze the relative effectiveness of particular features and strategies in meeting locally identified needs. Analysis of differential quality in implementation is also instructive in assessing whether schools do what they say they want to do and how well it is done from the perspectives of the clients. Descriptive ethnography is especially well suited to qualitative description and interpretation as evidenced by the classic community study tradition in sociology and by historical ethnographies of Native Americans done by generations of students trained by Franz Boas at Columbia University. None of this classic research on community character and change was outcome oriented nor hypothesis-testing research. Rather these studies carefully described the conditions and interpreted realities and processes of change, eventually allowing others to generalize and predict or to conduct theoretical or evaluative studies. Given the political content of language policy in the United States and misperceptions as to the inherent diversity among federally supported bilingual programs, descriptive and comparative study seems appropriate to "tell the inside local story of what happens over time, and why it happens," and to caution educational and psychometrically oriented researchers from overgeneralizing based upon synchronic studies.

Lewis (1966) described how San Francisco came to be presenting its changing community character rather than assess whether it achieved metropolis status or was better than much smaller communities. Goldschmidt compared two agricultural communities to study the influence of corporate and family-based agriculture, revealing insights as to how these communities were different and alike and what shaped and characterized their realities. Similarly, this comparative study looked at examples of bilingual programs generally perceived to be relatively successful and to have similar features, in order to explain what is at work in each site, and how and why they might be similar or different in quality of implementation. Thus replication of certain features and practices might eventually be generalized to other sites and programs.

The Question of Audience

The research team's goal was to provide descriptive stories to many different audiences, including (1) the two communities and school people in both sites who cooperated by allowing us to study them; (2) bilingual education practitioners interested in discoveries and improvements in practices; (3) researchers curious about the issues, methods or particulars of this study; (4) policymakers, legislators, and public service agencies; and (5) the general public.

The research describes the school and community environments and shows how sampled bilingual programs mediate and innovate between the two. The descriptive nature of the data makes it useful for various practitioners, affected client communities, and academic and applied researchers.

The first audiences for whom the research is intended are the people in Parlier and Milwaukee. Their continuing concerns helped to shape the research, and the data collected address problem areas and success stories in need of documentation and analysis. The research results were used to assist the local schools and communities to consider policies and improvement of practice, and the research team was committed to follow up with technical assistance in explaining findings and offering recommendations.

State and federal policy makers are interested in critical issues of comparative effectiveness of bilingual education practices, local control of the curriculum decision-making process, and cost-effectiveness of special program efforts. Bilingual education practitioner groups are interested in quality control factors among personnel, program options and their consequences, ways of strengthening links between home and school, and means of achieving maximum compatibility and school success in program efforts. Community audiences include school board officials, parent groups, and community organizations in the two sites and elsewhere. Parent groups are particularly concerned about educational equity and the protection of their children as human subjects in research.

Fellow researchers share multiple concerns related to studies in bilingual practice settings. There are major theoretical debates that require different case materials for treatment and testing. Researchers are also interested in the planning variables involved in the notion of linguistic and cultural compatibility in learning environments. Also important to the research community are the contributions of particular studies to long-term research efforts in the field.

The Research Project, which was broadly based, inductive, and eclectic, should prove valuable to others as an example of a qualitative study of communities, schools, and bilingual programs using ethnographic and sociolinguistic methods. To the extent possible for descriptive research, it is sensitive to the above concerns and issues. Our straightforward priority has been to design and carry out research that satisfies high standards of quality. The descriptive data are accurate and reliable insofar as means for quality control have been possible. The data are available for analysis and use by a wide variety of audiences.

Selecting Two Sites

As stated earlier, this Project involved a two-site design, because the research team was committed from the beginning to a comparative method, which is integral to an anthropological approach and serves to maintain a cross-cultural perspective. A multi-community focus allows for greater comparative opportunities in the research than would concentration on a single community and helps to account for variations in bilingual programs, sociolinguistic variations, and the ethnic differences within the Latino community.

In discussing multi-community research projects, Pelto (1970:256) states:

> These studies often preserve the design features of intensive community description, but a number of additional objectives concerning intracultural variation and controlled comparison are achieved by adding extra communities to the analysis.

Mary Berry (1977:26) also notes that

> We need to do more research on the problems of the Spanish speaking community, and be particularly mindful of the differences within the community—the differences between the problems found by Puerto Ricans and Chicanos, wherever they happen to be.

In this Project, the substantive tasks of research implied the importance of understanding variations of language and culture, and of quality of the programs. The Latino community in the United States was too large for one-site analysis, and within-group diversity could be better understood by contrasting descriptive data from more than one site. The communities selected—Parlier, California, and

Milwaukee, Wisconsin—exhibited contrasting features that were relevant to the dominant concerns of the research:

* Parlier is rural, with a small school system; Milwaukee is urban, with a large school system.
* Parlier's program is relatively recent and in a critical stage of development; while Milwaukee's has the maturity of ten years' experience.
* Demographically, Parlier consists of Chicanos (approximately 90%) and Anglos; Milwaukee is a mixture of Anglos, Blacks, Puerto Ricans, and Chicanos, allowing study of the complexities of the relationships among these groups.
* Power positions in Parlier are occupied by bilinguals; while in Milwaukee these are occupied by monolinguals.

As can be seen in Tables 1 and 2 below, each district has a program that formally satisfied criteria in Level I, Significant Program Features, which are innovative. The two sites contrast with regard to criteria in Level II Community/School Features (see Tables 1 and 2). Each site ranks high on the criteria for Level III, Research Potential, including available resources, interest among school and community, prior contact by research team, and overall potential for illustrating major issues.

Table 1. Level I Criteria: Homogeneous Variables

Bilingual Program	Milwaukee Bilingual Program Innovative Features		Parlier Innovative Features	
	Present	Absent	Present	Absent
Goals & Objectives	X		X	
Staffing	X		X	
Curriculum & Instruction	X		X	

Table 1. Level I Criteria: Homogeneous Variables (ctd.)

Bilingual Program	Milwaukee Bilingual Program Innovative Features		Parlier Innovative Feature	
	Present	Absent	Present	Absent
In-Service Training	X		X	
Parent Participation	X		X	
Evaluation	X		X	
Institutionalization	X			

Table 2. Level II Criteria: Comparative Variables

	Milwaukee	Parlier
Maturity		
High	X	
Low		X
Size and Type of Community		
Urban	X	
Rural		X
Center of Decision-Making		
Non-Bilinguals	X	
Bilinguals		X
Ethnic Mix		
Heterogenous, including Blacks	X	
Homogeneous, not including Blacks		X

Table 3. Level III Criteria: Parsimony Variables

	Milwaukee	Parlier
Available Research Resources		
High	X	X
Low		

Table 3. Level III Criteria: Parsimony Variables (ctd.)

	Milwaukee	Parlier
Interest by School & Community		
High	X	X
Low		
Prior Contact by Research Team		
High	X	X
Low		
Overall Potential for Illustrating Major Issues		
High	X	X
Low		

Research Framework

Anthropological Approach

Anthropologists have historically been interested in formal and informal learning situations as integral aspects of their ethnographic study of cultures. Some have given emphasis to enculturation and socialization processes across cultures (Henry 1955); a few others have explored cultural theories of learning (Cole 1971; Gearing 1973). A general area of the literature is referred to as "the anthropology of education" and is characterized by a history of case studies on culture and education (e.g., the Holt, Rinehart series edited by George and Louise Spindler). For many decades anthropologists in the United States have followed similar paths in the study of Latinos.

The Bilingual Education Community Study Project emphasized an anthropological approach, concentrating upon the cultural dimensions of research and utilizing a holistic view, the comparative method, and ethnographic fieldwork techniques.

Ethnography

Specifically related to this research is the fact that educators and anthropologists have begun to merge their fields and concerns by focusing upon the use of fieldwork techniques and ethnographic methodology for educational research and evaluation. Reference guides to this latter trend take the form of annotated bibliographies (Hill-Burnett 1974, Wolcott 1972), and fieldwork procedures manuals (Cassell 1978; Arvizu and Gibson 1978). Several workshops and seminars have paid attention to ethnographic evaluation, including the Monterey Workshop in July 1976 (Tikunoff and Ward 1977), and the 1978 pre-American Anthropol.gcal Association Conference workshop in Los Angeles.

Trueba advocates the use of ethnography to understand the social context of bilingual education:

> The crucial idea behind my insistence on the social context of bilingual education is that learning, achieving, and cognitive development of culturally different children is not a language problem per se . . . familiarity with the child's (mono- or multi-) cultural environment can best give him the opportunity for a normal emotional and cognitive development, regardless of the number of languages the child is exposed to during his formative years. By implication, bilingual education programs will not be successful because of their language (first or second) instruction alone, but, primarily, because of the congruence between the school environment and the experiences the child brings from his home and community environment. . . . If we can deal with our own cultural biases, anthropological research can bring about an understanding of the nature,the process and the outcomes of bilingual education as perhaps no other discipline can. Careful documentation of the conditions outside of school, under which children eligible for bilingual programs best learn, could contribute to an understanding of the children's responses to formal educational interventions in school (Trueba 1978:7–8).

The term "ethnography" means different things depending upon who is using it, and which audience is being addressed. According to Wolcott, an educational anthropologist, "An ethnography is, literally, an anthropologist's picture of the way of life of some interacting human group; or, viewed as process, ethnography is the science of cultural description" (Wolcott 1975). To sociolinguist Dell Hymes, ethnography is a mode of inquiry for the "discovery of knowledge," a systematic search for specific information, including an explicit procedure, the use of contrastive insight, and presentation of a general interpretation. To our research team, ethnography was simply a tool for systematic description, inquiry, and explanation.

The ethnographic task of this Research Project was eclectic in form and procedure, informed by the decades of experience of anthropology in community studies (Redfield 1943, Lewis 1959), and by the more recent experience of researchers in the "ethnography of schooling" (Spindler 1973; Kimball 1965; Gearing 1973; Hill-Burnett 1972–73; Wolcott 1975). A mixture of traditional ethnographic tools was used, each for its respective strength in contributing to the overall balance of quality in the technical means of data collection. The categories of basic data collected included traditional areas of concern to both community studies and studies of "school culture." However, priority was given to procedures more specifically designed for describing and studying the sociolinguistic and cultural interactions and compatibilities between community and school as related to exemplary bilingual educational programs.

The work of Doug Foley (1977) is an excellent guide to diachronic study of the Latino community and school, particularly the topical themes of historical reconstruction of power relationships in the community which affect its schools. The Parlier site was quite similar in many characteristics to Foley's North Town, and it was possible to replicate much of Foley's ethnographic approach, providing a historical context for viewing a bilingual education program. John Ogbu's (1974) seminal work in Stockton also was appropriate as a model to follow in the study of a multiethnic urban community. He contextualizes his analysis of social and structural relations in minority education through rigorous standards of community study. The Milwaukee site was characteristically quite similar to Stockton, and the research drew upon some of Ogbu's design.

Critical areas not fully developed by Foley and Ogbu which received close attention in this research were:

1. Focus upon an exemplary bilingual program—innovative features, characteristics, processes, personnel, pragmatics of development, and implementation.

2. Sociolinguistic inquiry that revealed the range of bilingualism, language use, and language attitudes as well as qualitative explanation of cultural variables involved in social interaction.

3. Comparative design that, through contrast, revealed the heterogeneous nature of the Latino community, the complicated, varying, and creative efforts toward realizing educational equity through bilingual education programs, and the real view of the world of policies, programs, and problems as seen by school people.

4. A qualitative, ethnographic test of the notion of cultural compatibility between communities and schools. Attention to the enculturation process in the family and the socialization process in the schools and community might help in understanding the qualitative dynamics of the research settings.

Symbolic Interaction

Ethnographic and sociolinguistic research may be conducted from a wide variety of theoretical frameworks, each with its related questions, particular methods, and special techniques. We chose to carry out the research within the framework of symbolic interaction (Geertz 1973), and actively to pursue the research in an inductive, descriptive manner, allowing for an introspective and recursive process to modify the work when necessary. A symbolic interaction framework enabled the team to study events and interactions within and between the schools and communities with some conceptual direction but without an overly restrictive theoretical bias. This compromise gave the research a balance between the traditional "outsider" perspective, sometimes understood as an "etic" or comparative context, and an "insider" perspective, sensitive to that which was significant and unique to those involved in the situation studied.

Through symbolic interaction, the research team began with similar assumptions and foci for inquiry. Significant symbols, events, and interactions were studied at the various important levels—e.g., individual (students, teachers, parents); institutional (family, community, school); and program (pre-history, implementation, future).

The sociocultural life of the community was studied through observation of processes, patterns, and changes in interaction within the activities and relationships in which people were engaged as well as through the instrumental linking agents and mechanisms mediating the dynamics of interaction. Thus the substance of meaning and the rhythm of people in action provided information that aided the research team in describing communities, schools, and programs as ongoing, interacting, sociocultural processes. This approach enabled the research team to compare, contrast, and contextualize in-school program phenomena with the backdrop of family, community, and macro-structural influences. Within the limits of resources, then, the research began as an idiographic case study (micro), evolved logically into a valuable multiple community comparison (macro), and addressed what was significant (in-depth and qualitative) in the actual research situation in a manner that was mindful of accountability to the various interests involved. Our use of the symbolic interaction framework is summarized in Table 4.

Table 4. Symbolic Interaction Framework

Areas of Interest   Units of Analysis

	Individual	Institution	Program
Significant Symbols	Students Teachers Parents	Family Community School	Pre-history Implementation Future
Significant Events	Students Teachers Parents	Family Community School	Pre-history Implementation Future
Significant Interactions	Students Teachers Parents	Family Community School	Pre-history Implementation Future

Significant Symbols in Parlier

Schools	Bilingual Programs	Community	Political Interaction
1. Team sports and Band	1. Outside Funding	1. Political Power	1. UFW grower affiliation
2. Stadium Lights	2. Bilingual personnel who relate to parents	2. Safety	2. Residence in Parlier- location & duration
3. Improvement of grounds and buildings	3. Performances by children	3. Economic	3. New and past ideologies
4. Fiscal solvency	4. Advisory committee meetings	4. Means of transportation	4. Individual opportunism vs. organizational group goals
5. Achievement scores	5. Bilingual notices and home visits	5. Health Services	5. Community services- police, health, religious

Significant Symbols in Parlier (ctd.)

Schools	Bilingual Programs	Community	Political Interaction
6. Vandalism suspensions	6. Motivation and attitude factors	6. Location of residence	6. Absentee ballots & precinct work
7. Attendance	7. Curriculum innovation	7. Linguistic and cultural competencies	7. City Council
8. Drop Outs & transfers	8. Staff devel., workshops/ waivers	8. "Respeto"	8. School Board
9. Success Models	9. District support (board & admin.)	9. Community/ family events- parades, balls, weddings	9. Leadership (elected voluntary)

Collaborative Model and Division of Labor

A collaborative model for conducting this research was necessary for several reasons. First, an interdisciplinary team effort involving personnel trained in sociolinguistics, anthropology, and education was required, since the perspective provided by each of these fields was relevant to the Project's research questions. Second, the research was conducted in two sites, requiring coordinated efforts at both, as well as at the Sacramento headquarters. Third, the research was conducted by four researchers, each contributing particular strengths and assuming lead responsibility for particular areas of research activity: Eduardo Hernández-Chavez was primarily responsible for sociolinguistic activity; Steve Arvizu was the lead person in community ethnography; Judith Guskin was the primary fieldworker and coordinator in Milwaukee, and Concepción Valadez concentrated on studying the schools and classrooms. Most importantly, however, the collaborative model for research was used because of the research team's commitment to involving and respecting the people in the sites as research colleagues.

There are many examples of researchers ignoring the input and involvement of the target community, and in some cases such research was harmful to those involved (Gough 1973; Horowitz 1974). Research situations involving controversy sometimes require that researchers address the dichotomy between humanism and science in practical ways. One problem faced by researchers in this study has been working with sometimes opposing individuals and groups, while maintaining our ethical standards of accountability, reciprocity, protection of human subjects and relative independence from sources of support. We chose a collaborative model for research in which the relationship between the researchers and the people whom they seek to understand goes beyond mere informed consent from the latter. In this model, the knowledge, experiences, and rights of cooperating residents are respected by concrete processes of research design.

Methodology

Multiple technical means for collecting and analyzing data and presenting findings were used, each for its respective power in revealing the kinds of data relevant to the research. The sum of techniques guaranteed a holistic view of the research problems considered through ethnographic and sociolinguistic analysis. No single technique or method was sufficient to study such a complex educational problem. In fact, our study faced some of the same difficulties as other research involving fieldwork methodology—selecting an appropriate combination of techniques matching the nature of the problem to be studied. Our combination of survey technique, participant observation, and intensive in-depth measures is common to fieldwork research. We conducted community study and school ethnography using complementary techniques to collect different forms of data on the same problems of the research tasks. These included a community survey, observation of community activities and events, life histories, review of documentary information, testing of students, biographical interviews, and participant observation. In large part, these data-gathering activities were designed to serve the purposes of both the ethnographic and sociolinguistic portions of the study. Insofar as was possible, each activity yielded information that was used for one or more aspects of the ethnographic and/or sociolinguistic analyses made. The major tools utilized were:

* Archive/document review
* Historical reconstruction by use of photographs
* Ethnographic filming of non-recurring events
* Videotaping of interaction
* Comparative interviewing
* Collection of topical life history
* Participant observation
* Aggregation of data from attitude questionnaires.

Identification of Exemplary Programs

This Project pre-selected two comparative sites for study: Parlier, California, and Milwaukee, Wisconsin. The procedure followed in selecting the sites included (1) defining an exemplary program; (2) developing selection criteria rationale, and (3) selecting two sites for the research.

Definition of "Exemplary"

We define an exemplary bilingual program as one that provides an example. Our goal in the selection process was to illustrate the qualitative dynamics at work in programs that bilingual educators would concur met commonly accepted criteria for bilingual programs. In simple terms, an exemplary program must exemplify and illustrate significant features, e.g., parent involvement, cultural relevance, instruction through the home language and English; although it need not necessarily show proof of outstanding performance or a high degree of effectiveness. A bilingual program is a key variable that reflects the congruence or lack of congruence between the world of the school and the world of the home and community. Within this definition, a distinction was made between the ideal (goals, objectives, and plan of operation of a program) and the reality of implementation, impact, and effectiveness.

Selection Criteria

Multiple references were utilized to develop selection criteria. The research team consulted with school officials, reviewed criteria from other research projects, and considered expressed concerns among practitioners, policymakers, and the general public.

The selection criteria developed include several layers of consideration: significant program features which are innovative, community/school features, and research potential of the sites. The following outline illustrates how we categorized the selection criteria.

Criteria for Selection

I. Significant program innovative features:
    a. Bilingual education goals and objectives
    b. Bilingual staffing patterns
    c. Curriculum and instructional practices
    d. In-service training
    e. Parent participation
    f. Evaluation
    g. Institutionalization
II. Community/School features:
    a. Ethnic mix
    b. Size and location
    c. Age of program
    d. Political activity
III. Research potential:
    a. Possibilities for answering major questions and issues

b. Interest among community and school
c. Expedient resources identifiable
d. Links with research team

The combined experience of the research team in the field of bilingual education approximates forty work years, a factor that encouraged the team to feel confident in identifying sites conducive to in-depth research. Collective experience, professional contacts, and intuition facilitated the identification of unique strengths and opportunities for research in each of the local settings considered.

Development of Instruments, Protocols, and Guides

Key-Informant Interviews. Interview schedules were designed to obtain a variety of preliminary information that would inform the community survey, the event observations, and the ethnohistorical aspects of the study. The information gathered in these interviews included personal data from the respondents, their perception of language use in the community, information about cultural events, historical events, and the schools. Each interview was between an hour and an hour and a half in length.

At each site, respondents included eight to ten key people. The persons to be interviewed were identified through prior conversation with school officials, teachers, city officials, and parents. The criteria for the selection of these respondents were that they be key people in the community and that they be knowledgeable about the community and about community events.

Results gained from these interviews provided an overview of the political, educational, and cultural life of the communities as well as information which would be incorporated into the community survey. They also assisted in identifying important community events for ethnographic observation. From these interviews, several key people in each of the communities were identified as subjects for in-depth interviews and life histories.

Language Attitude Questionnaires. It was of interest

to learn how language attitudes varied among children from different ethnic groups who either were or were not enrolled in a bilingual education program. It was also important to know whether language attitudes affected language learning and academic achievement and, if so, in what way.

Instrumentation was preceded by a review of previous work on language attitudes, particularly the work of Lambert (1972) and his colleagues in Canada. The language sub-study drew heavily on this work, although the instruments were adapted for use among Mexican-American and Puerto Rican children in the United States.

Lambert used three principal techniques: a modified matched guise, a language motivation questionnaire, and a sociolinguistic orientation questionnaire. The matched guise technique used recordings of selected bilinguals, each speaking in both languages. The subject was to evaluate the speaker on a series of characteristics along a scale from negative to positive. In the present study the matched guise technique was not used, since it was extremely difficult to find speakers who were perfectly balanced in both Spanish and English. In addition, this study included a third variety—the use of code switching. Thus a Language Variety Evaluation was devised, employing dominant speakers of the three varieties. Each recorded a monologue, with identical content, for each variety of speech. The order of the six voices was then arranged at random, and subjects were asked to evaluate them on the characteristics we had chosen. Characteristics for the Language Variety Evaluation were selected from a list of characteristics provided by students from another city with a Mexican-American population very similar to Parlier's. The voices for the recordings were also chosen from the same school. This was done to eliminate the possibility that students who were doing the evaluation might recognize an individual voice.

The Language Motivation Questionnaire asked students to judge the relative importance of Spanish and English for each of ten different functions. These functions were selected by a procedure similar to that followed for the selection of characteristics used in the Language Variety

Evaluation. The Sociolinguistic Orientation Questionnaire asked students to state their preference, in particular kinds of relationships, for speakers who used Spanish, English, or code switching.

Sampling procedure made use of class lists which were obtained from each of the bilingual and non-bilingual classrooms in grades one through six in the target schools. Permission slips were sent to the parents of each of the children in those classes. Those children whose parents did not return permission slips or who denied their children permission to participate in the study were then excluded. From the remaining population, eight children from the bilingual program and eight children from the non-bilingual program were selected for each grade.

Administration of the three-instrument battery required two sessions of twenty minutes each. The first session was devoted to the Language Variety Evaluation, which involved listening to the voices and judging the characteristics. The second session was devoted to the Language Motivation Questionnaire and the Sociolinguistic Orientation Questionnaire. The language variety evaluation was administered to all students individually through headsets. The language motivation and sociolinguistic orientation questionnaires were administered to first-graders individually, and in groups of four to five children in grades 2–6.

Encuesta Sobre Lengua y Cultura. The community survey conducted was first conceived as a relatively short sociolinguistic questionnaire that would include questions about language attitudes and attitudes toward bilingual education. Prior to developing the questionnaire, a review of a number of sociolinguistic and sociological interviews was conducted. These included the National Chicano Survey conducted by Carlos Arce at the University of Michigan as well as sociolinguistic questionnaires developed by Joshua Fishman, Dennis Bixler, Domingo Dominguez, and others. Following this review, it became evident to the investigators that a brief questionnaire would not be adequate for our purposes. Such a questionnaire necessarily would be superficial in nature and would require the collection of similar data in other ways. The time and effort required to conduct such a short questionnaire could not be justified in view of the amount and quality of information needed. Consequently, it was decided to expand the scope of the survey from a relatively short questionnaire to an in-depth interview that would range across a wide variety of topics. These included demographic information, language use, language attitudes, language learning and proficiency patterns, social organization and cultural values, and education, including bilingual education.

An interview schedule was developed, both in English and Spanish. This schedule included the topics to be explored in the interview, sample wording for the questions in English or Spanish, and suggestions for probes to be used in particular situations. Care was taken to use a variety of Spanish that would be appropriate for the Mexican-American communities in Parlier and Milwaukee and for the Puerto Rican community in Milwaukee.

The families to be interviewed represented a sub-sample of the families whose children participated in the language attitude study. This procedure was followed for several reasons. The sample for the attitude study was taken from the school records and was selected randomly from bilingual and non-bilingual classes in first through sixth grades. Thus, the interview sample also had these same characteristics. Using the sub-sample of the children in the attitude study also permitted us to gain a great deal more information about those same children than was available through school records. Moreover, the children and their parents could be compared with respect to language proficiency, language use, language attitudes, cultural values, and attitudes toward education.

Not all of the families who participated in the attitude sub-study were included in the interview. Due to these restrictions as well as to time and resources, it was only possible to interview fifty families. Many of the families moved between the time of the attitude sub-study and the interview. Some of the families could not be located because school records were incomplete; many did not have telephones, and some families declined, for one reason or another, to participate.

Administration of the interview itself took between

one and one-half and two hours. It was conducted, insofar as possible, as a conversation with both parents of the focus student. The conversation centered on each of the topics and questions in turn, allowing the respondent to answer freely and in as much detail as desired. In this way, not only was information obtained on as many of the topics as possible, but in-depth qualitative information was obtained on those topics about which each family had particular knowledge. A problem with this procedure was that exactly the same kind and amount of information was not collected from each of the families, and there was a lack of strict control over the consistency of the questioning. Nevertheless, such a procedure is fully appropriate for an ethnographically oriented study, and what was lost in consistency was more than recovered in richness of information. In addition, frequent discussion sessions were held with the interview teams throughout the data collection period, during which such problems were analyzed and adjustments made.

In contacts with families in the communities, great care was taken to explain the purpose of the interviews and how the results were to be used. It was also explained to each family that their responses were to be kept strictly confidential. However, in keeping with the investigators' collaborative research philosophy, it was made explicit to each respondent that the results of the study would be made available to the community. This is particularly important in ethnic minority communities because of the general feeling that researchers are interested only in their professional advancement, not in sharing their results with the people they study.

During the course of the interviews, the investigators learned of some families' pressing needs. It was made clear to the interview teams that their primary responsibility was to conduct the interview, not to engage in social work. Nevertheless, they were encouraged to assist people insofar as it was possible to do so, and it was expected that they would follow through in any such commitment they made.

Document Review

Review of a variety of documents facilitated historical reconstruction and comprehension of summary data regarding the overall circumstances and conditions in the schools and communities and aided in the qualitative interpretation of what was occurring at the research sites. Each document reviewed was considered in terms of the author's purposes, audience, and relevant circumstances. For example, Chris Arce's HUD final report for the City of Parlier was not written with the bilingual program and education policy decisions in mind. Yet it contained invaluable information concerning community needs, attitudes, and desires.

Examples of documents which we reviewed were data on specific school district characteristics available through the State Department of Education, minutes of community meetings and advisory committee meetings, results of program reviews, census data, economic reports, newspaper accounts, and school records. Since we were interested in interpreting and explaining the quality of life in the areas studied, we looked for major features of the community and schools, significant events that had shaped present relationships. If schools are microcosms of the society and communities in which they exist, then documents about the social life and characteristics of the community and region should contain contextual and historical information with rich potential for understanding the dynamics at work within the schools. Some documents, such as school records, were treated with full confidentiality and sensitivity and were invaluable in yielding comparative data on dysfunction signals, e.g., school attendance, suspension rates, or vandalism of school property as well as on standard measures, such as racial and ethnic surveys, staffing characteristics, academic achievement levels, and expenditures per pupil. Some school records gave measures of innovations within the organization in terms of numbers of alternative education programs and quality of efforts beyond the average for the region. Language proficiency and educational information was collected for all children in the bilingual programs in grades K–6 and, for all children

of parents participating in the survey, language proficiency
scores in English and Spanish, reading and mathematics
scores from standardized instruments, course grades,
attendance records, and disciplinary records were collected.
We regarded document review as a secondary source of
data and used it to guide our primary fieldwork.

Observation of Events

Analysis of the preliminary interviews and the
community survey gave an overall picture of the significant
social groups in the community, the meaningful events
which create a context for social interaction, and the
varieties of language used. From the twenty-five events
reviewed, we selected five which could best yield information
relevant to the study. These either recurred frequently or
were major single events involving the home, school, and
community; these events were observed intensely, in
substantial detail, and over a period of time.

The purpose of these observations was to gather
objective data on the use of language varieties and on
social groups and their interactions in order to supplement
the results of the survey with more concrete data about
what is important and why. The research methods varied
depending on the type of event but included personal
observations and note-taking, tape-recording, interviewing,
and still photography, filming, and videotaping. In addition,
community persons familiar with an event were asked to
explain and interpret particular aspects of it.

Life Histories

This technique has traditionally been used to
document the important experiences of famous people
(Langness 1965). In anthropology, however, life history has
been a tool for explaining cultural phenomena of a
particular community, especially when informed by related
fieldwork and knowledge of the group studied (Kluckhohn
1945). Life history may be a rather straightforward
chronological account of what has happened to an
individual, in which the material gathered and presented

is primarily descriptive and unstructured by the researcher (Radin 1963). It may also be highly subjective and qualitative in providing insight into significant symbolic events, people, or topics (Dyk 1938; Lurie 1966). With a great variety of models for documenting life history, our research utilized a comparative, topical approach to life history technique (Arvizu 1978). This assured the research team of similar substantive data on topics and questions pertinent to the research tasks. A combination of interview, naturalistic observation, and projective inquiry helped us to obtain multiple data measures related to the information selected.

Visual Approaches

Ethnographic filming (Heider 1976) was utilized as part of participant observation and event analysis. However, the level of use of photography was less extensive and intensive than that which John Collier, Jr., used in his educational ethnography of a school serving Eskimos (Collier 1967). Because of resource limitations, we used a combination of 35mm still photography and videotaping, the latter mostly for the study of community events and for interviews. We used the procedures recommended by Sorenson of the Anthropological Film Center, Smithsonian Institution, for inductive documentation of naturally occurring life and activity in various communities with modifications similar to those in past Cross Cultural Resource Center ethnographic film efforts. Unfortunately, the amount of ethnographic filming done was limited by financial constraints.

Summary of Findings

The purpose of conducting descriptive, non-evaluative research is to explain, rather than predict or to test hypotheses. In this project, the two-site design provides for description and explanation of two bilingual programs with established similarities and distinctive qualities, encouraging a contrasting and comparative analysis of findings and the development of hypotheses to be tested by further research. In some instances, comparative ethnography reveals similarities, and in other instances it reveals distinctions between sites. Although further findings are expected through subsequent analyses, in the following six major areas the qualitative studies reveal discoveries worthy of synthesis as findings: (1) Diversity, (2) Participation, (3) Dysfunction and Incongruence, (4) Innovation, (5) Unexpected Results, and (6) Conflict and Social Cohesiveness.

1. Diversity

Diversity appropriately describes certain aspects of the findings because the two sites were selected for study based upon their similarities in bilingual education program features (homogeneous variables), their built-in differences (contrasting variables), and their potential for providing an understanding of critical issues in bilingual education (parsimony variables). Also important is the fact that these are programs that function in Latino community settings; and as recent research indicates, considerable diversity can exist within and between these communities. Equally significant is the fact that bilingual education, as a consequence of federal leadership and legislation, is an experimental and demonstration program that encourages local districts to design and implement bilingual programs through grants competition and discretionary distribution of resources. Thus, even though both sites studied have used Title VII funding and possess minimal features associated with bilingual education programs, each program is different in the way it was created, in its implementation, and in its ultimate impact. Therefore, our analysis shows major differences between the two sites in community vigilance, board policy, personnel practices, and ethnohistory.

Bilingual education through federal legislation and regulations requires the participation of parents and community representatives in the initiation and conduct of bilingual programs. Even though both sites complied with the legislative mandate and regulation requirements, the research team found profound differences in the quality of parental and community involvement between the two sites. The phrase "high community vigilance" best describes the character of community involvement in Milwaukee, as the energy of parents and community has been relatively continuous and consistent in the various phases of development of the bilingual program there over the past fourteen years. By contrast, in Parlier, the parent and community involvement in bilingual education has been relatively symbolic and sporadic and inconsistent in direction and results. (See participation section for further details.)

School Board policy in the two sites differed to a significant degree in nature and clarity. In Milwaukee, at the beginning of the bilingual program, the Board developed and approved a policy to establish a maintenance bilingual education program. This policy evolved from considerable public debate, court litigation, and tension among parents and community and School Board members. The general public was well aware of the policy as a consequence of city-wide town meetings, widely publicized controversial court communications, intense Board meetings in which the substantive aspects of the bilingual program were debated, and wide distribution of the written policy to Latino parents. Most people interviewed had a fairly clear understanding of the Milwaukee public schools' policy on bilingual education, even though there was considerable controversy over the creation of the policy and multiple attempts were made to revise it. It is also important to recognize the general sociopolitical context of this public debate. Civil rights activity was high in the public consciousness during this period of the early seventies, and there was considerable support from the community at large for the notion of "equal opportunity" represented by bilingual education.

In Parlier, the creation of the bilingual program saw an implicit, almost hidden Board policy of transition to English that was sufficiently vague so as to satisfy (1) parents who thought the program was teaching their children Spanish, (2) parents who thought the program was teaching their children English, and (3) the School Board, which tolerated the program because of its general potential for helping with English acquisition, with the understanding that it was not necessarily building bilingualism.

This ambiguity in Board policy is in part a consequence of attempts by most of those involved to avoid controversy in a community shaken by intra-and inter-ethnic turmoil. Two additional factors were crucial. First was the decidedly different sociopolitical climate of the late seventies from that of several years earlier. Economic and external political issues were now paramount, and there was a general sense that civil rights groups had made about as much progress as they were entitled to. A majority group backlash was beginning to set in. A very important second factor was the historically severe level of suppression of the Chicano group in this extremely conservative rural community, recent political takeover of the city council and school board, and subsequent factionalism among Chicano subgroups. Chicano activists were impelled to protest inequitable conditions, protests that the established power structure was equally impelled to resist. The result was direct confrontation, little chance of reasoned negotiation, and a bitter aftermath.

Thus the bilingual education staff, with deliberately moderated support from the bilingual superintendent, was frequently faced with implementing a transitional bilingual program that had contradictory goals, a shifting character, and different meanings for different people. The policy was not publicly debated nor widely discussed in the media at the time the program was created. Parents were relatively uninvolved in the initiation of the program, even though an active community advisory committee existed.

A very important element in the development of both bilingual programs was the staffing pattern in each site. In both cases, the programs were able to recruit individuals who were exceptional in their overall backgrounds, training, and experience. However, the quality of personnel in Milwaukee was different from the overall character of personnel in Parlier. Milwaukee developed a long-range affirmative action plan which, with the participation of parents and community leaders, recruited new bilingual teachers who were fully certified and possessed bilingual competencies. The program grew slowly and deliberately, concentrating teachers and expanding by grades vertically and horizontally, with quality control and permanence built into staffing plans.

In Parlier the staffing pattern was understandably different. The bilingual program had existed for a shorter period of time and had grown laterally and, nominally at least, through K–12 in a three-year period; this required short-range staffing, use of in-place teachers on waivers, and an imported core support staff. The hiring was characterized by temporary opportunity and necessity. The teachers who had experience and training in bilingual education were in the position of needing to help others, which created stress, dissipated energies, and raised anxieties. As a result, by the third year of the program, the core bilingual support staff and key bilingual teachers were burned out and lost to the district, resulting in a major turnover and loss of continuity in the program.

The contexts in which the two bilingual programs began were markedly different, as exemplified by the ethnohistory of each community. Milwaukee is a well-established and politically stable industrial community, with a relatively positive history of receiving waves of ethnic immigrant groups, a tradition of ethnically distinct neighborhoods, and public display of diverse ethnic symbols, e.g., churches, festivals, and social groups. Early German and Polish language schools were created with the goal of language maintenance. The changes in Milwaukee's power structure have been reasonably subtle, with individuals' ethnicity a public but minor factor in access to power.

There is also a sense of history in Parlier; however, its particulars are characteristically briefer and more laden with conflicts. The multiple waves of people who have settled in Parlier have struggled to survive, conquer, and dominate an adverse environment, among ethnic groups that have historically been averse to one another.

In Parlier, assimilation pressures to Americanize and gradual alienation and polarization combined to create a hidden ethnicity which was ultimately a major factor in political upheaval and change in the community and school. Contact between groups has historically been characterized by more conflict and change than in Milwaukee. People in Parlier have a great sense of what has existed before, a basic dissatisfaction with the present and a vision of the future. However, the negative inter-ethnic interactions in Parlier have contributed to a climate in which public discussions of ethnicity relate to exploitation, ethnocentrism, and political confrontation. White flight, the exodus of English-monolingual, middle-American students, is recognized in the Parlier Joint Unified School District. There is a pattern of conflict and change which is markedly compressed by revolt, resistance, and political action by historically disenfranchised Chicanos. The bilingual program in Parlier was not a central cause for conflict and factionalism, as the program was implemented with careful strategies to avoid controversy. However, the already existent conflict and polarization within the community played out in a struggle over leadership of the schools.

Thus, the environmental pre-conditions in these two communities differ in a manner which has affected both the dynamics of interaction around the bilingual programs and the meanings attached to linguistic and cultural symbols by various groups.

2. Participation

The concept of participation underlies the bilingual education movement in general and was a factor generally seen in the research in Milwaukee and Parlier. If the monolingual schools had been successful with Latino students at either site, the need for a bilingual program might not exist. In these communities, as in other parts of the United States, the bilingual program was created in an attempt to make the schools more responsive to the needs of Latinos. The Study shows an increase in participation level by Latinos in the educational process and a greater engagement by students, teachers, and parents in the learning process. These results are primarily due to (a) the use of multiple means of communication, (b) cultural relevance in the curriculum and in extra-curricular activities, (c) parental and community involvement, and (d) bilingual education personnel.

Multiple sources of data indicated a high interest in school on the part of students in bilingual programs at both sites. The results of interviews with parents and teachers indicated that student attendance in these programs was greater than the average for other students in other programs. The extent of contact between home and school appeared to be more frequent and of higher quality than that which normally occurs within each district. There were some indications that there was less vandalism to bilingual program classrooms than to other classrooms in public school buildings. The frequency and duration of suspensions and inter-student conflicts among students within bilingual programs in both sites was less than for school and district averages. These indicators may have been affected by the use of bilingual personnel, increased school-home contact, and relevance in curriculum. Interview data suggested an improved school climate as a consequence of bilingual education programming.

As indicated above, parental involvement at the two sites was found to be qualitatively different. In Milwaukee, parents participated in creating the program, designing the curriculum, hiring personnel, monitoring and evaluating, establishing policy, and solving critical implementation problems. The Milwaukee program invested consistently more than Parlier's in community liaison personnel and parent training. In Parlier, parents were involved in proposal review after development by staff and consultants. The attendance at advisory committees was very high at both sites, especially when student performance was concerned. However, parental involvement in Parlier was limited and excluded major policy formation, hiring and curriculum decisions, and formal evaluation. In fact, many parents in Parlier were relatively uniformed about the current status of the bilingual program.

The bilingual education programs in both sites were able to demonstrate the ability to increase students' and parents' participation level in school activities. Bilingual program students were more engaged in learning activities than comparable students and parental participation in school visits and events was substantially more frequent than the average for the districts.

3. Dysfunctions

Dysfunction is the inability to complete a proper action, and a lack of fit and correspondence among important elements in the educational process. In both sites, descriptive ethnography and sociolinguistics have revealed an incompatibility between school and community; the resulting dysfunctions have been minimized, though not eliminated, through bilingual education programs. Bilingual programs in both sites mediated linguistic and cultural differences and overcame some important barriers between the home and school. In both sites the schools' overall holding power for Latinos is low, with some signs of improvement associated with bilingual education programming.

The overall characteristics of the schools in Milwaukee and Parlier are incompatible with the overall characteristics of their students, families and communities in several key ways, illustrated by the following chart:

Schools	Communities	Bilingual Education
1. English-Speaking Environment	2. Spanish-Speaking Environment	1. Bilingual Environment
2. Monocultural "Middle American"	2. Multicultural Environment	2. Cross Cultural Environment
3. Mostly non-Hispanic Staff	2. Diverse Groups	3. Diverse but mostly Latino staff

A similar linguistic and cultural pattern was found at both sites. The schools have historically been monolingual and monocultural, staffed by personnel whose backgrounds have been different from that of their students, and historically dysfunctional for a large percentage of Latino students who have not achieved as well academically as other students. Large numbers of limited English speakers and non-English speakers appear to have affected the mean academic achievement scores of Latino students in regular school programs. By contrast, in the bilingual programs, English and Spanish are used for communication and instruction; a "culturally relevant" curriculum is provided, and staff with backgrounds similar to the students' are utilized, all of which benefits the students by minimizing learning dysfunctions. The overall effect of the bilingual program is to mediate between two systems which are often incompatible—the school system and the community/family system. The bilingual programs offer illustrations of gains in achieving congruence in learning, and some examples of improved achievement. Academic achievement gains were greater in classrooms operated by well trained and fully certified teachers, even though all classroom data demonstrated academic progress for the majority of the students, most of whom were assessed to be more difficult learner populations due to limited English proficiencies. However, the bilingual programs are not uniformly successful in every individual case nor in each classroom in a manner sufficient to reverse the general patterns of the districts in the schools in which they operate. There is some evidence that the school climate becomes safer and more participatory in character with bilingual education programming. However, it appears that some of the effects of a bilingual educational approach require more than a few years of measurement to illustrate clear growth and academic development beyond the average. Perhaps a longitudinal design would uncover a more complete story of impact, particularly concerning the issue of drop-out rates and comparative academic achievement.

4. Innovations

Although both sites exhibited distinctive qualities and innovations in the development of bilingual programs, they shared a number of similar characteristics. Both programs used two languages in innovative pedagogical approaches.

The teaching methods, although basically similar to non-bilingual classroom settings, appeared to have greater diversity and more power to engage LES/NES students than did the average classrooms in the districts. The participation and involvement of parents in both sites increased the level of communication between the school and the home, a factor which argues strongly for bilingual capabilities among school personnel apart from language acquisition tasks. Both programs implemented a differentiated staffing plan that utilized bilingual aides and resource staff in addition to regular and bilingual teachers. The resources available for curricular experimentation appeared to be greater than average and of benefit to teachers in greatest need. In addition, the testing and use of data for educational planning appeared to be greater within each bilingual program than in the district as a whole.

5. Unexpected "Spinoff" Effects

In most experimental educational programs, there is a strong possibility of the occurence of effects in unexpected areas, and bilingual education in Milwaukee and Parlier did reveal some significant unanticipated developments, as evidenced by their absence from original program goals and objectives in district documents. The major significant variable which affected the success or failure of each program was the quality of participation of parents and community. Ironically, in an interactive sense, the greatest unexpected effect of the bilingual program story in both sites was its relative effect on parents and community.

In Milwaukee, parents and community began interacting with the schools in an adversary manner; after thirteen years of struggle and negotiation, they have realized a partnership/steward role with regard to the bilingual education program. In the process, they have sharpened their organizing and negotiating skills and have formed and developed a cadre of people knowledgeable in dealing with schools. Understanding of the limits and potential of schools appears to have grown over the years among those parents who have been involved in bilingual education issues. In this sense, unrealistic confrontation and non-productive conflict have diminished in Milwaukee, even though parents' attention to school activities has increased. Parents have learned how the school system works, and they have become pro-active, democratic, and consultative in educational decision-making.

In Parlier, the story at first appears to be the opposite of Milwaukee's. After the "Chicano takeover" of the City Council, the election of some Mexican-American School Board members, and the appointment of a Mexican-American superintendent, the community relaxed its attention to school affairs, relying upon bilingual administrators to get the job done within the schools. Staff and consultants were also required to plan and develop programs like bilingual education with minimal input from parents and community. The trust placed in the schools developed into an undercurrent of dissatisfaction and a sense of malaise over what was and was not happening in them. Parents who were very supportive of the principle of bilingualism began to lose faith in the bilingual program, and parents who supported ethnic equity in the schools' operation began to withdraw and transfer their own children to neighboring private schools and school districts. There appeared to be a pattern of controlled community involvement in Parlier, which mediated against the generation of regular healthy criticism for district and program decisions. In addition, inconsistent interaction, consultation, and training were a function of staff and teacher turnover and resources invested in parent training. There seemed to be a closed attitude among some school people regarding information, a factor which added to distrust and antagonism. Thus, in the interaction between the Parlier schools and important portions of the Parlier community, what had begun as an era of conditional trust in 1977 had changed to reaction and conflict in 1980. The net effect was another community conflict over control of the schools, which resulted in a new School Board with very different philosophies and concerns.

In both sites, bilingual programs have been associated with tension between the schools and the community. However, both programs have served to facilitate, each in a different way, parental participation and the empowerment of disenfranchised portions of the community.

6. Conflict and Social Cohesiveness

Bilingual education in Parlier is one of many educational experiments intended to overcome traditionally unresponsive schools through innovative pedagogical strategies. Parlier is an excellent place to study bilingual education in order to understand how a program can mediate incompatibilities and build congruence between the school's characteristics and those of the home and community. It is also beneficial to study the process of implementing an experimental bilingual program for a better understanding of the interactions, dynamics, and variables important to effective education.

Parlier's bilingual program is not outstanding in performance and achievements; neither is it necessarily a model program that other districts should adopt in their communities. But for Parlier, the bilingual education program is a consequence of community/school conditions and the community's social structure, as mediated by the bilingual education program staff. As measured by the ideals of the bilingual education movement, the program has fallen short in several key areas. However, in comparison to other bilingual education programs, Parlier's has a special value in that it can help us to understand problems in implementation, innovative success, and practices needing improvement. Also, the study of Parlier helps us to examine conflict and social cohesiveness as part of the context in which bilingual education occurs.

Conflict and social cohesiveness are phenomena that exist in every community and school to some degree, being aspects of natural processes at work among people as they interact and struggle to survive. This is not a story worth telling to most logical, intelligent people. An important story well worth hearing, however, is how conflict and social cohesiveness was related to bilingual education in Parlier, California, and what can be generalized from a particular location and study to other locations and other studies.

Within the study's framework of symbolic interaction,

symbols are objects representing and carrying meaning; interaction is the dynamic process of acting and not acting when in contact with others. The world of objects in this portion of the study relevant to conflict and social cohesiveness includes the following: (1) those symbols related to bilingual education; (2) symbols relevant to major family, community, and school events; (3) symbols important to school/community interaction; and (4) symbols relating to political interaction between and within groups. (See chart on Significant Symbols in Parlier on pages 96–97).

Parlier, California, is an almost perfect place to study bilingual education in a community context. It is a small community, full of life and interaction typical of many valley towns; yet it is also unique in its particular history involving the political empowerment of Spanish-speaking people and controversy over educational matters. The people of Parlier all care about what happens in their schools and community. There is an unusually strong commitment to improving the quality of life in the community and the quality of education offered to the student population.

Although bilingual education has been an issue in community-school strife, it is not the cause of such conflict. Conflict in this setting is a consequence of (1) inequities in social structure, (2) long-term alienation and non-participation, (3) lack of adaptation by schools to changing student populations, and (4) individual opportunism. In this case, conflict is defined as a direct physical action of confrontation or an indirect action of resistance to the established order. A clear distinction must be made between conflict and creative tension. The latter is carefully mediated by brokers from vested interest groups, and is expected as an aspect of participatory democracy in U.S. society. The former is non-controlled *choque*, demanding immediate and profound change.

The long history of conflict among groups in Parlier, California, precedes the initiation of the bilingual education program, which was operational between 1976 and 1979. In fact, conflict in this rural agricultural community continues to the present without a formal bilingual education program.

The big question, then, is the role of bilingual education in this community, which has undergone numerous cycles of turmoil and transformation over the years. The bilingual education program was designed as an interface mechanism between the basically monocultural and monolingual English-speaking schools and mostly Mexicano-Chicano and Spanish-speaking population. The bilingual program functioned well in this regard, given the clear implementation problems of capacity building and quality control in personnel and the need for nurturing and support by the infrastructure of the schools and community. The bilingual program's success as an interface depended upon (1) a supportive, clear, and consistent policy from the different levels of government; (2) understanding and support from parents and community; and (3) a well-trained and highly skilled set of educators.

In Parlier, indicators of dysfunction between schools and homes diminished during the period of the bilingual program. Parents participated more in school affairs; student attendance, achievement, and attitudes improved; and incidence of conflict diminished. The original objectives of the bilingual program were satisfactorily achieved. However, the long-lasting effects of the program are questionable. School Board opposition affected implementation. Staff turnover removed organized bilingual education momentum within the schools, and parents have become relatively uninformed about school activities related to bilingual education programming. Tension among individuals and groups continues and has undergone a recent surge. Years after the end of Federal funding and after a period of leadership struggles among the school board and administrators, bilingual education is a programmaitc and political concern to Parlier residents and educators. Bilingual education program features, however, continue to be an important major issue in the political dynamics of schooling in Parlier. The concept of effective bilingual education still exists in the minds and hearts of some parents in the district, and it could again become a means for future innovation and problem-solving. For a brief time period the bilingual program served as a strategy for mediated change in a community and school system under considerable internal stress.

The phrase "social cohesiveness" connotes togetherness and connectedness. In this case, it refers to a social order that is a consequence of mutual understanding, cooperation, and basic ground rules for "*respeto.*" Cohesiveness has occurred in various forms in Parlier, within and among groups over history, and is presently manifested in the ideals conceived by parents, community people, educators, and political leaders. Social cohesiveness has been observed in Parlier in both community and school events and appears to thrive under conditions where (1) those in power respect diversity, (2) family and religious rules are at work, (3) cultural compatibility is emphasized, and (4) skilled "go-betweens" are present to mediate problems.

Social cohesiveness is affected by important processes within communities and schools. One of the important processes involved is clear communication, as manifested by linguistic, cultural, and social competence. Social cohesiveness is less likely to occur in circumstances where many people cannot communicate through mutual language and similar social expectations or in cultural circumstances where interlocutors are unable to achieve equivalent meanings from the same symbols, interactions, and behavior.

Implications of the Study

The Research Project has produced several important discoveries with implications for further research. First, situational, historical, and contextual variables need to be considered when bilingual programs are described and analyzed within community contexts. Second, the experimental nature of bilingual education efforts has stimulated great heterogeneity among bilingual education programs, which must be taken into account in future research. Third, there is further need for longitudinal and qualitative designs in the research and evaluation efforts in bilingual education; diachronic (historical) analysis greatly enhanced our understanding of the two sites studied and their unique and similar attributes. Implementation of exemplary and effective bilingual programs appears to be an evolutionary, on-going developmental process, which means that effectiveness measures are more meaningful when the proper time frame is used for analysis. Fourth, the role of parents and community in the success and/or failure of bilingual education programs must be considered in order to obtain a complete picture of what is happening in particular programs. Fifth, there is a great need for the systematic documentation and study of spin-off effects of bilingual education programs on students, school climate, and community development. It is hoped that future studies of bilingual programs will give greater attention to these important areas.

Endnotes

1. Dr. Steven F. Arvizu, Dean, Graduate Studies and Research, California State University, Bakersfield. Dr. Eduardo Hernandez-Chavez, Cross Cultural Resource Center, California State University at Sacramento. Dr. Judith Guskin, University of Wisconsin-Parkside. Dr. Concepción Valadez, University of California, Los Angeles.
2. The detailed description of the research project is contained in four volumes of the Final Report. The volumes include the following:
Volume I: Executive Summary. This volume highlights major findings of the study and the data on which they are based. Findings and conclusions illustrate program structure and the direction and approach to bilingual education as exemplified in the case studies.
Volume II: Non-Technical Report. This volume is specifically addressed to the two communities which were sites of the study. It consists of photographic and videotape records of important community events and a summary of findings interpreted in a manner appropriate for general audiences.

Volume III: Description of programs, schools and communities. This report presents ethnographic and sociolinguistic description of the programs, schools and communities, analyzing compatibility and incompatibility within and among them, and describing program characteristics, implementation effectiveness and evaluation.

Volume IV: Technical Report. This report is an overall technical guide indicating where backup data are located within the other volumes for assertions made in the executive summary.

3. The educational condition of Latinos and other language minority students has created a need to know which innovative practices of programs are effective and why. The Bilingual Education Community Study Project is but one of many research projects sponsored by the Federal Government to seek answers to questions about the operation of bilingual programs. As a means of coordinating diverse research efforts sponsored by different agencies, a task force on research was created to assist in directing and coordinating the national research agenda of the government in the field of bilingual education.This coordinating unit was the Part C Task Force and included representatives from the National Center for Educational Statistics, National Institute of Education, Office of Bilingual Education and Minority Language Affairs, and other entities involved in research. The research is specifically descriptive and non-evaluative as required by the sponsoring agency, the National Institute of Education, now called the Office of Educational Research and Improvement.

4. Comprehensive critiques of anthropological studies of Chicanos are given by Romano (1968), Vaca (1970), Rocco (1972), and Arvizu (1979). For discussion of the relationship between culture and education see Torres-Trueba (1978), Arvizu (1979) and Carter and Segura (1979). For traditional "outsider" qualitative experiences of anthropological study of community and school involving Chicanos, see Foley (1977) and Ogbu (1974). For innovative "insider" examples of anthropological research models for the study of community and school involving Chicanos see Arvizu (1978), Rios (1979), Vigil (1978), and Valadez (1978). The work of Steve Arvizu and Jay Schensul (1977–1979) in both Chicago and Connecticut serves as examples of outsider/insider collaboration in the study of communities and agencies.

References

American Instutes for Research
  1977   AIR Study: Evaluation of the Impact of ESEA Title
          VII Spanish/English Bilingual Programs. Palo Alto,
          Calif. American Institutes for Research.
Arvizu, Steven F., ed.
  1978   Grito del Sol: Decolonizing Anthropology. Berkeley:
          Tonitiuh International.
  1985   Education and Empowerment: An Analysis of Higher
          Education for Hispanics in the Future. In The State
          of Hispanic America V. Oakland, CA: National Hospice
          Center for Advanced Studies and Policy Analysis.
Arvizu, Steven F., et al.
  1977   Conceptual and Theoretical Tools. Monograph I of
          Demystifying Culture Series. Sacramento: Cross
          Cultural Resource Center, California State University,
          Sacramento.
  1977   Methodological Tools. Monograph II of Demystifying
          Culture Series. Sacramento: Cross Cultural Resource
          Center, California State University, Sacramento.
Carter, T., and R. Segura
  1979   Mexican Americans in School: A Decade of Change.
          New York: College Entrance Examination Board.
Cole, Michael, and John Gay
  1972   Culture and Memory. American Anthropologist 74(5).
Collier, John
  1967   Visual Anthropology: Photography as a Research
          Method. New York: Holt, Rinehart and Winston.
Duran, Richard
  1983   Hispanics' Education and Background: Predictors of
          College Achievement. New York. College Entrance
          Examination Board.
Dyk, Walter
  1938   Son of Old Man Hat. Lincoln: University of Nebraska
          Press.
Epstein, Noel
  1977   Language Policy and Affirmative Ethnicity.
          Washington, D.C.: Institute for Educational
          Leadership.
Estrada, Leo
  1986   Anticipating the Future Demographics of Hispanic
          America. Policy Paper. Tomas Rivera Policy Center,
          Claremont Graduate School, Claremont, Calif.

Foley, Doug
  1977   From Peones to Politicos. Austin: University of Texas Press.
Gearing, Fred
  1973   Where We Are and Where We Might Want to Go: Steps Toward a General Theory of Culture. Council on Anthropology and Education Newsletter.
Geertz, Clifford
  1973   Interpretation of Cultures. New York: Basic Books.
Geogh, Kathleen
  1973   World Revolution and the Science of Man *In* T. Warren, ed. To See Ourselves: Anthropology and Modern Social Issues. Glenville, Ill. Scott Foresman.
Harrington, Charles C.
  1980   Bilingual Education in the United States: A View from 1980. New York: ERIC/CUE Urban Diversity Series, ERIC Clearinghouse on Urban Education.
Heider, Karl
  1976   Ethnographic Film. Austin: University of Texas Press.
Henry, Jules
  1955   Cross-Cultural Outline of Education. *In* J. Hill-Burnett Anthropology and Education: An Annotated Bibliography. Human Relations Area Files.
Hill-Burnett, Jacquetta
  1974   Anthropology and Education: An Annotated Bibliography. Human Relations Area Files.
Horowitz, Irving
  1974   The Rise and Fall of Project Camelot: Studies in the Relationship between Social Science and Practical Politics. Cambridge, Mass.: MIT Press.
Kimball, Solon T., comp.
  1974   Culture and the Educative Process: An Anthropological Perspective. New York: Teachers College Press.
Kluckhohn, Clyde
  1945   The Personal Document in Anthropological Science. *In* The Use of Personal Documents in History, Anthropology and Sociology. Gottschalk, L., C. Kluckhohn, and R. Angell, eds. Bulletin 53 of the Social Science Research Council. New York: Social Science Research Council.
Lambert, W.E., and G.R. Tucker
  1972   Bilingual Education of Children: The St. Lambert Experiment. Rowley, Mass.: Newbury House Publishers, Inc.

Langness, L.L.
    1965   The Life History in Anthropological Science. New York:
            Holt, Rinehart and Winston, Inc.
Lewis, Oscar
    1965   San Francisco: Mission to Metropolis. Howell North
            Books. 1966
Lurie, Nancy, ed.
    1966   Mountain Wolf Woman, Sister of Crashing Thunder:
            The Autobiography of a Winnebago Indian. Ann Arbor:
            University of Michigan Press.
Moll, Luis
    1980   See chapter in this volume.
Ogbu, John
    1974   The Next Generation: Ethnography in an Urban
            Neighborhood. New York: Academic Press.
Olsen, L.
    1988   Crossing the Schoolhouse Border: A California
            Tomorrow Policy Research Report. San Francisco,
            Calif.
Pedraza, P., J. Attinasi, S. Poplack, and A. Pousada
    1980   Social Dimensions of Language Use in East Harlem,
            New York City: Centro De Estudios Puertorriqueños
            (Language Policy Task Force), City University of New
            York.
Pelto, Perti
    1970   Anthropological Research: The Structure of Inquiry.
            New York: Harper and Row.
Pifer, Alan
    1979   The Annual Address of the Carnegie Foundation. New
            York: Carnegie Foundation
Radin, P.
    1933   The Method and Theory of Ethnology: An Essay in
            Criticism. London: McGraw-Hill
Redfield, R.
    1930   Tepoztlan: A Mexican Village: A Study of Folklife.
            Chicago: University of Chicago Press.
Rios, Sam
    1978   An Approach to Action Anthropology: The Community
            Project, C.S.U.S. In Grito Del Sol: Decolonizing
            Anthropology. S. Arvizu, ed. Berkeley: Tonatiuh
            International.
Rocco, R.
    1970   The Chicano in the Social Sciences: Traditional
            Concepts, Myths and Images. Aztlan 1 (2):75–97. Fall.

Romano-V., Octavio I.
1971   The Anthropology and Sociology of the Mexican-
        Americans: The Distortion of Mexican-American
        History. *In* Voices: Readings from El Grito: A Journal
        of Contemporary Mexican American Thought, 1967–
        1971. O.I. Romano (ed.) Berkeley: Quinto Sol
        Publications, Inc. Pp. 43–56.
Spindler, George D.
1973   Burgbach: Urbanization and Identity in a German
        Village. New York: Holt, Rinehart and Winston, Inc.
Tikunoff, W.J., et al.
1980   Review of the Literature for a Descriptive Study of
        Significant Bilingual Instructional Features. San
        Francisco: Far West Laboratory for Educational
        Research and Development.
Torres-Trueba, Henry
1979   Bilingual Multicultural Education and the
        Professional: From Theory to Practice. Rowley, Mass.:
        Newberry House Publishers.
Torres-Trueba, Henry, and Steven Arvizu
1979   Bilingual Education: Theory and Practice.
        Champagne-Urbana: University of Illinois.
Troike, R.C.
1978   Research Evidence for the Effectiveness of Education.
        Washington, D.C.: National Clearinghouse for
        Bilingual Education.
Trueba, Henry
1989   Raising Silent Voices: Educating the Linguistic
        Minorities for the 21st Century. New York: Newbury
        House Publishers.
Vaca, N.
1970   The Mexican American in the Social Sciences: 1912–
        1970 Part I. El Grito 3(3):3–24. Spring.
Valadez, Senon
1978   In Search of a Perspective: An Apology Long Overdue.
        In Grito del Sol: Decolonizing Anthropology. S. Arvizu,
        ed. Berkeley, Calif. Tonatiuh Publications.
Vigil, James Diego
1980   From Indians to Chicanos: A Sociocultural History.
        C.V. Mosby Company.
Wolcott, Harry
1975   Criteria for an Ethnographic Approach to Research
        in Schools. Human Organization 34(2) Summer.

Zappert, L.T. and B.R. Cruz
    1977   Bilingual Education: An Appraisal of Empirical
            Research. Berkeley, Calif.: Bay Area Bilingual
            Education League.

The Context of Bilingual Education in Milwaukee: Complex Ethnic Relationships in an Urban Setting

Judith Guskin[1]

Introduction

This chapter conveys the attitudinal, political and community context of bilingual programs in Milwaukee in 1981, after the first decade of competitive federal funding for such programs. The use of the ethnographic present is demonstrated in this chapter's report of that context as it was being formed during the period of this study. The author conducted the interviews on which this chapter was based as a member of the team of the N.I.E. Two-Site Bilingual Community Study described earlier in the chapter by Arvizu et al. As the previous chapter described the methodology of that ethnographic research, including the development of the sociolinguistic interview schedule used to tap attitudes to language use and inter-ethnic relations reported below, this chapter will focus on the voices of the Black, White and Hispanic residents from interviews at one of the two sites: Milwaukee.

The Urban Context

Urban ethnic relationships are particularly complicated today as attitudes toward ethnicity are changing. As immigration continues, ethnicity is being recognized as enduring—not as the "parochial" and divisive barrier to progress and to rational planning that it has been considered in the past but as an important factor in American social, cultural, and political life which is not likely to disappear.

Continuing in-migration to cities has a variety of consequences. It supports language maintenance by incorporating newcomers who must use their native language for survival, but it can also make host communities more intolerant of language and cultural differences. Newcomers affect the existing ethnic populations by providing a need for the employment of bilinguals and professionals, but they also create some strain between different generations and different social class groups. Migration patterns also affect residential patterns. If there is limited housing available for poor people, an ethnic group that is stigmatized by skin color, language, or other factors may become increasingly segregated.

In cities across the United States, the relationship between Blacks and Whites affects the attitudes of Whites toward other minority populations, and the other minority groups need to consider their relationships to Blacks. As the combined ethnic and racial minority population outgrows the White population in more and more cities, the functioning of the cities becomes critically dependent on the relationships among these groups. The kinds of coalitions that are possible and the perceptions of one group's goals by another become issues that cannot be ignored. While Whites may for the most part continue to control business activities and political decision-making, some Blacks and Hispanics have in the past two decades attained positions of importance.

The relations between Blacks and Hispanics vary: for example, Hispanic school board members in Chicago held up desegregation planning when it was not seen as serving their interests, whereas in Los Angeles coalitions supporting desegregation have included Blacks, Whites, and Hispanics.

In order to identify important aspects of ethnic relationships in Milwaukee and to highlight the way in which they may help explain social relationships, attitudes, and the implementation of bilingual education, selected aspects will be outlined; then more specific information from the Milwaukee research will be presented and discussed.

Our cities are mixtures of people coming from different countries or different regions of a common homeland; they may have different customs, dialects, and ideologies. Generational differences are also important. Furthermore, the way the host community perceives the various ethnic and linguistic groups can affect their members' own awareness of commonalities and differences within and between groups and thus influence interaction. Although each city is unique in its particular ethnic mix and relationships, there are commonalities among them. The issues presented in this analysis of inter-ethnic relationships in Milwaukee, for example, are common to other cities as well: stigmatization of language, degree of residential segregation and its consequences, relative size of the Hispanic population, and the changing identities of the Hispanics themselves.

Stigmatization of Language

One of the major problems for bilingual education in this country has been that a large proportion of the general public has stigmatized speaking a non-English language as somehow un-American and often expresses anger at the use of a non-English language that they cannot understand in public domains. What is the reality in Milwaukee?

Milwaukee is a city where many languages have been and continue to be spoken. This is particularly true of the South Side, the port of entry for immigrants. With the exception of Hispanics, most residents who live on the South Side no longer speak the languages of their grandparents, but they know people in the neighborhood who do. While some remember that their parents spoke another language, they do not, for the most part, speak any language other than English themselves.

Linda Steiner (1981) discussed Milwaukee organizations which teach Mandarin, Croatian, German,

Greek, Polish, Latvian, Hebrew, Serbian, Slovak, and Ukrainian. These are primarily affiliated with churches, and are offered after school and on weekends. Some of the groups have been offering language classes for many years, while others are relatively new; this suggests a continuing pride in ethnicity as well as some efforts toward language revival. Most of the people who participate in such programs are members of the particular ethnic group involved, and many of the classes combine language teaching with cultural activities. Although most of these programs are private and church-affiliated, the public schools also offer language-immersion programs in Spanish, German, and French as well as bilingual programs.

According to Steiner, many people in Milwaukee value languages other than English. However, the interviews we conducted in the spring of 1981 show a range of attitudes. Some non-Hispanic parents on the South Side do not highly value native language maintenance, and English is seen as entirely sufficient for themselves and their children. Others have more complex attitudes and do support maintenance of the home language.

For example, Sandra, a single parent with a large family living on welfare, remembers that her parents spoke Polish at home when she was little, although they stopped as she grew up. While she can still understand a little Polish, she does not speak, read, or write it. She wishes that she could speak it more fluently and is sorry that she is gradually forgetting what she knew. She understands that Spanish-speakers have a strong desire to continue speaking Spanish. Her sister is married to a Mexican and took lessons in Spanish because he speaks it at home. Sandra feels positively toward bilingual education, but she sees it as serving only Hispanic children who do not speak English. At one point she tried to enroll her child in a bilingual program but was told that she could not. She says, "I'd be glad if my kid could talk Spanish. . . . I wish she could, because this way she could understand everything that's going on [in the neighborhood]." However, she feels that those who do speak Spanish at home and in their classrooms should speak English as much as possible outside them, "so they'll learn it."

Mary, on the other hand, does not support language maintenance. She is of mixed European ethnic heritage; her parents spoke Bohemian but did not teach their children to speak it. While she sometimes wishes that she could speak it, she does not feel this is important. She also perceives that Hispanics care about retaining their language, and although she hopes they will speak it less in the future, "I think you'll still hear more Spanish, because they seem to stick very strongly to their own way." She does not see this as positive: "I think everyone should speak English. That's the way it has always been in this country."

Most of the twelve non-Hispanic Whites of varying European ethnic backgrounds living on the Near South Side who were interviewed felt negatively about the idea of Spanish being spoken in public. They reported that they were angry and frustrated with Hispanics with whom they came into contact, whether at work or in the neighborhood, because Hispanics spoke Spanish in their presence. The following statements convey their feelings:

> Nancy: They should try to be the same as everybody else, they should talk like everybody else . . . if you let them into the U.S., they should start talking English.
>
> Sue: I figure, if you got something to say let us talk where we all understand. When they're around people who don't understand they should talk English, because they can talk English. I had that run-in many times.
>
> Millie: That's a bad subject for me. I don't like them people. Because they don't talk English. If they want to be in the U.S., they should talk the language . . . these people don't want to learn the English language . . . they should try to become as American as they can . . . I hate it [hearing more Spanish in the neighborhood].
>
> Gloria: I think they should join the rest of us as soon as they can . . . everything's put

in English and Spanish and I don't
believe in it . . . they're pampered. It's
hard to deal with people like that because
they don't understand you, and I'm not
going to stand for an hour and try to
explain something to somebody and
they've been here for five years already.

Dave: I was never brought up with either
Mexican or Puerto Ricans and I find the
hardest thing for me to cope with is, if
they're going to live here, why not speak
our language, instead of, in front of
people like me and my wife, all of a
sudden they're speaking English, then
they're back to speaking Mexican or
Puerto Rican, or whatever it is. And it
seems like that's where most of the
trouble is in this area. If they're going
to be here, they should get accustomed
to our ways, our language, and use it.
How they speak in their own homes is
their business. But when they're out on
the streets, I've seen a lot of it—starting
fights, especially in taverns and that. You
know, they're speaking to you in English
and all of a sudden a buddy will come
in, and there's a fist fight over it, because
one party doesn't understand what the
other is saying. . . . I would always
assume that they had something to hide,
because if they could speak English to
me one minute, why couldn't they speak
it to me when a friend came around?

As these quotations illustrate, the speakers see
Hispanics as foreigners who were "let into the U.S," ignoring
the fact that most are U.S. citizens. They are not "like an
American person" unless they speak English. The speakers
find it unacceptable and threatening that someone knows
some English but still speaks Spanish with his or her
friends in public places. These White residents of the South
Side have begun to feel like a minority group in their own
neighborhoods and do not like this.

Many informants are aware that Spanish-speaking

people want to hold on to their language and are willing to condone this but only if the use of Spanish is restricted to the home.

Josephine:	It's something they have to keep. The Polish, French, German—all of 'em, they all keep in touch with that.
Sue:	They should learn English. They can keep Spanish at home, but they should teach their kids English.
Millie:	I'm not saying that they should drop their language completely. There are many kids for many years that have grown up with double language— English and whatever. I think it should still be done.
Gloria:	In public, I think they should use English, but in their homes and so, let them use Spanish. They can keep it as long as there's a limit on it. For their personal selves and their own family; if they want to keep it and write it, or whatever they want to do, fine.
Ann:	They want to keep Spanish to talk with their family, but they have to be taught English so they can communicate with the outside world.
Dave:	I know they're both [Mexican and Puerto Rican] very clannish groups. I think they should try to adapt. They can keep their cultural heritage and that, but adapt to our way of life also. It's fine to stick to traditions, and that, but you've got to live in the neighborhood, so why not speak the same language . . . when my great-grandmother came here, they had to learn different ways, so I think that Hispanics should learn different ways.

Several informants mentioned that another language, either German or Polish, was spoken in their homes when they were little but that it was not taught to them. People report still hearing some of these other langauges being spoken on the South Side. However, the area is becoming more and more Hispanic, and most informants expect that more and more Spanish will be spoken. Almost all of these families have relatives and friends who live in the suburbs and would like to leave for the suburbs themselves.

Three families interviewed presented a different attitude toward language use. One had previously enrolled their children in Bruce Guadelupe, the community school that has a bilingual program. The school later moved out of the neighborhood; the family wanted to enroll their children in the nearby public school's bilingual program but did not think this would be allowed. They felt that Hispanics should use both Spanish and English in public as well as in the home. Another family has foster children, both Mexican and Black, and likes the fact that these children are being exposed to cultural and linguistic differences. These parents spoke explicitly about trying to overcome their earlier prejudices, which they said they had been given by their own parents. The third parent was a Native American brought up by her grandmother, who spoke only an Indian language. This woman had a Puerto Rican boyfriend and was aware of prejudice toward Puerto Ricans on the South Side. She felt that it was important to respect linguistic and cultural differences.

Most of the Hispanic families who were asked about Anglo attitudes toward the issue of Spanish perceived correctly that many Anglos did not want them to speak the language in public places. They believed that Anglos felt frustrated because they could not understand what was being said. The data from these interviews indicate that a majority of Hispanics report that they do, however, use Spanish in public places. If they are talking to Anglos they will use English, but they prefer Spanish for shopping and for speaking to friends downtown or at work even when Anglos are present.

The Hispanic adults interviewed valued the use of both languages in all domains—on the job, for official business, in school, for shopping, to converse with other Hispanics, and in community activities. To some extent,

Hispanic parents whose children had not been enrolled in bilingual programs placed slightly less value on the use of Spanish for all these, but even they saw Spanish as important. Observation confirms that they do in fact speak it in public domains.

This is true among the youth as well, although they also speak a great deal of English. Those participants in the high school bilingual program who were surveyed said that both languages were important for many functions, including "for a happy life," "for education," "for political influence," "for reading for pleasure," and "for speaking to friends" (most reported that the majority of their friends were other Hispanics). According to 75% of the students, however, Spanish was more important for communicating with parents.

In conclusion, there is a discrepancy between the views of the Hispanics and Whites who were interviewed concerning the use of Spanish in public. Hispanics value bilingualism for its own sake and consider the use of both Spanish and English desirable in all domains: at home and at work, in shopping, and so on. Most Whites tolerate language maintenance only if it is confined to the home; in fact, they resent the use of Spanish in public if they feel that the speakers can also speak English. The main reason for this attitude among the Anglos seems to be a belief that the speakers are saying nasty things about them. Hispanics are generally aware of these attitudes, but they consider the language spoken by the person they are addressing to be more important than the ease of a bystander who does not speak Spanish. Hispanics make adjustments, but the value of being able to use both languages and the continuing presence in the community of people who are Spanish-dominant lead them to speak Spanish often in public. Whites feel that this is making them "a minority" in their own neighborhoods, and they don't like this.

The Consequences of Residential Segregation

Whose neighborhood is it? Perceptions of places may or may not correspond to their physical realities, especially with respect to changes in population. Mexican Americans have lived on the South Side for a long time as have many different Eastern European groups and relatively fewer Blacks; yet the area has been and continues to be seen by many residents, as well as people from other parts of the city, as a Polish community. Some parks and schools have Polish names, but there are no streets with Mexican names. Mexican Americans have been seen in the past as a small and probably temporary population.

However, it has now become clear to most people that changes have been taking place on the South Side, especially during the last decade. More Hispanic-owned businesses are opening, and a large number of social service agencies in the area which serve the Hispanic population. Some churches have moved out of the area; most have remained, and have found their parish memberships increasingly Hispanic. Hispanics are now a majority in two of the Catholic churches on the Near South Side. One former church social hall is now a large Hispanic recreation center, in which over 80% of the membership is Hispanic with the remainder Anglo.

The ways people perceive their commmunity can affect the way they perceive themselves, and whether they feel fraternally toward the other people who live there. If they feel secure in the community and see others "like themselves" living around them, they may have a sense of ownership and feel that they "fit in." If, however, they feel that people "like themselves" are moving out, that it is becoming less safe for them to live there, and that they are becoming a minority in the neighborhood, then they may feel less comfortable physically and psychologically. It is still their neighborhood—or is it?

Images of communities, especially ethnic urban ones, tend to persist for a long time, even if the communities themselves change. Hunter (1924) has studied persistence and change in ethnic communities in Chicago. He stresses the need to see such comunities in terms of symbolic interaction:

> Although the local urban community is an external object, a "social fact," nonetheless it

arises from a process of social interaction. In short, it is a social product. The symbolic definition and identification of local communities, like the individual identity formation of Mead and Cooley, is a process of symbolic interaction. Names and boundaries used as identifying symbols of social units require shared definitions that are often worked out in the communication and interaction of residents from juxtaposed areas. The "looking-glass self" has its parallel in the "looking-glass community."

To Hispanics in Milwaukee, the South Side is the largest and oldest *barrio*, the place to hold events, just as they did years ago, and to go to restaurants and visit friends. It is also the site of those schools which have the largest Hispanic student populations. To many of the Whites who have recently come from the rural areas of Wisconsin, the same part of town may only be a stopping-off place on the way to the suburbs; they rarely interact with their Hispanic neighbors. To other Whites, particularly old timers of Polish and German backgrounds, this was their part of town but is now changing in ways they do not necessarily like. These old-timers often sentimentalize the past.

Demographic data show that the Hispanic population of the South Side has been growing, and that currently over 50% of the Hispanics in Milwaukee—about 13,136 persons—live there. They make up 50% or more of the population in four census tract areas on the Near South Side, while in the larger geographic area they make up only about 18% of the population. This pattern is not unusual for Hispanics; in a study of 35 cities conducted by Moore and Mittleback (1972:80), Mexican Americans were in every instance less segregated from Whites than were Blacks.

The schools with the largest Hispanic enrollment are located in these changing neighborhoods. Also, Hispanics feel that the 1980 census has underestimated the population, according to a newspaper article by Mary Ann Esquivel (1981). Preliminary figures for the 1980 census report 29,343 Hispanics, while Hispanics themselves feel that the figure should be around 45,000.

Most outsiders see the South Side area as predominantly Polish, with a small Hispanic population which is believed to be the result of recent immigration. In *National Geographic Magazine,* an article entitled "Milwaukee: More than Beer" (Levathes 1980) refers to the South Side as Polish and conservative. It includes a photograph of a South Sider with a Polish last name cutting his lawn; he speaks about the ethnic community of the neighborhood. The author states that neighborhoods in Milwaukee have been ethnically divided from the very beginning: "German, Irish, Polish, and Italian immigrants created distinct neighborhoods." He also notes that things seem to be changing: "More recently, Black and Latino communities have arisen." He provides no information about the numbers or values of these groups, which in fact are not new to the city. Regarding recent changes, he quotes a South Side priest who says, "My funerals are all Polish. My weddings and baptisms are all Latino." From the priest's point of view, this is indeeed a changing area.

Those South Siders who have lived in the area for a long time are aware of the change. To them, the neighborhood was once a place where "everyone knew everyone else." If a young man misbehaved, someone down the street would tell his parents about it.

> I think one of the things about growing up in a neighborhood like this was that you didn't dare do anything wrong, because you knew doggone well that the neighbors knew who we were and they were going to come back to your parents and let them know about you.

Life centered around church-related activities and social events sponsored by the local neighborhood tavern. If a South Sider were looking for a neighbor, he would most likely look in the tavern or in a nearby bowling alley. Whole families might be down there, not just the men:

> There was a time I could name every single person that lived in the houses down the way here . . . I think I know four families now that are still here, that have stayed in the neighborhood.

These old-timers speak of the kinds of values that the *National Geographic* article highlighted as persisting for them: family, honesty, discipline, hard work, and friendly interaction. These values are reflected in well-tended lawns and in the institution of the local tavern, of which there are over 1,595 in the city. Some old-timers feel that their Hispanic neighbors "fit in" and share at least some of these values: they also work hard, and they care about their families. Other Whites do not believe this. Some feel that today's youth is "running wild," while the more stable and younger families are moving to the suburbs. "The children have no one to play with anymore." These people no longer see the taverns, streets, and bowling alleys as safe, family places. However, as one informant put it, they still feel a strong loyalty to the area, "almost a defensive pride." They try to keep their lawns neat and to keep up a network of friendships with other old-timers. They resent newcomers who do not follow their patterns. As one informant put it:

> The old German and Polish stock down here keep their lawns and houses in immaculate condition and the younger, newer people coming in don't have quite the same values . . . and sometimes it irritates the neighbors.

The difference here is not merely the values suggested by lawn care but the identity of the lawn's owner, which is more significant. This involves feelings of threat because newcomers are different in many ways, although the old-timers are not sure how different they are. Lawns are used as a neutral way to express this fear. The same informant continued with his analysis of the "newer people" by differentiating those who had similar values from those who did not. "This may not be so important," he said, but "you know that you're on the same wave length." If you know that "they're different from you," then you "just leave each other be." Most Anglos see Hispanics as different from themselves, although they claim to know little about the differences.

Hispanics see this issue differently. Housing remains

one of the area's biggest problems. There have been some
efforts at cracking down on absentee landlords and some
rehabilitation of existing buildings, but problems persist.
People do not have the money to move or to fix up the
old houses. A newspaper article (Rummler 1981) quoted
one Hispanic who grew up in the neighborhood and now
works with a social agency:

> I can appreciate them restoring it and stuff, but
> the people who live here can't afford that . . .
> we can't do it. When you've got six kids, working
> in a tannery, underinsured, trying to get your
> kids an education, it's hard to think of
> rehabilitating your house.

Some old-timers believe that Hispanic adults want to leave
the city to return to Mexico or Puerto Rico and that this
is why they maintain Spanish. According to these people,
although Mexicans have children and grandchildren, they
still think of Mexico as home, not the South Side. The old-
timers see this as inappropriate. The renunciation of dreams
of returning to the homeland is part of adaptation; again,
Hispanics do not fit the pattern the old-timers expect.

Interethnic Interaction

Those Hispanics who have grown up on the South
Side have a different perspective. They do remember getting
along with Anglo children in school and having some Anglo
friends, but they also remember fights between Whites
and Hispanics, as well as between Mexicans and Puerto
Ricans. Some recall that those who were predominately
Spanish-speaking had the most difficulty in those years.
"I used to cry a lot," said one girl who did not know
English before she went to school. Another informant
recalled that her Anglo acquaintances had more money
than her own family did, and this created uncomfortable
comparisons:

> We tried, I know my parents tried their best, but
> still when you would go into another person's
> home, being Anglo they would have everything,

and you go back home and you don't have all
of that. I rememebr I used to take this young
boy to school, and every day his mother would
give him chocolate with milk, that Hershey, and
I thought to myself, "Why can't I have a glass
of milk with chocolate syrup being poured in
there?" . . . every day I would go and they would
have bacon and eggs, and all of that . . . I was
getting paid, I think it was a quarter a week, to
take him to school . . . they were a well-to-do
family . . . very nice people, they would give us
lots of things . . . but still, when I would see
that early in the morning . . . I would say "Oh,
I hope she offers me some," but she never did,
you know. I was just there waiting for him
. . . so it was little things like that, that stick
in my mind.

One informant recalled her children growing up in
the 1950's; because they were "Spanish," they would speak
Spanish to each other.

They would get beat up 'till finally I . . . just got
down to brass tacks and taught them how to
fight back. Sometimes they say "turn the other
cheek" . . . but my kids weren't going to get beat
up all the time.

Some Whites in the neighborhood did not fight with the
Hispanics. Friendship among White and Hispanic youths
who grew up in the neighborhood exists, and exists today.
However, contact does not always lead to friendship and
often leads to antagonism.

Hispanics and non-Hispanics interact more today in
some of the churches as well as at work, and there are
some social agencies which serve both groups, but there
is also a lot of ethnic separation. As one informant put
it, "everyone is turf-oriented." Ethnic boundaries are
maintained in spite of contact.

Interactions in the Schools. Some of this orientation
spills over into the area's schools. The Junior High School
on the South Side has been a scene of conflict between
the groups. The bad image suffered by this school was

overcome somewhat when a Hispanic principal who worked with both White and Hispanic parents was hired. However, there are still parents and students who refer to the school as "rough" and speak of tensions. There is still a good deal of vandalism—over $60,000 worth last year—and there have been many fights, some between groups. "Anglos girls would be attracted to Latino boys, and then the Latin girls would attack them," said one informant. There is a local gang, the Cobras, which is reported to take money from the students. Most of its members are Hispanic, but not all. Currently, there is reported to be much less fighting in the school because of the strict rules set up by the Hispanic principal as well as the extensive human relations and multicultural training provided to the staff. Today the school is 46% Hispanic, double the percentage of Hispanics in the neighborhood near the school. The population of Hispanics in the area has grown, however, from 8% to 23% in ten years.

In the elementary schools there is some name-calling but few fights based on ethnicity. White and Hispanic children interact on the playground, although they are most likely to be found playing with their own classmates, as students are generally assigned to activities as whole classes. In effect, this means that Hispanics in the monolingual English classrooms interact more often with non-Hispanics than do Hispanics in the bilingual classrooms. However, when Hispanic parents were asked about their children's friends, more than half felt that their children related well to all groups, including Anglos (non-Hispanic Whites of varying European backgrounds), who currently make up about 35% of the student population. Few parents stated that their children related only to Hispanics or only to Anglos.

Within the teaching staff, there is still some indication of ethnic cleavage. Although the basement lunchroom is common "turf," some Hispanics choose to stay in a bilingual room, where they can speak Spanish, share ethnic food, and feel comfortable. Some Anglos also stay by themselves. Interaction does take place, and people are polite to one another, but there remains a sense that one building houses two quite separate staffs and programs and that each remains separate to some degree.

There are positive signs of cooperative efforts in both the schools and the community as a whole. Responding, perhaps, to a growing awareness that many Hispanics are here to stay, some Anglos are trying to find ways to adapt. In one elementary school in an area of the South Side where few Hispanic families live, more than 75 children are learning Spanish; most of them are Anglos. The Anglo parents are enthusiastic about the program, and many of them attend weekly classes at the school to learn Spanish themselves. In another school which is predominantly Hispanic, a monolingual teacher recently requested a year's leave of absence to go to Mexico; she had decided that she needed to learn Spanish and wished to live and study it there in order to learn it fluently.

Interaction in the Community. Other signs of growing cooperation between Anglos and Hispanics include joint participation in neighborhood revitalization projects, such as the nationally recognized Walker's Point historic preservation site, where, for instance, a branch bank plans to re-open with a bilingual manager.

Common problems also remain. Taverns continue to be a source of concern for both Hispanic and Anglo residents. Both groups agree that the old family-oriented taverns are changing. Men standing around outside taverns are a source of anxiety for families in the neighborhood, whether the taverns are owned by Hispanics or Anglos. Unemployment only makes this situation worse.

There are also, of course, Whites who do not wish to recognize and adapt to the changing ethnic population of the South Side, many of them old-timers, as mentioned above. According to demographic data and the report of a local historian who has interviewed many people on the South Side, there is "still a substantial core" of old-timers, especially Poles, who do not wish to move but who do not interact with the newcomers. But there are many Polish organizations still active in the community, and many old-timers also participate in church activities, such as bingo or church festivals. Since the churches are growing more integrated, the old-timers do interact with Hispanics through these activities.

In summary, Hispanics are not as segregated as Blacks, but increased contact does not mean that the poeple who live in the neighborhood consider it integrated. Patterns of interaction are still primarily based on ethnic affiliation. Different organizations serve different populations, and where membership in these cuts across ethnic lines—in the Catholic churches, for example, in public schools, and at work—there has been some evidence of tension. For the most part, a live-and-let-live attitude prevails. Hispanics and non-Hispanics do shop in some of the same restaurants and drink in some of the same bars, but Hispanics also have their own establishments. There is some intermarriage between Hispanics and other groups, but figures on the incidence are not available. Cooperation certainly exists; however, for the most part, people keep to their own groups.

Some Hispanics find their increasing population on the South side advantageous, since this supports the provision of services, including bilingual programs, and gives the Hispanic minority some visibility within the city. They seek pride and respect for the group as a whole. Some Anglos, however, do not like the fact that the Hispanic community is growing larger and say they resent feeling like a minority. Some Anglos will attend "Fiesta Mexicana" and even march in the Annual Mexican Independence Day Parade; but many older South Siders would rather see things as they were in the past, the way these people remember them, when one was more likely to hear Polish on the street than Spanish, when these other ethnic groups "owned" the neighborhood.

Those Anglos who have arrived more recently seem to look forward to the day when they can afford housing in the suburbs, although they prefer the South Side with its concentrations of Hispanics to the other low-cost housing areas, which are primarily Black.

The Relative Size of the Hispanic Group, Compared to Blacks

The presence of a large Black population in a city is a factor in the relations between Whites and Hispanics, in the ways Hispanics see themselves, and in their relations with Blacks. Questions are raised as to how resources are and should be shared as well as what is necessary for educational success. Blacks often do not understand the importance Hispanics place on language maintenance. They may also feel resentful because they perceive that Whites accept Hispanics more easily than they do Blacks. However, many Hispanics have to cope with the clear stigmatization of skin color in American society, with the assumptions of both Whites and Blacks concerning Hispanics' attitudes and feelings about skin color, and with the fact that they are seen as both White and non-White, as a cultural or racial group as well as primarily a linguistic group.

Milwaukee's South Side is usually seen as primarily Polish, and the inner city as primarily Black. The bridge which connects the two areas across the Industrial Valley is called "the longest bridge in the world, since it connects Poland with Africa." It also connects the predominately Puerto Rican area with the predominantly Mexican area, but no one characterizes it as a link between Mexico and Puerto Rico. Such images are partly the result of the size of an ethnic group, and neither Hispanic group is quite large enough for that kind of image-making.

While the degree of Hispanic integration is usually seen in terms of Hispanic-White boundaries as these are maintained by both groups, this is clearly only a partial consideration of the question in a pluralistic society in which there is also a much larger minority group. Whites are the arbiters of comparisons between Blacks and Hispanics; they have responded to Blacks with greater fear and avoidance. There are opportunities for coalition-building betwen the two groups as well as competition, but they remain generally separate.

Historically Hispanics and Blacks have not interacted closely, and until recently neither group has stressed the need for increasing their mutual understanding. Blacks often cannot understand why the language issue is so important to many Hispanics, and they also feel that Hispanics are trying to "cash in on" Black efforts to change institutions which remain under White control. Many Blacks feel some clarification is required concerning Hispanic views on variations in skin pigmentation and on the physical diversity that exists within the Hispanic population. They may ask, "Is a Black Puerto Rican Black?" By which they mean, "Is he on our side of the Black-White conflict?"

While Hispanics constitute about 4% of Milwaukee's population, Blacks constitute 23%. Hispanic population growth since World War II has been continual but so has the constantly increasing Black growth rate. In 1960, Blacks made up only 8% of the city's population; by 1970 this was 15% and by 1980, 23%. The Black community remains segregated; housing patterns indicate that while some Blacks have moved into adjoining suburbs, most have remained in the central city. A recent editorial in the *Milwaukee Journal*, entitled "Suburbia—Why So Very White?" (August 1, 1989) cited the fact that 70% of all Blacks were concentrated in one sector and pointed out that "metropolitan Milwaukee continues to hold a place on the dishonor roll of the nation's most racially segreagted areas." A comparison with cities of similar size showed that of 16 such cities, only the White suburbs of Pheonix, Arizona, had a smaller population of Blacks than Milwaukee. A comparison of census data from 1960, 1970, and 1980 shows increasing segregation. There has been an increasingly heavy concentration of Black families in the Central City, due to an increase in the Black population and a simultanous outflow of White families to the suburbs. (There are, however, very few Blacks on the South Side of the city.)

Blacks have attained some political power over the last decade, both in the city council and in the School Board. Hispanics have, by contrast, been unsuccessful in both areas despite their attempts. Some are not happy with some Black Board members' attitudes and wish they could have Hispanic representatives. Increasing Black influence makes Hispanics want greater influence, too, but both groups are aware that Hispanics do not as yet have much influence. They are also aware of their differences.

The few occasions on which Blacks and Hispanics have worked together to try to achieve the same goals have not been significantly successful. A few community leaders in both groups have spoken out about encouraging cooperative efforts and have managed to increase the dialogue and avoid conflict; but most issues have remained primarily Black or primarily Hispanic. During desegregation, for instance—clearly a Black issue—Hispanic leaders tried to convince their own community that it made sense to cooperate with Blacks and Whites in order to protect their own bilingual programs. Their limited success allowed Whites to take Black concerns more seriously than Hispanic ones during this case.

The segregation of Black and Hispanic communities extends into the city's schools. Black staff who have been assigned to predominantly Hispanic schools, for instance, can generally work well in most environments but would prefer to work in schools with predominately Black populations. Similarly, a Mexican teacher who was assigned to a predominately Black North Side school did adjust, but she asked as soon as she was able to for a transfer to the South Side. Blacks do not see the South Side as their part of town; similarly, while the North Side is "home" to many Puerto Ricans, for Mexicans it is someone else's "turf."

As desegregation is considered a Black issue, so bilingual education is a Hispanic one. Black leaders have learned about bilingual education from their Hispanic colleagues, and many of them are positive in their attitudes. They see the need to improve the achievement of minority youth as a common cause; they also perceive the growing size of the Hispanic population. Other Black leaders, however, are not so ready to support bilingual education. While they do not explicitly say that the money used for such programs should go to Blacks, they do feel that the programs are too costly and have little benefit, especially for those Hispanic children who already know some English. Some of these Blacks are on the Board; others are principals of schools which have bilingual programs. They have influence over both the funding and implementation of bilingual programs, so their opinions carry considerable weight. These opinions are often surprisingly similar to those of the South Side Whites quoted above.

Blacks' Attitudes to Bilingual Education

The following sample of attitudes toward bilingual education by Blacks who are somewhat knowledgeable about such programs may therefore be more supportive of them than most. They have worked with Hispanics on community committees and in schools. The child of one respondent has been enrolled in a bilingual program for over four years. In general, those sampled are supportive of the idea of learning another language, although none have studied Spanish themselves. One community leader, for example, said:

> I believe it is critical to learn a language. I, among other people, really feel unfortunate in a sense that they didn't have this push toward bilingual years ago when I was going to school, and I believe it is a handicap not to be able to, especially in this country when you have Hispanics who are going to make up a large portion of our population.

Another Black leader indicated that learning another language should be a part of everyone's education and could be a first step toward bridging cultural differences. A Black teacher said a second language was valuable because it strengthened one's own language; she planned to take intensive Spanish during her sabbatical. None of the Blacks interviewed understood or spoke Spanish, but they were somewhat embarrassed about this, and thought it would be better if they did.

The differences between Blacks and Hispanics over the issue of bilingual education were defined during a conference of Milwaukee's Black and Hispanic leaders in 1980, hailed in the September 1980 issue of *Nuestro* magazine as an indication that these groups were becoming more open to exploring common issues. One participant commented that "Blacks really hadn't known much about bilingual education and Latinos hadn't understood Black sensitivities." The meeting was seen as an opportunity to discuss these differences.

One Black community leader, for instance, said that he felt bilingual education was useful only for Hispanics, as a means of helping them achieve more academically. He was not concerned if bilingual programs led to increased segregation for Hispanics, for he felt that schools should focus on providing quality education: "All schools should be good schools, regardless of [their] being all Black or all Hispanic." A simple reassortment of racial or ethnic bodies did not amount to integrated, quality education, and the speaker felt that schools integrated in that sense might not provide better education.

Another Black leader in the schools held similar views: mixing Blacks and Whites in the same building did not necessarily provide better education, so why worry about segregating Whites and Hispanics? This respondent, however, differed in his views toward the maintenance approach to bilingual programs; he felt that this was not a good idea, because it cost too much and was too hard for teachers to implement. He didn't like the fact that the bilingual program "wants to be separate."

One Black activist felt that what was needed most in educational reform at this time was an acceptance of people's differences, "treat[ing] them appropriately in terms of their needs." He saw the main purpose of bilingual education as an "effort to reach out to those kids in their native language, which is comfortable, in order to help them make their transition to tackle English." He would encourage Black friends to place their children in bilingual programs because of their humanizing influence: "It's an experience that everyone should go through." He added, "I believe that most Blacks are sympathetic because being a minority they are aware of some of the preferences that minorities have to have in order to cope. Just like I have had Title I for a number of us to achieve in school." He felt that the small number of non-Hispanics in bilingual programs was due to a lack of public education.

Another Black teacher who had a good deal of contact with bilingual education did not feel that pupils in such programs made as much progress as Hispanics in monolingual programs, because these students were more

Spanish dominant and the programs inappropriately protected them.

> Now, when I was in a Black school, and a child came in and didn't know very much English, never once would we say "well, you know, probably at home broken English is spoken."

He saw bilingual education as an excuse to protect Hispanic children. He questioned whether it was to the child's benefit to learn Spanish, since the demands the child faced in the world would require English:

> I think somewhere along the way we have forgotten about the child. . . . It would be nice if we could all get together and say, "Now look, when these kids go to get a job, or even when they reach junior high school or high school, if they cannot fill out that application they won't hand them one in Spanish and say, 'Here, dear, fill this one out in your language.' It's going to be in English."

He felt that many of the older Spanish-dominant children would not be able to do this for a long time.

This Black teacher also felt that the Hispanic students were too conscious of ethnicity:

> The children are really on this all the time. Much more than any other race that I've been around. They seem to be totally absorbed with this [question of who is] Puerto Rican or Mexican. They'll even look at me, with my coloring, and ask if I'm Puerto Rican or Mexican and when I say "American," they're totally confused.

This teacher admitted that part of the issue was the students' awareness of race and their wish to make it clear to their teachers that they were not Black.

> Some of the kids do have the hair and the skin that, if you didn't know that they were bilingual you would assume that they were Black, but I

> do notice that they really want to let you know
> their identity. They don't want you to confuse
> them as being anything else but Latino, you
> know—they want to keep that straight. I have
> one little, cute boy who's very, very dark and I
> said to him "Do you speak Spanish?" and he
> said, "Oh yes, I'm Puerto Rican. I'm Puerto Rican,"
> and I mean, he wanted me to know, because it's
> very easy to look at him and think, you know,
> he might be Black.

This respondent was aware that he was never informed about bilingual education in any systematic fashion and still did not know how the program worked. He was also open to learning:

> At this point I don't know what I think about
> it. It's new, and it's different, and I'm learning.

However, this teacher said he would feel more comfortable in an all-Black school.

Among the Blacks interviewed was one parent whose child was enrolled in a bilingual program. He felt informed about the program and was in favor of it. He saw few differences between Hispanics and Blacks:

> Most of them want to have the same things that
> we do—their kids [to] get a decent education and
> make something out of their lives. I think both
> groups are having a tough time, Hispanics and
> the Blacks, are really. I think they are similar
> because they got to fight for whatever they want
> and we have to fight for whatever we want. It's
> just fight, fight, fight. Looks like each group is
> fighting for some rights.

This man's son had been in a bilingual program for four years, could understand Spanish, and was doing well in English and other subjects as well. The child's friendship with a Hispanic boy in the neighborhood led to his enrollment in this program. His father said, "He is doing great in it." The child spoke some Spanish at home and sometimes watched a Spanish television show; he translated it for his brothers and sisters. The boy's father had disussed this with his own friends and they were also positive about it. Other members of the family were also learning Spanish, and he would recommend that other Black parents enroll their children in the bilingual program.

In conclusion, the Black population in Milwaukee is large and highly segregated; although they still do not have influence commensurate with their numbers, they have made some gains in political influence and the establishment of Black-oriented programs during the last decade. Minority/majority issues have usually been Black/White issues or Hispanic/White issues rather than fought by both minorities in coalition. The leaders of both groups have tried to play a broker role and have taken public stands regarding the need for coalition strategies. Hispanics make it a point to attend the Urban League banquet and to concern themselves about issues which are important to Blacks.

Blacks do not usually publicly attack bilingual education in the interests of fostering cooperation with Hispanics. Some Blacks, in fact, fully support it, and a few actually enroll their own children in these programs. Other Blacks do, however, see these programs as draining resources from others and are less enthusiastic about them. Since several of these individuals have influence over program implementation, their lack of support can cause problems for bilingual education from time to time.

Changes in Ethnic Identity

Ethnic identity and the language of the home have become a badge of pride for Hispanics in Milwaukee, not a source of shame. Many Blacks, however, want them to choose sides in the fight for equity for minorities; most Whites want them to act like other White ethnolinguistic groups in Milwaukee, eschewing displays of language and culture outside the home. Officially, Milwaukee's Hispanics are designated "non-Black" with regard to desegregation programs; other state and local programs designate them a "minority group."

Hispanics' continuing difficulties in breaking out of

the lower segments of the labor market represent a combination of barriers, including discrimination and lack of educational achievement. Spanish, on the other hand, remains useful in many situations; it ties Hispanics to family, friends, and community. Moreover, if racially differentiated minorities do surrender cultural identity and language, according to Eduardo Seda Bonilla (1973), they become only marginally acceptable to their own comunity while still largely unaccepted by White society. Hispanics are not fully "White," although they are often considered "non-Black"; some individuals may be able to "pass," but the group is not accepted as a whole by the majority society.

Using Spanish consciously as a force for identification and unity is one means by which Hispanics can struggle for identity as members of a distinct minority group within the context of a Black-White-Hispanic city. Differences among Mexicans and Puerto Ricans must be subordinated in order to accomplish this new self-identification as Hispanic or Latino.

Changes in ethnic identity are part of the adaptive patterns of most groups living in cities, particularly minorities. On Milwaukee's South Side, the many changes in the decades of the 60's and 70's have led to a growing cohesion within the Hispanic community. Bilingual education has been part of this process of adaptation.

When they first arrived in Milwaukee, Mexicans depended on kin networks as well as on a mutual aid society for Mexicans. Programs geared toward the community as a whole reinforced Mexican identity as did the local newspaper, which looked to Mexico as the source of information and to Mexican culture as the arbiter of behavioral norms. As increasing numbers of Puerto Ricans come to the city, however, and community agencies developed, there was a shift from Mexican identification. Store fronts now display both the Mexican and Puerto Rican flags; South Side organizations hire Puerto Rican staff and serve Puerto Rican families in the area as well as Mexicans. A bilingual newspaper represents local and national Hispanic concerns, not only Mexican issues.

This does not mean that Mexicans and Puerto Ricans have sacrificed their separate identities. Each group does retain separate spheres of interaction; they patronize separate bars, and the congregations of some churches are predominantly Mexican, while others are mostly Puerto Rican. Children know who they are and are quick to say so. Puerto Rican teenagers sign "P.R." after their names when they sign in at the local recreation center; there are occasionally fights between Puerto Rican and Mexican youths, though not so often as in the past. Why do these fights occur? Said one parent, *"Machismo es la causa."*

Hispanic parents are aware that it is not possible to teach everyone to speak the same kind of Spanish, that there are differences in pronunciation and vocabulary, and that bilingual teachers will not necessarily be from their own group, but they do not feel much concern about this. They do feel that bilingual teachers should speak "good" Spanish and also be able to communicate with the parents themselves, but they understand that the teacher will speak that variety of Spanish that seems most comfortable to him or her. They realize that in order to adapt to their new environment, Hispanics have to make adjustments and get along. In the words of one parent:

> A Mexican believes Mexican Spanish is best, but a Puerto Rican believes Puerto Rican Spanish is best. . . . It all depends on how they were raised. . . . We have different values; but we are all human and equal. We are all Latinos.

Thus despite some continuing separatism, the Hispanics recognize that Mexicans and Puerto Ricans have common problems in adapting to their new situation in the Midwest. They have succeeded in interacting in many domains—in schools on the South Side, in work settings, most of which employ both groups, in their community center and in health centers as well as in their relationship with the dominant society. From its inception, for example, the leaders who organized the City Wide Bicultural Advisory Committee were aware of the need to bring both Mexican and Puerto Rican groups into the organization and continue to do so.

Some theorists define ethnicity only as a product of

early socialization processes which perpetuate sentiments, values, and customs from the home. However, another perspective toward ethnicity is illustrated by the conscious establishment of ethnic unity in the interests of obtaining political power. In Milwaukee, Hispanic youths are adapting their ethnic backgrounds, expressed in their family lives, to the real contact and conflict situations they face in public. Having been defined as a coherent ethnic group by the dominant society they have deliberately consolidated themselves in order to enhance their opportunities.

This self-identification of Hispanics acording to their language is, then, fostered by the dominant society. The process of ethnic consolidation has been successful partly because it began during the late '60's, a period dominated by activist youth who were willing to take risks and to confront authority. The youth movement in society at large facilitated the adaptation of ethnicity, allowing the establishment of a coherent group that could tap into the powerful emotional impulses of language and cultural pride; it also provided such groups with instrumental strategies for coalition politics, thus encouraging a sense of fraternity in order to work toward common goals. This coherence was reinforced by success: it became clear to all concerned that a united and numerically larger Spanish-speaking group was more effective in modifying policies and programs than the smaller Mexican or Puerto Rican groups had been when working alone. Further, because people felt themselves related by their language, they played down their ethnic differences. Young people could "belong" to this community even if they did not speak Spanish well; they belonged simply because they were Hispanic.

Language, then became a unifying link among Milwaukee's three *barrios*, serving to reduce the social distance that had previously been reinforced by residental separation. This mutuality of interest fostered secondary associations, such as an increased sense of responsibility for newcomers. Bilingual education and the newly created Hispanic agencies replaced, to some extent, the newcomers' dependence on family and friends from their own home towns for help and emotional security. These new structures did not replace the *familia unida* but supplemented it,

providing services to those who did not know English—
for which concurrently, bilingualism became an employment
asset—and keeping those who were losing Spanish in touch
with their "wider family."

Another aspect of ethnic identity is the
intergenerational stress that carries over from both
discrimination and immigration itself. Hispanic youth today,
however, have institutional as well as family supports which
reinforce their ethnicity. As their community's organizations
have developed, opportunities to express ethnic pride have
grown. While values and language behavior do continue
to change and tensions between teenagers and their parents
remain, rejection of one's ethnicity is not considered
necessary for success in the community. This is a
considerable difference between the Hispanics and the more
established and assimilated White ethnic groups—the Poles,
the Germans, and others—mentioned above.

Hispanic parents usually desire that their children
retain their culture, thus maintaining their ties to their
families in the city as well as elsewhere. As one parent
put it, "It is important, because you are what you are."
Families in Milwaukee do invite relatives from Puerto Rico
to stay for extended periods of time, and they themselves
go to Puerto Rico, or Mexico, or Texas, whenever possible
for vacations and for support during family crises. These
parents expect that, living in Milwaukee, their children
will change and that they will speak more English, which
the parents consider valuable. By self-report and from
observation both in and out of school settings, Hispanic
youths of all ages use a great deal of English. Younger
children and newcomers of any age continue to use more
Spanish, and switch to Spanish during outbursts of anger,
while explaining something to a friend who is Spanish
dominant, or in talking to a parent. Most of the students
in the high school bilingual program who were asked about
their language use indicated that they used both languages
with friends but mainly Spanish with older people and
parents. They also indicated that they place a high value
on bilingualism. No matter what their own use patterns
and dominant language were, these teenagers said that
speaking two languages was something to be valued.

Institutions such as the 800-family United Community Center, which runs programs to address such problems as drug use and teenage pregnancy, play an important role in providing youth and family activities, bringing teenagers and parents together. Community leaders have also tried to provide visibility and rewards for youths who do well in high school and to support those who go on to college; thus in many ways it is advantageous today for a successful student to stress his ethnicity rather than deny it. The Spanish Speaking Outreach Institute provides a support network for Hispanic college students; more than 600 now attend the University of Wisconsin-Milwaukee, and there are more at other area institutions. Education is considered an important means for upward mobility: none of the youths interviewed aspired to jobs in the foundries or tanneries but rather to a wide assortment of positions, including professional ones. Unlike their predecessor immigrants, these youths may receive financial help, public recognition, and, eventually, better jobs if they are bilingual and proud of their ethnicity. Even if they do not enroll in a bilingual program, its existence validates bilingualism itself, which, in turn, affects community norms. Although bilingualism is considered especially necessary for newcomers, it is not rejected by the generation born in the United States, particularly since it is considered important in maintaining generational ties. Speaking Spanish may be stigmatized by Anglos but not within the Hispanic community.

Another observation which can be made from the rise of Hispanic ethnicity is the success with which, by changing stigma into pride, this community has prevented the internalization of the dominant society's negative attitudes and has won attention and gained resources from the larger society. Since the late 1960's, Milwaukee's Hispanics have been developing media for public displays of pride in their language and culture. A monthly bilingual newspaper, for instance, includes in its Spanish and English articles information concerning national Hispanic conferences and reports, as well as local concerns, business advertisements and job information. It joins Hispanics to one another and to the national Hispanic community.

Another local newspaper, *The Milwaukee Journal*, regularly carries a "Latin Corner" which provides information concerning community leaders and issues. Radio programs in Spanish have increased. The city's public schools now publish all important informational materials in Spanish as well as English.

The Hispanic community also organizes major events, such as the Fiesta Mexicana, a September 16th parade, and a Christmas show at the city's Performing Arts Center, in which thousands of Hispanic and non-Hispanic citizens participate. There is a Latin American Chamber of Commerce, formed in 1969, that includes doctors, architects and lawyers as well as small shopkeepers, which has seen success in such efforts as lobbying for state legislation to re-open a bank on the South Side. Thus the Hispanic community has succeeded in keeping its own middle class involved in the process of asserting ethnic pride, which is important because they function as brokers with the dominant society's institutions: non-Hispanic businesses and organizations also give money to support event and program expansions on the South Side, and when the Milwaukee Ballet relocated there, Mexican dancers performed at the opening.

These are some instances of the ways in which Hispanics have gained greater visibility for their language and culture in the city. While discrimination and stigmatization remain, the Hispanic community has come a long way in its efforts to make the public aware of its needs and in ways that reinforce its' members ethnic pride as well as win additional resources. Bilingual education programs are one important example of what has been accomplished. People feel that these are part of a positive era of reform. As a former editor of the bilingual newspaper *La Guardia* said,

> It is now clearly recognizable that Latinos are on the threshold of one of the most potentially dynamic eras of their history in America.

Successful bilinguals provide a visible example of pride and a link to the resources of the majority society. If these people continue to use both languages and remain in touch with their communities, they contribute to an evolving ethnic identity which maintains key features of the minority culture while adapting to and succeeding in the dominant society. Such people serve as role models for Hispanic youths, enabling them to see that they can succeed without rejecting their parents' values and language. Also, bilinguals provide influential outsiders with a means of negotiation through people with whom they feel comfortable, and they will share more information and provide more resources if they feel that successful persons are involved.

In Milwaukee bilinguals have come to study in the area's colleges and remained in the city after graduating. They have provided leadership in the push for bilingual education, as well as for other community concerns. Their knowledge networks extend beyond the city, connecting the community with information sources and resources which have proved valuable. In Schermerhorn's (1969) terms, " The degree of enclosure has been changed and there are greater possibilities for integration of the minorty group." It is also important that bilinguals who are educated and middle class can relate to Hispanics from all of the disparate groups within the Hispanic community. Thus Cubans, Puerto Ricans, and Mexicans are able to work together, modeling a new Hispanic identity to supplement their various national ancestries. While some conflicts continue, the behavior of these individuals provides a public display of cooperation and encourages it among the rest. People work together on the boards of various agencies, plan the writing of proposals for funding, and meet with agencies to obtain resources. They provide an essential element of group cohesivenesss.

Bilinguals' relations with the dominant society give them access to information which they can relay back to their communities, enhancing the success of reform efforts. If people know whom to influence, they may be able to effect change without resorting to conflict and confrontation. This is exemplified by the late 1970's in Milwaukee, when the initial stages of confrontation were followed by a brief period of consolidation and development.

In addition to their role in joining people from the

Mexican and Puerto Rican communities and connecting them as a whole to Anglos and their resources, bilinguals can train others in leadership roles in the community. Training programs such as one in Milwaukee for parents related to bilingual education facilitate the development of friendships between Mexicans and Puerto Ricans who are working toward a common goal, increasing group cohesiveness, and, in turn, heightening the response of the dominant society. Milwaukee's policy of providing assistant principal positions to Hispanics enhances the school's ability to communicate with Hispanic students and parents; indeed it is based on the assumption that such middle-class Hispanics, whether they be Puerto Rican or Mexican, can act as effective brokers toward their community.

In Milwaukee, Hispanics have dealt with the issue of "Who represents the community, really?" by fostering the growth of multiple leaders from different backgrounds who publically demonstrate cooperation in the interest of achiving common goals. Bilingual education has been a key factor in the development of this cohesiveness, in which middle-class bilinguals have played an important role.

Parallels may be found between the situation in Milwaukee and Smith's (1975) analysis of change in the bridging of divisions between Cape Verdians and other Portuguese immigrants in Northeastern cities. Adaptation to the urban environment required that the Portuguese communities' internal splits be resolved, allowing its members to work toward common goals. In both situations, the improvement of their children's education was a particularly important goal for both old-timers and newcomers, for Blacks as well as non-Black Portuguese. A new identity as Portuguese was created in order to achieve this goal.

It seems that the fact of people having multiple identitites, which is a reality of American life, is less important than their interpretation of the conflict or congruence among them. These multiple identities, including ethnicity, continue because our society has allowed some degree of structural separation to exist. According to Gordon (1964), there is a degree of cultural pluralism in our society which makes it acceptable for one's primary relationship to remain within the family and traditions of one's own group. While this is the society's general pattern, Gordon believes that Americans need to be reminded that cultural retention for all groups does have a place in their system.

This degree of separation is functional, especially for newcomers. It is the basis for their adjustment to the urban milieu. Gordon stresses that the dominant society's institutions should accept this with good grace while providing opportuities for broader contacts with societal institutions for those who wish to take advantage of them. Instrumental skills, such as knowledge of the English language, should be provided so that people may be empowered as citizens, but this can be done without harming the traditions of the home. Some degree of change within ethnic groups is inevitable because of members' contact with other values and other ways of doing things. The challenge, Gordon says, is to provide a healthy psychological and sociological environment, so that youths need not reject their parents and their parents' values while they are learning to adjust to the dominant society.

The situation for urban minority groups who face discrimination on the basis of their language and color is somewhat different. They must adapt themselves to a society in which these characteristics are stigmatized. In addition, when their numbers are few, they must find resources to improve community and individual advancement. Additional difficulties arise with linguistic differences, racial differences, and generational differences within the group itself. Separate values and traditions may remain, but advancement demands the building of internal cohesion. One's identity as a Hispanic becomes just as significant as one's Puerto Rican or Mexican American background.

Visions of the Future

Milwaukee's Mexicans and Puerto Ricans feel, for the most part, that there are sufficient similarities among Hispanics to allow this internal cohesion to develop. While history, food preferences, color, music and sometimes, religion—there are more Protestants among the Puerto Ricans, although the majority are Catholic—create differences between these groups, they find similarities in their language and cultural styles, especially as compared with Anglos. Both Mexican and Puerto Rican informants felt that Hispanics were "warmer" than Anglos, and that all Hispanics shared common problems. They saw language variation as the natural consequence of growing up in differing situations but considered the differences relatively minor, involving only vocabulary—the use of different words for the same thing. These people were aware of conflicts among themselves and other Hispanics, but they stressed cooperation.

One community leader, for instance, said that it was important to avoid emphasizing the differences between constituent groups because of Hispanics' need to be pragmatic to accomplish difficult organizational tasks. He has been involved in organizing bilingual education programs and other efforts in two communities in the Midwest.

> When I see a mission that needs to be accomplished, I'll do whatever it needs to take care of it. . . . I believe in a pluralistic society and I believe that each ethnic group has something to offer to the composition of the community and that each one should have their own personal pride and that no one is better than the other. There are some people who think more nationalistic, that do not see any good in any other group, and that's the type of mentality that can hinder more than help, because they are not willing to compromise or work with any other philosophy, and that's a problem.

Although factions make organization difficult, he does not feel that such internal differences interfere with program planning and the provision of services in Milwaukee. He sees that the problems that arise are the result of a lack of tolerance and understanding; however, he believes that people learn about other groups, even adopt their speech as the natural consequence of the urban experience. He believes that this process should be considered enriching. For example, although he is Chicano, his young daughter interacts with Pureto Ricans and is beginning to speak as they do.

> You know with my child it's something that I have experienced, and I have not made her feel that she was doing something wrong. I was fascinated that she was acquiring the Puerto Rican way of speaking, but at the same time I reinforced that that was one way of saying it, and we said it another way, so that she understood that what we were teaching her at home was something that was relating to our experience, and something that she was learning in a Puerto Rican home was something additional to complement her.

He believes that teachers and parents should be sensitive about this issue and avoid allowing differences in identity to promote divisiveness or prejudice.

Time has also been a factor in the creation of a Hispanic identity. According to some informants, as more contact has occurred and more resources have become available, less conflict has arisen in the community. According to one Puerto Rican leader, for instance, there were more divisions earlier, when Puerto Ricans first began coming to Milwaukee in large numbers.

> I feel that the Hispanic community has grown a lot. I think they've gone through a lot of pains in growing. I think that there was division in the Hispanic community between Chicanos and Puerto Ricans. I felt that division was caused, I would say, mostly because of funding. The Chicanos had been here longer than the Puerto Ricans, and they were in charge of agencies. And many of the people that the agencies were helping were Chicanos. And so when Puerto Ricans came, it was kind of "we were here first," and some of the goals and objectives that they had for their people, according to some of them, not all, were not in their minds applied to the Puerto Ricans.

The speaker felt that the fact that Puerto Ricans are American citizens, while some Mexicans are not, was an example of these groups' different needs and, consequently, their different foci of concern. Bilingual education, however, was a common concern:

> There were certain things that pulled the community together. Bilingual education was one of them . . . I think they learned that education is important. I would say the most decisive one. Because once the kids were educated, then you could try to get them into jobs.

The variations within the Hispanic community do, however, cause some difficulties for the bilingual teacher. The teacher must be aware of the linguistic and cultural differences, as well as generational ones. This leader, who has been a bilingual teacher, dealt with this problem:

> A bilingual teacher must know the different kinds of backgrounds of the children—the different countries. She has to know, for example, when she gets a migrant child, that is completely different from getting a Mexican or Puerto Rican child that comes from a very solid, established home, or a child that comes from a Puerto Rican or Mexican background that was born here, who has never seen Mexico or Puerto Rico, and yet you're talking about culture. And when you look at it, their culture is here, it's Anglo culture, except for what they have at home, that is Spanish culture. So when you talk about a palm tree, many kids have never seen a palm tree. You see what I mean? So a teacher has to be very aware of the type of children she has in her classroom. Just because they happen to be Hispanic doesn't mean they're all the same. So she has to put in a lot of time and effort to get to know her children. And in order to get to know her children, she has to get to know the family.

A community made up of people with commonalities

and differences must maintain a balance between its internal differences and the cohesiveness required for the achievement of common goals—a common identity, such as being "Hispanic." In Milwaukee, Mexicans and Puerto Ricans, urban and rural people are grouped together for programs and services. Those persons and agencies providing such services, such as bilingual teachers, are faced with a challenge: to make their services effective, it is necessary that the person or agency recognize the community's internal diversity; yet this must be done without creating divisiveness.

A number of articles have stressed the difficulties involved in understanding issues of ethnic identity and how it may be changing among Hispanics. Writers of these articles have observed changes within Hispanic populations in the Midwest (West and Macklin 1959), and within upwardly mobile groups generally (McDonagh 1959). The assimilation theory has been reexamined in its application to the Hispanic experience: for example, Arce (1981) points out that existing conceptual definitions are inconsistent; that some researchers use various kinds of behavioral measures, while others use value orientations based on traditional Mexican values. Difficulties are also caused by the failure to distinguish among such concepts as cultural awareness, cultural loyalty, and self-identification. He suggests that we know little about the precise nature of these concepts, and that too much research has been done with college students.

Estrada, Garcia, Macias, and Maldonado (1981) point out that Chicanos now inhabit every state in the Union; furthermore, during the 1980's almost half of the Chicano population will come to reside outside the five southwestern states. In discussing the Midwestern situation, they suggest, as this article has done, the changes taking place in Chicano self-identification:

> Midwestern Chicanos, finding themselves among non-Chicano Latinos, necessarily interact, but not always easily or without hostility and suspicion. New patterns, however, are becoming evident as efforts at cooperative ventures are made. Chicanos

in Milwaukee, Chicago, and Detroit, for example,
discovering that they face problems similar to
those of other Latinos, seek to create coalitions
that form the basis for a national Latino thrust.
These contacts have understandably progressed
further among Cuban, Puerto Rican, and Chicano
leaders at the national level than at the local
level, particularly as the strategy of nationally
organized coalition-building has spread.

Some of the national leaders who have been trying
to create greater understanding among Hispanics of all
backgrounds have come from Milwaukee. They have been
advocates for change in the city, including the establishment
of bilingual education programs, and have therefore had
to deal with such problems as nationalistic attitudes,
ignorance, and prejudice, which sometimes impede coalition
building. With their assistance, an extensive bilingual
program has been established for a Hispanic population
which has inhabited Milwaukee a long time but which has
been continually changing. Hispanics in this urban context,
aware of the diversity of their own community, are adapting
creatively to the realities they face. Parents and community
leaders recognize the importance of tolerance and
understanding of the differences among them. Conflicts do
continue, but people prefer to emphasize cooperation.
Hispanic community organizations continue to reflect their
leaderships' ethnicity and politics to some extent as well
as the role these leaders played in the early days of
confrontation with the dominant society. However, the
membership, staff, and boards of these organizations
usually reflect the "Latino" reality of the city.

The Midwest will continue to serve as an excellent
setting for further study of Hispanic identity—its continuity,
its evolution within constituent groups, and the changes
in it which result from the contact among these groups.
Milwaukee's Hispanics are adapting to a complex urban
setting in which they make up a growing segment of the
population. They are seen and often stigmatized by Whites
as a single, alien entity, "The Spanish." Blacks consider
Hispanics both competitors for resources and potential
partners in their own push for change. Among themselves,

they are Puerto Ricans or Mexicans, but they are also "Latinos" striving to reconcile community development and improvement in an urban setting with a sense of belonging and with their traditional respect for the family.

Endnote

1. Dr. Judith Guskin, Adjunct Associate Professor of Anthropology, University of Wisconsin-Parkside, at the time of writing. Now President of Vision Quest Productions, Los Angeles.

References

Arce, Carlos H.
 1981 A Reconsideration of Chicano Culture and Identity: Daedalus. Spring:177–191.
Eidheim, Harald
 1969 When Ethnic Identity Is a Social Stigma, *In* Frederick Barth, ed. Ethnic Groups and Boundaries: The Social Organization of Cultural Difference. London: Allen and Unwin.
Esquivel, Mary Ann
 1981 State Latinos Fear Impact of '80 Census. The Milwaukee Journal 29 March.
Estrada, Leobardo F., F. Chris Garcia, Reynaldo Flores Macias, and Lionel Maldonado.
 1981 Chicanos in the United States: A History of Exploitation and Resistance. Daedalus, Spring:103–131.
Gordon, Milton M.
 1964 Assimilation in American Life. New York: Oxford University Press.
Greeley, Andrew M.
 1974 Ethnicity in the United States. New York: John Wiley and Sons, Pp. 295–296.

Hunter, Albert
  1974   Symbolic Communities. Chicago: The University of
          Chicago Press.
Levathes, Louise
  1980   Milwaukee: More than Beer. National Geographic
          158(2). August.
McDonagh, Edward C
  1959   Status Levels of Mexicans. Sociology and Social
          Research 33:449–459 July. as reported in Arce.
The Milwaukee Journal
  1981   Suburbia—Why So Very White? 1 August.
Moore, Joan, and Frank G. Mittleback
  1972   Measuring Residential Segregation in 35 Cities. In
          The Changing Mexican-American. Rudolph Gomez,
          ed. Pp 80–89. El Paso: University of Texas Press.
Nuestro
  1980   Brown and Black: Collision or Coalition?
          September:19.
Rummler, Gary
  1981   Area of the Past Now Has a Future. The Milwaukee
          Journal. 19 July.
Schermerhorn, Richard A.
  1969   Comparative Ethnic Relations: A Framework for
          Theory and Research. New York: Random House.
Seda Bonilla, Eduardo
  1973   Ethnic and Bilingual Education for Cultural Pluralism,
          In Cultural Pluralism in Education. Madelon D. Stent
          et al., eds. New York: Appleton-Century-Crofts.
Smith, M. Estelle
  1975   A Tale of Two Cities: The Reality of Historical
          Differences. Urban Anthropology 4(1):61–72. Spring.
Steiner, Linda
  1981   Ethnic Groups Talk Up Language Studies for
          Children. The Milwaukee Journal. 16 September.
West, Stanley A., and June Macklin
  1979   The Chicano Experience. Boulder: Westview Press.

Bilingual Education in a Chinese Community: An Ethnography in Progress[1]

Grace Pung Guthrie[2]

Introduction

It is commonly acknowledged that bilingual education is highly politicized and controversial. On the one hand, its proponents swear by it despite any inadequacies found through empirical investigations of specific programs. On the other hand, opinions and articles utterly hostile to bilingual education abound despite all the good things which studies say have happened to students in such programs. One columnist called bilingual education a "monstrous educational boondoggle" introduced by Chicano and other minority politicians who stood to gain most from it (McCabe 1981). Efforts have been made to evaluate the effects of bilingual programs objectively. Unfortunately, however, the findings from these studies have created even more confusion and controversy regarding the success or failure of bilingual education in serving this country's language-minority children.

One problem is that many studies have attempted to evaluate bilingual programs by comparing their participants' achievement test scores to those of monolingual control groups. These efforts failed to take into account such issues as the myriad variations of bilingual programs in design and intent; the actual implementation of programs; the real attitudes among administrators, teachers, parents, and students involved in the program; and the interactions of the participants, the program, and the school and larger environment. Little wonder that the results from these studies often contradict one another and generate more confusion and controversy. With the recognition of the serious limitations of these traditional statistical studies, ethnography has gradually gained importance as an alternative methodology to discover the inner workings of a bilingual program, its immediate and larger contexts (the school, community and larger society), and the interactions of various human and environmental elements involved in the program.

Our project, "Ethnography of Bilingual Education in a Chinese Community," is a step in this direction. We plan, through long-term participant observation in and ethnographic interviews with members of the target school and community, to describe, analyze, and explain the introduction and implementation of the bilingual program, the perceptions of it among community members, and its potential effects in the school and community. We hope that our attempt to describe and illuminate as holistically as possible the complex variables and factors that influence and interact with the implementation and outcome of bilingual education in an urban Chinese community may help us gain insights into various facets of the bilingual education movement and programs in other communities.

Before examining the research design and methodology of the study, let us first consider what ethnography is and is not.

Ethnography

In the simplest terms, ethnography is the study of culture. It is, as Bauman (1972) defined it, "the process of constructing through direct personal observation of social behavior, a theory of the working of a particular culture in terms as close as possible to the way members of that culture view the universe and organize their behavior within it." In Malinowski's words, the goal of ethnography is "to grasp the native's point of view, his relation to life, to realize his vision of his world" (1922).

Ethnography has been the traditional tool used by Western/European anthropologists in studying cultures other than their own. Only recently has it been used to understand the various cultures within our own complex society. Yet Goodenough (1976) points out, "multiculturalism is present to some degree in every human society." American society has traditionally been portrayed as a melting pot; it might be more accurately understood as a chef's salad, consisting of various ingredients mixed together. Each element is part of the whole yet maintains its own distinct color and flavor. Different ethnic groups follow contrasting cultural rules in their daily lives; so do different occupational and social class groups. Ethnographic research that has focused on various segments of this society has revealed distinct argots and implicit or explicit rules for acting, perceiving, and evaluating operating in each.

Recently, the value of ethnographic research in understanding childrens' educational processes has also become clear. As Hymes states:

> What happens to children in schools appears to depend on how the children interpret their world, given such categories as they have available. To find out what they see and do, to convey that knowledge in a way that permitted some of the texture of their life and world to come through, would be what I mean by ethnography (Hymes 1978:172).

Philips (1974) carried out an ethnography of communication in the school and community of Warm Springs Indian Reservation and discovered the "invisible culture" that governs these Indian children's classroom behavior. Ethnographies of classroom interactions with Odawa children (Erickson and Mohatt 1977; Mohatt and Erickson 1981), with Athabaskan children (Van Ness 1981), and with Chicano children (Cazden et al. 1980) have all demonstrated the usefulness of the ethnographic approach in understanding the classroom experiences of mainstream and minority children. (For more papers on classroom ethnography, see Trueba, Guthrie, and Au 1981).

The scope of ethnography may vary from the investigation of culture in a complex society with various social institutions, to the study of a single social organization, or a single social situation, even to the intensive microanalysis of a few minutes of a reading lesson (McDermott 1976). Hymes (1978) identified three types of ethnographies as defined by the project's research focus. Comprehensive ethnography seeks to describe the total way of life in a community—its customs, rituals, beliefs, organizations, artifacts, and so forth. Topic-oriented ethnography focuses on selected aspects of the target community's culture, its educational or economic system, for example. Hypothesis-oriented ethnography starts out with a set of hypotheses generated from previous ethnographies and understanding of a particular culture.

Project Objectives

Our project is located within the middle range on the continuum from macroethnography to microethnography. It is not an attempt to produce a comprehensive ethnographic description of the total culture of the target community. It is topic oriented, and, after the initial stage of fieldwork, hypothesis oriented as well. The goal of the study is to describe as completely as possible the educational processes of a group of Chinese-American bilingual children in their bilingual program, their school, and their community. In order to do this, we need to describe the pertinent characteristics of the bilingual program, school system, and community served by the school. Our objectives are these:

1. We want to know how the bilingual program is organized and under what philosophy it operates. How do children enter and leave the program? What constitutes their education in the program? What do the administrators and teachers intend the program to be?
2. We wish to describe the school system of which the target school is a part. We need to know,

for instance, the system's policy on bilingual education, the system's size, and how much freedom the school has in establishing its own programs.

3. We want to describe the community. We are interested here in the different sorts of language and cultural groups in the community and whether they also represent different regions. We will also seek information about the community's economic structure— its bases, and what most of the parents of the schoolchildren do for a living.

We also need to investigate the attitudes toward bilingual education among those people involved, including teachers, students, school administrators, parents, and other members of the community. We might search for differences in attitude in terms of language background, national origin, socioeconomic status, and length of residence in this country. Ultimately, we wish to describe how these attitudes affect the rationale, design, implementation, and results of the bilingual program.

In addition, we want to determine the effects on bilingual education of:

1. interactions among teachers, students, parents, and school administrators
2. the sociocultural dynamics of the school, the various sociocultural groups constituting the immediate community, and the wider community.

Research Design

The following section describes the ethnographic research design adopted to accomplish these objectives.

Methods and Procedures

Ethnographers differ from other social science researchers in that they tend to follow a cyclical rather than linear pattern of investigation. A linear research design begins with a well-defined problem and very specific hypotheses. These definitions are operationalized, and research instruments are designed before the researchers go out to the field to collect data or test subjects. Finally, data are analyzed, conclusions drawn, and results reported. Ethnographers, on the other hand, work more like explorers of a new territory. They enter the frontier territory with only a general problem in mind and a general goal—to understand and chart the territory. They can only plan their course of investigation in a preliminary way. They may follow a certain direction at first but change course after having evaluated the initial data. They have to analyze the information they gather to discover new questions and to elicit directions for the next phase of fieldwork. Thus the research process moves in a cycle that is repeated again and again until the project nears completion (see Spradley 1979, 1980).

The following figure illustrates the cyclical pattern of research activities in our ethnographic project. Each of these activities will be explained in detail in this section.

Entering the Field

Malinowski (1922) advised serious ethnographers to remain "in as close contact with the natives as possible, which really can only be achieved by camping right in their villages." In our case, we did not have to literally camp out. We did attempt from the very beginning of our project, however, to set up our office right in the middle of the community selected for it. Unfortunately, this building was not available for rent until the fourth month of our operation. We therefore concentrated our early fieldwork on the target school. Using the school as our base camp in our evolving exploration of the community, our researchers were gradually initiated into community life through the school personnel and parents.

After our project had been cleared by the school district's research department, we approached the target school's principal for a face-to-face presentation of our

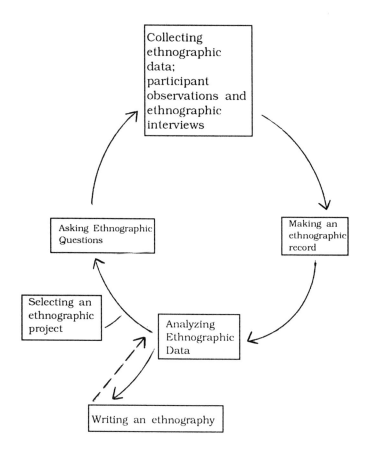

The Ethnographic Research Design
(adapted from Spradley, 1980)

research project. The principal had sounded quite reluctant at first over the phone. A number of other projects had been conducted in his school in recent years, and he was afraid that the school had already been overstudied. In the interests of both teachers and pupils, he was opposed to allowing any more researchers to come in and interrupt the school routine. Finally, after a long telephone conversation, he granted us an interview. During the interview, we presented the goal and methodology of our project, emphasizing the naturalistic character of our methodology, which is not disruptive. We promised not to usurp instructional time and to help the teachers out as well. We pointed out that working as instructional aides was an integral part of our research methodology. The principal finally gave us the go-ahead but left it to us to persuade the teachers to participate in the study.

Next, before beginning our classroom observations, we had to convince the curriculum director and the teachers of the validity and usefulness of our research. Once again we presented our research rationale, goal, and methodology as clearly as we could. We made sure they understood our sincerity and our enthusiasm for learning from and working with them. They were all interested in learning our exact schedule, so that they could incorporate our presence into their lesson plans. We definitely wanted to be of help to the teachers who had kindly agreed to let us into their rooms, but we also asked them to allow us to simply observe for the first week or so. As we became more and more familiar with the teachers' styles and classroom routines, we gradually took on the role of participant observers in the life of the classroom.

We initially observed only the second and fifth grade bilingual rooms. Then we realized that it would be fruitful for comparison purposes to observe the regular (non-bilingual) rooms at the corresponding grade levels and therefore added two classrooms to our observation list. The two regular rooms were observed for only two weeks each, however. Such comparative observation helped us put what we had seen in the bilingual rooms into proper perspective. At the beginning of the third month, we also gained access to the sixth grade bilingual room when it was recommended to us as an exemplary one. At present, all three bilingual rooms have been scheduled for long-term participant observation.

We are very grateful for the openness, warmth, and cooperation extended to us by the teachers and school administrators. After our initial contact with the school administrators, we were told that we would not be required to check with them every step of the way, and that we could go in and out of the classrooms as long as the teachers agreed. In his monthly bulletin, the principal asked all the teachers to assist us in our research efforts. To reciprocate such favored treatment we made sure that we took nothing for granted and did our best to be helpful and sensitive to the needs of the teachers and students. We also carefully matched the backgrounds and personalities of our researchers with the teachers' in order to ensure the development of rapport and to maximize the classroom ethnographer's role as an aide/researcher.

Each of the assistant ethnographers was introduced into a classroom by doing joint observation with the principal ethnographer for a whole school day. Thereafter these assistants, each of whom was responsible for one classroom, were encouraged to trust their own intuition and sensitivity in building their personal rapport with the teacher, the aide, the students, and other school staff. They were frequently advised to act—to move around in the classrooms, for example, and talk to the teachers, aides, students, and even parents—only when they felt they could do so comfortably and unobtrusively. We regularly held post-observation conferences to compare our field experiences, insights, and difficulties. The principal ethnogrpaher carefully reviewed the assistant ethnographers' field notes during the first month of observation, providing feedback regarding the strengths and weaknesses of their observations and notes prior to the next observation.

To avoid disturbing the classroom structure and routine, only one regular observer was assigned to each room. From time to time, however, by special arrangement with the teacher, the principal ethnographer continues to observe the class with the regular participant observer to check on his or her observations' reliability.

In short, our three assistants have been trained, through constant feedback and encouragement, to operate independently. In the process, they have provided the project with multiple entries into our fieldsite.

Through formal and informal school contacts, we were introduced to such key community informants as directors of community agencies, a former schoolteacher, and a parent who was known as the "Ambassadoress of Chinatown." These informants have been instrumental in our being allowed to participate in all sorts of community fairs and organizational meetings. Now that our office is located on the second floor of a newly renovated historical building at the heart of the Chinese community, in the midst of such community service agencies as the local Chinese Community Council, the Asian Community Mental Health Service, the Asian Health Service and so forth, we literally live and work among the natives. In the months ahead, as this project continues, we will be intensifying our community participant observation and interviewing.

Participant Observation

All of us are participant observers, to a certain degree, in our daily activities and interactions with people. But usually we become too much a part of the cultural scene and take its rules for behavior and interaction for granted and therefore cease to be effective observers. When we are confronted with new or unfamiliar situations, on the other hand, we tend to sharpen our observations and are better able to see tacit rules at work. At a new field site, ethnographers at first work only as observers, recording in detail all the activities verbal or non-verbal communications, and physical characteristics of people and places. Gradually, however, they participate more and more in the natives' activities and thus become full-fledged participant observers. Participation in a group's cultural activities is necessary to experience events and activities directly, to get the feel of what the natives go through, and to perceive and record the unfolding of events in depth. Without a certain degree of participation the ethnographer can only make observations from an outsider's viewpoint and can never really be in touch with the natives.

The participant observer differs from the ordinary participant, however, in that he or she consciously tries to maintain the role of an observer, to be aware of the tacit rules at work, and to take into account, not only immediate actions but also the contexts in which they take place, to be conscious of experiences, as at once both insider and outsider; to reflect critically on his or her experiences, and finally, to meticulously record what he or she sees, hears, thinks, and feels.

Our researchers assumed the roles of non-participant observers during the field visits, carefully recording as many behavioral and contextual details as possible. In the target classrooms, however, as we became more familiar with the classroom routines, and as the teachers and students became more comfortable with us, we came to participate more and more as aides. The degree and form of participation has depended largely on the individual teacher's style and preference. In general, we help out whenever we are asked to do so and in the way the teacher suggests. When we do not have specific tasks we make ourselves available to all the students, answering their questions, for example, and reading stories to or with them. In one classroom, our researcher is responsible for teaching a reading group bilingually twice a week. When the regular aides are absent, our researchers participate even more in the classroom life. When it becomes theoretically interesting to us, we also observe ESL classes; however, our role in these small group observations is largely non-participant.

We are participating more and more in the community as we have recourse to libraries and service agencies and as we become customers of shops and restaurants, members of local organizations, and friends of the natives. For example, we regularly attend the meetings of a city-wide Asian educators' association and of the school district Chinese bilingual parents' organization. Occasionally, we also attend church and community fairs.

From our initial open-ended, unprejudiced observation and record-keeping, we have gradually become more and more focused. As we have become more attuned to the cultural scene, we have been able to identify specific events which seemed significant and, thus, appropriate for closer observation. At present, we are in the process of examining data collected from these observations. As we progress in our data analysis, we may find selective aspects of events that require further consideration and renewed and even closer observation. Because of the scope and forms of this project, we will observe and analyze only a few cultural domains in depth while conducting general descriptive observation for the entire period of fieldwork.

Ethnographic Interview

The ethnographic interview is both a science and an art. On one level, the ethnographer has to know which questions to ask in order to elicit the responses that can shed light on the life and world of the natives. On another level, the ethnographer must be artful in the way he or she asks questions so as not to jeopardize the carefully cultivated rapport with the natives. Without knowing the art of ethnographic interviews, the ethnographer, no matter how well-armed with theoretical tools and carefully considered questions, may not be able to elicit any meaningful responses—or any responses at all.

On the topic of interviewing, Spradley advised (1979) that,

> It is best to think of ethnographic interviews as a series of friendly conversations into which the researcher slowly introduces new elements to assist informants to respond as informants. Exclusive use of these new ethnographic elements or introducing them too quickly, will make interviews become like a formal interrogation. Rapport will evaporate and informants may discontinue their cooperation. At any time during an interview it is possible to shift back to a friendly conversation. A few minutes of easy going talk interspersed here and there throughout the interview will pay enormous dividends in rapport (Spradley 1979:58–59).

To conduct a successful ethnographic interview, the ethnographer must be very sensitive to the needs, moods, and personalities of his or her informants and alert to the changing contexts of the conversation and the setting. Last but not least, he or she must be creative and flexible in asking questions. The ethnographer should also be open to the informants—bringing personal experiences into the interview, for example, especially when the informants express interest in knowing these things. This is a fair trade of information and a great way to build rapport.

Questions put forth in survey research and other types of social science interviews are almost always preconceived by the researchers and use the technical terminology and phrasing of social scientists. In ethnographic interviews, on the other hand, questions are generated from fieldwork experiences in the informants' native culture and are asked in their own language.

Again, Spradley (1979) points out very clearly the ethnographer's non-ethnocentric and non-threatening techniques:

> Ethnographers adopt a particular stance toward people with whom they work. By word and by action, in subtle ways and direct statements, they say, "I want to understand the world from your point of view. I want to know what you know in the way you know it. I want to understand the meaning of your experience, to walk in your shoes, to feel things as you feel them, to explain things as you explain them. Will you become my teacher and help me understand" (Spradley 1979:34)?

As the principal ethnographer in this project, I often remind our researchers to learn from the people we study and to avoid making evaluations and judgments during the course of participant observations and interviews. Our informants have consequently come to believe in our sincere desire to discover their ways of seeing and doing things. I have myself experienced the benefits of this approach, as my informants have expressed their appreciation of an attitude which is not condescending or arrogant as researchers often seem to be. Some informants were very reserved and guarded at first in my interviews of them. But when they sensed my genuine intereste and enthusiasm they relaxed, and often, at the end of the interview, they were surprised to find how much they had talked.

We have conduted three major types of ethnographic interviews for this study—key-informant, semi-structured, and informal—each with its own special purpose and method.

  1. Key-informant interviews. These were open-ended, get-acquainted interviews with such people as the directors of community service agencies, active members of the community, such as the "Ambassadoress of Chinatown," and several parents. We did not begin with a fixed set of questions but rather allowed the informants to point out to us the various aspects of life in the community. As we grow more and more familiar with the educational issues and concerns of the community, we can return again and again to ask these informants more specific questions. In the meantime more contacts are being made, and more key informants are being identified for future in-depth interviews. With a few exceptions, all key-informant interviews have been audiotaped and later transcribed. In general, these interviews last from an hour to an hour and a half.

  2. Semi-structured interviews. After the first three months of participant observation and open-ended interviews of key informants, we decreased our field activities to take stock of all the exploratory ethnographic data we had gathered. We set up preliminary coding categories to reduce the huge amount of data (see the section on data analysis) and wrote a summary overview of it. After the preliminary data analysis and debriefing sessions on the researchers' impressions, reflections, and perceptions, we postulated tentative hypotheses.

Based on these hypotheses, three semi-structured sets of interview schedules were designed for student, teacher, and community member and parent interviews. These were structured so as to ensure consistent data collection across respondents but were also sufficiently open-ended to maximize interpersonal sensitivity and to encourage the informants to express themselves as much as possible in their responses to the questions and probes posed.

The Student Interview was used with all students in the three target bilingual classrooms (N=92). The researchers were advised when asking questions to be aware of situational factors and sensitive to the individual child's particular background. The children's personal data had been collected during the participant observation phase.

The first four or five student interviews were not taped. After comparing notes, we made the decision to tape the rest. To our surprise, most of the students enjoyed the interview more and became more talkative when they knew they were being taped. The interviews were conducted in English or Cantonese, depending on which language the child felt comfortable speaking. After each interview, the interviewer transcribed all probes, questions, and responses recorded onto the tape.

The Teacher Interview has been used so far with 22 of 24 homeroom teachers in the school. We have also interviewed two ESL teachers and the one Prep teacher (who takes over each homeroom teacher's class one hour a week so that the teacher can prepare for his or her lessons), totalling 25 teacher interviews thus far. We used three slightly different sets of semi-structured interviews for bilingual teachers, regular teachers, and Chinese-American regular teachers.

The interviews, all taped, lasted anywhere from 45 minutes to two hours. Most of the teachers were willing to be taped. A few expressed some reservations about it at first but agreed after we expressed once again the purpose of this research and guaranteed to protect their privacy and anyonymity. Often, after the tape recorder was turned off, the informants became really talkative and touched upon more controversial topics on their own initiative. These comments were entered into field diaries after the interview.

The interviews usually began with an exchange of greetings and personal information. The researcher then explained the purposes of the interview, after which the tape recorder was turned on for the duration of the interview. It should also be noted that in addition to those questions provided by the interview schedules, additional questions arose naturally from the flow of the conversation and often led to even more probes along the same lines.

For the Community Member/Parent Interview, a more detailed and structured interview schedule has been devised and is being pilot tested. Because we anticipate interviewing from 100 to 150 people, we think the more structured format will help considerably to speed up the data collection and analysis processes. The pilot testing seems to indicate, however, that while the questionnaire serves well for the sociolinguistic component of the project, it may be too limiting for eliciting ethnographic data. At this moment we are revising the questionnaire as well as considering taping all the interviews so that we can capture the community members' and parents' words and views more truthfully. A decision must be made either to interview more people with relatively superficially coded data in the style of a record survey or to interview fewer people, with all the richness of ethnographic data captured on tape.

3. Informal ethnographic interviews. Throughout the course of participant observation, we have conducted informal ethnographic interviews with teachers, aides, students, other school staff, and community members. These interviews have not been scheduled and planned ahead of time; they have occurred spontaneously during participant observation. Whenever the time and place seem right, our ethnographers engage the natives in conversation and then ask questions relevant to our study (but pertinent to the conversations at hand). None of these informal interviews have been taped; they have instead been integrated into the observation field notes.

Ethnographic Records

Recordkeeping has been critical to every aspect of the ethnographic research procedures described above. An ethnographic record may consist of maps, films, pictures, documents, field notes, diaries, and interview transcripts. All facets of research, from field notes to decision-making, are carefully recorded and filed. These records provide the data used for ethnographic analysis and serve as the bases for the writing of the ethnography—the final product of the research. In this project, recordkeeping has taken four major forms: field notes, logbooks, interview schedules and transcripts, and analytic records.

Field notes were taken during or immediately after participant observation. Our ethnographers have been encouraged to note as many sights, sounds, and activities as possible during the initial stage of observation and to take verbatim accounts of conversations whenever able. When the context of the activities observed is particularly important, a detailed description is provided. Often, an additional diagram or map of the setting is carefully constructed and included in the field notes. Furthermore, all field notes are clearly dated and paged; the original and duplicate copies are stored separately. Announcements, instructional materials, and/or other documents collected in the field are attached to the same day's field notes.

Logbooks record those daily activities, impressions, reflections, and incidental observations and interactions that each ethnographer feels may be of relevance to the project. The logbook is used like a field diary; each researcher is left relatively free to choose what will be recorded. The principal ethnographer reads all the logbook entries and asks that especially interesting accounts or reflections be typed up and duplicated. When completed, the principal ethnographer collects the logbooks and files them. They then provide a useful index of research activities carried out during the course of the project.

Interview schedules and transcripts serve as a third form of documentation. All taped interviews are transcribed, typed, and duplicated for the record. The more structured interviews, employing interview questionnaires, are directly recorded on the questionnaire documents; no transcripts are made unless the interview turns out to be particularly informative. The researchers are encouraged to write on the margins of the questionnaire any additional contextual or personal information that may be of interest to our inquiry.

Analytic memos and summaries are critical to the ethnographic process. As field notes and interview transcripts are read and digested, analytic memos, suggesting ways of categorizing and analyzing the data, are maintained; these in turn become an ethnographic record for further analysis. Periodically, we write summaries of what we have observed, heard, and concluded. Besides serving as a record, these analytic memos and summaries pose new questions for future observations and interviews and keep us fresh in the field.

In addition to the above four major types of record, we have also collected various maps, documents, newspaper clippings, and literature to supplement data gathered from our fieldwork.

Analyzing the Ethnographic Data

Early in our study we established, by reading field notes and interview transcripts, a set of preliminary coding categories to help reduce the multitude of data we had amassed. These categories were entered in the margins of the documents in pencil so that they could be changed to reflect new orders of classification as new insights and understanding emerged. A set of tentative hypotheses, or cultural themes, was derived from this first stage of data reduction. In order to substantiate them, we began to conduct ethnographic interviews with various key informants and members of the school and community. Many of these interviews, including those of teachers and students, have been completed. Those involving community members are still in progress.

At the same time the interviews were begun, our researchers, armed with the tentative hypotheses, re-entered the field and conducted more focused participant observation. For example, from our initial observations it had become clear that non-English-speaking (NES) children were often segregated and isolated within the bilingual classrooms. They were usually seated together at one corner of the classroom, and given instruction—elementary English as a Second Language (ESL) lessons—by the aide. Since their English was not strong enough for them to start the reading series prescribed for the regular classes, they did not participate in any reading groups at all. This initial observation led us to more focused study of the manifestations this sort of isolation or segregation took. We also conducted interviews with all the students in the target bilingual classrooms to see whether the NES children were indeed isolated from the rest of the class. If so, did they suffer in their self-concept, and was their progress in the acquisition of English and other school subjects consequently affected? This question led to another: Did these NES children, isolated into a non-reading group, ever get a chance to move into the regular reading groups or even into the top reading group in the bilingual classrooms? If they did, how long did they take to get into the mainstream in their classrooms? A comparative question comes to mind: Did NES children fare better in being integrated into their classrooms, if they were not in such a bilingual program? To answer these questions, even more focused observations and interviews will be required.

This process of data collection (participant observation and ethnographic interviews), data reduction, ethnographic analysis, further data collection, and data analysis will be repeated again and again until a clear picture of the target culture emerges. Only then can a definitive ethnography be written about bilingual education in this school and community. However, leading ethnographers and field researchers suggest that writing a description of the culture under study as soon as possible and before the completion of the fieldwork has some merit. (Malinowski 1922; Spradley 1979, 1980; Schatzman and Strauss 1973). As Spradley (1980) points out:

> It is well to recognize that what you write is true of every ethnographic description: it is partial, incomplete, and will always stand in need of revision. Most ethnographers would do well to set aside the feelings that writing is premature and begin the task sooner rather than later. In the process of writing one discovers a hidden store of knowledge gained during the research process (Spradley 1980:160).

The next section of the paper constitutes an attempt at a preliminary ethnography of bilingual education in a

Chinese community. It is a summary overview of what we have observed and found. Since we began our ethnography from the school site and gradually expanded into the surrounding community, the work at this stage may seem a bit lopsided. As our community fieldwork intensifies, however, our description will become more balanced and complete.

Little Canton:
A Preliminary Ethnography

Little Canton is a thriving Chinese community in Cherrywood, California. Its population density may not be as great as that of the famed Chinatown in San Francisco; nevertheless, few observers can fail to notice the hustle and bustle of business activities here, especially in contrast to the immediately surrounding areas. Little Canton always seems busier and noisier and more crowded with traffic than any other area in the city, with the possible exception of downtown during the rush hours.

Walking through the crowded streets here, one often feels as if one were in the Orient. Besides the great number of Chinese store signs (with English translations) and the continual business transactions and traffic, about 90% of the people on the streets of Little Canton are Asians of every description: highly acculturated and sophisticated professionals; traditional Chinese shopowners, with their eager and enterprising air; Chinese peasant women, carrying babies secured to their backs with long pieces of cloth; and newly arrived refugees, still wearing their tribal costumes of Southeast Asian countries. Only during lunch or dinner hours does one observe a majority of non-Asian faces in Little Canton.

Little Canton proper consists of approximately six city blocks in which most of the restaurants, bars, clubs, and markets are located. In the evening, their lights and neon signs stand out against the semi-darkness of the abutting business areas. In contrast to the dark and menacing areas nearby, Little Canton seems to be an island of warmth and safety. It is particularly busy on weekend nights, when the restaurant crowd comes in for Chinese dinners, and on Sundays when Chinese families from the neighborhood or from nearby cities and suburbs gather to attend church, to shop, and to enjoy their Sunday teas or dinners.

There are four Christian churches in Little Canton proper, and many families come back here to attend one even after they have lived away from the neighborhood for many years. There is also a Buddhist temple on the edge of Little Canton, but the temple is not so popular as a gathering place. The four churches offer various sorts of day care, bilingual Bible classes and services, and, in response to the urgent language needs of a constant influx of immigrants from Hong Kong, China, and Vietnam, free evening lessons in English as a Second Language (ESL). These ESL classes are usually taught by American-born Chinese (ABC) members of the church, or by ABC high school or college students.

The Cherrywood Chinese Community Council (CCCC) was originally founded by the pastor of the Presbyterian church, who recognized the new immigrants' need for English and other survival skills. Now the CCCC, funded by the United Way, the city, and several federal sources, offers ESL, survival skills, and citizenship and CETA training classes, as well as free employment and income tax services. It has become a popular center for the Chinese and (ethnic Chinese) Vietnamese immigrants in the city of Cherrywood, and there is a long waiting list for the classes.

Cherrywood Unified School District (CUSD) also operates a Neighborhood Center adult school in Little Canton. This school is housed at the Chinese Community Center which has been the Chinese after-hours school for many generations of children here. (CUSD only borrows the classroom space from the Chinese Community Center, and is not otherwise connected with it.) The CUSD offers adult English classes at quite a few neighborhood centers in the city, yet most of the Chinese immigrants prefer the one at Little Canton, so that here, too, there is always a long waiting list. One of the English teachers at the Neighborhood Center explained that it is very convenient

for these immigrants to come to Little Canton to learn
English and afterwards do their daily shopping. The English
classes are also focal points of social activity, where people
go to meet relatives and friends.

The Chinese Community Center (CCC) houses, then,
two different schools: The neighborhood center adult school,
which operates from 9 A.M. to 3 P.M., and the Chinese
school for children, open evenings from 3 P.M. to 7 P.M.
Every morning at about 8:30, after dropping their children
off at one of the church day care centers, at the Little
Canton Children Center, or at King School (the community's
elementary school), a group of immigrants begins to
congregate in front of the CCC, waiting for the door to
open. They come out of their classes at 3 P.M., head for
the day care centers and King School to pick up their
children, and do their grocery shopping before going home.
Meanwhile, starting at 2 P.M., Chinese children have begun
to gather at the gym or in the hallways at CCC to wait
for their Chinese classes to begin, at 3, 4, or 5 P.M. Most
of these children come from King School, which is only
two blocks away. Because of the practice of split reading
groups, some primary graders are let out at 2 P.M., while
the rest of the school lets out at 3:00.

There are six different levels of children's Chinese
classes at CCC. Each class lasts for two hours per day.
Often these children have to wait for two hours after their
regular school to start their Chinese lessons, and some
have to wait for another hour or so after the lessons end
for their parents to pick them up. As a result, these children
have very long days, usually including two to three
unsupervised hours during which they play at the gym,
eat snacks in the hallways, or do homework in the library
until the adults come out of their English classes.

Those working parents who have enrolled their
children at the Little Canton Children's Center are
considered lucky, for the waiting list here is reputed to
be many years long. The parents drop their children off
there every morning on their way to work. When King
School, across the street, opens at 9:00, the Children's
Center teachers walk the K–3 graders over. (For some
children, the school day starts at 10:00 because of the

practice of split-reading among the primary grades.) At the end of the school day, the Center teachers escort these children back to the Center.

One of the reasons for the overcrowding of King School (which will be described later in this paper) is the presence of the Children's Center and the Chinese School in the community. Both the Children's Center and the CCC provide sorely needed supervision and care to the children of working parents. The combination of King School with either the Children's Center or CCC is too attractive for the parents to resist, leading to many incidents of falsified addresses in order to get into King School. The Children's Center also provides non-resident children from outside the King School's service area with a legal address that allows them to attend King School.

There seems to be a great deal of learning going on among both adults and children in Little Canton. They either work or go to school for the bulk of their day. Some unemployed recent immigrants attend school from morning to night (9 A.M. to 9 or 10 P.M.). They try to get into every possible class in order to learn English. This zest for learning English is also evinced among the children, even though both Chinese immigrant adults and children occasionally express great difficulty and frustration in doing so. All the immigrants interviewed so far in our project consider English the greatest obstacle in their adjustment to American life.

It is interesting, however, that Cantonese is used at the cafes, restaurants, banks, social service agencies, medical facilities, and other business establishments in Little Canton. There is now even a Chinese theatre to serve the community. No English is really needed to survive in Little Canton, but the immigrants seem to consider it a temporary and transitory place of residence. While they enjoy the convenience and security of Chinatown, they intend to move away when they become more affluent, as successful residents have traditionally done. They realize that English is essential to their upward mobility. All the immigrants interviewed considered Cantonese very important while they resided in Chinatown but saw English as even more essential.

King School

King School is very much at the heart of Little Canton. For years it has had an excellent reputation in the education of Chinese children. Its official capacity list is supposed to be 500; however, at the latest count, it had an enrollment of 735. The school facility is being stretched to the limit. This overcrowding is the result of many factors besides those mentioned above—its excellent reputation, and its proximity to Little Canton Children's Center and the Chinese Community Center. Many parents also choose King School over others because of its large proportion of Chinese students and faculty. King School has 14 Chinese-American teachers out of a faculty of 28 as well as a Chinese-American principal, nurse, and secretary, and a large number of bilingual Chinese aides. More than half its students are ethnic Chinese. Many Chinese parents therefore feel safer sending their children to King School.

It has also frequently been pointed out that many parents falsify their addresses in order to send their children to King School, so that they may take advantage of its maintenance Chinese bilingual program. They feel that their children will be more safely sheltered in this program's all-Chinese environment, free from the drugs, violence, and disciplinary problems which plague many urban classrooms. They feel that their children will behave better and learn more here. Another reason commonly given for the popularity of the school's bilingual program is that the parents, who often speak very limited English, if any, feel more secure interacting with Chinese-speaking teachers and aides. However, while the Chinese bilingual program has enjoyed quite a measure of support from the community, it has also stirred its share of controversy. To understand this, a discussion of bilingual education in King School is in order.

Bilingual Education at King School. Because of its large proportion of non-English-speaking/limited-English-speaking (NES/LES) children, the entire school sometimes seems to be a giant bilingual program. According to the latest count of the school population, there are 431 ethnic Chinese students out of a total enrollment of 735. All 431 ethnic Chinese students are classified as NES or LES. And there is still a constant influx of NES/LES children from China, Hong Kong, or Southeast Asia. There are nine bilingual classrooms at King School—one at each grade level (K–6), plus a 1-2 and a 3-4 combination class. These nine classrooms can accommodate at most 288 students, with an official maximum classroom enrollment at 32 each. That leaves about 150 NES/LES students to be absorbed by the regular (monolingual English) classrooms. This number does not include the newly arriving NES/LES students or those who are not Chinese. Regular classroom teachers interviewed have repeatedly pointed out the increasing proportion of the NES/LES children in their classrooms. One of them reported that 29 of her 30 children were NES/LES.

The school has wrestled with the problem of placing these children for a long time. There is contention between the regular and bilingual teachers as to who should have these children in their classrooms; this particular conflict will be discussed in detail later in this report. The principal's approach has been to adopt the following policy: (1) pull-out ESL lessons are provided to NES/LES children from both bilingual and regular classrooms, and (2) the regular teachers are allowed to share the bilingual aides, whose time used to be spent exclusively in the bilingual rooms. This practice makes the regular rooms function rather as partial bilingual classrooms. Both bilingual and regular teachers have pointed out that the whole school is practicing some sort of bilingual education and that there are two types of bilingual programs in the school:

1. the partial bilingual program, including all those "regular" classrooms sharing bilingual aides, and ESL classes; and
2. the full maintenance bilingual program, which is comprised of the 9 self-contained bilingual classrooms.

The fact that there are actually two types of bilingual programs in the school is, unfortunately, not commonly observed. The term "bilingual program" usually refers only to the bilingual program proper—the maintenance program.

Consequently, both the regular and the bilingual teachers have habitually failed to see their shared problems and characteristics (e.g., ESL help for their NES/LES children and shared bilingual aides). They have carefully maintained their separate identities. This polarization of bilingual and regular teachers has been routinely observed by our researchers and has also been pointed out by many teachers themselves in our interviews of them. The division of the school into two distinct, hostile camps is in many respects a result of the ways in which the school's bilingual program has developed.

History of the Bilingual Program. The bilingual program at King School was begun in 1971, after the school district had successfully obtained Title VII funding through a joint effort with three other neighboring school districts. The four school districts formed a consortium which developed its own model of bilingual education to be implemented in the participating schools. A few Chinese teachers from King School (ethnic Chinese, bilingual but not biliterate) were involved in the proposal writing stage. After the proposal was funded, however, these teachers were not able to teach in the new bilingual program because the funding stipulated that participating teachers must be both bilingual and biliterate in the children's first language. These senior Chinese teachers were asked instead to provide in-service training to their two bilingual and biliterate instructional aides, so that the latter might become full-fledged and accredited bilingual teachers.

These two instructional aides were thrust unwittingly into the bilingual program in the summer of 1971. After in-service training during summer school, they had to go literally from door to door to recruit students for the bilingual program. The program officially started in the fall of 1971 with two bilingual classes, K and 2. The two aides had been working with K and 2, respectively; therefore, it was logical that they run the K and 2 bilingual classes. The next year, when the original K class of children entered first grade, a first grade bilingual room was added to the program and a new bilingual K room was formed. Thereafter, following the maintenance model of the consortium program and the natural progression of grades, a new bilingual room was added to the program every year. By 1976, the bilingual program was comprised of 7 classrooms—one class for each grade from K to 6.

This growth process was not without problems. From the very beginning of the program, the regular teachers at the school felt alienated and "put down" (this term surfaced again and again during interviews). They felt great disappointment and injustice: while they were instrumental in the program's establishment, they suddenly became "not good enough" to teach once the program was funded. From the regular teachers' viewpoints, the aides-turned-teachers were not sufficiently qualified and experienced to teach in the first place. They found it even more difficult to see these bilingual teachers safe and secure in their teaching posts, while they themselves, in spite of their seniority, had to face the threat of being dismissed from year to year. Furthermore, bilingual teachers had special Title VII funding for all sorts of instructional materials, and their rooms were well supplied. The regular teachers, however, were not allowed to share the "rich" resources. There was also much jealousy over the presence of full-time bilingual aides in the bilingual rooms. Because of shrinking budgets, the regular teachers did not have even half-time aides. This feeling of injustice and jealousy was a common theme in interviews with the regular teachers. It does not appear to be specific to this school or district, however, but seems to be prevalent in many.

The bilingual teachers, on the other hand, felt that they were the products of circumstances and should not be the targets of such animosity and hostility. It was difficult enough to have had to learn to teach bilingually on the job and attend school at the same time to obtain their credentials; they found it doubly hard to work in an environment where they were openly looked down upon and isolated. What they really needed was all the help they could get in starting the new program. One of the two aides-turned-teachers recounted how they had to work and meet after school and on weekends and how enthusiastic they were for the first few years. She also recalled how she and the other original bilingual teacher became "burned out" and left the school as a result of the contentious atmosphere.

The former principal of King School was commonly
recognized as a strong supporter of the bilingual program.
Perhaps because of his own bilingual ability and Chicano
heritage, he gave unqualified support to the maintenance
bilingual program model developed by the consortium.
Ethnic Chinese teachers in the regular classrooms, however,
have pointed out time and again how inappropriate this
model, which was developed for Spanish-speaking children,
has been for the bilingual Chinese children. A leading
Chinese teacher at the school complained that "the
guidelines of the program were not designed by anyone
in the Cherrywood office. They were designed by the Spanish
folk over in Burton City (the neighboring city). "King School's
two aides-turned-teachers were the only non-Spanish
speakers in the bilingual credential in-service training
program run by the consortium in 1971. Most of the
training was conducted in Spanish and was reported to
be rather useless to the Chinese trainees. They had to rely
very much on their own resources and on the help of the
former principal. He apparently gave much more time and
attention to the bilingual program than to the regular one
and held separate staff meetings with the bilingual
personnel. When confronted over this by the regular
teachers, he explained that "If you have a sick child, you're
going to give him more attention." This practice of separate
staff meetings became a tradition, further alienating the
rest of the school from the bilingual component.

It is frequently pointed out that the Chinese bilingual
program was really a school within a school. It had its
own staff meetings, separate guidelines, and a separate
source of funding. It also followed directions from the
consortium, and, as one teacher pointed out, "they really
didn't have to dance to the tune that we [the regular
teachers] were required to."Since the Title VII funding for
King School's bilingual program ended in 1980, the program
itself has been in a state of limbo. It still maintains its
separate identity but is perhaps not as strong as in the
past. The bilingual teachers still refer to themselves as the
"Consortium" (actually the consortium's acronym) teachers
and refer to their program as the consortium model—a full
maintenance program.

Despite the current Chinese principal's efforts to integrate the two programs, neither party is ready to resolve their longstanding feud. An observer soon discovers that the regular teachers do not socialize with their bilingual colleagues and that the latter consider the current principal an arch-enemy of their program's survival. As a result of our initial observation that the school leadership was more supportive of regular staff and that the regular teachers directed a spiteful tone toward the bilingual ones, we postulated a tentative hypothesis that there was a stigma attached to the bilingual program. However, in the light of new understanding gained from more focused observation and extensive interviews with the teachers and students, this original hypothesis had to be modified.

Stigma or Something Else?

In order to test our tentative hypothesis that the bilingual program was stigmatized, we re-entered the field for more focused observation. We conducted interviews with all 92 students in the three target bilingual classrooms and 26 teachers of the entire staff of 28. The picture we obtained from these interviews was quite different from what we had hypothesized. Most of the regular teachers did find fault with the bilingual teachers' qualifications and teaching experience and particularly with their inability to provide proper English language models for the children. (There may be some truth to this criticism when levelled against specific teachers.) However, in the context of all that was said, it appeared that this spitefulness may very well have arisen from the regular teachers' insecurity concerning their jobs' continuity and concurrent jealousy over the bilingual program's contrasting stability. The bilingual program does not appear to be stigmatized at all.

On the contrary, the bilingual program is said to have the more able students. It is also noted for having few behavior problems, enabling the bilingual teachers to spend more time on teaching and less on discipline. Most of the regular teachers have pointed out that the bilingual program has a more stable and homogenous population due to its maintenance nature: the children stay in the program from K to 6, and they do not have to leave it unless their parents request that they do so. As discussed earlier, most Chinese parents want to keep their children in the bilingual program; thus the bilingual classrooms are always full and cannot take in any new students. Yet, given King School's location at the heart of Little Canton, new NES/LES immigrant children are of course constantly trickling in. With the bilingual classes full, these new students can only be placed in the regular classrooms. This has been an additional source of conflict between the regular and bilingual teachers.

Our researchers have found further evidence against any stigma attached to the bilingual program in the comments made to them by staff members. In spite of his reputation as an enemy of bilingual education, the principal has on many occasions praised certain of the bilingual teachers, calling them the best teachers in the school. Many of the regular teachers, too, have readily conceded the bilingual teachers' expertise in teaching NES/LES children. A few of the regular teachers who are strong proponents of the ESL program and strongly emphasize the importance of proper English role modelling in English language development cannot help but praise the professionalism of some of the bilingual teachers and aides.

In our student interviews, we found that bilingual students tend to stick together; they do not socialize with students from the regular classrooms. They seem isolated from the rest of the school, but this does not appear to be the result of any stigma attached to their group. The bilingual students express no feelings of inferiority about themselves or the program; their classrooms are so self-contained that there seems to be little opportunity for them to compare the differences between bilingual and regular classes.

Re-evaluating our initial hypothesis as well as evidence that supported that hypothesis and taking into consideration our new insights, we must now postulate that there is a stigma attached only to being NES/LES. The following is a discussion of the treatment of NES/LES children in the school, and the fights between regular and bilingual teachers over who should have to teach them.

The Problems of NES/LES Children. From the first day of our fieldwork, we have observed the isolation and segregation of the NES/LES children in the bilingual classes. They tend to be seated in a corner of the room and assigned to work on their own or with the aide or the participant observer. The bilingual teacher is usually occupied with the rest of the class. As far as we have been able to observe, the bilingual teachers tend to work only with the Fluent English-Speaking (FES) groups (the regular reading groups).

This is not to say that the bilingual teachers may not have very good reasons for structuring their classes in this way. Given time constraints, perhaps it is valid for the teacher to work with the majority of students. Perhaps it is educationally sound to group the NES/LES children together for special ESL lessons until they are sufficiently proficient in English to join the rest of the class. There are, of course, very real constraints on the teacher's time and energy in dealing with many different levels of English proficiency and reading in the classroom. The teacher must in some way prioritize tasks. The accredited teachers may feel that their own time and expertise is better spent with the FES children. The NES/LES children can obtain help from the bilingual aides, whose English may not be good enough to handle the FES reading groups but is sufficient to give the NES/LES children some rudimentary lessons.

However sound the reasons may be behind the practice of segregating them from the mainstream classroom life, these NES/LES children still feel the stigma of separation. They have been observed, time and again, to have sensed their isolation and segregation due to their lack of English proficiency. This segregation is not confined to the classrooms but is also apparent on the playground. Play groups often form along language proficiency lines. In class, there have been occasions when teachers have actively tried to integrate the NES/LES children into the activities—by seating NES/LES children among the fluent English speakers (FES) children, for example. However, the NES/LES children still experience alienation from the rest of the class. The FES children have even been observed to mistreat their NES/LES counterparts; the latter have often expressed inferiority over their inability to learn English, and to speak it as well as the others.

One negative result of the teachers' lack of attention to these NES/LES children is that their progress is not often noticed or praised. The children tend to stay in their non-reading groups (that is, at the pre-reading stage) for the whole year. Unless the aide or the participant observer intervenes, bringing certain children's progress to the teacher's attention, these children may very likely be tracked and branded as "dummies" for the rest of their school lives.

In May 1980, when the end of the cycle of Title VII funding became known, there was a proposal submitted by the regular teachers, with the principal as the leading proponent, to have all the NES and low LES children placed in the bilingual classrooms. The regular teachers' argument was that bilingual classrooms were meant for NES/LES children, according to the state and federal regulations and that the bilingual teachers were better equipped to teach them.

The bilingual teachers were furious about the proposal, and mobilized over 100 parents to "kill" it. One admitted to us that the bilingual teachers had "reacted violently, strongly against the plan, because we felt a lot of hatred at that time." Apparently, at the height of the conflict, during a meeting in which the argument grew particularly heated, some bilingual teachers reportedly said, "We don't want to teach only the dummies." In the course of our observation and interviewing, quite a few teachers, both regular and bilingual, have admitted to the difficulties of teaching the NES/LES children and their unwillingness to do so. However, on this occasion, when the bilingual teachers inadvertently called the NES/LES children "dummies," the regular teachers became incensed and were all up in arms. This incident intensified the conflict between the two camps and was mentioned repeatedly in the interviews.

It is once again time for the schools to prepare plans for the coming year. At King School, the bilingual teachers are expecting another battle. Some, however, have grown so tired that they do not want to fight any more. One said that if the school and community were not ready for a maintenance Chinese bilingual program, she was ready to adopt a transitional model: It was simply too hard to try to do a good job under such suspicion and hostility. Another bilingual teacher admitted at one point that the proposal might not be a bad idea for the students, provided the class size were small and the duration limited to one year or six months. However, when asked later on whether she would agree to the plan if it were re-submitted, she said that she would not come out and say that, that if she had to gather the parents again to oppose the program, she would do so—but tactfully.

It seems, then, that it is ultimately up to the parents to decide the future of the bilingual program at King School. As one teacher said, "If we don't have any parents supporting bilingual education, it would just be no bilingual education." We must therefore ask what the parents and community really want, who the vocal parents are, and whether they are really representative of the community views. Furthermore, do the parents know what kind of bilingual program they want and for what purpose?

As our study continues, we are seeking answers to these and other questions. We are now conducting interviews of parents and community members and hope to have some conclusive evidence in the near future.

At this stage in our fieldwork, we were struck by the importance of staff relationship to the proper development and growth of a program, especially an innovative one. When a new program is initiated, special care must be taken in preparing the entire school staff and in securing their good will and understanding; otherwise the program will encounter numerous unnecessary roadblocks. As Troike concluded after reviewing various research results in bilingual education, "Even a well-conceived program may fail, however, if it operates in a hostile environment which negates all of the positive signals the teacher and the curriculum transmit to the child" (Troike 1981:503).

We are not saying that the bilingual program at King School is a failure or that it is going to fail; we are merely stating that the unintended consequences of a haphazard and other-initiated introduction of that program have worn out a few hard-working, conscientious, and dynamic bilingual teachers. Some have left the field of teaching altogether. Some have stayed on but feel they have been put on the spot and have had to prove and defend themselves, year after year. They have had to prove, in particular, to their non-bilingual colleagues that they are competent teachers in English by working very hard on improving their students' English proficiency—often to the sacrifice of Chinese instruction. The real time spent in instruction in Chinese or in Chinese lessons has gradually dwindled over the years. In a school environment largely hostile to the idea of maintaining Chinese in public classrooms, some of the less confident bilingual teachers have gradually accepted the arguments of the school's leading teachers and have used more and more English in their classrooms, almost to the total exclusion of Chinese. A few have admitted in informal interviews that they really wish they didn't have to teach Chinese at all, feeling that their disadvantaged children need all the time they can spare for English, and there are only so many hours in a day.

The bilingual teachers' struggle against the placement of all NES/LES students in their classrooms should not be taken to mean they did not care about these children. On the contrary, we found that they were deeply concerned for the children's future. Often the teachers' own personal experiences in struggling to learn English and adapt to the mainstream culture made them very sympathetic to these children's plight. However, they already had their hands full having to deal with many different reading groups in both Chinese and English (for a detailed description of the Chinese bilingual classrooms, see Guthrie, 1985). They did not believe they could manage having all NES/LES children in their classrooms. Legally, one-third of each bilingual classroom was entitled to be comprised of FES students. The bilingual teachers did not understand why, if they were successful in raising their students' scores, they should be punished by losing their top achievers. Because of the intense competition between the bilingual and the regular programs, the bilingual teachers needed their best performers to prove their own and their program's success, since there were no other measurements of success available.

The principal informed us that the school population over the past few years has consisted of approximately 60% Chinese, 20% Southeast Asian, and 20% others (Blacks, Chicanos, and Whites). From the known student population characteristics unique to the school and community, one may safely say that at least two-thirds of the children are NES/LES. That means, consequently, that King School should therefore have more bilingual teachers and classes than the present ratio of one bilingual to two regular classes. At present, we are not sure whether it is the difficulty of finding qualified Chinese bilingual teachers or political considerations that have prevented the district and school administration from creating more bilingual classes. However, it seems that it is the bilingual teachers' right to stand up for themselves and to safeguard quality education for their students by enlisting parental support.

Ironically, the parents of the NES/LES children did not ask for bilingual education in King School ten years ago; the first bilingual teachers had to go from door to door to recruit parents and students. Now that the parents have learned to appreciate the bilingual program—for whatever reason, and whatever that program may be in its actual implementation—they have become a force to be reckoned with. The school leadership has been observed to make efforts to sell these parents the traditional non-bilingual program. The Chinese-American parents' traditional respect for authority, including school authority, may make them easy targets for manipulation. If the decision is ultimately left to them, the survival of King School's bilingual program may depend upon which school authority manages to communicate with and convince these parents of the validity of his or her program.

Endnotes

1. The research reported here was supported by the National Institute of Education, Dept. of Education, under Contract No. 400-80-0013 to ARC Associates, Inc.
2. Dr. Grace Pung Guthrie is a Project Director at the Far West Laboratory for Education Research and Development, San Francisco. This paper was written for a presentation at the annual meeting of the American Educational Research Association in Los Angeles, California, April 17, 1981.

References

Bauman, R.
    1972   An Ethnographic Framework for the Investigation of Communicative Behavior. In Language and Cultural Diversity in American Education. R.D. Abraham and R. Troike, eds. Englewood Cliffs, N.J.: Prentice-Hall.
Cazden, C.B., R. Carrasco, A.A. Maldonado-Guzman, and F. Erickson
    1980   The Contribution of Ethnographic Research to Bicultural Bilingual Education. In Current Issues in Bilingual Education, 31st Annual Georgetown University Round Table on Language and Linguistics.
Erickson, F., and G. Mohatt
    1977   The Social Organization of Participation Structures in Two Classrooms of Bilingual Children. Paper presented at the Annual Meeting of the American Educational Research Association. New York, April.
Goodenough, W.
    1976   Multiculturalism as the Normal Human Experience. Anthropology and Education Quarterly 7(4).
Guthrie, Grace Pung
    1985   A School Divided: An Ethnography of Bilingual Education in a Chinese Community. Lawrence Erlbaum Associates.
Hymes, D.H.
    1976   Ethnographic Monitoring. Symposium paper delivered at the Multilingual/Multicultural Materials Development Center, California State Polytechnic University, Pomona, Calif.
    1978   What Is Ethnography? Sociolinguistics Working Paper #45. Austin, Tex.: Southwest Educational Development Laboratory.

Lewis, O.
    1963   Life in a Mexican Village: Tepoztlan Revisited. Urbana:
            University of Illinois Press.
Malinowski, B.
    1922   Argonauts of the Western Pacific. London: Routledge.
McCabe, C.
    1981   Charles McCabe Himself. The San Francisco
            Chronicle. March 9 and 10.
McDermott, R.P.
    1976   Kids Make Sense: An Ethnographic Account of the
            Interactional Management of Success and Failure in
            One First-Grade Classroom. Unpublished doctoral
            dissertation. Stanford University.
Mead, M.
    1928   Coming of Age in Samoa. New York: Morrow.
Mohatt, G.V., and F. Erickson
    1981   Cultural Differences in Teaching Styles in an Odawa
            School: A Sociolinguistic Approach. *In* Culture in the
            Bilingual Classroom. H.T. Trueba, G.P. Guthrie, and
            K.H. Au, eds. Rowley, Mass.: Newbury House.
Philips, S.U.
    1974   The Invisible Culture: Communication in the
            Classroom and Community on the Warm Springs
            Indian Reservation. Unpublished doctoral dissertation,
            University of Pennsylvania.
Schatzman, L., and A.L. Strauss
    1973   Field Research: Strategies for a Natural Sociology.
            Englewood Cliffs, N.J.: Prentice-Hall.
Spradley, James P.
    1970   You Owe Yourself a Drunk: An Ethnography of Urban
            Nomads. Boston: Little, Brown.
    1979   The Ethnographic Interview. New York: Holt, Rinehart
            and Winston.
    1980   Participant Observation. New York: Holt, Rinehart
            and Winston.
Spradley, James P., and Brenda Mann
    1975   The Cocktail Waitress: Women's Work in a Male
            World. New York: Wiley.
Trueba, H.T., G.P. Guthrie, K.H. Au, eds.
    1981   Culture and the Bilingual Classroom: Studies in
            Classroom Ethnography. Rowley, Mass.: Newbury
            House.
Van Ness, H.
    1981   Social Control and Social Organization in an Alaskan
            Athabascan Classroom: A Microethnography of

Getting Ready for Reading. *In* Culture and the Bilingual Classroom. H.T. Trueba, G.P. Guthrie, and K.H. Au, eds., Rowley, Mass.: Newbury House.

Individual Differences in Growing Up Bilingual

Ana Celia Zentella[1]

How is "bilingual" defined? Who is a fluent bilingual? How do you become bilingual? What relationship exists between bilingualism and cognitive development?

After a spate of research in bilingualism over the last twenty years, we still do not have complete answers to these questions because of the myriad variables involved in the complex process of becoming bilingual. We search for answers not only because they present challenging linguistic issues, but because of pressing educational problems: there are presently over 3 million children in U.S. public schools who cannot understand English well enough to be able to study in English-only classrooms, and that number is expected to increase rapidly during the next decade. The educational programs specifically designed to benefit these students are being dismantled just as research on bilingual children in and out of school is shedding new light on the linguistic nature of bilingualism and on its social and cognitive correlates (Skutnabb-Kangas 1981, Hakuta 1986, Harding and Riley 1986, Genessee 1987). Studies influenced by the work of Dell Hymes (1962) and modeled after those of Susan Philips (1972) and Shirley Heath (1983) have shown that the lack of fit between the communication patterns and the cultural learning styles of the community and those of the school are in part responsible for such dismal educational statistics as the 80% drop-out rate for Puerto Rican students. In the face of renewed national pressures to make children choose one language and one culture—the dominant one—and to focus research on classroom or school studies, I would like to make a plea for the kind of educational research that incorporates community ethnography so that links may be made between the cultures of the home and the school in ways that strengthen both.

My own work among Puerto Ricans in East Harlem, "*El Barrio*," is a study of language in the community context (Zentella 1981a). Even though I was born and raised in a similar Puerto Rican community in New York City, it required two years of participant observation to unearth some of the patterns that lay beneath the surface of life in *El Barrio* and to recognize the complexity of some apparently obvious variables such as personality, experiences, and cognitive skills. What follows is an insider's view of growing up bilingual in a low-income Puerto Rican community and the dizzying number of factors involved.

El Bloque

The most striking initial impression one has of *el bloque*, as the block is called, is of constant activity and interaction. Somebody is usually around, and something is usually happening. In the midst of trash-strewn streets, overflowing garbage cans, ripped-out doorways, and gaping mail boxes, members of several intimate social networks gather against the backdrop of three five-story tenements. These buildings house approximately 100 people, including the 19 families with 34 children that were the principal focus of my study.

Age and sex are the basic linking factors in local social networks, for both children and adults. Each network has its own favorite space and time on the block for socializing, but good weather brings everyone down to "*janguear*" ("hang out") for a while. When the Spanish-dominant women, those between thirty and sixty years old, come downstairs to chat, they congregate in the hallway vestibules that house the mailboxes and face the street. The Spanish-dominant men of the same age sit across the street under the block's two trees on warm days; on most days they stand or sit around the domino table and parked cars in front of the two *bodegas* (grocery stores) that separate the tenements and the numbers parlor. The young "dudes," English-dominant lovers of salsa music in their early twenties, lean against the parked cars in front of the tenements or the housing projects across the street with their prized "boxes" (over-sized radios). Younger mothers, English-dominant women in their late teens and early twenties, sometimes lean against other cars or sit on the narrow two-step entrances to the buildings, with their baby carriages parked alongside the steps. Teenagers congregate in the pinball alley or move to sit on car fenders for private discussions. The young children (3–12 year olds) have the run of the block. They whirl about from one area to the next and thus may be subject to the supervision of people from any one of the networks. As a result, the children are intermittently addressed by monolingual standard or non-standard Spanish speakers, monolingual standard and non-standard English speakers, and bilingual and bidialectical speakers of both languages. The children respond to the older adults in accordance with the community norm "Speak the language spoken to you," which is required by both the presence of monolinguals and the cultural importance of "respeto" (respect). Among themselves the children usually speak English; but they also alternate Spanish and English at an average of 25 code-switches per hour for many important discourse functions. The greatest diversity of linguistic behavior and code-switching occurs outside on *el bloque.*

At Home

When we enter the homes on *el bloque,* we find four distinct communication patterns differing in terms of the language(s) that the parents speak to each other; the language(s) the parents speak to the children, and vice versa, and the language(s) the children speak among themselves. The major patterns are diagrammed in Figure A.

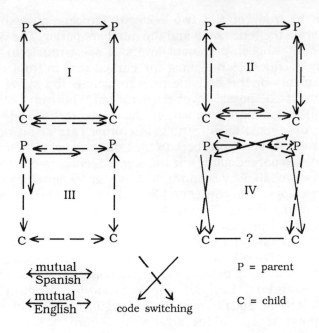

FIGURE A Patterns of Communication at Home

I.   The parents speak only Spanish to each other and the children; the children respond to their parents in Spanish but they speak Spanish and English to each other (5 families, 8 children).

II.   The parents speak Spanish to each other and the children, but one of them sometimes speaks English as a second language to them; the children respond in both languages, preferring Spanish for their parents and English for each other (9 families, 14 children).

III. The parents usually speak English to each other and to the children, but one parent speaks some Spanish to them; the children respond in English and speak it to each other (3 families, 8 children).

IV.   The parents code-switch frequently among themselves and to their infants who are just learning to speak (2 families, 4 children).

Individual Differences in Growing Up Bilingual

In the majority of the families (patterns I and II, representing 14 of the 19 families), the children hear their parents speak Spanish at home to each other and are always spoken to in Spanish by at least one parent. This is true of 69% of all of the children of *el bloque*. The parents in these groups had migrated to the mainland after spending their youth, including early adolescence, in Puerto Rico. These children are the ones who most closely approximate the "one language/one environment" principle in that they must speak Spanish at home to at least one parent, but they speak English outside the home. Among these families we find a greater percentage of fluently bilingual children, i.e., children who can speak at length as easily in one language as in the other; but they also include older children who are more fluent in English than in Spanish.

Parents who were born and raised in New York City, or who left Puerto Rico before late adolescence, or married an Anglo (one mother) mainly speak English to each other and their children. This is true of three families with 8 children among them. As expected, English-dominant and even English-monolingual children are found in these families, but they also include some children who are Spanish-dominant or fluent bilinguals.

The interaction in the homes of the two young couples in their early twenties who were born and/or raised in New York City is characterized by frequent code-switching between English and Spanish with each other, using more English than Spanish, and with their four young children (IV). Unfortunately, these children were too young to speak much of anything during the study; but their incipient vocabulary consisted of words from both languages.

As you can see, it is difficult to make accurate predictions about the level of children's bilingual fluency based on language patterns of the home. This is because our brief description of the patterns in each group of families is adequate only as a sketch of one of the principal communication patterns in which the children participate every day. It is not correct to assume that children in Groups I and II do not speak much English with adults in a home setting or that Group III children do not interact in Spanish with adults while doing chores, eating, and so on. This is because families do not raise their children in nuclear units isolated from the neighbors. Rather, the entire block is like a clan, due in part to the fact that nine of the 19 families with children are members of the same family, related by blood, marriage, or *compadrazgo* (ritual kinship). Two other family groupings link four more families to each. Within such family groupings there is constant visiting, exchanging, and sharing; the children are as likely to be found in one living room as another. The other families on the block are incorporated into the network because all children have the run of most apartments. Whenever people out on the street are unsure of the whereabouts of a child in a building, the problem is resolved by calling up the stairwell; the child appears from any one of a number of doors.

In sum, contrasting language patterns at home may not be good predictors of children's language proficiency levels. Children within each group may or may not develop similar language abilities. It is true, as the diagram indicates, that the children of group I speak more Spanish to each other than those of Group III, i.e., it seems that the use of English among the children increased in proportion to the extent of English understood and spoken by their parents. By the end of the study, however, the school-age children in Group I were speaking to each other predominantly in English despite the fact that their primary caretakers did not demonstrate visible improvement in their English skills. Nor are these isolated cases; communication in English is the norm for school-age sisters and brothers among Puerto Ricans in the United States. The principal exceptions are among those siblings who migrated to the United States during or after their teen years. This holds true even for older sisters and brothers who have subsequently lived more years in New York than in Puerto Rico. For example, those who arrived at fourteen and sixteen still speak Spanish to each other at forty-two and forty-four, or sixty-two and sixty-four. They may, however, speak only English to their children. In this way the Puerto Ricans are similar to the other linguistic minorities in the United States whose fate has been to lose their mother tongue by the third generation. More significant, however, are the differences that may interfere with or impede the expected replacement of Spanish. Primary factors involve macro social and economic issues such as the rate of the flow of migration to and from Puerto Rico, residential patterns, out-marriage rates, female and male employment opportunities, public housing desegregation policies, and urban renewal. In the block that is home to our subjects, the prevalent configurations of these factors favored the continued presence of Spanish during the period of the study. For example, a greater number of residents came from Puerto Rico than left; the overwhelming majority of households included Puerto Ricans only (one Anglo spouse was the only exception); and the tenements allowed for frequent and extensive interaction among the families and included empty apartments that were made available to newly arrived relatives. The presence of one dominant family network intensified the residents' complex and dense relationships, and the high percent of unemployed residents contributed to the continuous presence on the block of members of diverse networks. Therefore, the children of all of the families were in continuous contact with Spanish monolinguals, with various levels of Spanish/English proficiency, and with various patterns of interaction outside their homes.

Differences in bilingual proficiency among children of different families are to be expected, but differences within families may be more surprising, particularly to those teachers who teach sisters and brothers in different classes or years. Such differences in siblings can be accounted for by many situational, educational, or cultural variables, with one factor of particular interest being the socialization of young Puerto Rican children into appropriate male and female roles. This process provides girls with more exposure to and participation in Spanish than their brothers because of their closer restriction to the house; the greater amount of time spent with the mother; play and friendships with other girls; caretaking responsibilities with infants; attendance at Spanish religious services; and inclusion in female discussions and activities, such as cooking, sewing, cleaning, taking clothes to the laundromat, and watching the *novelas* (soap operas). The work of Labov (1972) and other sociolinguists has consistently indicated that females are more sensitive to the link between language and social status and thus are more likely to follow the appropriate norms in the community. This is corroborated on the block and is more apparent as the girls grow older and take up mother roles, becoming more bilingual in the process. Their fluency in Spanish improves as they learn to carry out those roles in Spanish, maintaining the traditional link between that language and caretaking and as they solidify their membership in the mature women's network.

Despite the immersion of females in Spanish-linked activities, the impact on all female children is not the same; that is, not all sisters speak Spanish equally well, nor do all brothers speak it poorly. Within each family one or more of its members will be subject to a number of Spanish or English influences to varying extents; this affects each child's personal language history and development. One child may visit Puerto Rico more frequently or for longer stays than others; one may be enrolled in a bilingual program and others may be in a monolingual English class; one may spend more hours out on the block while others are more confined to the apartment; one may identify more with African-Americans than with Puerto Ricans, or one may participate in religious programs that require literacy in English or Spanish. Other major factors include identification with either Puerto Rico or the United States as a whole and racial identity as Black, White, *jabao*, *trigueño*,[2] or other.

As if this staggering variety of situational variables were not enough, they also interact with cognitive and social variables that help determine who becomes a proficient bilingual. Lily Wong Fillmore's (1983) two-year study of Cantonese and Spanish-speaking children in school, from kindergarten to second grade, demonstrated how difficult it is to gauge the respective weight of cognitive, social, and situational variables. We know that they all contribute to the process of becoming bilingual, but we do not know in what proportion each contributes or what interactions may exist between such variables.

The situational variables in the school setting include the organization of the class—whether it is learner- or teacher-centered, for example, and the mix of its students— in terms of the number of limited English-proficient students and Spanish monolinguals. These situational variables correspond to such variables in the community setting as families' language patterns and children's participation in diverse networks.

The social and cognitive variables that Wong Fillmore identified as helpful in language learning are the same for these children both in school and in the community. The cognitive abilities that are required to discern the patterns of the units, the structure, and the meanings that make up language include memory, inductive reasoning, mental flexibility, and pattern recognition. The social abilities needed to become bilingual are those that allow speakers to engage in the indispensable sustained interactions that provide language learning practice: this requires sociability, outgoingness, and talkativeness. As you might expect, Wong Fillmore found that high ratings in the social and cognitive abilities were characteristic of children who picked up their second language easily, but this was not always the case. Her most important finding was that variation in language learning ability is widespread and greater than expected, regardless of cognitive and social ratings; what some children learned in eight months took others who scored higher, and were therefore considered "brighter," two to three years to learn. Contrary to popular belief, differences in the rate of language acquisition can be unrelated to intelligence or motivation.

The effect of the social situation in which the language learning occurs is another factor that must also be taken into account. In the Wong Fillmore study, whole classes turned out to be full of predominantly "slow" or "fast" learners because the organization of the class and the mix of students proved very influential. She concluded that the most effective classroom in which to learn a new language is one in which there is an open, learner-centered atmosphere with a mix of language-proficiency abilities. This type of classroom allows students maximum interaction with an adult speaker on a one-to-one basis, and it provides exposure to peers with more developed language proficiency.

This, of course, is similar to the situation just described for *el bloque*, but it is *not* what the children of el bloque encounter in their school experiences. All of their classrooms are either teacher-centered English monolingual classes or teacher-centered bilingual classes. Furthermore, Migdalia Romero's (1983) study of a sample of the bilingual schools in *El Barrio* has documented that 60% of the teachers' talk is in English. Neither type of classroom stimulates language learning to the maximum, although the bilingual classes do allow the children to socialize with a mix of students that is more representative of the block than the English monolingual classes.

I did not look for correlations between the types of classrooms in which the children of *el bloque* were placed and their level of bilingualism, but two facts in this regard are worth noting. In contrast to Richard Rodriguez's (1982) belief that the public person can be developed only via the public language, English, and not in bilingual classrooms, the best students in the study were also the most fluent bilinguals, as determined by language proficiency tests in the school, peer ratings, and my own evaluation. The star "performer," Maria, a popular 8-year-old who was born and raised in *El Barrio*, read above grade level in both languages and was generally a good student; she was in a bilingual class for Intellectually Gifted Children (IGC) at the time the study began and continued in IGC classes for the next two years. The best speakers of Spanish and English among the boys also received the best school grades. The second point is that there were children who spoke Spanish and English well who went to English monolingual classes, but they could not compete in reading Spanish with the students from the bilingual classes. Maria and other students from bilingual programs were called upon to read such materials as signs, advertisements, greeting cards, and letters from Puerto Rico aloud in Spanish for older children who spoke it well but who learned to read only English in school. It is well known that "reading is the single most crucial skill through which all students achieve success or encounter failure in schools" (Benitez 1985:6); the literacy efforts in bilingual classrooms are essential to the development of the academically successful as well as public English persona, contrary to Rodriguez's claim.

Effective reading strategies are built upon children's spoken language, but when the children of *el bloque* enter the schools, their oral bilingual skills are not seen as assets. They feel under attack because they speak Puerto Rican Spanish, because they speak Black English Vernacular (BEV), and because they mix these together. This is the case even in bilingual classes, because few of the teachers are aware of the features of varieties of Caribbean Spanish, or the rule-governed nature of non-standard dialects, or of the process of becoming bilingual that characterizes the community.

Research on bilinguals out of school has rarely grappled with the complexity present in *El Barrio*. In the past, longitudinal studies of bilinguals have often been case studies of individual middle-class children in nuclear families, often the children of researchers (Ronjat 1913, Leopold 1949, Fantini 1976). Most often these children learn their languages in strict adherence to the one language-one environment principle, usually speaking a different language to each parent, or one language in the home and the other outside. When bilingual communities have been studied, they too seemed to compartmentalize their languages, either along the lines of classic diglossia or in accordance with topics, locales, or domains. Such previous studies of communities with stable economic, demographic, and social parameters cannot be adequately compared to the language experiences of *el bloque* (Pedraza, Attinasi, Hoffman 1980), nor can those of individual middle-class children. Incorrect assessments will result if the bilingualism of lower working-class children who are considered non-White and who come from territories that have been politically subjugated by the United States (e.g., Puerto Ricans and Chicanos) is judged by a standard based on European, White, and/or middle-class immigrants of a previous generation. Comparisons with such inappropriate models lead to negative attitudes, evaluations, and inappropriate placements in educational programs. If teachers are unprepared for the kind of bilingualism acquired when many people speak different varietes of two languages to children, they may be prone to blame the acquisition process for any or all educational failure and even to believe that bilingualism causes cognitive dissonance. Too many educators continually tell parents that their children will become confused if they are raised bilingually. Yet the contrary is true, i.e., not only can people learn a second language as competently as a native speaker, but proficiency in one's first language does not hinder the acquisition of English or any second language, rather it fosters it (Cummins 1981). In addition, being bilingual has demonstrated cognitive assets even when the children are more proficient in one language than the other, as Hakuta's research (1986) with lower-class Puerto Rican children in Connecticut has substantiated.

It is precisely the complexity of the *vai-ven* (go-come) migration caused by Puerto Rico's colonial status pattern, the push-pull of economic, educational, and social forces that keep most members locked in poverty, the experiences that alternately reinforce Spanish or English, and the cultural membership in the "*dos* worlds/two *mundos*" (Padron 1982) that characterize the process of growing up bilingual in *El Barrio*. The most productive definition of this process as it operates in the Puerto Rican community is John Attinasi's concept of "interpenetrating bilingualism," or the fluid and creative use of all of the environmental language resources at hand without the purist separation of languages and without the wholesale condemnation of the varieties spoken with/by uneducated Spanish speakers or by English speakers, including BEV (Attinasi 1983:10).

The question of cultural identification is central in this process. The children of *El Barrio* love people who speak Spanish and people who speak English, they love Puerto Rico and New York, and they feel like both Puerto Ricans and New Yorkers. They learn to admire members of the community who are fluent in both languages and for whom code-switching is one of the ways of speaking.

Attempts to judge or interpret this process via principles that work for other types of communities but are inadequate for communities such as the one under study, run the risk of mislabelling and wrongly stigmatizing behaviors. Even worse, such attempts fall short of capturing the strength and diversity of the language abilities of children like those of *el bloque*, and decisions based on such research can contribute to their failure to achieve in the schools.

Endnotes

1. Dr. Ana Celia Zentella is an Associate Professor at Hunter College of the City Univeristy of New York (CUNY) as well as the Graduate Center of CUNY.

2. In North America the social construct of race is dichotomous, that is, White or Black (sometimes termed non-White). In Latin America there are more than forty terms for groups with differing proportions of Indian (Native American), European and African descent. *Jabao* and *trigueño* are two of these terms [editors' note].

References

Attinasi, John J.
  1983   Language Attitudes and Working Class Ideology in a Puerto Rican Barrio of New York. Unpublished manuscript.
Benitez, Diane
  1985   A Bilingual Monoliterate?: Implications for Reading Instruction. ERIC/CLL News Bulletin 8(2).
Cummins, James
  1981   The Role of Primary Language Development in Promoting Educational Success for Language Minority Students: A Theoretical Framework. Los Angeles:

California State University, Office of Bilingual, Bicultural Education, California State Department of Education.

Fantini, Alvino E.
1976 Language Acquisition of a Bilingual Child: A Sociolinguistic Perspective (to Age Five). Brattleboro, Vt.: Experiment Press.

Fillmore, Lily Wong
1983 Who Needs Bilingual Education to Learn English? Paper delivered at National Association for Bilingual Education, Washington, D.C. February 17.

Genessee, Fred
1987 Learning through Two Languages. New York: Newbury.

Hakuta, Kenji
1986 Mirror of Language: The Debate on Bilingualism. New York: Basic Books.

Harding, Edith, and Philip Riley
1986 The Bilingual Family: A Handbook for Parents. London: Cambridge University Press.

Heath, Shirley B.
1983 Ways with Words. London: Cambridge University Press.

Hymes, Dell
1962 The Ethnography of Speaking. In Anthropology and Human Behavior. T. Gladwin and W.C. Sturtevant, eds. Washington, D.C.: Anthropological Society of Washington. Pp. 13–53.

Labov, William
1972 Sociolinguistic Patterns. Philadelphia: University of Pennsylvania Press.

Leopold, W.F.
1949 Speech Development of a Bilingual Child: A Linguist's Record. 4 vols. Evanston, Ill.: Northwestern University Press.

Padron, Henry
1982 Dos Worlds/Two Mundos, poem presented at the N.Y.S. Convention of the National Congress for Puerto Rican Rights, November 17, SUNY, New Paltz. Reprinted in Hermanos Latinos 13 #2, December 1982, SUNY, New Paltz.

Pedraza, Pedro, John Attinasi, and Gerard Hoffman
1980 Rethinking Diglossia. Working Paper #9. New York: Centro de Estudios Puertorriqueños, City University of New York.

Philips, Susan U.
1972   Participation Structures and Communicative
        Competence: Warm Springs Children in Community
        and Classroom. *In* Functions of Language in the
        Classroom. C. Cazden, V. John and D. Hymes, eds.
        New York: Teachers College Press.
Rodriguez, Richard
1982   Hunger of Memory: The Education of Richard
        Rodriguez. New York: Bantam Books.
Romero, Migdalia
1983   Significant Bilingual Instructional Features Research:
        Teacher/Student Talk. Paper delivered at National
        Association for Bilingual Education, Washington, D.C.
        February 17.
Ronjat, J.
1913   Le dévéloppement du langage observe chez un enfant
        bilingue. Paris: Champion.
Skutnabb-Kangas, Tove
1981   Bilingualism or Not: The Education of Minorities.
        Avon: Multilingual Matters.
Zentella, Ana Celia
1981a   Hablamos los dos. We Speak Both: Growing Up
        Bilingual in El Barrio. Ph.D. dissertation. University
        of Pennsylvania.
1981b   Language Variety Among Puerto Ricans. *In* Language
        in the USA. C. Ferguson and S.B. Heath, eds. London:
        Cambridge University Press.
1985   The Value of Bilingualism: The Puerto Rican
        Experience. *In* Language of Inequality. Joan Manes
        and Nessa Wolfson, eds. The Hague: Mouton.

An Ethnographic Study of Home/ School Role Conflicts of Second Generation Puerto Rican Adolescents

Marietta Saravia-Shore and Herminio Martínez[1]

Introduction

This chapter[2] reports the findings of an ethnographic study of lower socioeconomic status (SES) second-generation Puerto Rican adolescents in New York City who dropped out of school and subsequently participated in an alternative high school equivalency diploma program. The chapter conveys, in the Hispanic adolescents' own words, their experiences and attitudes toward schooling and the reasons they dropped out and subsequently re-enrolled in the high school equivalency course. A major theme of discussion is their feelings about their dual roles as adults with head-of-household responsibilities outside of school and as adolescents required to follow rules meant for minors inside school walls.

Underlying this duality is the clash between the conflicting value systems of their homes, their peers on the street, and in the social system of the school, which leads to conflicting expectations for Puerto Rican adolescents in these three domains.

Theoretical Framework

The theoretical framework of this study situates schooling within the context of the larger society of which it is a component (Comitas and Dolgin 1978). Following the model of the school as a social system described in the ethnographies of Lacey (1970), Rist (1973), and Ogbu (1974), this study seeks to describe the patterns of expectations for adolescent behavior in several social contexts: the home, the street, the workplace, and the school. It also explores the patterns of interaction among teachers and lower SES second-generation Puerto Rican adolescents in a public high school and in an alternative high school setting.

The authors have been guided in their analysis of social interaction in the classroom by the theoretical perspective of Grannis (1967, 1978), who views the school as a model of the larger society. Grannis contends that urban schools for lower SES students tend to prepare them for the routinization and close supervision of lower-echelon jobs, whereas suburban schools prepare their students for executive-level, responsible jobs, and hence construct situations where students have more responsibility for their own learning and for decisions about the allocation of their time. One way of constructing such a situation, for example, is the use of contracts for independent or team projects over an extended period of time.

Susan Philips (1972) has documented the effects on student classroom participation of various ways of structuring interaction, which she has termed "participant structures." Grannis (1967) identified several such structures in the classroom that reflect the allocation of resources in the larger society. He points out how student access to such resources as books and materials can be either direct or mediated through the teachers and how control over time, pace of work, and movement can be either under sole control of the teacher, joint control of students and teachers, or determined entirely by the students. Similarly, task selection or allocation can be controlled in any of these ways.

For the purposes of this paper, the period of adolescence is viewed in a cross-cultural perspective (Mead 1928; Fortes 1938; Firth 1936) as socially and culturally defined. As Firth wrote in his study of the Tikopia:

> Entry into adult life involves the realization of social obligations and the assumption of responsibility for meeting them. What initiation does is to set a time on the way to manhood—often only approximately the time when the parallel physiological changes are due to take place—and by bringing the person into formal and explicit relations with his kindred, confronts him with some of his basic social ties, reaffirms them and thus makes patent to him his status against the days when he will have to adopt them in earnest (Firth 1936:433).

By contrast, in the different sociocultural contexts of the Hispanic home, the ghetto street and the urban school, there are conflicting definitions of adolescence, and thus contradictory expectations of lower SES Hispanic adolescents.

The literature on the socialization of lower SES Hispanics living in large urban ghettos documents the assumption of adult responsibilities by very young children, with vivid examples in such life histories as Piri Thomas's *Down These Mean Streets* (1967) and *Up from Puerto Rico* (Padilla 1958). Older siblings, particularly girls, are expected to act as surrogates for parents who work outside the home or whose large families necessitate this caretaking. A carefree childhood is virtually unknown as adult responsibilities pile up on youngsters, and the harsh realities of life with limited economic resources are all too evident to them on ghetto streets and in overcrowded homes.

Similarly, adolescence brings other adult responsibilities early—for some, the responsibilities of parenthood, for others, self-support or support of younger siblings. At school, however, the situation may be totally different, with no recognition of the students' near-adult or adult status in other settings. One way in which distance, and thus social control (Lacey 1970), is maintained by high school teachers and administrators is to treat adolescents as children in need of close supervision and monitoring through stringent school rules, and to deny them the rights and privileges of adults. It is hypothesized that the resulting role conflicts among adolescent Hispanic students lead either to frustration, aggression and violence, or to their withdrawal from the situation, for example, by dropping out of school.

Another factor to be considered is the Hispanic adolescent's perceptions of the opportunity structure of his or her community and the job market. As documented by Ogbu (1974), adolescents who know of the racial and ethnic prejudices which lead to job discrimination against Blacks and Hispanics and the resulting high unemployment rate in their communities may have little motivation to sustain their participation in school. When they perceive it to be so much more difficult for a member of an oppressed minority group than it is for other persons to obtain a job or even to obtain further education or vocational training to increase the possibilities of employment, dropping out may seem to be a reasonable choice.

Methodology

This study followed an ethnographic approach in which the investigator was an on-site observer in the school and the surrounding community. Over a period of ten months, after gaining access to the alternative school, the investigator observed its classrooms and hallways, walked around the immediate neighborhood with some of the students, and hung out in front of the school. Patterns of seating and interaction were recorded in the classrooms and informal conversations were held with the teachers, administrators, and counselors to learn about their perceptions of the students. On the basis of informal discussions with students, an interview schedule was developed and employed among 18 male and 15 female students. The interview elicited student experiences and attitudes toward schooling, sex, work, and family life.

Interviews were conducted in English or Spanish or both, depending on the situation and the student's preference. The interviewer used the interview schedule as a basis for questions but did not strictly adhere to it, since it was important to establish and maintain trust; therefore the interviewer answered questions as well as asked them and shared feelings.

Program Description

The site of this ethnographic study was a community-based organization in a low-income neighborhood in New York City. Of the various youth-oriented programs sponsored by this organization, the General Equivalency Diploma program was selected because of its population and its history of achievement. Interviews were conducted with community members, administrators, teachers, and previous program participants prior to the selection of this particular program.

The requirements for program eligibility included: (1) family income below poverty guidelines, (2) age range between 16–21, (3) application through appropriate channels, and (4) completion of a three-week probationary period. The program is two-fold, including both preparation for a General Equivalency Diploma and part-time work in various non-profit institutions. Students spend 15 hours a week in classroom instruction and 15 hours at work-sites such as hospitals, clinics, and day-care centers. The positions they hold include receptionist, typist, maintenance worker, general office worker, and library worker. Students earn a stipend of $175 every two weeks, representing 30 hours of work per week at the minimum wage.

Classroom Observations

Three classrooms were observed over a period of ten months. Two characteristics of the classroom that were immediately notable were the small size of the groups— from nine to ten students—and the absence of noise. There was task-oriented participation, discussion, and student demonstration of problem-solving in algebra at the blackboard, but there was no "kidding around." This group of former drop-outs was one of the best-behaved groups of high school students the observer had ever seen.

In this alternative school setting, rules, regulations, and restrictions were de-emphasized. Instead, emphasis was placed on the student's goals. These students had enrolled voluntarily to prepare to take and successfully pass the GED exam for a high school equivalency diploma. Thus, the teachers did not demand obedience—"you have to do this homework"—but rather stressed the positive consequence of doing the homework, which would be to reach the student's goal. When students came in late or without their homework, apparently angry and ready to fight the expected put-down or reprimand, their tardiness was ignored and their presence simply acknowledged.

During follow-up interviews, teachers explained that this was a deliberate strategy. They were interested in creating a classroom of adults. The teachers mentioned that their students often had other responsibilities, but that they were also responsible for doing their homework. It was expected that they would do this work, since it was the students themselves who wanted to pass the exam.

In class the teachers would emphasize this goal, which was clear and well defined. There was a lot of talk about the test; for example, "Listen, you've got to get this down pat. They usually have two or three of these problems, and it's worth five points." A student chimed in, "That's right, I missed passing by five points."

One of the students' complaints about their previous schooling was that the work did not lead to a clear goal, that it was "all over the place." It should be noted that these same students were now working diligently on abstract tasks apparently unrelated to their daily lives, such as algebra problems. However, they had made the connection between their learning algebra, passing the algebra component of the exam, and the diploma's significance to their lives.

The classroom's bulletin board featured a list of people who had taken and passed the GED exam. Among these were students from the neighborhood who had attended this alternative school, and everyone knew some of them. All the students in the program, which has a good reputation in the community, had been referred to it by someone who had already gone through it.

The lack of restrictive rules and regulations in the classroom was evident in the following ways: students could get up and walk out of the classroom to go to the bathroom or out for a smoke without asking permission. They could smoke in class; they had direct access to materials and did not have to ask the teacher's permission to obtain them. They were expected to work, but the pace was left up to them. If a student had not had time to do the homework, he or she was nevertheless asked to participate in class by trying to solve the problem rather than being excluded from participation.

If a student missed a day, however, the teacher referred him or her to one of the best students for notes. Thus, rather than being rewarded with extra attention from the teacher, the student was "punished" by being made to ask a better student for assistance. On the other hand, when a student needed further clarification or assistance to understand the process or concept being taught, the teacher would either take class time to assist him or her or make an appointment to do so afterward.

The following observations convey the tone of the class:

• The emphasis on individualized instruction required that each student be actively involved in his or her own work while the teacher worked with other individuals.

• The teacher's presence was not essential to the learning nor to discipline. In several instances, the teacher left the room and the students continued working in absolute silence.

• Students paid attention to instructions with, for the most part, no interruptions. Mutual respect was apparent.

• All the students asked questions at various points.

• There seemed to be great independence regarding behavior. Students smoked, left the room without requesting permission, and exercised their own judgment regarding completion of assignments, selection of some reading material, etc.

• There was a noticeable emphasis on responsibility.

After many conversations with teachers, the observer concluded that there is general agreement among them concerning student motivation. One teacher's perceptions of the problems facing adolescents in school may be summarized thus:

• After many years of involvement with the system, she feels that teachers' lack of concern is a real problem. "This sickness has spread to the majority of teachers." There are many reasons for this lack of concern, but they certainly reflect the system's inability to deal with "different students."

• There is a general attitude of low expectations toward Black and Hispanic students. It is assumed that they will never achieve certain goals. The standards of the educational system are therefore constantly lowered, which has a circular effect damaging to the students as well as to the schools.

• "The assumption is that schools which are all Black and Hispanic are inferior!" Therefore, teaching in schools with this population is equivalent to teaching in a setting where learning is severely limited.

• The school plays a more important role in the lives of these students than most people realize. "The school is successful if it can provide the kind of association many of these kids are looking for. If they can find someone to talk to, this usually makes the difference."

According to this teacher, individualized teaching represents

> the only possibility for the successful instruction
> of inner-city students. You can't just go through
> the curriculum, or forget that it does exist, but
> rather there needs to be constant clarification of
> concepts and building on each student's
> knowledge. I find myself clarifying concepts that
> they were taught in high school, but could not
> understand. Then they gave up or left school.
> There are many things that have to be clarified
> before you can move on. Besides, a lot of attention
> is to be given to the whole student.

Student Talk

We now turn to the students' interpretations, in their own words, of their experience. These quotations from students have been organized into the following categories:

- Student Attitudes toward the Alternative High School
- Student Perceptions of the Previous School
- Student Perceptions of Being an Adult and Being Treated as a Kid
- Student Comments on Prejudice and the Conditions of Puerto Ricans
- Student Aspirations

Student Attitudes to the Alternative School

There was a consensus among the students that the alternative school they were attending was a good place for them. The teachers cared; the content was more challenging and demanding; and they were learning.

> This place is quite different. You have a lot of students there, but not here, and I like that. Also, the teachers have a real interest in teaching. They care if you pass or not.
>
> I like it here because they teach you more. I did not know how to do fractions. I could hardly multiply or divide. Here I was doing algebra. My reading is better. My notebooks are filled. Before, they only had drawings and blank pages. I write a lot now. If I am told to study, I do it. I remember things now. Before, I used to forget all the time.
>
> I like the education here. Each teacher is easier, but they push you. They make believe you are in college. It's training you to be independent in your thinking. They don't let you take breaks and all that.

Students' Perceptions of the Previous School

The students generally evaluated their previous high school experience much less favorably than their current schooling at the alternative high school. Criticisms of the previous schools concentrated on teacher favoritism toward the better students, teachers' lack of respect, care or concern for students, and the repetitiveness of their instruction. The following comments are illustrative of these opinions:

> Most of the teachers only cared about the smart kids. Others did not care. They would tell you that you always had an excuse, that you were wrong or something. They would always argue, argue with you, but never listen. I was in-between—I was not very smart—but not too stupid.
>
> I can't think of anything I really liked about school. As I told you, it was very packed and boring. They'll make you take a test, then start the term teaching stuff on the test, then learn it again, then test you again, and on and on.
>
> They never tried to help the bad students. If you fail, it's just too bad. They didn't understand. They had no individual understanding. They tried to get loud and rowdy. Playing the part of super-cool. If you want to learn, fine; if not, fuck you. They only gave attention to two or three; the rest could go to Hell. They cared for the two or three smart ones, the goodies. The rest of us—forget it.
>
> No, I wasn't doing well. When you need help, they [teachers] don't give it to you. They teach you things over and over again.
>
> Before, in a way, I thought it was important to do well. But I gave up.
>
> In a way I didn't care. Now they try to help me so I feel better. I care more. Here they encourage you, they talk to you. Over there, as long as they get paid, they don't care.
>
> I disliked the teachers' attitudes. They don't give a shit and a damn, either you learn or not.

I was told a million times, "I get paid, whether you learn or not, as long as I sit at this desk." And that's just what they did many times. If the class was noisy, he just sat behind that desk and did nothing.

They don't respect us. They make believe they are listening, then erase it all from their mind. They don't register a fucking word.

Those guys [the teachers] didn't care about the students. In Catholic schools, yes. They were on your back all the time. They wanted you to be somebody. If they had to pull your ear, they did. Even if they had to pull your ear. In high school, if you wanted to do it you did; nobody really cared whether you made it or not. If you could not make it, that was just tough.

They [teachers] don't understand the problems we have. They are into their own generation and the problems that are happening are different now.

Some teachers don't care. But that's only 10%. You can tell the way they treat you, the way they talk to you. They put themselves up there, and you are down here. But we are all human beings.

Most teachers don't respect students, so how can they expect to be respected?

The younger teachers understand the problems of the students. But if they are old, forget it. A lot depends on how they talk. If the words are too hard, then you don't understand what they mean. If they are too easy, then you get angry because you don't want to be treated like a baby. You don't want people to sweet-talk you. You need to talk to people at their level. I like people to talk straight, to tell me the truth without bullshit; because, if they lie to me now, what's going to happen when I grow up?

Some teachers think that we [adolescents] have inferior minds. Maybe we seem that way, but it's the school, the home, the environment. It's like a big puzzle that we have to put together. But teachers don't understand what's going on in our heads.

I quit because it was hard. They had too
many unnecessary classes. Gym classes and stuff
you don't need for your future. They had all kinds
of shops. Then, they told me I needed so many
credits. But they put me in classes for half credits.
At the end, they told me I needed seven credits.
I had passed my courses, but I had been sick.
They told me that I had been out too much. I
have asthma and I would miss class. It's also
a long walk. If you are late three times, you are
out. If you are out, you fail the term. I was put
into the eleventh grade for two years because I
was out. I said I was not going to take gym. They
said I had to take it. I argued with the principal
and then walked out. They didn't try to stop me.

Those teachers don't give a shit. All they do
is check attendance. They never asked you how
you were feeling: if you were sick. You know—
to make you feel wanted. When I was sick [with
asthma]—the teacher would say that every letter
was a fraud. He would not accept it; take me
to the office, to the counselor; then they would
call the hospital. Finally, my doctor got really
mad and said to them that he had his work to
attend to. What a waste of time!

Students' Perceptions of Being an Adult and Being Treated as a Kid

The students generally expressed annoyance at being
treated as kids in their previous high schools, while carrying
the responsibilities of adults (such as supporting
themselves) outside school. A representative selection of
such feelings as expressed by the students follows:

I see myself as a young adult. Not completely an
adult—because by the government, I am a minor.
There are things I can't do because I don't have
the schooling or experience. . . . My boyfriend
is a long ways from being an adult. He thinks
that everything will always be available to him.
I hate to see what will happen when it doesn't.
Everything is fantasy. If you don't live in reality,
it will pass you. You'll never get anywhere.

. . . Some people see me as an adult. Others don't. . . . Some people treat me like a kid. When they talk to adults, they do it on a higher level, but when they talk to you so sweet. As I told you, that bothers me. I like to hear things straight. No lying, no bullshit.

It's difficult to say when a man becomes a man. A lot of guys act very young. A woman becomes a woman the day she has a child. She can't come back on it. It is here and is a part of her. . . . A boy becomes a man around eleven. That's when the system begins to change. But he is not fully until he takes responsibility for himself. As for a woman, this happens when she can take care of herself and keeps her self-respect.

By 18 years, you ought to support yourself, regardless of whether you are a man or a woman. . . . I am an adult. Since I was 13, I had a lot of responsibility on myself. My mother never told me what to do. I learned all about life—the birds and the bees and all that—in the streets. I went through a lot. That's one thing I will make sure to do with my kids—give them all the advice they need. I want them to learn from me.

My mother, to this day, doesn't see me as an adult. We never talked woman-to-woman. As I told you before, I learned everything on my own and kept it to myself. . . . Any responsibility makes you grow up. But there are always more responsibilities for the woman. She has to look out for both, for the kids, for the home, to make it work.

I work at a hospital—in the Accounting Department. Before that, I never did anything too serious. I worked at McDonald's, Macy's card shops. I call it more serious because of the responsibility. What you do wrong can have consequences.

I support myself, but my mother gives me room and board. Once I start getting paid there, I want to give her some money.

Everybody—man or woman—should provide for themselves by 15 or 16. In a way I think that I am an adult. I am not in my twenties. But I can do anything a older person can do. I can do a lot of things.

I think that my family sees me as an adult. They don't treat me different from anybody else.

I think that when you are matured, you can take care of yourself. When you can take care of things that get in your way then you are a man or a woman.

A man should be on his own by 18. By 16 he's got to be out there realizing what life is all about. Women at 14 because they mature faster. But both out by 18 to make it by themselves.

Yes, I consider myself an adult. I hope others see me that way. I handle my income, my rent and all that.

I think I'm an adult. I can deal with problems I could not deal with [before]. I use to say "fuck it and let someone else solve it." Now I solve it. If I can't, I ask for help and I learn to solve my problems.

Now that I'm in school they see me as a man. Before, my own family would put me down. I make my own decisions. Now they even ask me my advice on things. Now, they see me as an adult—and my friends too.

When you can deal with a decision, you are an adult. When you can take on something and see it through. It's got nothing to do with work. What separates a kid from a man or woman is the way they handle responsibility.

They [teachers] don't care. They are going to get paid for it no matter what happens to us. She would file her nails and say, "I will get paid—you want to make noise, go ahead." She should have taken the disrespectful people out of the class and taught the others.

Yes, they [students] had freedom. You could leave when you wanted. They didn't care.

They [teachers] treat you like kids. For example, if you don't do a little thing then it's, "I will fail you, I will call your parents, I will send a letter," like that. Here they help you if you want, if you don't want, they don't; they let you be. But you feel the responsibility because they care and it is up to you.

They treat us like kids. The same in the other years when we were small. They don't think that you have problems. But that you need sleep or food or something like that. They can't understand that if your parents fight you don't sleep. They don't want you to talk about it. "You don't sleep—get out of here!"

No, teachers treated us like we were still kids. I remember in one class, they made us fold our hands. And you know—they make you feel dumb, stupid. They call you stupid in a way. They keep saying, "You still don't know this! I taught it five times already." You feel like saying, "Hey if we knew it, we would not be here!" That's why so many kids drop out of Metropolitan. And let me tell you a lot of those—I know them—they are not dumb. They are just tired. Some are dumb, but a lot of them are not. I know.

Student Comments on Prejudice in School

The students' experiences of teacher prejudice directed at Black and Puerto Rican students are expressed below:

A lot of White teachers in that school were against Puerto Ricans and Blacks. In their conversation they always put them down. "The Whites and Chinese are smart, the Blacks and Puerto Ricans dumb." And that's all there is to it.

There was prejudice, but they are careful not to show it. If she would pick a student to do something special, she would pick her nationality, White. That's to do it right. Not give anyone a chance to do things.

I think that they were a bit prejudiced, they knew we were Black and Puerto Rican. They weren't going to kill themselves for us. They are always comparing you to Mr. White, but I am not him.

Some teachers are a bit prejudiced. The Chinese girls got a lot of attention, because they are smart, you know. They would ask them, "Why were you out? Did you understand the work?

That's O.K." My biology teacher hated me. My art
teacher was nice. Understood.

They would say things like "Do you want to
be like the other Puerto Rican women who never
got an education? Do you want to be like the
rest of your family and never go to school?"

Student Perceptions of the Conditions of Puerto Ricans

The living conditions of Puerto Ricans in the school's
neighborhood were perceived as depressed—crime and drug
ridden, with high unemployment, offering the students little
opportunity for any change. Statements illustrating these
feelings follow:

> The situation of Puerto Ricans is bad. Look at
> the number without work. It could get better if
> someone gave them jobs, a place to live, hope.
> A lot of people complain about teenagers getting
> high, being on the streets, but they won't help
> you get a job. I went to many places until I got
> tired. They tell you "I will call you."
>
> The condition of Puerto Ricans around here
> is terrible. No change is possible around here.
> You have to move away. If they got together like
> the White people, they would come in and tear
> it down.
>
> I live in *El Barrio*. I like it and I don't. There
> are lots of good people there, but also muggers.
> It's terrible how people put up with things, with
> dirt, the cold, muggings.
>
> The condition of Puerto Ricans is horrible.
> A lot want a better life but get worn out. I don't
> think anything will ever change that much. There
> are too many things keeping us down. I want to
> make it. I want to move to a nice place uptown.
> To Park Avenue. Why not?
>
> Yes, I want my kids to stay in school, study
> a lot, and not live around here. This place is not
> good for raising kids. There are lots of drugs
> around here. These kids know about sex and all

that before they should. They are learning too fast. That's why there are so many pregnancies. There is a lot of crime. Not all to get drugs. There is crime for food, medicine, clothes. People don't have enough to put on their back. They feel that it is worth the risk rather than to spend ten years working to get something small. People also rob for food for their stomachs. It's not all for drugs.

A lot of Puerto Ricans came here to the land of opportunity. I would stay in my homeland. By leaving they are not going to be any better here. The situation is bad here. I hope it changes soon. They better do something otherwise overpopulation and crime are going to go up.

Puerto Ricans and Blacks argue. If they got together we would not have this position. Nobody is doing nothing about it. This is a big dumping hole. If we live we live, if we die we die.

Student Perceptions of School

The following interview took place in the hallways of the alternative school. The discussion centered around the student's perception of school and the reasons why he had dropped out of school.

I went in for broadcasting, and they put me into printing. They told me that after the first year I could go into braodcasting because there was no room. After that they told me that there was no room. I didn't want printing. I didn't like it. I was bored.

I was there two years and then I had it. There is a racial problem here. You see a White class and, hey, they are learning and I want to get in it. No chance. I am not getting what I came here for. What should I stay here for? Even if I do all this, it's not what I want and what they accepted me for. I don't want just a certificate. I want a diploma. That's how it was explained to me by my teachers; but people don't want you there. So what the hell are you doing there?

All my teachers were White. Some—one—was poor. We still keep in touch. He is in Albany. He cares. There was something special. He talked to everybody. You don't see that in most teachers. They don't give a damn. That is why you see people dropping out.

What good are counselors? All they talked about is what you passed or failed. And then they tell you to go to night school. When you complain they tell you that you'll find the time.

Finally I brought my mother in. She doesn't speak too well, but I was there. They treated her like a piece of fucking shit, man. I finally got so angry and said, "Hey, that's my mother. You can't treat my mother that way."

I collapsed into tears in the Principal's office. I was going to jump him. Just to have a chunk of him. They were bullshitting me. I was made a fool of. Even my mother said that if I got arrested it would be the only time she would have been on my side.

I am glad I left. Here I am getting a chance. It's not a pretty school. But to me this is better. You know people, their mind, they got a goal. In school there is a lot of competitiveness. Hostility is a way to get attention and get rid of your frustrations.

I had good grades, good references. They want you there. Just to have you there for the rep of the school. I started to play hooky. Then they show they don't give a damn. All they tell you is you are failing, failing, failing. They don't understand.

The same thing more or less happened to all the people there. My brother—they threatened to send him to another school. Then they did. Then he dropped out. He couldn't keep up.

All teachers do is pull pencil on you. They don't treat you like a human being. I deserve more respect. They use power on you. They stick with the ones that are doing O.K. The more they pull pencil on you, the more anger and resentment there is. You are embarrassed. That's why a lot of people yell back at teachers, wave their fingers in their face and all that.

They don't teach. They are always pushing the good ones. You got a problem. They tell you to get somebody's notes. Get X to help you. They don't deal with your problems, just tell you how good someone else is and threaten you.

If you try to explain is no good. You feel the pressure of subjects, grade, moving, moving pressure, pressure. This brings violence to the schools. Kids got problems and all they get is more pressure and harassment. Teachers don't care. If you got problems you don't want threats— you won't make it. You will fail. You need understanding and help.

I want to finish and get a job. My parents are going back to Puerto Rico. They just don't understand it here. I want to stay and work so I got to get my diploma and a job.

A girl leaving for Buffalo University brought me here. We all bring each other.

We did not want to say to our parents, forget it. So we played hooky. I did not go to school for a month. Me and my friends use to play basketball and in the winter go to 42nd Street to the movies. We got money from the parents. Some of us had jobs part time. We were going to save money and go to California. One of us had money—his father had a lot of money put away for when he was twenty-one. I think that his father was in organized crime. He had a lot of money in the house.

We were going to take it and go to California. All in one apartment. Taking our time getting there. We were going to take Amtrak. It stops in a lot of cities. We were going to take our time. We wanted a break. His father found out. That was the end of it.

We were not into mugging or stealing. That was not our thing. We just needed enough money to go to the movies in Times Square. They are cheap in the morning.

When people talk about a high school dropout they make you sound sick or something. Did they ever get bored or give up on something? There is a reason for it.

Student Aspirations

Approximately half of the students want to go to college. They would like to earn more money than they have thus far and to have easier work. The other half would like to learn a trade that would enable them to earn more money.

Many students realize that a General Equivalency Diploma is not enough to help them make it. This can be very discouraging for them. Many also feel that "The White man always controls, so why bust my ass?" One says, however: "I try to tell them [the other students] that only if we work harder than they [the White majority] did and do can we have some control." Still another has said, "I will be out in the street with a diploma in my hand." These are common feelings among the students; however, they are not prepared by their environment or by the schools for the complexities of the world in which they will have to function.

Implications

An editorial Essay in the April 6, 1981, issue of *Time* magazine identified a trend: that many parents are putting aside their child-care responsibilities in order to develop an alternative life-style—in effect, reliving their adolescence—while adolescents are becoming more like adults. One in seven adolescents has drinking problems; many adolescents combine concern about jobs and future with cynicism about the way this society works. One adolescent was quoted as saying,

> We've got to look out for ourselves. Nobody else will. The politicians or whatever, those in power are out for themselves. The main thing is taking care of your business, having a job and knowing what to do with the check at the end of the week.

Time posed an interesting question: "Is it possible that society, moved first by alarm about its children and then by disenchantment, has subtly begun the process of disestablishing youth simply by turning everybody to adult ways promptly at puberty?" While we may disagree that "alarm and disenchantment" are the primary factors involved, it seems important to determine whether or not the trend suggested by *Time* exists—whether adolescence is indeed being "disestablished" and, if so, to what extent and for which groups of people. But contemplation of such a study of social change makes it apparent that the baseline itself is not well-understood.

Anthony Burton has suggested, in an article published in *Anthropology and Education Quarterly* (1978), the need for developing an anthropology of the young. Concerned that the culture of the young may have been ignored in anthropological research concentrating on schooling, Burton suggests an inquiry targeted toward understanding and explaining their lives. He states that anthropology must develop approaches which "regard the young as subjects of their own existence rather than as objects of the efforts of school systems." As can be seen by this chapter, we agree with that suggestion and that a new analysis of the cultural patterns of the young is needed but stress that such an analysis must be sensitive to their varying socioeconomic realities. The cultures of the young differ depending upon their economic class and whether or not they are members of oppressed minority groups as defined by Ogbu (1974).

Burton (1978) has also noted the same phenomenon we found among Puerto Rican adolescents:

> There are many people in state-level industrial societies who are adult in most important senses, but who have not yet completed their school attendance through twelfth grade, under what are often dependent and even humiliating circumstances. It is necessary that they do so because of a technocratically derived cultural norm which specifies that one must survive this quasi-ritual in order to avoid being defined as "young."

Similarly, Glasgow, in *The Black Underclass* (1980), has suggested that there should be a rethinking of high schools' goals to make them more relevant to the demands of today's society and marketplace:

> It must recognize the special differences of today's inner-city urban youth (who seek earlier marriages, independent functioning, and incomes and who hence need earlier job market entry) and the special obstructions (structural, racial, market constrictions, skills deficits and vocational underexposure) that impede their chances to secure a living. Educational alternatives—such as schools without walls, various work-education combinations, school apprenticeship, earlier technological training and a broad range of differentiated routes to achievement—must be explored (Glasgow 1978:188–189).

We would add that continuing attention must be paid to the racism, sexism, and class biases in our society which are reflected in schooling, in research design as well as in policy implementation. It is equally important to attend to the double and sometimes triple burden of prejudice which must be borne by ethnic and language minority youngsters in a society which often seems to harbor negative attitudes towards its youth. To start where we have may seem obvious, but is in fact rare—by listening to young people, and letting their concerns emerge from their own talk. The lack of such research is perhaps itself some indication of a societal attitude toward our young people.

Some strategies for the educational involvement of minority youth may also be derived from the comments of these Puerto Rican adolescents which reflect the conflicts between those expectations of them expressed at home or in the workplace and those expressed by regular school personnel. Those who participated in our study articulated again and again the importance of being accorded adult freedoms and responsibilities in the school setting. These are to be carefully distinguished from the "freedom" to do what one pleases proffered by teachers who "don't care."

In summarizing the ways in which these students perceived the alternative school as facilitating their learning more fully than did their regular school, the following factors seem to have been most salient:

- The teachers cared about the students and were concerned that they achieve the goal of passing the GED exam.
- The school's social organization emphasized students' decision-making and their responsibility for the ways they spent their time; rules concerning time, such as promptness, were de-emphasized—for example, students did not have to account for being late.
- Goals and tasks were clearly defined, and students and teachers shared them.
- Models of success were in evidence in the form of photographs or lists of previous successful students.

The cultural values of the families of these Puerto Rican adolescents which conflicted with those propagated by their schools may be summarized thus:

- Adult responsibilities are delegated by the parents from an early age.
- Limited-English-speaking parents expect the child to serve as a Spanish/English interpreter to guide them through the rules, regulations, and requirements of the English-speaking world.
- The value accorded to intra-family support, which includes the delegation to older siblings of the responsibility for caring for younger ones as parent surrogates, also hastens the process of becoming adult in Puerto Rican families.

To what extent are these family value constellations shared by other immigrant groups and minority groups? How widespread among adolescents of other cultures is this conflict between the parents' expectation that their offspring be an adult and the high school staff's that he or she be a monitored adolescent? These are questions which suggest further ethnographic research concerning adolescents of different cultures.

Endnotes

1. Dr. Marietta Saravia-Shore is Director of the Cross-Cultural Literacy Center, Institute for Urban and Minority Education, Teachers College, Columbia University. Dr. Herminio Martinez is Associate Dean of the School of Education, Baruch College of the City University of New York.
2. This paper was presented at the Annual Meeting of the American Educational Research Association, Los Angeles, California. April 16, 1981.

References

Burton, Anthony
    1978   An Anthropology of the Young. Anthropology and Education Quarterly. Washington, D.C.: Council on Anthropology and Education. 9(1). Spring.
Comitas, Lambros, and Janet Dolgin
    1978   On Anthropology and Education: Retrospect and Prospect. Anthropology and Education Quarterly (Washington, D.C.) 9(13).
Firth, Raymond
    (1936) 1966 We the Tikopia. Boston: Beacon Press.
Fortes, Meyer
    1938   Social and Psychological Aspects of Education in Taleland. London: Oxford University Press.
Glasgow, Douglas
    1980   The Black Underclass. San Francisco: Jossey-Bass.
Grannis, Joseph
    1970   The School as a Model of Society. In The Learning of Political Behavior. Norman Adler and Charles

Harrington, eds. Glencoe, Illinois: Scott, Foresman and Company.

1975   Community, Competence and Individuation: The Effects of Different Controls in Educational Environments. IRCD Bulletin. New York: Institute for Urban and Minority Education, Teachers College, Columbia University 10(2). Spring.

Lacey, Colin
1970   Hightown Grammar: The School as a Social System. Manchester: Manchester University Press.

Mead, Margaret
1928   Coming of Age in Samoa. New York: W. Morrow.

Ogbu, John
1974   The Next Generation: An Ethnography of Education in an Urban Neighborhood. New York: Academic Press.

Padilla, Elena
1958   Up from Puerto Rico. New York: Columbia University Press.

Philips, Susan
1972   Participant Structures and Communicative Competence: Warm Springs Children in Community and Classrooms. *In* Functions of Language in the Classroom. Courtney Cazden et al. New York: Teachers College Press.

Rist, Ray
1973   The Urban School: A Factory for Failure. Cambridge, Mass.: MIT Press.

Thomas, Piri
1967   Down These Mean Streets. New York: Knopf.

Time
April 6, 1981.

Bilingualism In and Out of School: Ethnographic Perspectives on the Determination of Language "Dominance"[1]

Pedro Pedraza and Alicia Pousada[2]

Introduction

Bilingual education programs must repeatedly assess their students' language skills, both for placement purposes and for evaluation of individual and program success. Most attempts to examine children's language repertoires depend on data from one context alone—either standardized tests of language dominance or quick surveys of home language use.

However, children are subject to competing influences from home, community, and school, and in order to assess their linguistic performances and/or capabilities accurately, it is vital to consider the entire scope of their language experiences in and out of school. Tests determine only a very restricted type of language ability (and that only if the child is able to get over his fear of the test situation and respond more or less naturally). Home language surveys are answered by parents who are asked to determine their childrens' language proficiency. Most are exceedingly brief and go no further than ascertaining the language most frequently used or the language preferred in the home.

What is needed is an approach which looks at the whole picture for the children and recognizes that this picture may change precipitously over time in response to transformations in roles, responsibilities, and opportunities for interaction. In our opinion, the most promising approach to a study of language use is an interdisciplinary one with a strong ethnographic base. The ethnographic component not only supplies the data needed for more quantitative sociolinguistic analysis but, even more importantly, suggests what is and what is not important to analyze (Erickson 1977).

The Study

For this reason, we of the Language Policy Task Force of the Centro de Estudios Puertorriqueños, Hunter College, CUNY, became engaged in a two-year-long research project which examined Puerto Rican children in various stages of bilingual language acquisition from an ethnographic, attitudinal, and quantitative sociolinguistic stance.[3] This project (Language Policy Task Force 1982) was an extension of a large-scale interdisciplinary study of adult language use in *El Barrio* in East Harlem, New York City (Language Policy Task Force 1980) and afforded us a unique intergenerational perspective through which to view language behavior in a bilingual community.

We will explain briefly the nature of this project and then move on to a consideration of some insights afforded by the combination of qualitative and quantitative methodology in the characterization of the very elusive concept of "language dominance."

From 1979 to 1981, we systematically followed the diverse activities of a group of sixteen elementary school-age children in East Harlem. All of these children were Puerto Rican (with the exception of one Central American) and were exposed to both English and Spanish in a wide range of settings. They were selected on the basis of (1) residence on the block we had been studying in depth for adult speech patterns, (2) grade level (we selected children from kindergarten through second grade when home influences are strongest, and fifth and sixth grades when peer influences are greatest), and (3) school program (monolingual or bilingual). The sample that resulted was composed of six girls and six boys from the younger age-set and two girls and two boys from the older age-set. Half were in bilingual classes and half in monolingual classes.

We began observation (both participant and non-participant) in the children's classrooms during the spring semester of 1979. Once we had gained the trust of the children and their teachers, we began taperecording them in their various school activities. When the semester finished, we followed the children onto the block and spent the summer getting to know them and their families. We taped the children in many different situations, alone with their closest friends, with their families, or with large groups of children out on the street. We remained with the children for some of the sessions, participating or not as the situation dictated, but for others left them with the recorder to do as they wished. When school resumed in the fall, we went back into the classrooms with the children, maintaining at the same time our presence on the block and in the homes. At the end of the fall term, we began administering various pyscholinguistic measures of language dominance and formal language attitude interviews with the children, their parents, and their teachers. The corpus of taped data that resulted from this fieldwork amounts to more than 160 hours of speech.

The sixteen children in our sample represent an abundantly varied group of individuals who embody in their different activities, family situations, interests, and language abilities the broad range of experiences available to children raised in an urban ethnic neighborhood. As we cannot treat each one separately here, we will examine in detail four who are of particular interest in determining their language dominance. But first, let us consider some of the problems inherent in measuring language proficiency and language dominance and then turn to the tests we utilized.

Approaches to Assessing Language Proficiency

While research has indicated that language proficiency is only one factor among many to be taken into account when determining the educational needs of limited-English-speaking children, bilingual education legislation and decision-making have been based upon this one factor to the exclusion of other sociocultural characteristics of speakers and communities (e.g. home environment, individual aspirations, cognitive development, ethnic identification, etc.). Nevertheless, there has been a proliferation of language proficiency assessment instruments since the Lau decision of 1974—more than 342 in this country alone, according to the Northwest Regional Education Laboratory.

Because of the difficulties inherent in measuring language proficiency (i.e., the number of parameters involved, the commensurability of these components, and the method of measurement), testmakers have focused on the most accessible features of language performance. As a result, most instruments measure vocabulary range or syntax and not functional uses of language, although such tests have been shown not to predict effective classroom participation or communicative competence.

A number of studies comparing instruments of various types have found that they measure different linguistic components and are only modestly correlated with reading or achievement tests. Despite these findings, schools continue to rely upon single tests, and evaluators of bilingual education programs persist in lumping together different scores and levels when reporting numbers of children of a particular proficiency, or when determining the effectiveness of the instructional program.

Even more crucial than inter-test comparability is whether the tests measure anything resembling actual language use. Rodriguez-Brown and Elias-Olivares (1981) conclude that language tests are not congruent with language use and that language proficiency cannot be described accurately unless assessed in naturally occurring communicative situations. For bilinguals, this means bilingual rather than monolingual contexts, in which their entire repertoire (including code-switching) is taken into account.

Actual patterns of language use become particularly salient when it comes to determining language "dominance." To say that a speaker is dominant in one language or the other is insufficient, because language ability must be assessed in a number of contexts with various interlocutors and different purposes. Depending on the criteria utilized, different assessments of dominance may be obtained. The definition of the dominant language as that in which a speaker feels most comfortable is subjective and variable and may be further complicated by the speaker's emotional attachment to a language. A speaker's ability to carry out certain tasks in a particular language is again variable as he may have different skills (oral and literate) in each of his languages. Actual frequency of usage can also be misleading, because a speaker may be forced out of circumstance to use a language other than the one he manipulates best. Moreover, frequency of usage may vary over time for any given individual. Defining dominance in terms of the language first learned or the language used at home raises further problems, since a child may use one language with his parents and another with his siblings, other relatives, and friends. Finally, use of relative proficiency or fluency presents the problem of establishing an objective standard by which to measure ability when more than one variety of each language exists in the same speech community and when speakers vary in their performance at different levels of linguistic structure, as documented by Zentella in this volume.

The Tests

Thus we see that testing of proficiency and determination of language dominance are far from simple matters. In order to examine these issues more closely, let us now turn to the tests administered to our sample. We will begin by scrutinizing the placement tests used by the school district, then look at the psycholinguistic tests we provided, and finally compare the children's performance on each.

Language Assessment Battery (LAB)

The LAB was developed as a placement instrument for bilingual programs governed by the Aspira Consent Decree in New York City (see Santiago 1977: 81–82). It was constructed at three levels—K–2, 3–6, and 7–12—and measures listening, reading, writing, and speaking. The 20th percentile is utilized as the cut-off point below which English proficiency is considered inadequate. Children scoring below the 20th percentile are given the LAB in Spanish, and if their Spanish scores are higher than their English by so much as one point, they are placed in bilingual classes. The test is repeated every year until the child passes the English part and can be moved into English-only classes.

There is considerable dissatisfaction with the test throughout the school system, and a replacement instrument (which is still inadequate) has recently been developed by the New York City Division of Bilingual Education. Among the many flaws in the format of the LAB is the priorities of skills being tested. The speaking test (which is not even administered in New York City due to lack of personnel and time) represents only a small portion of the battery, although this ability is ostensibly the most crucial to program placement. The writing test, on the other hand, which measures one of the last skills to be acquired, is given the greatest emphasis. What appears to be at issue throughout is vocabulary and experience with substantive facts and realms of existence which may not bear any relation to any domain of knowledge encountered by children in school or at home. None of the sections appears to tap any real life abilities or distinctions or to measure the kind of speaking proficiency a child needs to function in school or outside. Nor is there any consideration of differences between examiners or students, which may lead to misunderstandings or "wrong" answers.

On the basis of these and numerous other problems, it appears that any placement done solely on the basis of the LAB test must be open to question and may endanger effective implementation of the bilingual program. Let us now consider the other tests.

Word Naming by Domain

The word naming task involves the elicitation of words in English and Spanish appropriate to particular domains and attempts to give a richer, more contextualized picture of bilingual abilities than is possible from global assessments.

The first application of the word naming test was in a large-scale study (Fishman, Cooper, and Ma 1971) of a bilingual New Jersey barrio in which Puerto Rican adults and adolescents were asked to name in one minute as many different words as possible referring to the domains of family, neighborhood, religion, education, and work, first in one language and then the other. In our adaptation of the test, we followed Cohen (1975) in reducing the amount of time and omitting the work domain. Dominance ratings in different domains were calculated for each speaker on the basis of difference scores. The test appears most useful in determining the relative size of the active vocabulary in each language, comparing the total output of the speaker, in one language or both, with that of other speakers, and indicating in which contexts the speaker's vocabulary in Spanish and English is most developed.

Its basic problem appears to be its reliance upon vocabulary listing, which has not been shown to be related to functional language proficiency. Furthermore, the design of the task seems to indicate a testing for recall and retrieval ability rather than for communicative competence.

Ambiguous Word Language Dominance Test

The Ambiguous Word Language Dominance Test (developed by Gary Keller) was designed to measure language dominance among Spanish/English bilingual students, 10 years old or older. It consists of a list of 100 randomly ordered words, 24 of which are ambiguous as to language (e.g., pie, dime). The remaining 76 words are evenly divided between Spanish and English. As the student reads the list aloud, the examiner checks off the ambiguous items according to whether they are pronounced in English or Spanish, omitting any pronounced in both languages. As with the domains test, difference scores are used to determine language dominance ratings.

We elected to use this test despite the fact that some of the children were under 10 years of age, since we knew that reading ability varied considerably and not necessarily according to chronological age. As it turned out, 11 of the 15 children tested were able to complete the test with varying degrees of effort.

There are several problems with the test which bear mentioning. First of all, it is based upon literacy skills which may or may not be present among a given group of children and have little bearing on conversational or oral expression. Further, the skill measured, that of reading a list, may have little relation to any desired reading skills targeted in a particular program. The test does not provide for dealing with the "padding" or non-ambiguous words, which are often pronounced as if they too were ambiguous. The location of these padding words tends to affect the ambiguous words as well, as there are stretches within the exam during which one language predominates; consequently, the ambiguous words in the vicinity are automatically included in that language as part of the overall reading momentum. Certain problems exist with the ambiguous words themselves, in particular their complexity (many are not common in the vocabulary of most elementary school children). A final and perhaps most serious problem is the lack of flexibility within the rating scale, which maintains that a score of 3 to -3, for example, is always that of a balanced bilingual, without taking into account the child who pronounces less than the full 24 ambiguous words with unmistakably English or Spanish phonology.

Cross-Validation of the Tests

Let us now look at the different ratings given for each child and attempt to validate them against each other as well as against observational and self-report data. In the full report of this study, we analyze each test in great detail and examine the correlation of the scores with what we know about the children from our constant observation over two years, from their own assessments of their abilities, and from their placement in particular programs. As space does not permit such a detailed consideration here, we summarize the overall comparison in Table A.

The most striking point about Table A is the variety of ratings obtained for each child. In many cases, the disagreements among ratings are of degree (bilingual versus one or the other language), rather than absolute (English versus Spanish) which indicates that the tests are at least in the right ballpark. However, it is precisely the distinction between balanced bilinguals and English or Spanish "dominants" which is often ignored in program placement and evaluation. It is not sufficient for a test to identify correctly the two extremes of the language spectrum; it should be able to determine which children are equally proficient in both of their languages.

All of the tests are better predictors of the language abilities of the children in the monolingual classes—that is, there are fewer contradictions among the ratings for these children than for those in the bilingual classes. Again, this is a case in which the tests perform better when measuring an extreme. The tests accurately reflect the fact that these children, though bilingual, are developing only one of their languages on a consistent basis and in a literate form, while the others are receiving reinforcement (not always equal) for both languages in and out of school.

If we take our observations as a base against which to compare the ratings from the other sources, we see that the closest correspondences come from self-report of most frequent language used and the word naming in the school domain. The LAB ratings do not agree at all with our observations for most of the children in the bilingual classes. The ambiguous stimulus is variable but less so

Table A
Language Dominance Assessments From Five Different Sources for Children in Bilingual and Monolingual Classes

Speakers	LAB	Word Naming by Domains:				Ambiguous Stimulus	Self-report Most Freq. Lang.	Observed Most Freq. Lang.
		Home	Neigh.	Church	Schl.			
Bilingual Classes								
Iris	N	S	S	S	S	S	S	S
Josie	E	E	E	E	B	sub. S	B	B
Dorcas	E	S	E	E	B	mod. E	B	B
Chico	S	S	B	S	S	—	S	B
Indio	S	B	E	B	S	mod. E	B	E—B
Flaquita	S	E	B	B	B	B	B	B
Juanita	S	E	B	B	B	B	B	B
Herminio	S	S	B	B	S	mod. S	S	S
Conejo	S	B	E	B	E	B	B	E—B
Monolingual Classes								
Pito	E*	E	E	E	E		E	E
Gordito	E	B	E	B	E		E	E
Baby	E							E
Ramon	E	E	B	B	E		B	E
Debbie	E	E	E	E	E	E	E	E
Linda	E	E	E	E	E	E	E	E
Maria	E	B	E	B	B	mod. E	B	B

E = English
S = Spanish
B = Both
N = Neither
— = Unavailable
* = test not given
English dominance
pre-supposed

than the LAB. Therefore, we can establish a tentative ranking of these measures in order of effectiveness or validity: first observations, then self-report, word naming by domains, ambiguous stimulus, and, least effective, the LAB.

Admittedly, this ranking is somewhat simplistic and based primarily upon the number of divergences from a standard—observation—which in itself may be questionable. Each of the measures has something to commend it and may be more appropriate in certain circumstances than the others. For example, while the Ambiguous Word Language Dominance Test is clearly impossible in cases where children have reading problems, it works well with biliterate children and is more finely graduated in its ranking than the others. The Word Naming by Domains Test is very limited in the type of language ability it measures; however, it measures that ability in a wider set of situations than do any of the others except for observation and self-report.

As generalized tables do not give a good sense of the population involved nor its complexity, let us now turn to a more detailed examination of 4 of the 16 children.

Specific Cases

Table B shows four of the sample children—Iris, Indio, Maria, and Conejo—and their language dominance as determined by performance on the different language tests, as well as self-report in school, home, and neighborhood and observed language behavior in the same three settings. As can readily be seen, there are a number of disagreements among the various assessments, particularly between the Language Assessment Battery and the others, yet program placement is made after consideration of only the scores on the LAB Test.

Some background information about each of the children will help clarify the table. Iris was five years old and in an English-only kindergarten when we began our study, despite being almost completely Spanish monolingual. As she put it, "No entendia ni papa" (I didn't understand a single thing). She was placed in that

Table B
Differential Indicators of Language Dominance

	School tests		Psych. tests		Home language		Block language		Schl. language			Overall	
	LiB test	schl. progr.	wrd. naming text	ambig. stim. test	reprtd. lg. used at home	obsrvd. lg. used at home	reprtd. lg. used on block with peers	obsrvd. lg. used on block with peers	reprtd. lg. used in schl. with peers	reprtd. lg. used in schl. with best friends	obsrvd. lg. used in schl. with peers	reprtd. lg. pref. overall	reprtd. lg. used most overall
Iris	N	M/Bi	S	S	B	S	S	S	S	B	S	E	S
Indio	S	Bi	B	E	B	B	E	E	B	S	B	E	B
Maria	E	M	E	E	B	B	B	B	B	S	B	B	B
Conejo	S	Bi	E	B	S	B	B	E	B	E	B	S	B

N = neither language

S = Spanish

E = English

B = both languages

M = monolingual

Bi = bilingual

kindergarten because she registered late and the bilingual kindergarten was overloaded. She remained very silent and withdrawn until placed in bilingual first grade during the second year of observation, where she began to blossom. It soon became clear that she was behind in most areas and ended up being put into the bilingual learning disabilities program. According to her LAB Test scores, Iris would have to be considered "a-lingual," scoring at the third percentile in both languages. Our observations indicated that this was clearly not the case. Iris is an animated and non-stop talker in Spanish. While she is primarily a Spanish speaker, she professes to prefer English and says that "Inglés es bueno porque en inglés tu aprendes y en español no aprendes nada" (English is good because in English you learn and in Spanish you don't learn anything). She has apparently internalized the often-repeated warning of her Spanish monolingual parents that English is necessary to succeed in this society and, as a result, tends to report more English than she actually can or does speak.

Indio was seven years old and participating in a bilingual bridge class of first and second graders when we met him. He is the only non-Puerto Rican child in the sample and was born of Central American parents. Indio is very verbal and alert. He has excellent Spanish and English skills but favors English despite considerable exposure to Spanish at home with his parents. He says that he does not like speaking Spanish because it is not challenging. As he puts it: "English is better cause Spanish you learn it fast. English, too, but it's difficult, you know." Despite his extensive English skills and outspoken preference for the language, Indio's LAB Tests register him at only the seventh percentile in English and the 86th in Spanish. He also reports using Spanish with his best friends in school but English with those on the block.

Maria was eleven at the outset of the study and participating in a monolingual sixth grade class. She was once enrolled in a bilingual mini-school for a short time during her second grade year. Soon afterwards she scored above the 20th percentile in English on her LAB Test, which automatically made her ineligible for bilingual classes. Her performance on the two psycholinguistic tests of dominance also indicates superior English proficiency. She feels that her Spanish is poor, since she was never given an opportunity to develop more than a slight written competence. Regardless of this, she can sustain long conversations in Spanish with little problem and does so often with her grandparents, baby sister, Spanish-fluent children on the block, and her best friend, who has recently arrived from Puerto Rico. She enjoys speaking both languages and would like to be in the bilingual program.

Conejo was eleven and participating in a bilingual sixth grade class when we began our study. He was born in Puerto Rico and came to New York City at the age of six. He uses Spanish at home with his mother and both languages with his sister and his friends at school or in the street, with English predominating. He identifies himself as bilingual and laughingly told us about how his teacher would always criticize him for code-switching in class: "I used to tell her, 'I talk BILINGUE.'" He tends to over-report his use of Spanish to some extent, counting occasional code-switches as speaking in Spanish. While we do not have information on his LAB scores in Spanish (he was absent), he only scored in the ninth percentile in English, an assessment which is hard to believe given his heavy involvement in peer groups containing both Black and Puerto Rican youths. He also states that he prefers to speak Spanish, perhaps because of his expressed awareness of and pride in being Puerto Rican.

There are several general trends visible even in this sub-sample. To begin, there is no match at all between the results of the LAB Test and the observed use of language in the home, or with peers on the block or in the school. There are very few correspondences between the LAB Test and the children's own reports of language use in the three settings. The psycholinguistic tests come closer to the observed language usage in all contexts than does the LAB Test, with the exception of Maria whose monolingual English educational background may account for the discrepancy between her observed skills and her test performance. Conejo's performance on these tests may also indicate the effect of his school background—in this case, the bilingual program.

This may require explanation. While we have little firm evidence that the bilingual program influenced the children's oral linguistic performance,[4] these data indicate a potential positive effect with regard to literacy and self-perception of language skills. It may be that Conejo, who acquired literacy in Spanish first, feels more secure about his Spanish skills because of an association made between literate and oral competence. Maria, whose literate skills are restricted to English despite having equivalent oral skills in both languages, may underestimate her Spanish ability for similar reasons. This suggests a relationship between literacy and linguistic self-perception that needs to be verified. Such a finding would serve as a pivotal argument for the role of bilingual education in the enhancement of self-esteem and give further support for programs that are directed toward the development of biliteracy as well as bilinguality.

Returning again to the trends in the data, we see that the reported and observed language use of the children in the home, block, and school settings are closely matched for Maria and Indio but vary for Iris and Conejo, who over-report their use of English and Spanish, respectively, for the reasons given earlier. Additionally, the indication of language preference for all the children does not correspond, for the most part, to reported overall language use or observed language use in any context. These data serve as further evidence of the influence of factors other than actual practice— e.g., questions of ideology (Attinasi 1979)— upon perceptions of language use.

Conclusions and Applications

As we have illustrated in this paper, language dominance is a concept that covers a wide range of language behavior and abilities. However defined, it is not static but changes with the speakers' varying conditions and life circumstances. Testing for dominance is fraught with difficulties, and existing tests all fail in some regard to tap the richness and complexity of the bilingual speaker.

In order to go beyond the limitations of these tests, a more critical look at the communicative skills demanded by the educational process is necessary. Research on the dynamics of language use in the classroom should attempt to determine those sociolinguistic factors most relevant for education.[5] In other words, the criteria for assessing language dominance should derive from knowledge of what occurs in a classroom or from the objectives of classroom instruction, not a priori definitions of dominance or language proficiency.

The remaining question is what concrete value this understanding has for the practitioner and what methods can be used to obtain the information needed for an improvement of actual daily practice.

The utility of the broadened conception of language dominance and proficiency presented here lies in part in achieving realistic language assessments that ensure accurate placement, determination of individual progress, and evaluation of program effectiveness. Different constructs of dominance and proficiency may be relevant for each of the above tasks. For example, the criteria used to determine what has been added to a student's verbal repertoire may differ from those used to check minimal entrance level skills. Educators should decide which construct of language dominance and proficiency is most valid for a given purpose and develop instruments or methods of assessment accordingly.

There exist various ways beyond testing of obtaining the information needed to enhance the perception of a child's language capabilities. Teachers can check the validity of a child's language assessment by listening to him in different settings among his peers, particularly those which are not teacher-initiated or controlled—for example, lunchroom or playground chatter. Special attention should be paid to language forms not used in class—the rhymes, jokes, raps, insults, and songs that characterize child-centered interaction and verbal play (Kirshenblatt-Gimblett 1976, Ervin-Tripp and Mitchell-Kernan 1977). A sense of the child's home language environment can be obtained by talking to parents, visiting the home, and seeing the child interact with his family. If home visits are not feasible, the child can be observed with his parents and siblings at arrival or dismissal time. Teachers can make a further judgment of dominance both in and out of class by listening to the children's code-switching. Both the amount and type of switching can be indicators of the child's dominance and the level of development of each of his languages.[6]

These are only a few potential techniques, and they cannot take the place of more extended, intensive inquiry. However, they do point to innovative, non-test assessments which are within easy reach of the teacher and closely allied to the ethnographic approach found useful throughout this project.

In sum, in this chapter we have considered some issues in testing language proficiency, a number of tests of language dominance, and the performance on them by a sample of sixteen Puerto Rican bilingual children. Comparison of test results with self-report and observation reveals considerable variation and inaccuracy, some due to problems inherent in the tests themselves and some the result of different patternings of bilingual skills among these children. The tentative ranking of the tests discussed in this paper as well as suggestions for non-test measures of language dominance are offered in hopes of contributing to an understanding of "language dominance" and "relative proficiency."

We have also attempted to present an example of how ethnographic research can lead to a more profound understanding of a specific educational problem—that of determining language dominance. Our experience in the field has shown us that ethnography has much to tell us about many other aspects of education, including the relation of school to community, parent participation in the educational process, the social organization of the school, and the integration of the bilingual program within the regular school environment.

We feel confident that an ethnographic approach will be an important element in future research in bilingual education, leading to the resolution of old problems and the avoidance of new ones. Perhaps with more research of this kind, research constructs like "language dominance," which are loosely tossed about as verities in legislative mandates may someday be translated into coherent and cogent educational policy that aids rather than hinders the progress of bilingual children in our society.

Endnotes

1. This chapter is a synthesis of two papers—one presented at the American Anthropological Association's annual meeting in Washington, D.C., on December 5, 1980, and the other presented at the Third Annual Ethnography in Education Forum at the University of Pennsylvania in Philadelphia on March 18–21, 1982.

We would like to acknowledge the valuable assistance of our colleagues at the Centro in the production and revision of the chapter.

2. Pedro Pedraza is Director of the Language Policy Task Force of Centro de Estudios Puertorriqueños, Hunter College of the City University of New York. Dr. Alicia Pousada is currently an Assistant Professor at the University of Puerto Rico.

3. The project was supported in part by the National Institute of Education, the Ford Foundation, and the City University of New York.

4. A perception common among some parents (especially those whose children are not in the bilingual program) is that the program hinders the development of English skills. Our observations indicate that all of the children, regardless of program, are acquiring English skills, testimony to the effects of living in an overwhelmingly English-speaking society.

5. It should be noted that the work of Erickson (1976, 1977), Carrasco, Cazden, and Erickson (1978), Shultz (1976), Carrasco (1980), and others in the ethnography of education is directed toward the investigation of this very question.

6. For further information on the analysis of code-switching, see Poplack (1978, 1979) and Sankoff and Poplack (1980).

References

Attinasi, J.
  1979   Language Attitudes in a New York Puerto Rican Community. *In* Ethnoperspectives in Bilingual Education Research: Bilingual Education and Public Policy in the United States. R. Padilla, ed. Yspilanti, Mich.: Eastern Michigan University. Pp. 408–461.

Carrasco, R.
  1980   Expanded Awareness of Student Performance in a Bilingual Classroom. *In* Culture and the Bilingual Classroom: Studies in Classroom Ethnography. H. Trueba, K. Au, and G. Guthrie, eds., Rowley, Mass.: Newbury House.

Carrazco, R., C. Cazden, and F. Erickson.
  1978   Social and Cultural Organization of Interaction in Classrooms of Bilingual Children: A Two Year Project. Working Paper. Harvard University Graduate School of Education.

Cohen, A.
  1975   The Sociolinguistic Assessment of Speaking Skills in a Bilingual Education Program. *In* Papers on Language Testing. L. Palmer and B. Spolsky, eds. Washington, D.C., TESOL. Pp. 173–186.

Erickson, F.
  1976   What Makes School Ethnography "Ethnographic"? Anthropology and Education Quarterly 4(1):10–19.
  1977   Some Approaches to Inquiry in School-Community Ethnography. Anthopology and Education Quarterly 8(2).

Ervin-Tripp, S. and C. Mitchell-Kernan, eds.
  1977   Child discourse. New York: Academic Press.

Fishman, Joshua A., R.L. Cooper, R. Ma et al.
  1971   Bilingualism in the Barrio. Bloomington, In.: Indiana University Publications.

Kirshenblatt-Gimblett, B., ed.
  1976   Speech play: Research and Resources for the Study of Linguistic Creativity. Philadelphia: University of Pennsylvania Press.

Language Policy Task Force.
  1982   Intergenerational Perspectives on Bilingualism: From Community to Classroom. Report to National Institute of Education. NIE-G-78-0091. New York: Centro de

Estudios Puertorriqueños, City University of New York (CUNY).

1980   Social Dimensions of Language Use in East Harlem. Working Paper #7. New York: Centro de Estudios Puertorriqueños, CUNY.

Poplack, S.
1978   Social and Syntactic Constraints on Code-Switching. Working Paper #2. New York: Centro de Estudios Puertorriqueños, CUNY.
1981   Revised version. *In* Latino Language and Communicative Behavior. R. Duran, ed. Norwood, N.J.: Ablex Publishing Corp. Pp. 169–184.
1979   "Sometimes I'll start a sentence in Spanish y termino en espanol": Toward a Typology of Code-Switching. Working Paper #4. New York: Centro de Estudios Puertorriqueños, CUNY. Also in Linguistics 18:581–618.

Rodriguez-Brown, F., and L. Elias-Olivares.
1981   Bilingual Children's Home and School Language: An Ethnographic-Sociolinguistic Perspective. Final report to NIE-400-79-0042.

Sankoff, D., and S. Poplack.
1980   A Formal Grammar of Code-Switching. Working Paper #8. New York: Centro de Estudios Puertorriquenos, CUNY. Also appears as Technical Report #945, Centre de Recherches Mathématiques, Université de Montréal.

Santiago, I.
1977   Aspira versus Board of Education of the City of New York: A History. New York: Aspira.

Shultz, J.
1975   Language Use in Bilingual Classrooms. Paper presented at the Annual Convention of Teachers of English to Speakers of Other Languages (TESOL). Los Angeles, California.

Bilingual Program Evaluation Policy: Implications From Ethnographic Research[1]

Marietta Saravia-Shore[2]

Introduction

This chapter is informed by several perspectives: experience in the alternating roles of program evaluator and bilingual program administrator; work within the paradigm of experimental research after study toward a masters degree in psychology and subsequent work within the paradigm of ethnographic research while completing a doctorate in anthropology.[3]

The perspective of Herbert Marcuse also informs this chapter. The limitations of many practices in evaluation and testing are clarified by Marcuse's critical analysis of empiricism. Marcuse (1964) was one of those who first uncovered the ways in which currently dominant modes of empirical research, by emptying concepts of all but their operational or behavioral meaning, dominate and abridge language and impede critical thought:

> the operational and behavioral point of view practiced as a "habit of thought" at large, becomes the view of the established universe of discourse and action, needs and aspirations (Marcuse 1964:15).

Empiricism is a mode of scientific domination in which "the treatment of concepts and their meaning is restricted to the representation of particular operations and behavior" (Marcuse 1964:12). Consider, for example, the definition

273

of the purpose of education provided by the Encyclopedia of Educational Evaluation:

> . . . since the purpose of education is to change the behavior of the learner, the objectives of instruction should be stated in terms of that behavior (Anderson 1975:182).

This reduction of education to behavioral change distorts the complex meanings that education historically has had and suppresses the history of the meaning of education. The full meaning of an education—to understand relationships, construct meaning, elicit insights, grasp the rules of a system or the implications of a theory, learn how to learn, develop a global perspective and cross-cultural literacy—may be reducible to behavioral objectives but in doing so much is lost. As Soltis (1984) has put it,

> The learner has felt and seeks again the good feeling of the mastery and understanding of a skill, or the consumatory experience of insight, appreciation, and understanding of ideas, or the thrill of discovering something not known before, or the feeling of accomplishment that comes with making sense of the world (1984:8).

Marcuse's critique of empiricism is still relevant today. Looking at the role of evaluators in North American society, one can see parallels to that of high priests in other societies in terms of their control of ideology. As an instance, W. James Popham, psychologist and former President of the American Educational Research Association (AERA), has written "Ten Commandments for Educational Evaluators," which reflect that the prior unquestioning belief in behaviorism in the "applied science" of evaluation is being challenged. Popham suggested that "educational evaluation is teetering on the brink of a heretical abyss" and that it's time for establishing "a bit of orthodoxy." In the same way that camp movies can laugh at and yet perpetuate cultural stereotypes, Popham's commandments satirize but also reinforce some evaluation cliches:

Make Measurable Thy Objectives
Make Criterion-Referenced Thy Measures
Render Proper Adulation to the Prophets of
Educational Evaluation
Honor Thy Decision Maker: Have No False
Decision Makers Before Thee.

I suggest that the first two "commandments" supported by Popham have significant limitations, which are discussed below. The option of framing evaluation as decision-making, alluded to in the fourth, however, has the merit of making the process of evaluation explicit; it identifies values, and recognizes that competing interest groups will attempt to decide what will be deemed valuable. In behaviorally-based evaluation, it is often the evaluators who are the implicit decision-makers, determining and selecting the outcomes (objectives) which the educational program will have; which of these are to be measured and reported; and, therefore, which will be emphasized in the curriculum. This phenomenon led MacDonald (1974) to conclude that in the field of education, evaluation is the tail that wags the dog.

The organization of this paper will follow that of a formative evaluation. We can ask, historically, where we have been in bilingual education evaluation, where are we, and where do we want to go? I suggest that a consideration of the process of inquiry in ethnographic evaluation provides heuristic approaches to the last question.

A Needs Assessment of Bilingual Education Evaluation

Where is evaluation today? We might first look briefly at the historical roots of evaluation, drawing out the assumptions underlying the perspective of behavioral evaluators. In their 1961 text, *Measurement and Evaluation in Psychology and Education*, Robert L. Thorndike and Elizabeth Hagen defined evaluation as follows:

> The term "evaluation" as we use it is closely
> related to measurement. It is in some senses
> more inclusive, including formal and intuitive
> judgement . . . and . . . the aspect of valuing—
> of saying what is desirable and good. Good
> measurement techniques provide the solid
> foundation for sound evaluation (Stufflebeam et
> al. 1971:27).

According to the *Encyclopedia of Educational Evaluation* (1975), Ralph Tyler was the first to define goals and objectives in behavioral terms and make them the basis of instrument development and evaluation. Thereafter, in the 1940's and 1950's, there was much concern and effort spent in helping teachers "to formulate their objectives in order to improve their tests and adapt their instruction to the needs of individual pupils" (Anderson 1975:143).

Educational evaluation has been dominated by the discipline of psychology. That has meant, historically, a behavioral perspective and a focus on the individual, with a de-emphasis on the perspective of groups. This should not surprise us, since the institution of evaluation reflects the larger economic and political institutions of our society, with their emphasis on the ideology of the individual, individual achievement, and the meritocracy. This ideology of the meritocracy, however, does not jibe with the reality of differential access to educational opportunities and economic benefits by different racial, ethnic, and socioeconomic groups in our society. Thus educational evaluation and testing have obscured the reality of differential access by different groups.

Program evaluation relies on the measurement of individual student achievement. Scores that yield numerical values can be grouped and statistically manipulated to find such data as group means, standard deviations, and standard errors of measurement. These statistical procedures lend scientific legitimacy to scores which were gathered on standardized tests usually designed for individual student achievement but used for group and program comparisons. The standardized achievement tests being used for program evaluation were not in fact designed for this use at all but rather to distinguish between individual students at different levels of achievement and predict further achievement. The process of achievement test development includes item analysis of field test results; only test items which distinguish "good" achievers from "poor" achievers are kept in the test. These standardized achievement tests of individual students are, then, inappropriate for the purpose for which they are now being used—program evaluation.

Oscar Buros, whose series of *Mental Measurement Yearbooks* are standard references, has written in "Fifty Years of Testing—Some Reminiscences, Criticisms and Suggestions"

> I think it's unfortunate that so much attention is being paid to predicting success at the next higher educational level, while less and less attention is being given to determining what was learned at earlier levels (1977:11).

Buros described the statistical procedures used in test item validation, such as discarding items which do not correlate with the total score, and concluded:

> Although these techniques are widely used by our very best testmakers, it is my thesis that these techniques have been harmful to the development of the best possible measuring instruments. These statistical methods of item validation confuse differentiation with measurement and exaggerate differences among individuals and grades. I would like to see their use discontinued.

In 1935 Buros had made a similar criticism:

> It seems inescapable that such methods of statistically validating achievement tests insidiously tend to strengthen the status quo, to impede curricular progress, to perpetuate our present grade classification, to differentiate rather than to measure, to conceal unlearning, and to give an illusory sense of continuous learning from grade to grade.

Subsequently (1977), Buros urged that our goal should be measurement, not differentiation.

> I suggest that achievement test batteries be of two types: tests for assessing the performance of groups and tests for assessing the performance of individuals. The group tests should be designed to measure the achievement of schools, school systems, or other groups having common objectives and learning environments. Since our interest is in groups rather than individuals each test could be quite short, requiring very little time to administer (Buros 1977:14).

Buros then described the possibility of matrix testing, with no student taking more than one subject. The time for an achievement battery would be reduced from as much as seven hours to half an hour.

Has Buros' criticism been heard? The move to criterion-referenced tests which can be more closely related to the curriculum being taught and thus are more appropriate in program evaluation seems to be a response to this criticism. But standardized achievement tests are still more prevalent as criteria for program success.

Social anthropologists such as John Ogbu (1974) and Colin Lacey (1970) have documented the function of testing and tracking (or streaming in Britain) in the replication of the current social structure within both the United States and Britain. This latent function of testing was also identified by Roger T. Lennon, a psychologist who was formerly director of testing for Harcourt, Brace, Jovanovich. "One goal of the schools is to perpetuate a culture. The tests are responsive to what citizens think the schools should be about" (Adams 1976:11). Lennon did not mention whether or not he had surveyed a representative ethnically or socioeconomically stratified sample of citizens to reach this conclusion about what is expected from the school system. What tends to be perpetuated by schooling and standardized testing is a justification, within the ideology of the meritocracy, for sorting students, stratification, and maintenance of the status quo in the social structure.

A different perspective on the definition of evaluation

was made in 1971 by the Phi Delta Kappa National Study Committee on Evaluation, of which Daniel Stufflebeam was Chair.

> Evaluation is the process of delineating, obtaining, and providing useful information for judging decision alternatives. Evaluation is also the process of ascertaining the relative values of competing alternatives (Stufflebeam 1971:40).

The *Encyclopedia of Educational Evaluation* (1975) had also noted that "Evaluation is a human judgmental process applied to the results of program examination" and that judgement is influenced by values (a root of evaluation).

Stufflebeam and his colleagues (1971:19) have argued that "the evaluator's traditional focus has been microscopic (the individual student, the classroom) rather than macroscopic (the school district, the state system, or the national network)." A related difficulty they noted (echoing Buros) is that instruments have been developed for use with the individual, while the concern is now with system data. This leads to still another problem: faulty aggregation of data. An evaluation of 50 pages is appropriate for one project, but the Department of Education needs to know about the nationwide effects of a particular funding program such as Title I or Title VII. Succinct Executive Summaries of the detailed data on project processes, student characteristics, and outcomes are most useful for policy decisions when backed up by a full report.

What then are the major problems in evaluation? We have identified: (1) the mystification of evaluators' power over ideology and decision making, (2) the ideology of individual merit supported by "individual" achievement tests that were actually constructed by inclusion of items that discriminate between groups which have more or less educationally enriched home backgrounds, not individuals who have or have not learned the school curriculum, (3) the use of those achievement tests developed for individual ranking and sorting to measure group achievement, and (4) the lack of theory and models. In their book, *Educational Evaluation and Decision Making* (1971), Stufflebeam and his associates identified some of these problems and posited that underlying everything else was "the lack of adequate theory" (1971:9). They found no "systematic treatment of evaluation design" and few models among which to choose (1971:8).

In terms of practice, Stufflebeam et al. noted that even the (then) United States Office of Education did not provide adequate guidelines for evaluating the programs which they fund and for which they require annual evaluations. Their guidelines requested:

> Describe the methods, techniques, and procedures which will be used to determine the degree to which the objectives of the proposed program are achieved and
> Describe the instruments to be used to conduct the evaluation.

They did not request that the evaluator determine which factors were involved in achieving or not achieving the objective and did not request recommendations for alternative implementation.

Two emphases in educational evaluation which are distinguished are product evaluation, in which the students' achievement is measured, usually with standardized instruments, and process evaluation, in which the educational program implementation is evaluated. In the evaluation model that is still prevalent today, the emphasis is on outcomes: educational evaluation still tends to be equated with measurement of student achievement, although there is an equally significant need for process evaluation.

I would argue that the most detrimental omission was that the guidelines did not require process evaluation, determining the degree to which the program was implemented as proposed, rather than simply whether or not its objectives were met. It would seem logical that before evaluating the outcomes of an educational program, one must ascertain whether or not the program had been implemented as proposed, and if not, why, and how it was changed. Since outcomes are presumably the result of the program implementation, a process evaluation enables users of the evaluation to see the relationship of the outcomes to processes in the program, such as administrative support procedures, or administrative blockage; personnel, time and resource allocation; teaching/ learning models; classroom social organization, coordination among components of the program and with other programs, and other program features that might be changed.

Where Are We Today?

The lack of process evaluations of bilingual programs was first identified by Saravia-Shore (1979). In 1980, in the *Forum* of the National Clearinghouse on Bilingual Education, Bernal reported on a conference by the Austin Evaluation and Dissemination Center: "Process evaluation is an area of evaluation which has not been well executed as a rule in Title VII programs." In 1988, in the same publication, O'Malley, speaking as director of the Evaluation Assistance Center East funded by the Bilingual Education Act, noted that "Program documentation is an essential but often neglected part of the evaluation process" (1988:3). He suggested that one of the three practices to improve evaluations of instructional programs for limited English proficient students was "program documentation or developing a clear description of instructional procedures and monitoring whether or not they are implemented as intended" (1988:1).

To see how far the field of evaluation of bilingual programs has come, one can review the 1989 Guidelines for Evaluations of Title VII (bilingual) programs developed by the Georgetown University Evaluation Assistance Center East. This Center, funded by the Bilingual Education Act to provide technical assistance in the area of evaluation, developed the Guidelines, adapted from recommendations by Lam and Gamel (1987), to provide recommendations to meet the requirements of the Title VII regulations concerning evaluation. The Guidelines go beyond student outcomes to program implementation and teacher and student characteristics to achieve the whole picture of the program and gather potentially useful data for replication of programs that demonstrate enhanced student academic achievement. One requirement, for example, is that the evaluation

> Provides information on the amount of time (in school years or months, as appropriate) participants received instructional services in the project and in another instructional setting, and on different instructional tasks.

A second requirement "Identifies special educational activities undertaken and the pedagogical materials, methods, and techniques used in the program." Related recommendations include "key instructional features" and the percentage of instructional time devoted to each language and identification of which subjects are taught in which language. Two other requirements ask for information on the background of the teachers and students: "Gives educational and professional qualifications of staff, including language competencies" and "Gives information on education background, needs, and competencies of project students." The relevant recommendations for students include not only language competencies in each language but socioeconomic status and years of education completed.

In terms of student outcomes, in addition to standardized tests, the Guidelines suggest such indices as "changes in the rate of student grade retention, dropouts, absenteeism, . . . [and] enrollment in postsecondary education institutions."

O'Malley suggested that at a minimum the aspects of the program that need to be documented were the activities that are expected to influence program outcomes, which could be done in an interview or with observation checklists. He noted that optional aspects that might require documentation were student and staff characteristics, "the setting or context," materials, and cost (1988: 3).

These 1989 Guidelines respond to Burry's (1979) review of the state of the art of evaluation of bilingual education programs for UCLA's Center for the Study of Evaluation which criticized the "failure to explore the relationships among instructional strategies, implementation techniques and program outcomes."

> Understanding these relations will require greater evaluator attention to delineation of program goal and attainment strategies, as well as consideration of program outcomes in addition to those of a purely cognitive nature. Reporting these relationships in a useful manner will require greater evaluator attention to program description and documentation. . . .

This is the arena where ethnographers, as I suggested earlier, can contribute the theoretical framework from anthropology and their experience in ethnographic documentation.

To summarize the problems identified in the "Needs Assessment" by Bernal (1980), Burry (1979), Saravia-Shore (1979), and O'Malley (1988), there is a lack of process evaluation data from bilingual programs with which to inform policy decisions. For example, there is a dearth of information on which bilingual education models are most appropriate for various categories of students.

This lack of process evaluation of the implementation of bilingual programs has been evident at the classroom level, the school organization level, and the district level. Burry has proposed that evaluators consider and explore "the relationships among instructional strategies, implementation techniques and program outcomes." "This kind of information has been requested in every major effort to evaluate bilingual programs. However, previous efforts have not successfully established these relationships."

What should be discarded? As a beginning, those evaluation designs conceived within the experimental paradigm which are based on the assumptions of random assignment of matched students to treatment and control groups. Burry (1979) concluded his review by stating "The use of true experimental design is usually not possible in a bilingual program evaluation. . . . ." Bilingual programs usually cannot be studied in a purely experimental fashion, because legislation prohibits the withholding of bilingual services from students who are defined by law as being entitled to such services. Therefore it is impossible to use in evaluation such statistical models as the analysis of co-variance, since "in this model one of the assumptions is random assignment (of students) to treatment and control group." For both legal and ethical reasons, Limited English Proficient students in need of bilingual education cannot be randomly assigned to non-treatment groups for comparative purposes.

We might also ask how programs can be legitimately or validly studied within the experimental design paradigm since the federal government has instituted Protection of Human Subjects provisions that require researchers to obtain the prior permission of subjects for their participation in a study. This procedure does not allow random selection of subjects, since they are now self-selected and a bias is present in every sample. However, this is too large a question to cover within the scope of this chapter; also, to date, Protection of Human Subjects covers only research, not evaluation.

For substantive discussions by Egon Guba and Yvonna Lincoln and Matthew Miles and Michael Huberman et al. of the experimental and ethnographic paradigms of evaluation and whether or not they should be used together, see Fetterman (1988 and 1986).

Where Do We Want to Go?

If the experimental paradigm of evaluation is not appropriate for bilingual education programs, we might instead consider complementing quantitative evaluation with ethnographic evaluation of the program. The definition of ethnographic evaluation encompasses the use of on-site participant observation and in-depth interviews of program participants to monitor the implementation of a program. Program processes can be identified, monitored, and documented in a variety of ways via ethnographic observation as recorded in field notes, photographs, and videotapes. Interviews are another way of ascertaining the impact or effectiveness of the program from the perspective of the students, teachers, and parents.

Participant Evaluation

I would suggest the term participant evaluation, which acknowledges the importance of the program participants as evaluators. Conversely, every evaluator, whether he or she wishes it or not, is a participant in the life of the program being evaluated and shapes its form. This phenomenon needs to be made explicit. The term "participant evaluator" calls attention to the process. The role of the ethnographic participant observer is a model for the role of participant evaluator as the dual role of outside/insider of a participant evaluator obtains. When working as an evaluator one may begin as an outsider, but there are numerous pressures to become an insider if one is on-site for any length of time, creating double-bind conflicts between participant and evaluator. This conflict is lessened if a policy decision is made to distinguish between certain formative evaluation information, meant to be used by the project staff to improve the program—which need not be reported—and the summative evaluation, which analyzes and reports the relationships between program processes and student, staff, and parent outcomes. Participant evaluator teams, consisting of an outside participant evaluator and staff members who are internal participant evaluators, may be more effective than either group alone in terms of ongoing formative evaluations. Bilingual program staff can be assisted with evaluation tools and techniques so that they may monitor the implementation of the program on a much more comprehensive basis than any outside evaluator would have time to do. Participant evaluation is thus a cost-effective form of comprehensive evaluation.

Another advantage of an ethnographic approach, particularly participant evaluation, is that the experience of "key informants," such as teachers and paraprofessionals, may be tapped to ascertain which instructional strategies, grouping patterns, participant structures, and classroom rules work for which students, supplementing the ethnographer's observations of relationships over a period of time. The collaboration between external and internal participant evaluators, such as teachers, also has the benefit of encouraging more reflective teaching. Whereas most evaluations rely solely on quantitative outcome data, these methodologies combine quantitative and qualitative data collection and analysis of program implementation and outcomes.

Ethnographic Evaluation of Program Implementation

In the latest (1991) presentation to the National Association for Bilingual Education, the Georgetown University Evaluation Assistance Center (EAC) East suggested that a portion of the evaluation report be devoted to Program Implementation. This section would indicate the "key features (those aspects of the program which are believed to be essential to produce the intended outcomes) of the instructional program and the way in which each feature is implemented" (1991:3). While various "research designs" such as Gap Reduction and Pre/Post with a Group Comparison were disseminated by the University of New Mexico College of Education EAC-West, there was no suggestion as to methodology for documenting program implementation except sample forms to collect the amount of instructional time by subject area, professional qualifications of staff, and a summary to fill in columns on project objectives, corresponding activities, instructional materials, and methods/techniques. No mention was made of the potential utility of ethnographic evaluation for documentation of program implementation.

Erickson (1974) has suggested that ethnography is particularly appropriate for the evaluation of bilingual programs, especially those concerned with students' development of full bilingualism. Referring to Dell Hymes' term, "the ethnography of communication," for the study of the variation in the rules of how to say what to whom in a whole range of situations within a speech community, Erickson proposed that such an ethnography would be particularly useful.

Erickson advanced two criteria for the evaluation of the "effectiveness" of maintenance and developmental bilingual programs:

1. the wideness of the range of different variants of both languages that students are encouraged to speak and actually do speak while attending the program, and
2. the percentage of total daily talk in the program by students in their mother tongue. By "encouraged to speak" I mean receiving social rewards (positive reinforcement) from peers and staff while the speaker is actually speaking. (Erickson 1974:12).

Underlying these criteria for a program that is effectively fostering language maintenance is the understanding, from the field of sociolinguistics, that different language varieties are appropriate in different situations. The language variety that is appropriate to use with one's grandmother is not as appropriate with one's classmates in the hallway as a more colloquial variety would be. If students are being "corrected" for speaking non-standard Spanish in the hallway with their peers, the program is not fostering home language maintenance. Erickson (1974) suggests that "language lesson periods" be specially marked by the teacher when refinement and development of standard Spanish is the goal, just as language arts periods mark the development of skills in English.

Erickson also suggested the method of placing a tape recorder in a child's backpack—the same method used by Pedraza and Pousada in their research on language usage in the classroom and other domains of a child's life, described in their chapter in this volume—as one of the best means of collecting samples of interactions between students, peers, and teachers to assess whether or not various language varieties were being encouraged.

The benefits of this kind of ethnographic evaluation in providing feedback to the staff on what they are actually doing were summarized by Erickson as follows:

. . . researchers found that in a bilingual
classroom in a program whose staff had the
manifest aim of fostering language maintenance,
the latent, informal classroom social structure
was such that Spanish speaking children got
more "payoffs" from speaking English than from
speaking Spanish, without either member of the
classroom teaching team (one bilingual in Spanish
and English) realizing that this "hidden social
structure" and "hidden curriculum" existed or
that it was contradicting what the teachers
thought they were doing (Erickson 1974:13).

In the evaluation of program implementation, the
focus is rarely on the social organization of learning. Yet
as such studies as those in this book have emerged, it
is clear that the way in which learning is organized is as
important as the content that is taught. In a September
1990 workshop by the Evaluation Assistance Center East,
the Director noted, "We know very little about questions
to ask concerning what is delivered to students."
Ethnographic, process evaluation is useful in identifying
such questions. Observation of the social organization of
teaching and learning may prompt questions about ways
students can "deliver" or elicit interpretations of experience
or knowledge from one another. Paired learning for problem
solving, for example, tends to elicit more active participation
than a teacher-centered classroom organization. Similarly,
when students are teamed at a computer to write, interview
each other, create a dialogue, or describe a picture in their
second language, they are each generating more language
than if asked to answer questions individually, in turn,
addressed to the whole classroom by the teacher. The
grouping for teams, games, and tournaments in which
teams of heterogeneously grouped students must rely on
each other and the learning of the whole group to achieve
their goal has implications for intergroup learning. Learning
Centers and group process models such as the
Descubrimiento program, in which students learn to
assume different roles in a small group conducting a
scientific experiment, such as reader of instructions,
organizer, setting up the experiment, experimenter,

recorder, presenter to the rest of the class, are other ways of organizing learners for more active learning. Are these roles and forms of interaction modeled and taught? Is cross-age peer tutoring observed?

The research reported by Carrasco, Maldonado-Guzman, and Moll in this volume demonstrates that the ethnographic documentation of classroom implementation through videotaping can also be useful to evaluators as a basis for discussion with teachers concerning what they are doing and to teachers in developing their own self-awareness by viewing themselves interacting with students in a videotape.

Needs Assessment

Another area of evaluation that can be enhanced with an ethnogaphic approach is needs assessment. A holistic needs assessment includes goal setting by program participants and parents. Stakeholders can best judge what they need in the context of what they want students, teachers, and parents to achieve, thus making their values explicit. After interviewing a sample of teachers, principals, paraprofessionals, and parents in an open-ended discussion of goals, an ethnographic evaluator can develop a survey based on the goals and objectives mentioned by all these constitituents. This survey can then be distributed to everyone involved to ascertain priorities among goals and the extent of consensus. This is one way in which the ethnographic interview informs the development of a survey instrument. After analysis, the quantitative results can then be given back to the participants or their representatives, who will then have a set of prioritized goals to guide further efforts. Moreover, such a formative district needs assessment can identify the human and institutional resources which are available to build upon, such as:

1. Bilingual teachers
2. ESL teachers
3. Teachers and administrators who have communicative competencies in languages other than English

4. Community members who would like to participate or mentor students in the bilingual program
5. Any programs that can serve as models
6. Facilities
7. Transportation
8. Support services such as guidance and counseling, remedial reading, etc.

Ethnographic Evaluation of Program Management and Articulation

Finally, I would like to discuss some specific recommendations growing out of the preceding discussion. Ethnographic participant evaluation would strengthen the processes suggested in the Evaluation Assistance Center (East) Guidelines by offering a methodology to document the implementation of the program in the classroom as well as the bilingual program management and the coordination of the program with the rest of the school.

In the SWRL Guidelines for evaluation, a "unique problem in evaluating bilingual education projects" was "identified," as "the difficulty in separating the influence of school and community contexts from the effects of project participation" (SWRL:46). To anthropologists or other researchers with a holistic perspective, this might seem a false problem.

The articulation of a bilingual education program with the ongoing monolingual educational program is an important factor in its implementation. To separate the influence of the school from the program is impossible: isolation of a bilingual program from the rest of the school is in itself a particular kind of relationship to the school which is the program's context. Therefore it is the relationship between the program and the school context which is significant in an evaluation rather than program implementation alone.

Integration into the life of the school or isolation from it as an add-on, transitional, temporary annex or pull-out, affects the bilingual program in numerous and vital ways—

in teacher's attitudes toward limited English proficient students, for example, and toward their native languages, and toward staff—which, in turn, affect bilingual students' attitudes toward themselves, school, and both languages. Nor would this be unique to bilingual programs, since all programs exist in the context of their school and district policies and practices. The extent of coordination of the bilingual program with the other programs in the school which may have related services is another aspect that is significant and can be evaluated more accurately if approached indirectly through observation as well as interviews with staff outside of the bilingual program.

The area of the effectiveness of project management procedures is also one in which ethnographic evaluation can play a significant part. Program management calls for participant evaluation by teams of outside and inside participant evaluators. One mode of evaluation of program management as a participant evaluator is through systematic, frequent participation in staff meetings. In such an arena, the participant evaluator can report feedback in a timely fashion, thus participating in suggestions for modification of the project. Moreover, evaluators can learn a great deal about the management and implementation of a project at staff meetings. Problems are often identified by the internal participants in their roles as participant evaluators. Staff meetings exemplify the social organization of the project; for example, blocks in the channels of communication or ambiguities in the lines of responsibility, role overlap, and role overload usually surface there.

The social organization of staff development is another area amenable to ethnographic evaluation. Are the teachers participating in in-service staff development programs paired so they can offer one another follow-up support when they are back in their classrooms? Will their role expand to teaching colleagues what they have learned? Do teams of teachers and administrators from a school participate in staff development together? What role do teachers have in the school? Do they participate in school-based management efforts so that their evaluation efforts can inform decision-making?

A focus on the users of the evaluation report suggests

some final remarks. Evaluations are done, not only to assist local staff and to inform parents and students but also at the request of the funding agencies, such as OBEMLA and, ultimately, Congress. One format that is useful for the latter audience is an Executive Summary. The Georgetown University Evaluation Assistance Center suggested a one-to-two page Executive Summary in their 1991 presentation to the National Association of Bilingual Education.

Another suggestion also comes from an ethnographic approach. Several anthropologists, including Dr. Steven Arvizu and Dr. Richard Warren, have utilized such visual media as videotape and film of the bilingual program to reciprocate the time and energy given by participants in those programs to researchers and evaluators when assisting the evaluators in their work. Bilingual programs can utilize these visual documentaries as orientations for new parents as well as for staff development with teachers new to the project. Where evaluators have access to resources such as film and videotape equipment, this mode of report/feedback to the bilingual program from an evaluator will often outlive the concurrent written evaluation report.

In sum, the implications of ethnographic evaluation for bilingual program evaluation seem quite broad. The limitations of a behaviorist, product-focused, non-contextual, and non-participatory evaluation model are clarified by an ethnographic perspective. As I have tried to demonstrate, the ethnographic perspective and its associated methodologies also provide some practical approaches to solving the problems identified in bilingual program evaluation as it is presently carried out.

Endnotes

1. Paper presented at a Council on Anthropology and Education Symposium: "Policy Implications of Ethnographic Research in Bilingual Education," American Anthropological Association Meeting, Washington, D.C., December 5, 1980, and revised for this book.

2. Director, Cross-Cultural Literacy Center, Institute for Urban and Minority Education, Teachers College, Columbia University.
3. I am indebted to Dr. Janet Dolgin, formerly of the Anthropology Program at Teachers College, Columbia University, for leading me to examine some implicit assumptions in my own practice as an evaluator.

References

Anderson, Scarvia B., Samuel Ball, Richard T. Murphy, and
    Associates
    1975   Encyclopedia of Educational Evaluation. San
            Francisco: Jossey-Bass.
Bernal, Ernest
    1980   Forum. Rosslyn, Va.: National Clearinghouse for
            Bilingual Education.
Bissell, Joan S.
    1979   Program Impact Evaluation: An Introduction for
            Managers of Title VII Projects. Los Alamitos: South
            West Regional Laboratory.
Buros, Oscar
    1977   Fifty Years of Testing—Some Reminiscences,
            Criticisms and Suggestions. Educational Researcher
            6(1). July–August.
Burry, James
    1979   Evaluation in Bilingual Education. In Evaluation
            Comment. Los Angeles: Center for the Study of
            Evaluation, University of California. 6(1). October.
Burry, James, et al.
    1980   Bilingual Evaluation Training Models. Los Angeles:
            Center for the Study of Evaluation, University of
            California.
Erickson, Frederick
    1974   The Politics of Speaking. In Notes from City College
            Advisory Service to Open Corridors. New York: City
            College. Winter.
Evaluation Assistance Center-West and Evaluation Assistance
    Center-East
    1991   Revising Title VII Evaluation Requirements:

Approaches Incorporating Multiple Assessments. Washington, D.C. OBEMLA Title VII Management Institute. January 9, 1991. Albuquerque, N.M.: EAC-West College of Education, University of New Mexico, and Arlington, Va.: EAC-East Georgetown University.

Fetterman, David M.
1988   Qualitative Approaches to Evaluation in Education: The Silent Scientific Revolution. New York: Praeger.

Fetterman, David, and Mary Anne Pitman
1986   Educational Evaluation: Ethnography in Theory, Practice and Politics. Beverly Hills: Sage Publications.

Lacey, Colin
1970   Hightown Grammar: The School as a Social System. Manchester: Manchester University Press.

Marcuse, Herbert
1964   One Dimensional Man: Studies in the Ideology of Advanced Industrial Society. Boston: Beacon Press.

Macdonald, James B.
1974   An Evaluation of Evaluation. The Urban Review (New York City: APS Publ.) 7(1). January.

Ogbu, John
1974   The Next Generation: An Ethnography of Education in an Urban Neighborhood. New York: Academic Press, Harcourt, Brace, Jovanovich.

O'Malley, J. Michael
1988   Using Evaluation to Improve Instructional Services for Limited English Proficient Students. NCBE Forum 11(4):1, 3. Wheaton, Md.: National Clearinghouse for Bilingual Education.
1990   Evaluating Title VII Projects. Presentation September 27–28, New York City.

Popham, W. James
n.d.   Ten Commandments for Educational Evaluators. Los Angeles: Instructional Objectives Exchange.

Saravia-Shore, Marietta
1979   An Ethnographic Evaluation/Research Model for Bilingual Programs. In Bilingual Education and Public Policy in the United States: Ethnoperspectives in Bilingual Education Research, Vol. 1. R. Padilla, ed. Ypsilanti: Eastern Michigan University.

Saravia-Shore, Marietta, and Steven F. Arvizu
1978   Executive Summaries of Research and Evaluations of Bilingual Education Programs. Washington, D.C.: Council on Anthropology and Education.

Soltis, Jonas F.

    1984   On the Nature of Educational Research. Educational Resarcher December:5–9.

Stufflebeam, Daniel L., et al., Phi Delta Kappa National Study Committee on Evaluation

    1971   Educational Evaluation and Decision Making. Itasca, Ill.: F.E. Peacock.

PART III

Constructing Classroom Contexts

On Ethnographic Studies and Multicultural Education[1]

*Henry T. Trueba and
Pamela G. Wright*[2]

Introduction

The purpose of this study is to review and assess the contributions of current ethnographic studies to a better understanding of the educational process in multicultural settings, focusing on microethnographic research. In pursuing this purpose, the chapter addresses the development of microethnographic research methods, the characteristics and findings of current microethnographic studies, and the overall state of the art of this field as it relates to education in multicultural settings.

Background

General Ethnography, New Ethnography, and Ethnography of Schools are approaches reflecting particular methodological and theoretical biases which produce different outcomes. Each of these ethnographic approaches has contributed to the development of microethnography.

Traditional Ethnographic Approaches

Ethnography has been described as the central task of fieldwork, which in turn has been considered the "hallmark" of cultural anthropology. The function of ethnography is the description of culture. At the core of this work has been a "concern with the meaning of action and events to the people" under study (Spradley 1979:3, 5).

Basic to the study of ethnography has been a distinction between an "emic" and an "etic" approach. These terms were coined by Kenneth Pike and defined by him as follows:

> In contrast to the Etic approach, an Emic one is in essence valid for only one language (or culture) at a time. . . . It is an attempt to discover and to describe the patterns of that particular language or culture in reference to the way in which the various elements of that culture are related to each other in the functioning of the particular pattern (Pike 1954:8).

Further:

> An etic analytical standpoint . . . might be called "external" or "alien," since for etic purposes the analyst stands "far enough away from" or "outside" of a particular culture to see its separate events, primarily in relation to their similarities and their differences, as compared to events in other cultures (Pike 1954:10).

Prior to the mid-1960's, ethnographers favored an etic approach whereby they assumed that all cultures had a uniform system of classification. Their method involved the observation of behavior in an effort to locate patterns of behavior that fit into the universal classification system. Strategies for analysis ranged from "pure induction" to combinations of inductive and deductive methods (Pelto and Pelto 1978:62).

During the 1960's, a group of social anthropologists who were trained in sociolinguistics began to develop the approach alternately called ethnoscience, the New Ethnography, and an emic approach to ethnography. A definition of ethnography offered at that time was:

> A discipline which seeks to account for the behavior of a people by describing the socially acquired and shared knowledge, or culture, that enables members of the society to behave in ways deemed appropriate by their fellows (Frake 1964:132).

This group of ethnoscientists often turned to linguistics in search of theoretical and methodological support in conceptualizing culturally bound behavior. This tendency has been explained as follows:

> It can be argued that of all the many aspects of culture, language is the easiest to study and its description the easiest to formalize . . . [and] it may be strategic first to try out new viewpoints and theoretical approaches on language and then see whether these approaches might also be applied elsewhere (Burling 1969:817).

As part of their emphasis on a strict methodology, the new ethnographers were concerned with issues of descriptive validity, reliability and exhaustiveness. They saw descriptive validity as being conditioned upon an emic analysis of ethnographic data; reliability as a congruence between the ethnographer's interpretation of observed behavior and the social meaning attached to that behavior by the actors; and exhaustiveness as an unncessary burden that ran counter to the selection of crucial ethnographic events essential to the understanding of a culture.

The new ethnographers argued that people "construe their world of experience from the way they talk about it" (Frake 1962:74) and that discourse analysis is therefore crucial to ethnographic description. They insisted that:

> By developing methods for the demonstrably successful descriptions of messages as manifestations of a code, one is furthermore seeking to build a theory of codes—a theory of culture. Since the code is construed as knowledge in peoples' heads, such a theory should say something of general relevance about cognition and behavior (Frake 1964:132).

What these ethnoscientists demanded was precision, specificity, and clear articulation between a theory of behavior and the ethnographic data from which it was drawn. Their major accomplishment was to "ground" ethnographic descriptions, with all their behavioral inferences and their implied theory of behavior, in the ethnographic evidence available through linguistic behavior in a given social context.

Ethnoscience based on discourse analysis was meant to discover categories, classifications, and discriminations relevant to the people under study, in an effort to arrive at an understanding of the cognitive system of the bearers of a culture (Sturtevant 1964). Studies of this type focused on religious behavior (Conklin 1964), beer making (Frake 1964), and firewood (Metzger and Williams 1966).

During the past three decades, the settings for ethnographic studies have changed from remote, non-Western locations to urban settings in our own major cities and, in many cases, to schools. This movement has necessitated changes in the methods and ideals of ethnography. As early as 1957, when anthropologists first moved toward the study of groups and institutions in complex societies, Alfred Kroeber charged that elements of "old-fashioned ethnography" such as ethnohistorical research, were being neglected, and that researchers were often unable to elicit data beyond the "expectable obviousnesses." Such criticisms are still made today; yet, despite them, traditional ethnographic methods have been successfully adapted to meet the needs of educational research.

Ethnography and the Schools

Those ethnographers who began to work in schools came from two distinctive backgrounds. One group consisted of traditional ethnographers who had done work in non-Western settings. The other group was made up of ethnographers who had been influenced by sociolinguists and by the methodology of ethnoscientists. The work of the second group will be considered in the next section.

Traditional ethnographers approached the study of

schools in much the same way they had the study of villages. By assuming that in both instances there existed a set of rules that governed behavior and underlay the social system, they asked themselves the same questions: What is the organization of everyday life? What do the different types of people do? What are their roles and responsibilities? What are the behaviors considered appropriate in interpersonal interaction? How does the overall system operate in its "holistic" sense (Erickson 1976:15–19)? These questions were often broad, ambitious, and unspecified. Studies in this tradition are exemplified by the work of Wolcott (1967, 1973), Burnett (1969), and Spindler (1971, 1974).

As traditional ethnographers continued this line of research, however, questions began to be raised about the validity of transferring the methods of standard ethnographic field work to the study of schools. An early effort in this direction was developed by Burnett (1973) in which she began to focus on specific, educationally relevant events and settings. Another move in this direction came from Erickson (1976). In this article, he applied Malinowski's categories for studying societies to the study of schools, concluding that "some of his [Malinowski's] principles of fieldwork and reporting can serve as a model for school ethnographers, but not his specific methods, for his social units differ from ours in both size and kind" (Erickson 1976:2).

Microethnography

The field of microethnography has developed as a logical extension of the new ethnography; it has been influenced by sociolinguistics, sociology, cognitive psychology, and, to a lesser extent, the ethnography of the schools. In contrast to previous linguistic efforts sociolinguists focused on the social context and dynamics of language use. Thus, sociolinguists such as Fishman (1966, 1970, 1972), Lambert and Tucker (1972), Labov (1966, 1972), Hymes (1964, 1967), and others dealt with the process of acquiring a language and using it in diverse social settings. Mackey (1970), Spolsky (1974), Shuy (1979),

Kjolseth (1973) and Fishman (1973) also dealt with the use of language in instructional contexts.

Sociologists and cognitive psychologists working in the late sixties and early seventies made other important contributions to the method and theory of microethnography. Ethnomethodologists such as Garfinkel (1967) and Mehan and Wood (1975) emphasized the importance of the structure of interaction in seeking to understand the regularity of behavior. Cognitive psychologists suggested that "differences in social organization and values influence the organization and manifestation of cognitive processes" (Scribner and Cole 1973), and that "cultural discontinuities introduced by formal education entail cognitive discontiuities in the organization of basic cognitive capacities" (Cole 1974:7).

In the early seventies, Cazden, John, and Hymes (1972) selected studies that applied linguistic concepts relevant to the use of language in classroom settings. Boggs (1972) and Philips (1972) addressed the issue of compatibility between the use of language in the home/community and in the classroom. Philips identified four participant structures, defined as "ways of arranging verbal interaction with students, for communicating different types of educational material, and for providing variation in the presentation of the same material to hold children's interest" (1972:377). This concept has substantially influenced the research design of microethnographic studies such as those by Mohatt and Erickson (1981), Van Ness (1977), and Mehan (1979). A strong conceptual effort to articulate method and theory appeared in the literature in the mid-seventies. Erickson (1976) provided a basis for a general understanding of the difference between traditional ethnography and ethnography in school settings. In the same year, Hymes (1976) addressed the applicability of ethnographic research to pragmatic educational concerns. These two contributions provided a necessary theoretical basis for the research that was to come in the following years. Florio (1976) sought to provide a unified theory of classroom interaction which would include the study of linguistic, cultural, and cognitive structures. She began with the question:

> Why [is it] that some children who seem
> intellectually and linguistically comparable to
> their classrom peers are unable to achieve success
> in important activities (1973:4)?

After reviewing concepts and models relating to classroom interaction found in studies by Ervin-Tripp (1975), Gumperz (1971), Gumperz and Hymes (1972), Sinclair and Coulthart (1975), Cazden (1974), Goffman (1961), Garfinkel (1967), Cicourel (1972), and Leiter in Cicourel et al. (1974), Florio concluded that each one touched on a critical aspect, but none dealt fully with interaction per se. The most apt description she found was Goffman's (1961) of face-to-face interation as a dance of identification. From this, the question became:

> What is it in the dance of identity that mediates
> what a child knows and can do in some contexts
> and the kind of performance (s)he eventually
> manifests in front of the teacher (Florio 1976:43)?

Florio concluded further that any comprehensive and unified theory of interaction must begin with the speech community, i.e., the classroom, as the basic unit of analysis, and must then deal with the social context in all its complexity in an effort to understand the "ways in which the social identities of teachers and children are in part generated by and help to create the quality of classroom interaction" (1976:46).

Erickson (1977) discussed the dichotomy between quantitative and qualitative research methodologies in education. He suggested that these methodologies could be combined by (1) textual analysis of ethnographic reports; (2) systematic ethnographic monitoring that would generate data capable of quantitative summary; and (3) interactional analysis based on video and/or audio tapes. Erickson and Shultz (1977) suggested that the ability to monitor contexts and contextual changes is an essential element of social competence. Bremme and Erickson (1977) addressed the relationship between verbal and nonberval behavior. They confirmed the position of Erickson and Shultz (1977) regarding students' need to identify changes in social contexts in order to exhibit appropriate behavior. Further, they stated that students must simultaneously attend to verbal and nonverbal behavior in order to successfully engage in classroom activities.

According to Erickson (1978), any description of interaction contains a theory of social interaction in its very structure and choice of words. Therefore, a high level of descriptive validity is esential for understanding the organization of classroom and of instructional activities. Erickson noted: "human learning is always mediated in social relationships . . ." [and] "all to face 'content instruction has *social* meaning as well as *referential* meaning" (1978:6).

Hugh Mehan (1978, 1979), writing from the sociologist's perspective, discussed his version of microethnography which he called "constitutive ethnography." According to Mehan, who draws on the works of ethnomethodologists such as Cicourel (1974); Garkinfel (1967); Garfinkel and Sacks (1970); Scheflen (1972):

> The central tenet of constitutive studies of the school is that "objective social facts," such as students' intelligence, scholastic achievement, or career patterns, and "routine patterns of behavior," such as classroom organization are accomplished in the interaction between teachers and students, testers and students, principals and teachers (Mehan 1978:36).

Comparison of Traditional Ethnography and Microethnography

When attemping to conceptualize the differences between previous and more traditional ethnographic research and the microethnographic research that is being done in educational settings today, it is helpful to compare and contrast their nature, scope, and methodologies. The most salient points of this comparison/contrast are presented in an abbreviated form in Table 1.

In conclusion, although microethnography is a continuation of previous ethnographic efforts, it differs drastically in its specificity of focus, its rigor of analysis via linguistic methods, and its emphasis on establishing relationships between inferences and observed behavior.

Selected Microethnographic Studies

The analyses which follow are based on fifteen microethnographic studies. The criteria employed in selecting these studies were the following: (1) comparability of method and theory; (2) relevance to educational issues; (3) quality of research design and data gathered; and (4) availability.

Description of Surface Characteristics

The children participating in these fifteen studies represented five ethnic groups: Hawaiian (2), Black (2), Anglo/Italian (2), Indian (3), and Hispanic (6). The studies were conducted in the following geographical areas: Illinois: Chicago (1); Oregon: Warm Springs (1); New York: New York City suburb (1); Canada: Ontario (1); Alaska (1); Hawaii: Honolulu (2); Massachusetts: Greater Boston (3); California: Santa Barbara (2); San Diego (4).

The projects ranged in duration from one month to four years; some events were drawn from ongoing studies. Specific information concerning duration was not available for all projects. However, the majority have extended for a period of at least a year.

Research was conducted in both in-school and out-of-school settings. The majority of the studies were conducted in-school, in primary classrooms: ten of these included first-grade students; several included kindergartners and second graders. Only three of the settings were bilingual classrooms, although Hispanic children were represented in other settings as well. Data were gathered in out-of-school settings in three of the studies.

Table 1
Contrasts Between Traditional Ethnography and Microethnography

TRADITIONAL ETHNOGRAPHY	MICROETHNOGRAPHY
Nature	Nature
1. Ethnography is seen as part of a unique discipline, accessible only to trained anthropologists.	1. Ethnography is the common patrimony of all social scientists, including educators.
2. Researchers acquire training primarily through extended field work experience, not through direct teaching.	2. Researchers acquire training in the classroom through direct teaching or through field work experiences focused on specific skills.
3. The aim is the study of social units with sizeable populations, mainly rural and not westernized.	3. The aim is the study of small, social units, primarily urban and westernized.
4. The focus is relatively flexible, holistic, general, and comprehensive.	4. The focus is on a particular type of interaction or clearly defined phenomena in specific settings.
5. It is primarily or exclusively qualitative and descriptive.	5. It is qualitative and quantitative; descriptive and interpretative.
6. It is socially insensitive in its attitude of science for its own sake, regardless of the implications of the quality of life of the people under study.	6. Science is seen as having a specific purpose, one that is congruent with and that can possibly contribute to the quality of life of the people under study.
7. Descriptions are seen as "objective" representations of reality.	7. Descriptions, by their very nature, contain a " theory of the events described."
Scope	Scope
1. An ethnography gives a full description of an entire tribe, community, or society.	1. An ethnography gives a description of culturally specific behaviors which are defined in a given social context.

TRADITIONAL ETHNOGRAPHY	MICROETHNOGRAPHY
Scope	Scope
2. It is an unbiased, objective description of the culture of a social unit through the eyes of an ethnographer; an etic description.	2. It is an understanding of the specific behaviors under study through the eyes of the people observed; an emic description.
3. It is holistic in the sense that it provides a general understanding of how the group operates and how values interrelate in the entire community, tribe, or society.	3. It is holistic in the sense that it identifies the functional relevance of critical incidents of behavior vis-à-vis the entire social unit under study; holism leads to the "social meanings" of behavior.
4. Ethnohistory is necessary to the holistic approach.	4. Ethnohistory may be helpful to the understanding of the behaviors under study, but it is not indispensable in the interpretation of the "social meaning" of behavior.
5. Efforts are intended to produce a complete account of a community.	5. Efforts are intended to explain only the behavioral characteristics of individuals in specific social settings.
Method	Method
1. Gathering of extensive ethnohistorical data is necessary.	1. Emphasis is on the detailed description of the phenomena at hand, here and now.
2. The unit of study is loosely defined as a community, a village, a tribe, or a society.	2. The unit of study is a specific group of individuals in a given setting such as a classroom, a factory, or a hospital ward in a concrete, interactional context.
3. It involves extended fieldwork, "playing the native" as a participant observer via total immersion in the culture.	3. It involves brief but intense and systematic data collection through videotaping, audiotaping, observations, and interviews.
4. It assumes static conditions, the "ethnographic present," where truth is relatively stable and expressed through regularity of behavior.	4. Each event is seen as part of a dynamic interaction wherein roles and meanings are continuously negotiated in the interaction.

Table 1 (ctd.)

TRADITIONAL ETHNOGRAPHY	TRADITIONAL ETHNOGRAPHY
Method	Method
5. Language is seen as part of the culture, or used for gathering information, often through an interpreter.	5. Language is crucial to the study of communicative interaction because through intense and sophisticated techniques of discourse analysis, the social meaning, the roles and status of the individuals under study are revealed.
6. Artifacts and "material culture" are inventoried and described exhaustively.	6. The physical environment is described only as an appropriate context in which to understand communicative behavior in interactional structures.
7. The relevance of information gathered is often questionable.	7. Only relevant information is gathered, and only for the purpose of explaining communicative behavior.
8. Emphasis is on objectivity and completeness; original data is not accessible or replicable; there is no clear explanation of methodological procedures.	8. No claims for completeness exist; data is available for re-examination for reasons of objectivity, validity, or reliability; methodological procedures are clearly described.
9. Intuitive observations are used to describe general behavior styles; data is not amendable to rigorous analysis or quantitative measures.	9. Sophisticated and exact methods of linguistic, paralinguistic, and kinesic analyses of communicative behavior are used to fully explain an interaction; data is often expressed quantitatively.
10. Observers' inferences are accepted without question; no documentation is offered, nor is there the possiblity to reanalyze the original data.	10. There must ba a demonstrable relationship between the observed behavior and its interpretation; data is accessible for secondary analysis to verify the validity of the observer's inferences.

The nature of the units of analysis varied. Some were structural, such as contextual shifts, participant structures and lessons; others were functional, including "getting ready" to read, teachers's communicative strategies, directives, and monitoring actions. The foci of the studies may be divided into four general categories as follows:

Teaching Styles/Cultural Congruence

Boggs (1972)
Van Ness (1977)
Au and Jordan (1981)
Mohatt and Erickson (1981)
Moll et al. (pre-publication draft)

Structural Studies/Sociocultural Roles of Interaction

Philips (1972)
Bremme (1976)
Mehan (1979)
McDermott and Gospodinoff (1979)

Issues Regarding Children's Social Competence

Shultz (1976)
Carrasco (1979)
Carrasco (1981)

Language Use/Communication-Miscommunication

Shultz (1975)
Cazden (1978)
Erickson (1980)

In many cases, studies were categorized according to relative emphasis. In fact, most of the studies have many common concerns. The general characteristics of the fifteen studies are summarized in Tables 2 and 3.

Table 2
Purpose and Focus of Studies

Study No.	Title/Date Published Researcher(s)	Purpose of the Study	Focus of the Study (is on)	Data/Length of Research
1	The Meaning of Questions and Narratives to Hawaiian Children—Stephen T. Boggs 1972	To investigate the hypothesis: it is unpleasant for s Hawaiian child to have a question directed toward him/her by an adult, within the context of understanding problems in learning to read.	communication exchanges between children and adults; circumstances in which they occur.	1.5 years Sept. 1966– Feb. 1968
2	Teaching Hawaiian Children to Read: Finding Culturally Congruent Solutions—Kathy Hupei Au & Cathie Jordan in press.	To describe the development, structure/content and success of a reading program developed for Hawaiian children based on the ideas of cultural congruence.	the communicative strategies used in the reading program	4 years 1972–1976
3	Language Use in Bilingual Classrooms—Jeffrey Shultz 1975	To illustrate language use strategies of children and teachers in bilingual classrooms & the implications of these strategies for bilingual education in general.	contexts in which students code-switched and their teachers' use of L1 and L2.	Not given
4	Talking Down: Some Cultural Sources of Miscommunication in Inter-racial Interviews—Frederick Erickson 1980	To illustrate how auditors' ways of listening can affect speakers' ways of speaking as they attempt to "explain" something.	cultural differences in the listening behavior of participants in inter- and intra-ethnic interviews	1970–?

Purpose and Focus of Studies

Study No.	Title/Date Published Researcher(s)	Purpose of the Study	Focus of the Study (is on)	Data/Length of Research
5	It's Not Whether You Win or Lose It's How You Play the Game: A Microethnographic Analysis of Game Playing in a K/First Grade Classroom—Jeffrey Shultz 1976	To present microethnographic research methods that have the potential to contribute to an understanding of the social organization of classrooms.	a child's social competence in playing tic-tac-toe and the teacher's perception thereof	1974–1976 Event taken from on-going study
6	Accomplishing a Classroom Event: A Microethnography of First Circle—Donald Bremme 1976	To demonstrate that sociocultural rules determine the appropriateness of interaction in the classroom	the structural organization of behavior during First Circle including rules for verbal participation	1974–1976 event taken from on-going study
7	Participant Structures and Communicative Competence: Warm Springs Indian Children in Community & Classrooms—Susan Philips 1972	To demonstrate that the social conditions that define when a person uses speech in Indian social situations are found in classrooms where Indian students frequently interact verbally, but are not in those where Indian students are silent.	different conditions for verbal participation at school and at community events	Not given
8	Cultural Differences in Teaching Styles in an Odawa School: A Sociolinguistic Approach—Gerald Mohatt & Frederick Erickson in press	To demonstrate that culture is an important factor in Indian children's school experiences and to apply these findings to teacher training	cultural differences in the teaching styles of an Indian and a non-Indian teacher vis-à-vis uses of time, style of directives, use of pauses	3 summers (teacher training)
9	Social Control and Social Organization in an Alaskan Athabaskan Classroom: A Microethnography of "Getting Ready" for Reading—Howard Van Ness 1977	To ascertain the usefulness of microethnographic research methods in understanding the workings of an Alaskan cross-cultural classroom	the organization of getting ready to read as a separate segment of the reading lesson	Not given

Table 2 (ctd.)

Purpose and Focus of Studies

Study No.	Title/Date Published Researcher(s)	Purpose of the Study	Focus of the Study (is on)	Data/Length of Research
10	Learning Lesson: Social Organization in the Classroom—Hugh Mehan 1979	To characterize the organization of teacher-student interaction in classroom lessons by describing both the structure of the lessons & the interactional work done by the participants while creating the structure	the organization of classroom lessons, and the establishment of social order in the classroom	1 year 1974-1975
11	You All Gonna Hafta Listen: Peer Teaching in a Primary Classroom—Courtney Cazden, et al. 1978	To analyze the communicative competence of four children by describing the strategies they used in their roles as tutors in communicating information to their tutees and managing interpersonal relationship in this setting	the tutors' performance via delivery of content and management of inter-personal relations	1 year 1974-1975 Event taken from on-going study
12	Aspects of Bilingual Students' Communicative Competence in the Classroom: A Case Study—Robert Carrasco, et al. 1979	To demonstrate the importance of basing an assessment of a bilingual student's communicative competence on his/her performance in a variety of classroom contexts and the efficacy of videotape analysis in accomplishing this broader based assessment	the tutor's performance while working with her tutee	1 year 1874-1975 Event taken from on-going study
13	Expanded Awareness of Student Performance: A Case Study of Applied Ethnographic Monitoring in a Bilingual Classroom—Robert Carrasco in press	To build teacher awareness of the communicative abilities/talents displayed by students in a variety of school contexts and the importance of using this broader perspective when assessing, planning teacher procedures/environments and setting expectations for children; the role of videotaping in accomplishing this	the process and results of ethnographic monitoring of one child's behavior in situations outside of the teacher's awareness	1 month April-May 1978

Purpose and Focus of Studies

Study No.	Title/Date Published Researcher(s)	Purpose of the Study	Focus of the Study (is on)	Data/Length of Research
14	The Construction of Learning Environments in Two Languages—Luis Moll, et. all. pre-pub draft	To see how curriculum and instruction, vis-à-vis the development of reading skills, are organized in a bilingual classroom & thereby to be able to pinpoint sources of interference in the development of second language skills	differences in the communicative strategies used in L1 and L2 reading lessons	1972 2 months
15	Social Contexts for Ethnic Borders and School Failure—R.P. McDermott & Kenneth Gospodinoff 1979	To demonstrate the functional role of miscommunication for both teachers and students and its relationship to political relation between different groups in the classroom and the community	the consequences of language differences in a variety of settings and a an analysis of one incident of miscommunication	Not given

Table 3

Setting, Population, and Research Methods

Study No.	Title/Date Published Researcher(s)	Setting	Population/ Individual Subjects	Data Gathering	Data Analyzed	Unit(s) of Analysis
1	The Meaning of Questions and Narratives to Hawaiian Children—Stephen T Boggs 1972	Hawaii in school 2 first grade classes 1 second grade class	Mainly Hawaiian students, a few Samoan & a few Caucasian students, a Caucasian teacher	1 participant observation 2 audiotaping Reading readiness exercises Day-long, bi-weekly visits	1 observations 2 recorded conversations with the observer, 37 conversations with 14 children 3 student performance on Reading-Readiness Assignment	1 question-answer interaction 2 response to questions in conversation & other verbalizations
2	Teaching Hawaiian Children to Read Finding Culturally Congruent Solutions—Kathy Hu-pei Au & Cathie Jordan in press	Hawaii KEEP experimental school	Primarily Hawaiian children in 4 consecutive years of grade 1		1 transcription of parts of 1 reading lesson 2 scores from 5 classes on the Gates-MacGinite Reading Test	1 reading lesson

Setting, Population, and Research Methods

Study No.	Title/Date Published Researcher(s)	Setting	Population/ Individual Subjects	Data Gathering	Data Analyzed	Unit(s) of Analysis
3	Language Use in Bilingual Classrooms—Jeffrey Shultz 1975	Suburb of Boston in school 1 first/second grade classroom	12 Sp. speaking students; two native Sp. speaking teachers, 2 native Eng. speaking teachers; 1 bilingual aide who was native Eng. Sp.	1 audiotaping 2 observation note taking	1 12 tapes of individual children (taping time 11–30 min) 2 transcription of videotape 3 teachers' rank orders of children's Sp. & Eng. speaking ability 4 language use of teachers	1 an utterance—one turn to talk
4	Talking Down Some Cultural Sources of Miscommunication in Inter-racial Interviews—Frederick Erickson 1980s	In school counseling settings Out of school Job interviews	5 white/black listener pairs 2 white/white pairs 2 black/black pairs	1 videotaping	1 9 tapes of interviews; 7 school counseling; 2 job interviews Total of 84 min.	1 instance, defined as LRRM+/- LR+r.n.p. or pp

Table 3 (ctd.)
Setting, Population, and Research Methods

Study No.	Title/Date Published Researcher(s)	Setting	Population/Individual Subjects	Data Gathering	Data Analyzed	Unit(s) of Analysis
5	It's Not Whether You Win or Lose, It's How You Play the Game A Microethnographic Analysis of Game Playing in a K/First Grade Classroom—Jeffrey Shultz 1976	Suburb of Boston, primarily an Italian-American community in school in K–1st Grade Classrooms	14 Kindergarten students; 11 first graders; 1 teacher; 1 student teacher	1 videotaping; 2 participant observation	1 videotape of tic-tac-toe game; 2 transcript of tic-tac-toe game	1 tic-tac-toe game; 2 utterances
6	Accomplishing a Classroom Event: A Microethnography of First Circle—Donald Bremme 1976	Suburb of Boston, primarily an Italian-American community in school in K–1st Grade Classrooms	14 Kindergarten students; 11 first graders; 1 teacher; 1 student teacher	1 videotaping; 2 participant observation	1 78 min. 50 sec. of videotape (taken from 40 hrs. on 5 days during '74–'75)	First circle (period of time)
7	Participant Structures and Communicative Competence Warm Springs Indian Children in Community & Classrooms—Susan Philips 1972	Oregon Warm Springs Indian Reservation In & out of school Reserve school grades 1–6 Non-reserve grammar school grades 1 & 6	a Warm Springs Indian children & adults; b Anglo students in grades 1 & 6; c Indian & Anglo teachers Warm Springs Indian Community	1 participant observation	1 Observations; 2 Field Notes	2 Participant structures

Setting, Population, and Research Methods

Study No.	Title/Date Published Researcher(s)	Setting	Population/ Individual Subjects	Data Gathering	Data Analyzed	Unit(s) of Analysis
8	Cultural Differences in Teaching Styles in an Odawa School: A Sociolinguistic Approach—Gerald Mohatt & Frederick Erickson in press	Canada Odawa Indian Reservation In & out of school 2 first-grade classrooms 4 Indian homes	a two classrooms of Indian students b two teachers—1 Anglo, 1 Indian	1 videotaping	1 Teacher = 11 hrs. of tape on 9 different days 2 Teacher+ 13 hrs on 10 different days, 16 tapes with sound 3 32 hrs. of tape in 4 children's homes	1 Major classroom activities 2 Directives / Monitoring acts 3 Pauses
9	Social Control and Social Organization in an Alaskan Athabaskan Classroom: A Microethnography of Getting Ready for Reading—Howard Van Ness 1977	Rural Alaska in school 1 kindergarten classroom	1 Kuyukon Athabaskan teacher 6 Kuyukon Athabaskan students 1 non-Indian student	1 videotaping	1 videotape	1 period called "getting ready to read"
10	Learning Lessons Social Organization in the Classroom—Hugh Mehan 1979	San Diego, Calif. in school 1 first second third classroom	1 classroom of students approx. 50% Chicanos, 50% Black 1 Anglo teacher 1 bilingual teacher	1 videotaping 2 observation field notes Taping 1 hr a day first week 1 hr. every 3rd wk. 9:74-3:75	1 14 hrs .of videotape	1 classroom lesson
11	You Are Gonna Hafta Listen Peer Teaching in a Primary Classroom—Courtney Cazdon et al. 1978	San Diego, Calif. in school 1 first second third classroom	The 4 oldest Black children in class	1 videotaping	1 4 tapes of instructional chains	1 instructional chain

Table 3 (ctd.)
Setting, Population, and Research Methods

Study No.	Title/Date Published Researcher(s)	Setting	Population/ Individual Subjects	Data Gathering	Data Analyzed	Unit(s) of Analysis
12	Aspects of Bilingual Students Communicative Competence in the Classroom & Case Study—Robert Carrasco et al. 1979	San Diego, Calif. in school 1 first second third classroom	Bilingual 50 dominant first grade tutor and her bilingual Sp. dominant tutee	1 videotaping	1 1 tape approx. 32 min.	1 instructional.l chain
13	Expanded Awareness of Student Performance: A Case Study of Applied Ethnographic Monitoring in a Bilingual Classroom—Robert Carrasco in press	Santa Barbara, Calif. In school Bilingual K classroom	Lupita,—a kindergartner K class—28 bilingual children bilingual teacher bilingual aides (3)	participant observation videotaping interviews/phone and in prison viewing session	1 2 hr. tape of Lupita during free time 2 teacher's response to tape during viewing session 3 interview with teacher	1 1 student-student interaction 2 teacher reaction introspection
14	The Construction of Learning Environments in Two Languages — Luis Moll et al. pre pub. draft	National City, CA in school 2-3 sister classrooms, one conducted in Eng. one in Sp.	1 top, middle & low reading groups working in Sp. and in Eng. total of 12 students 2 teachers —1 bilingual, 1 Eng. monolingual 2 aides—1 Eng. dominant, 1 Sp. monolingual	1 videotaping	1 videotapes of several reading lessonsz	1 reading lesson 2 teacher communicative strategies
15	Social Contexts for Ethnic Borders and School Failure—R.P. McDermott & Kenneth Gospodinoff 1979	Suburb of New York City in school First grade classroom	Top, middle, bottom reading groups and 1 Puerto Rican boy	1 Observation/field notes 2 Super 8 film 3 Videotape Data collected frequently		1 reading lesson

Table 4
Summary of Findings

Study No.	Date Published Researchers	Summary
1	Boggs 1972	This study deals with the cultural appropriateness of behavior in adult-child interaction. The findings suggest that Hawaiian children perceive it as basically unpleasant and risky to answer individually directed inquiries from adults. When the adult, however, is receptive, children may volunteer information or initiate a conversation. If an adult addresses the entire group, it is safe to respond as a member of that group.
2	Au & Jordan in press	This study documents that effectiveness of the communicative strategies used to teach reading comprehension to Hawaiian children and the cultural congruence between these strategies and talk story—a common Hawaiian speech event
3	Shultz 1975	The findings of this study indicate that the students' choice of language is primarily determined by his/her perception of the language ability of the person(s) to whom he or she is speaking; and, teachers used Spanish as a marked language and English as the regular language with obvious advantages.
4	Erickson 1980	The findings of this study show that listening response patterns of Blacks and Anglos are culturally different and that these differences lead to hyper-explanation on the parts of Anglo interviewers which is perceived as an insult by Black interviewees.

Table 4 (ctd.)
Summary of Findings

Study No.	Date Published Researchers	Summary
5	Shultz 1976	This study shows that the teacher arrived at a judgment about a kindergartner's level of social competence based on a small percentage of observed behaviors in the first days of school.
6	Bremme 1976	This study represents a classroom event called First Circle in all its contextual circumstances and establishes the rules for appropriate participation of children during teacher's time and student's time.
7	Philips 1972	This study indicates that the verbal participation of Indian children in the classroom is contingent upon the cultural congruence between the participant structures of the classroom and those of the community.
8	Mohatt & Erickson In press	This study points out the cultural differences between an Indian and a non-Indian teacher in the ways they use time, issue directives, monitor behavior and allow for student responses.
9	Van Ness 1977	The findings of the study point to the smoothness of the transition from the previous lesson into the reading lesson as resulting from cultural congruence between teacher and students communicative patterns.

Summary of Findings

Study No.	Date Published Researchers	Summary
10	Mehan 1879	This study analyzes the structural organization of classroom lessons, the procedures used to maintain classroom order and the skills needed for competent student participation.
11	Cazden, et al. 1978	This study showed that children who were successful tutors used communicative strategies that involved establishing an asymmetrical power relationship with their tutees and implied the acceptance of the responsibility to share their special knowledge with their tutees.
12	Carrasco et al. 1979	This study's findings point to the danger of misassessing the communicative competence of bilingual children by using their performance in teacher-led activities as the only basis for their judgment.
13	Carrasco In press	This study reinforces the importance of expanding the basis on which a teacher makes judgments about bilingual students' competence to situations which are not within the teacher's usual awareness.
14	Moll Pre-pub. draft	The findings of this study indicate that a lack of congruence between the communicative strategies used to teach reading in the first and second languages impedes acquisition of second language reading skills.
15	McDermott & Gospodinoff 1979	The conclusion of this study was that apparent on-going miscommunication in the classroom is in fact a communicative accomplishment and a reflection of the political and economic relationships between diverse groups in the community.

Discussion

Of the fifteen studies, those focusing on the organizational structure of teaching-learning transactions were conducted by Bremme (1976), Mehan (1979), and McDermott and Gospodinoff (1979). The main point of Bremme's study was to identify the two contexts called "teacher's time" and "students' time" and the rules for appropriate participation in each. Mehan's study yielded the structural organization of classroom lessons as well as the basic procedures and improvisational strategies employed by the teacher to maintain classroom order. McDermott and Gospodinoff's (1979) detailed analysis of reading lessons given to top and bottom student groups revealed how the postural configuration of the group members contributed to or impeded their successful completion of the lessons. This group's findings are related to Susan Philips' (1972); in her study she identified four participant structures and their differential effect in obtaining student participation in teaching-learning transactions, as well as some of the strategies teachers employed to encourage full participation.

The second group of studies contributed to an understanding of the importance of cultural and linguistic congruence in teachers' instructional strategies. Boggs (1972) found that Hawaiian children were very uncomfortable when asked to respond to individually directed queries, but that they were willing to talk as members of a group. Au and Jordan (1981) documented the effectiveness of a reading program in which an integral teaching strategy was based on a common Hawaiian speech event called "talk story." Philips (1972) found that Indian students were far more willing to participate in instructional activities when they were organized in groups or when the teacher was available for student-initiated consultations. Shultz (1975) identified the child's perception of a listener's language ability as a major determiner of language choice when code-switching. Finally, Moll et al. (pre-publication draft) inferred that children's ability to develop second language reading skills depended on the congruence between the communicative strategies used in first and second language reading lessons. These studies have shown that a measure of linguistic and cultural congruence between the teacher's patterns of classroom interaction and those of the students is necessary for the latter to develop the skills and the desire to participate fully in learning activities.

The third group of studies also dealt with cultural congruence, but primarily in terms of the teacher's management style. Mohatt and Erickson (1981) found differences in the ways in which an Indian teacher and an non-Indian teacher conceptualized their roles. These differences were reflected in the amount of time each allotted to activities such as "getting ready" and "cleaning up," in the ways they chose to direct and monitor behavior, and in the time they allowed for children to answer questions and comply with directives. Van Ness (1977), in observing an Athabaskan Indian teacher with six students, found that the ease with which a transition was accomplished and the lack of any exercise of overt control were indicative of a high degree of congruence between the teacher's expectations and the students'. These studies also suggested the advantages for classroom management resulting from congruence betwen the teacher's strategies and students' expectations of culturally appropriate behavior. The principle stressed here was that classroom management was contingent upon the common understanding of the roles and responsibilities of the teacher and student, which were culturally defined.

A final study dealing with the concept of congruence was made by Frederick Erickson (1980). In his study he stressed once more the idea that even the most fundamental rules of participation, such as listening and response patterns, are culturally determined and different for Blacks and Anglos, thus creating a potential for gross misinterpretations. He therefore implicitly reinforced the principles of cultural congruence by stressing the need to understand the nature of interethnic communication.

The last group of studies dealt with the processes by which teachers make judgments about their students' levels of social competence. Shultz (1976), Cazden et al. (1978), Carrasco et al. (1979) and Carrasco (in press) all reported that it was common for teachers to form judgments about their students' social competence in the early part of the school year, based on limited information. This was considered extremely important for bilingual and Black students, who often demonstrated a higher level of competence in peer interaction (occurring outside the teacher's awareness, and thus lost to her as a basis for judgment) than in teacher-student interaction. These studies stressed the following theoretical principles: (1) that social and linguistic competence is demonstrable in the appropriateness and degree of participation in classroom interaction, and (2) that the degree of participation and the level of competence are intimately related to each other and to the learning opportunities provided by the teacher.

Summary

The contributions of the fifteen microethnographic studies chosen for analysis and the theoretical and methodological trends they have established represent a major accomplishment in the field of educational research. Classroom interaction has been studied as a dynamic process of on-going teacher-child and child-child interaction. This process has, in turn, been examined as being determined, defined, and interpreted by its various structural and functional contexts. The three major focal emphases involved have been social competence, cultural and linguistic congruence of interactional patterns, and underlying structures and structuring processes of social interaction.

While all these studies have aimed at a high degree of descriptive validity, not all have been equally successful in achieving it; yet this is essential to the relevence of their contribution to an understanding of the educational process. Descriptive validity continues to concern ethnographers and microethnographers. It is a question of the "validity of the theory embedded in description" which has become "a highly structured and systematic enteprise involving rules of evidence and inference . . ." (Erickson 1978:1). The argument is that in the final analysis, descriptive validity is a matter of "functional relevance" in an emic sense (Hymes 1977; Erickson 1978).

To make sense of an event described ethnographically is indeed a test of the theory of social meaning attached to the observed behavior by the researcher. To be an emic description, it would have to interpret the observed behavior in terms of the actor's perception of the social facts. Thus, a description of a culture of the classroom would be valid only if it made sense to the classroom participants, and if it explained the structure or patterning of behavior in various contexts. As Erickson has so eloquently stated, "the theory entailed in a description of a connected sequence of events across time is in essence a theory of its social organization" (Erickson 1978:5).

The contention of the present discussion is that the level of descriptive validity of microethnographic research as a whole depends on the functional relevance of its findings to the understanding and implementation of educational practices. The assumption is that, to the extent that the studies included in this project analysed and established one or more of the following relationships, they contributed to the functional relevance of microethnography and, therefore, to its level of descriptive validity. These key relationships are:

1. a relationship between the interpretation of the social meaning of interactions and the observed behavior.
2. a relationship in which the teacher's behavior and the students' behavior are seen as jointly constructing the learning environment, and
3. a relationship between children's acquisition of social competence and the cultural congruence of patterns of classroom interaction.

Because these relationships presuppose an understanding of the nature and importance of the context of social interaction and result in the production of social facts, both context and social facts should be considered. Context is a dynamic, interactional notion and is understood as a determinant of human behavior. The context of classroom interactions is not a static set of situations devoid of persons interacting or the physical and human surroundings alone. Context consists primarily of individuals interacting and, by their interaction, defining the function and meaning of an interactional event. More specifically, a context is constituted by an accumulation of linguistic, paralinguistic, and kinesic features and proxemic shifts.

The verification of the relationship between the interpretation of the social meaning of interactions and observed behavior is the basis of descriptive validity, because it conditions the process of establishing inferences that are grounded in the ethnographic data. To the extent that this relationship is demonstrated, ethnographic analysis will have credibility. Because microethnographic data remains accessible, other researchers can assess the strength of this relationship by conducting their own analyses (Mehan 1979).

The assumption that teachers control the learning environment runs contrary to the second relationship, wherein the learning envirnment is seen as a joint interactional accomplishment of all participants. In order for a description of teaching-learning transactions to reflect reality, the active role of all participants must be recognized.

The third relationship relates to the idea that the social knowledge required for social competence in classroom interaction is best imparted in culturally and linguistically meaningful terms. This principle is reflected in the findings of many of the current classroom microethnographies. It is carried to its logical consequences in the selection and use of teaching strategies that are culturally and linguistically congruent with children's previous experiences.

A final consideration deals with the objective social facts of education. Influenced by the ethnomethodological tradition, some microethnographers have insisted that educators have failed to recognize the ways in which the objective social facts, such as students' achievement, their intelligence, and their choice of career paths, as well as the routine organizational patterns of behavior, "are accomplished in the interaction between teachers and students" (Mehan 1979:18). These researchers have therefore studied the "structuring activities and the social facts of education they constitute rather than merely describing recurrent patterns or seeking correlations among antecedent and consequent variables" (Mehan 1979:18). The recognition of the relationship between observed behavior (structuring activities) and the interpretation of the social meaning of behavior (the production of social facts) is the central concern of the process of grounding microethnographic theory in microethnographic data.

In the ultimate analysis, the descriptive validity of microethnographic research will depend upon the explanatory power of the descriptions of classroom interaction and their contribution to an understanding of educational processes.

Conclusion

In the foregoing analysis and discussion, we have noted:

1. the importance of the context of interaction to an understanding of the dynamic nature of the teaching-learning process;

2. the need for teachers to broaden the base from which they assess children's social competence, particularly that of racial and ethnolinguistic minority children;

3. the close relationship between a teacher's assessment of a child and the nature of the educational program planned for him/her, therefore, the critical importance of an accurate assessment;

4. the importance of structuring classroom interaction in ways that are culturally and linguistically congruent with children's previous experiences, as a first and necessary step in learning to communicate appropriately in intra-ethnic and inter-ethnic situations; and

5. the unique role of the underlying rules that govern the structuring of classroom organization and interaction and the fact that a knowledge of those rules is required for full participation in the learning process in a given classroom.

The contributions of microethnography in the schools described above have indeed substantially influenced the field of educational research. They have helped researchers and educators to reformulate some educational problems, such as the issues of the achievement and motivation of racial and ethnolinguistic minority students. For the first time in educational research, there seems to be a grasp of some of the crucial issues in classroom interaction that affect children's learning. This is not a minor accomplishment.

Challenges still lie ahead, however—including the application of microethnography to more specific problems in the understanding and implementation of educational practices and policies. Microethnography is a valuable instrument in educational research, but in some instances it has been far removed from the reality of day-to-day educational practices and therefore less sensitive to the need to redirect research efforts and designs to issues urgently needing attention. Research would be especially valuable in the following areas.

1. linguistic/social competence as it affects achievement and cognitive growth;

2. language loss and language acquisition and their effect on motivation to participate in learning activities;

3. bases for teachers' assessments of students' social and academic competence;

4. causes, nature, process, and outcomes of miscommunication in teacher-child and child-child classroom interaction;

5. teachers' patterns for rewarding and reinforcing students' behavior and the relationship between their effectiveness and their cultural congruence with the students' home culture;

6. teachers' styles of expressing affection and care to their students and the effects of these expressions vis-à-vis the children's culturally patterned expectations;

7. effectiveness of various strategies to cope with discipline problems across different cultural settings; and

8. skills and strategies employed by teachers in settings with racial and ethnolinguistic minority students in which the students participate fully and achieve at a high level.

The ultimate test of microethnography as a useful research tool in educational research will be its capacity to influence the nature and quality of the educational process.

Endnotes

1. The editors acknowledge with appreciation the permission of Dr. Richard Light, then editor of the *NABE Journal* published by the National Association of Bilingual Education, to publish this article which first appeared in the *NABE Journal*, Vol. V, No. 2, Winter 1980–81.

2. The researchers involved in these studies were associated with the following schools and/or regions: Rockefeller University, New York, R.P. McDermott and Kenneth Gospodinoff; Harvard Graduate School of Education, Cambridge, Massachusetts, Courtney Cazden,* Frederick Erickson, Jeffrey Shultz, Donald Bremme, Robert Carrasco; University of Pennsylvania, Susan Philips; Sinte Gleska College, Ontario, Canada, Gerald Mohat; University of Alaska, Howard Van Ness; University of California at San Diego, Hugh Mehan, Luis Moll, Courtney Cazden,* Robert Carrasco;* Hawaii, Stephen Boggs, Kathy Hu-pei Au, Cathie Jordan. The asterisks indicate people who had secondary research affiliations. In the past few years, some of these researchers have moved to other institutions.

At the time of writing, Dr. Henry T. Trueba was Chairman, Department of Multicultural Education, and Pamela G. Wright was a doctoral fellow, both in the College of Education, San Diego State University, San Diego, CA 92181. Dr. Trueba is currently Professor in the Division of Education of the University of California, Davis.

References

Au, K., and C. Jordan
    1981.   Teaching Reading to Hawaiian Children: Finding a Culturally Appropriate Solution. *In* Culture and the Bilingual Classroom: Studies in Classroom Ethnography. H.T. Trueba, G.P. Guthrie, and K.H. Au, eds. Rowley, Mass.: Newbury House.

Boggs, S.T.
    1972   The Meaning of Questions and Narratives to Hawaiian Children. *In* Functions of Language in the Classroom. C. Cazden, V. John, & D. Hymes, eds. New York: Teachers College Press.

Bremme, D.
    1976   Accomplishing a Classroon Event: a Microethnography of First Circle (Newton Classroom Interaction Project, Working Paper 3). Unpublished manuscript, Harvard Graduate School of Education.

Bremme, D. and F. Erickson
    1977   Relationships Among Verbal and Nonverbal Classroom Behaviors. Theory into Practice 16:153–161.

Brice-Heath, S.
    1982   Ethnography in Education: Toward Defining the Essentials. *In* Children In and Out of School: Ethnography and Education. P. Gilmore & A. Glatthorn, eds. Washington, D.C.: Center for Applied Linguistics.

Burling, R.
    1969   Linguistics and Ethnographic Description. American Anthropologist 71:817–827.

Burnett, J.H.
    1969   Ceremony, Rites and Economy in the Student System of an American High School. Human Organization 28:1–10.
    1973   Event Description and Analysis in the Microethnography of Urban Classrooms. *In* Cultural Relevance and Educational Issues. F. Ianni & E. Storey, eds. Boston: Little Brown & Co.

Carrasco, R.
    1981   Expanded Awareness of Student Performance: A Case Study in Applied Ethnographic Monitoring in a Bilingual Classromm. *In* Culture and the Bilingual Classroom: Studies in Classroom Ethnography. H.T.

Trueba, G.P. Guthrie, and K.H. Au, eds.   Rowley, Mass.: Newbury House.

Carrasco, R., A. Vera, and C. Cazden
1979   Aspects of Students' Communicative Competence in the Classroom. *In* Latino Language and Communicative Processes. R. Duran, ed. Norwood, N.J.: Ablex Publishing Co.

Cazden, C., V. John, & D. Hymes
1972.   Functions of Language in the Classroom. New York: Teachers College Press.

Cazden, C., et al.
1978   You All Gonna Hafta Listen: Peer Teaching in a Primary Classroom. In Children's Language and Communication. W.A. Collins, ed. Hillsboro, N.J.: Lawrence Erlbaum.

Cicourel, A.
1972   Basic and Normative Rules in the Negotiation of Status and Role. *In* Studies in Social Interaction. D. Sudnow, ed. New York: Free Press.

Cicourel, A. et al.
1974   Language Use and School Performance. New York: Academic Press.

Cole, M.
1974   Toward an Experimental Anthropology of Education. Council on Anthropology and Education Quarterly 5:7–11.

Conklin, H.C.
1964   Ethnogenealogical method. *In* Explorations in Cultural Anthropology: Essays presented to George Peter Murdock. W.H. Goodenough, ed. New York: McGraw-Hill.

Erickson, F.
1976   What Makes School Ethnography Ethnographic? Anthropology and Education Quarterly 4:10–19.

1977   Some Approaches to Inquiry in School-Community Ethnography. Anthropology and Education Quarterly 7:58–69.

1978   On Standards of Descriptive Validity in Studies of Classroom Activity. Paper presented at the Annual Meeting of the American Educational Research Association, Toronto.

1980   Talking Down: Some Cultural Sources of Miscommunication in Interracial Interviews. *In* Research in Nonverbal Communication. A. Wolfgang, ed. New York: Academic Press.

Erickson, F. and J. Shultz
  1977   When Is a Context? Some Issues and Methods in the
          Analysis of Social Competence. Quarterly Newsletter
          of the Institute for Comparative Human Development
          I:5–10.
Ervin-Tripp, S.
  1977   Language Acquisition and Communicative Choice.
          Stanford, Calif.: Stanford University Press.
Fishman, J.
  1966   Language Loyalty in the United States. The Hague:
          Mouton.
  1970   Bilingual Education in Sociolinguistic Perspective.
          TESOL Quarterly 4: 215–222.
  1972   Language in Sociocultural Change: Essays by Joshua
          Fishman. Stanford, Ca: Stanford University Press.
  1973   Bilingual Education: What and Why. Florida FL
          Reporter Spring/Fall, 13–14:42–43.
Florio, S.
  1976   Issues in the Analysis of the Structure and Quality
          of Classroom Interaction. Unpublished manuscript,
          Harvard Graduate School of Education.
Frake, C.
  1962   The Ethnographic Study of Cognitive Systems. In
          Anthropology and Human Behavior. T. Gladwin and
          W.C. Washington, eds. Washington: Anthropological
          Society of Washington.
  1964   Notes on Queries in Ethnography. American
          Anthropologist 66:132–145.
Garfinkel, H.
  1967.   Studies in Ethnomethodology. Englewood Cliffs, N.J.:
          Prentice Hall.
Garfinkel, H. and H. Sacks
  1970   The Formal Properties of Practical Actions. In
          Theoretical Sociology. J. McKinney and E. Tiryakian,
          eds. New York: Appleton-Century-Crofts.
Goffman, E.
  1961   Encounters: Two Studies in the Sociology of
          Interaction. New York: Bobbs-Merrill.
Gumperz, J.J.
  1971   Language in Social Groups: Essays by John J.
          Gumperz. Stanford: Stanford University Press.
Gumperz, John J. and D. Hymes
  1972   Directions in Sociolinguistics, the Ethnography of
          Communication. New York: Holt, Rinehart and
          Winston.

Hymes, D.
1964   Directions in (Ethno-) Linguistic Theory. American
        Anthropologist 66:6–56.
1967   Models on Interaction of Language and Social
        Settings. Journal of Social Issues 23: 8–28.
1976   Ethnographic Monitoring. Paper Presented at a
        Meeting of the Multilingual/Multicultural Materials
        Development Center Symposium, Pomona, California.
1977   Qualitative/Quantitative Research Methodologies in
        Education: A Linguistic Perspective. Anthropology and
        Education Quarterly 8: 165–176.
Kjolseth, Rolf
1973   Bilingual Education Programs in the United States:
        For assimilation or Pluralism? In Bilingualism in the
        Southwest. P.R. Turner, ed. Tucson: University of
        Arizona Press.
Labov, W.
1966   The Social Stratification of English in New York City.
        Washington, D.C.: Center for Applied Linguistics.
1972   Sociolinguistics Patterns. Philadelphia: University of
        Pennsylvania Press.
LaFrance, M, and Mayo, C.
1976   Racial Differences in Gaze Behavior During
        Conversation. Journal of Personality and Social
        Psychology 33:547–552.
Lambert, W., and R. Tucker
1972   Bilingual Education of Children: The St. Lambert
        Experiment. Rowley, Mass.: Newbury House.
McDermott, R.P., and Gospodinoff, K.
1979   Social Contexts for Ethnic Borders and School Failure.
        In Nonverbal Behavior. A. Wolfang, ed. Toronto:
        Ontario Institute for the Study of Education.
Mackey, W.
1970   The Description of Bilingualism. In Readings in the
        Sociology of Language. J. Fishman, ed. The Hague:
        Mouton.
Mehan, H.
1978   Structuring School. Harvard Educational Review
        48:32–64.
Mehan, H.
1979   Learning Lessons: Social Organization in the
        Classroom. Cambridge, Mass.: Harvard University
        Press.

Mehan, H. and Wood, H.
  1975   The Reality of Ethnomethodology. New York: Wiley-
          Interscience.
Metzger, D. and Williams, G.
  1966   Some Procedures and Results in the Study of Native
          Categories: Tzeltal Firewood. American Anthropologist
          68:389–407.
Mohatt, G. and F. Erickson
  1981   Cultural Differences in Teaching Styles in an Odawa
          school: A Sociolinguistic Approach. In Culture and
          the Bilingual Classroom: Studies in Classroom
          Ethnography. H.T. Trueba, G.P. Guthrie, and K.H.
          Au, eds., Rowley, Mass.: Newbury House.
Moll, Luis et al.
  1980   The Construction of Learning Environments in Two
          Languages. Laboratory of Comparative Human
          Cognition. Unpublished manuscript, University of
          California at San Diego. [See Moll et al. in this volume]
Pelto, P. and Pelto, G.
  1978   Anthropological research: The Structure of Inquiry
          (2nd Ed.). Cambridge, Mass.: Cambridge University
          Press.
Philips, S.
  1972   Participant Structures and Communicative
          Competence: Warm Springs Indian Children in
          Community and Classrooms. In Functions of
          Language in the Classroom. C. Cazden, V. John, and
          D. Hymes, eds., New York: Teachers College Press.
Pike, K.
  1954   Language in Relation to a Unified Theory of the
          Structure of Human Behavior (Vol. 1). California:
          Summer Institute of Linguistics.
Scheflen, A.
  1972   Communicational Structure. Bloomington: Indiana
          University Press.
Scribner, S. and M. Cole
  1973   Cognitive Consequence of Formal and Informal
          Education. Science 182:554–559.
Shultz, J.
  1975   Language Use in Bilingual Classrooms. Paper
          presented at the meeting of Teachers of English to
          Speakers of Others Languages (TESOL), Los Angeles.
Shultz, J.
  1976   It's Not Whether You Win or Lose, It's How You Play
          the Game: A Microethnographic Analysis of Game

Playing in a Kindergarden/First Grade Classroom (Newton Classroom Interaction Project, Working Paper 2). Unpublished manuscript, Harvard Graduate School of Education.

Shuy, R.
1979   On the Relevance of Recent Developments in Sociolinguistics to the Study of Language Learning and Early Education. NABE Journal, 4(1) Fall.

Spindler, G.D.
1976   Anthropology and Education. Council on Anthropology and Education Newsletter 2:1–2.

Spindler, G.D., ed.
1974   Education and Cultural Process: Toward an Anthropology of Education. New York: Holt, Rinehart and Winston.

Spolsky, B.
1974   Speech Communities and Schools. TESOL Quarterly 8:17–26.

Spradley, J.
1979   The Ethnographic Interview. New York: Holt, Rinehart and Winston.

Sturtevant, W.
1964   Studies in Ethnoscience. American Anthropologist, Special Publication 66:99–131.

Van Ness, Howard
1977   Social Control and Social Organization in an Alaskan Athabaskan Classroom: A Microethnography of Getting Ready to Read. Unpublished manuscript, Harvard Graduate School of Education.

Wolcott, H.F.
1973   The Man in the Principal's Office: An ethnography. New York: Holt, Rinehart and Winston.

Wolcott, H.F.
1967   A Kwakiutl Village and School. New York: Holt, Rinehart and Winston.

Making Contexts: The Social Construction of Lessons in Two Languages

Luis C. Moll, Stephen Diaz,
Elette Estrada, and
Lawrence M. Lopes[1]

Introduction

A major goal of bilingual multicultural education programs is the improvement in academic performance of children of limited English proficiency or of children from cultures which differ significantly from the majority culture. An important assumption underlying such programs is that certain types of classroom interactions are required to produce positive academic outcomes for these students. The nature of these required interactions has never been well specified, but they presumably involve strategies that will promote academic progress while simultaneously fostering the comprehension and use of the second language. The problems Latino children have in school, as described by Carter and Segura (1979), strongly suggest that traditional English monolingual classrooms lack the structural arrangements, curricula, and teacher-student interactions necessary to promote effective learning. Hence the need for bilingual programs.

Existing bilingual programs, however, have not generally brought about as much improvement in school performance as their designers expected. Cummins (1979), among others, has suggested that to make bilingual education effective, research should be directed toward identifying those conditions under which bilingual learning experiences are likely to retard or accelerate areas of school achievement. This task is especially urgent at present, given the public concern which bilingual programs have generated.

The research reported here has been designed as an attempt to break away from summary measures of classroom performance and to see how curricula and instruction are organized in a bilingual program. We videotaped classroom lessons in a school that seemed to provide an excellent case study of children's experiences in a bilingual program. In this program, children were taught for part of each day entirely in Spanish and entirely in English for the remainder. Two teachers, one English speaking and one bilingual, allowed us to observe and compare their implementation of lessons. The focus of our attention was reading. We sought to specify the variations in communicative activities that constituted the reading lessons and to pinpoint those features of the lessons that helped or hindered the development of second-language skills. The results suggest the need to organize and coordinate lessons in ways specifically designed to take advantage of the children's existing strengths.

Theoretical Framework

Our study was influenced by two theoretical approaches based on the idea that learning and teaching are complementary aspects of education and that education is accomplished as a system of interactions. The first is the microethnographic approach to the study of schooling; the second is the socio-historical approach to the study of learning and development. Each approach provided a means to systematically study the content and organization of learning sessions, to identify areas of difficulty, and to suggest interventions for beneficial change.

Microethnography

On the one hand, our study relied on microethnographic research techniques utilized, for example, by Mehan (1979) and McDermott and Roth (1979). These studies are similar to traditional or general ethnographies because they illustrate ways to study people's actions and the concrete circumstances under which these actions take place (c.f. Erickson and Mohatt 1980). However, microethnographies usually focus on specific behavioral interactions in specific institutional settings, and do not attempt to describe a whole way of life. Traditional ethnographies provide general and full descriptions of events through extended fieldwork, the use of native informants, and long-term participant observations. Microethographies, however, usually rely on the use of videotapes, supplemented by participant observations, to provide detailed descriptions of the behavioral interactions of individuals in specific contexts.

A basic premise of microethnographic studies is that social events such as classroom lessons are interactional accomplishments (McDermott and Roth 1979). Therefore, a primary goal of such studies is to describe lessons or other important educational events by characterizing the interactional work of the participants who assemble them (Mehan 1979; Florio and Erickson 1980; Au 1980).

A microethnographic study seeks to "locate" the participants' activities as part of the context in which they occur. From this perspective, context is not limited to the participants' physical location or characteristics, although these are clearly influential. Context is also constituted by what the participants are doing, which is only partly conditioned by where and when they are doing it (Erickson and Shultz 1977; McDermott and Roth 1979). This interactional approach to context is particularly attractive in studying classrooms in which students may differ ethnically from their teachers and in which two or more languages may be spoken with various degrees of fluency. It provides a principled way to analyze the communication system the teacher has set up to implement the classroom lessons; but it also takes into account that whatever the student does influences the teacher and that both are largely influenced by, and in turn construct, the context in which their interaction takes place (Watzlavick, Beavin, and Jackson 1967).

The Socio-Historical Approach

We have also relied upon the theoretical and empirical notions developed by Soviet investigators belonging to the socio-historical school (Vygotsky 1978; Wertsch 1985), and in the work of our colleagues at the Laboratory of Comparative Human Cognition (1983) regarding the relationship between culturally organized experiences and learning.

We found these ideas particularly relevant to the study of classroom interactions because they emphasize the significance of interactions between people in learning and development (for a review, see Wertsch 1979). At the heart of this approach is the analysis of learning in terms of interactions embodied in distinct, culturally organized activities. In the study of any learning activity, the unit of analysis is the act or system of acts by which learning is composed (Leont'ev 1973; Talyzina 1978). Consequently, a critical task in the analysis of classroom behaviors is the careful and detailed description of different forms of educational activity (e.g., story time, arts and crafts, a reading lesson, etc.), and its constituent acts. The sequence of these acts is collaboratively assembled by the teacher and the students. Such a sequence includes the teacher's initiation of questions and the students' complementary answers, as well as sub-sequences, such as finding a word on a page and reading it. These sequences may also be examined for the content and social distribution of specific educational tasks.

We have been particularly influenced by the implications for instruction drawn by Vygotsky. Vygotsky (1978) argued that as children internalize the kind of help they receive from others, they eventually come to use these means of guidance to direct their own subsequent problem-solving behaviors. That is, children first perform the behaviors appropriate to completing a task under someone else's—usually the teacher's—guidance and direction, before they can complete the task competently on their own. This shift in the control of the task constitutes learning. To say that a child is working independently is roughly equivalent to saying that he is carrying on an interaction "in his head."

Vygotsky called such systems of interactions as those embodied in many instructional tasks "zones of proximal development." He defined these zones as

> the distance between the actual developmental level as determined by independent problem solving and the level of potential development as determined through problem solving under adult guidance or in collaboration with more capable peers (1978:86).

Applying Vygotsky's concept to the study of formal learning environments such as classroom reading lessons, the student's entrance skills, as perceived by the teacher, and the instructional materials presented for use in the lesson combine to set the lower boundary of the zone. The skills that the teacher wants the child to master, and the embodiment of those skills in the instructional materials used in the lesson, constrain the upper end of the zone. The way the teacher organizes interactions between children and text in order to move them from lower to higher levels of the zone (or "reading level") is the focus of our attention.

Soviet research has identified other characteristics of classroom zones of proximal development which have important implications for the study of bilingual classrooms. The first is derived from Vygotsky's view (1978) of the relation between learning and development as part of a single, interactive process, in which learning is transformed into development which then provides the foundation for further learning. In instructional activities, zones of proximal devlopment are constructed precisely so that learning can precede development. Teaching which is oriented toward developmental levels that have already been reached is likely to be ineffective (Vygotsky 1978). Good teaching, however, is that which provides students with learning experiences which are in advance of development.[2] Instruction should be prospective; it should create a zone of proximal development. Otherwise, it trails behind development rather than coaxing it along and becomes ineffective. Instruction should not run too far ahead of development, either, or the result will be chaos (Siegler and Richards 1981).

Talyzina (1978) reminds us that although instruction leads development by means of the content of the knowledge to be acquired, such content does not directly produce development; it is always mediated through the teacher, who distributes tasks and regulates student communicative/learning activities. Development is, then, accomplished through the organization of learning activities which are appropriate to the content of the instruction as well as to the student's developmental level. This is a highly complex undertaking, since each school subject has its own specific relationship to the child's level of development (Vygotsky 1978). The relationship varies as the child moves from one level of achievement to another, and, in the case of bilingual instruction, from one linguistic context to another.

The socio-historical/interactional approach that informed our study of the development of children's skills in the bilingual classroom has influenced our observations in at least three important ways. As Dowley (1979) has pointed out, (1) one does not look inside the child for the origins of intellectual skills; instead, one looks at the child-adult interactional system as the source of help that produces change. To this we would add that (2) these interactions must be studied in relation to the content and the objectives of the specific lessons, since it is the relationship among social organization, content, and the child's initial skill level that creates effective zones of proximal development. Finally, (3) one looks for evidence that particular zones (e.g., particular lessons) are providing those interactions that should, theoretically, be the basis of learning.

Research Procedures

The Setting

Our study was conducted in a combined second- and third-grade classroom in a school south of San Diego, bordering on Mexico. This school has implemented a "maintenance" program aimed at promoting academic development in two languages. Two "sister" classrooms were involved in the study—one with a Spanish curriculum, the other with an English one. During the course of the day the children received reading instruction in Spanish, their native language. They also went to the English classroom for oral language and reading lessons in their second language. Only those children who had been judged sufficiently fluent in English to take an active part in lessons were enrolled in this dual arrangement. Native Spanish- and English-speakers were mixed for such activities as art, music, and recess, but otherwise instruction was conducted in separate languages and in separate classrooms. This instructional arrangement was ideal for our project, because it gave us the unique opportunity to observe how the same native Spanish speakers participate in reading lessons given in two distinctive language and instructional settings.[3]

The Participants

After several days of preliminary observations and consultations with the classroom teachers and their aides, we videotaped several reading groups. In each classroom, the children were divided into three ability groups, as defined by their teachers. We especially focused our attention on twelve children who appear regularly in the videotapes in both classrooms. Three of the children were predominantly Spanish-speaking; the rest functioned with ease in both languages. This narrow focus made it possible to collect data on the same children performing in several related classroom contexts and in both languages. We were particularly curious about what kinds of zones of proximal development characterized the children's reading lessons in Spanish and in English.

The teachers' criteria in determining the composition of the reading groups varied. The Spanish teacher classified the children largely on the basis of her conversations with them and by having them read to her. The English teacher relied more on previous teachers' reports and recommendations. Interestingly, neither teacher paid much attention, if any, to language dominance test scores.

The Spanish teacher was a Mexican-American female and a fluent bilingual. Her instructional aide was a monolingual Spanish-speaking female from Mexico. The English teacher was an Anglo, English-monolingual male. His instructional aide was a predominantly English-speaking Mexican-American female. In keeping with the instructional model, the English teacher and his aide spoke to the children only in English. The Spanish teacher and her aide spoke exclusively in Spanish.

Observations and Analysis

Our primary research strategy was to contrast the children's reading experiences in Spanish and in English. We videotaped the high, middle and low ability groups as they performed in each language setting. The goal was to videotape the twelve target children at least twice in each classroom. We collected a total of twenty hours of videotaped data.

Our analysis proceeded in two directions. First, we focused on the three different teacher-defined ability groups within each classroom setting. These "ability-level" contrasts are extremely important, because distinctions made among ability groups (and individuals) are the foundations upon which curricula are implemented: educational materials and activities are correlated to the children's designated categories to create the lesson plan—the teacher's "blueprint" for the zones of proximal development that he or she wants to create. The three systems employed here gave us an idea of the changes that constitute the development of reading skills.

Second, we contrasted each ability group across the two different language and instructional settings. We quickly formed the impression that the children encountered markedly different instructional environments when they went from Spanish to English. But, as we will make clear, more than a change in the language of instruction is responsible for these differences. The general focus of instruction changed when the children moved from the

Spanish to the English classroom. Our basic claim will be that instruction in reading English takes place at a level of reading skill well below the children's general level of development. Substantiating and explaining the reasons for this situation will be the task of the remainder of this paper.

The Spanish Classroom

In this section, we will describe the organization of reading lessons in the Spanish classroom for each of the three ability groups, and provide examples of the teacher-student interactions that constitute these lessons.

The Low Group

The major emphasis of the lessons in this group was to teach phonetic decoding skills and pronunciation. Although the children were seated together and formed a distinct ability group, the teacher provided instruction on a one-to-one basis. In the example below, the student reads the words aloud; when the teacher notices he or she is having difficulty, she intervenes by providing single words to help him or her continue.[4]

1.	Child (C):	How are we going to the beach? Today we . . .
2.	Teacher (T):	We'll . . .
3.	C:	We'll go by tra . . .
4.	T:	train
5.	C:	train, said the mother. Lucy and Ringo see . . .
6.	T:	seem
7.	C:	seem happy (singular—"contento") too.
8.	T:	happy (plural—"contentos")
9.	C:	happy (plural) too.

The analysis of the videotape reveals that in addition to simplifying the child's reading task by sensitively providing correct words when the student hesitates, the teacher also provides auxilliary help. For example, the child in the example above reads while covering those lines to come with a piece of paper. This helps him to focus solely on the specific line he is reading. At certain times, the teacher will take over this function by moving the paper along the lines, thus simplifying even further the demands made by the task on the student.

This instruction at the level of decoding is carried out in many instances without any explicit assurance that the children understand what is being read. The teacher checks on comprehension by constructing educational sequences designed to familiarize the children with the process of examining the story's content. (Answering comprehension questions becomes a primary activity in the more advanced groups.) In the following examples, the teacher questions the student after he has read a story about a family trip to the beach.

1. Teacher (T): OK, tell me what was the story "To Swim" about?
2. Child (C):   That they are going to swim . . .
                 I mean in the morning they are going to go swim.
3. T: mm-uh. And does it seem by seeing this (pointing to the picture) that they are enjoying themselves? Or not?
4. C: Yes.
5. T: How do you know that they are having a good time? What do you see that shows they are having a good time?
6. C: The sand and the ocean.
7. T: Yes, because it says that the sand and ocean are pretty, but in the faces here (points to picture), how are they?
8. C: They are happy.
9. T: The faces are happy. True? They are not sad.

The child has no problem with the initial question (1–2). The next question (3) is whether the children in the story are enjoying the beach activities. Note that the teacher points to the illustration when she asks the student to confirm whether or not the children are enjoying themselves. The student answers affirmatively (4). Then the teacher asks the student to show how he reached his conclusion that the children are enjoying themselves, and urges him to examine the illustration in order to answer (5). When the student answers inappropriately (6), the teacher directs him by pointing to the specific part of the illustration from which he can derive the answer and asks him a question directly related to the illustration (7).

It is important that the teacher works with these children on comprehension exercises, even though they experience decoding difficulties. The format of the question-answer exchange is typical of lessons at more advanced stages; however, the form of this exchange between the teacher and the low group child is not typical of advanced classes, since the teacher often ends up supplying answers. Here we have a clear example of behavior in a zone of proximal development, sometimes called scaffolding (Wood, Bruner, and Ross 1976). The teacher asks a question at some level of difficulty and, finding that the group, or certain children among it, can't interact appropriately at that level, will fill in "parts of the task" until the group's instructional level is met (see also Cole, Dore, Hall, and Dowley 1978; Mehan 1979). Teachers "fill in" or provide assistance in many ways, some of which we are tempted to describe as "social." In the example above, the teacher even points out to the student the precise part of the illustration involved as an aid in responding to the comprehension question.

The Middle Group

In contrast to the low group, the middle group's lessons primarily involved teacher guidance in promoting reading comprehension, supplemented by instruction concerning how to answer fully and effectively. In the following example, the teacher has asked each child to read a question from the book to the child next to him. The response must be correct in both content and form—in this case, a complete sentence.

1.	Teacher:	I want you to ask Marcos this question.
2.	J:	Do you put a letter in the mailbox?
3.	M:	Yes, I put a letter in the mailbox.
4.	T:	Very good. You ask Question Two.
5.	J:	Do you place a letter in an envelope?
6.	A:	Yes, I place a letter in an envelope.
7.	T:	Very good. Okay, Number Three.
8.	A:	Do you have to give stamps to the mailman?
9.	J:	No, you do not have to give stamps to the mailman.
10.	T:	Or, I don't give stamps to the mailman. Number Four.
11.	M:	Does the mailman write the letters?
12.	A:	No.
13.	T:	In a complete sentence.
14.	A:	No, the mailman does not write the letters.
15.	T:	Very good. Number Six.

This activity gives the students early and very explicit practice in the basic question-answer exchanges (often to known-answer questions) so common in formal lessons.

In this example, the children assume a more complex role in the interaction than the lesson format of the low group requires. They assume (via the use of the book as script) the roles both of questioner and respondent. The teacher's role also clearly changes in three aspects: the emphasis on word or sentence level comprehension is different; she does not have to perform the task at this level herself; and she uses the reading materials, rather than oral discourse resources, to mediate her interactions with the children. In the above example, the children are not only made to use the questions in the book to ask their own but also to construct the form of their responses as modelled in the book. In the next example, also from the middle group, the teacher asks the questions, but the children are asked to answer without looking at their notebooks or at the textbook—in other words, without material help. Their answers, consistent with the model the teacher has created, are given in the form of complete sentences, and faithfully reflect the content of the story.

The added ingredient of question-answer formats provided from memory is not free of problems; this is reflected in the interaction. In at least one instance, the teacher provides both question and answer for the student, thus duplicating the function of analagous behaviors with the lower reading group.

1. T: What kind of . . . I am going to ask the question and you are going to answer it in complete sentences, without looking at your books because I want to see if you remember what happened in the story. What kind of bird is the penguin?
2. C: The penguin is a very famous kind.
3. T: Let's see, yes, no. What does he do, what does he not do?
4. C: The penguin cannot fly, only . . .
5. T: Very good, that's the kind of bird, the bird that does not fly. Very good. How are his feathers and what color are they, Ali?
6. C: The penguin's feathers are black.
7. T: Are what?
8. C: Black.
9. T: And are they long or short? The penguin's feathers are black and short, right? OK, how are his wings?
10. C: His wings are short.
11. T: Very good, short. Where do they live, Marcos?
12. C: The penguins live in colonies.
13. T: Very good, you have studied. Where do they lay their eggs, Angelica?
14. C: In their nests.
15. T: In their nests, right. Do they (the book) tell us how many eggs they lay?
16. C: Ten.
17. T: Okay, and, what do penguins eat, Alice? Complete sentence.
18. C: The penguins eat fish.

Although the children are not looking at the materials, they are able to answer the questions correctly. With some reminders, they can also phrase their answers within the complete sentence form, as the teacher requires. After the lesson terminates, the teacher asks the children to write out answers to the questions found in the text. She makes

it very clear that they must incorporate the structure of
the questions into their answers.

The High Group

The high group's lessons consist of yet more complex
demands on skill. The most obvious change is that these
children are required to write book reports. But there are
also qualitative changes in the teacher's interactions with
the students as part of reading itself. In those activity
sequences which are common to all three groups, such
as question-answer sequences regarding text, the questions
asked of the high group are more spontaneous and informal
than the others' have been. That is, the questions are less
text bound; they do not come straight from the book.
Instead, the teacher pursues questions that arise from her
exchanges with the students and the topics developed by
these exchanges. Furthermore, the emphasis is now on
the communication of generalizations drawn from the
reading, and the teacher makes fewer requests for complete
sentences. In the following example, the teacher begins a
combined evaluation/instruction activity after the group
has read a poem about a cobbler.

1.	T:	Sandra, what is this poem about?
2.	C:	About a cobbler.
3.	T:	What is he doing?
4.	C:	Using his hammer.
5.	T:	Right. /Tipi tapa/, who is making that sound?
6.	C:	The hammer.
7.	T:	The hammer, right. Does the poem say that he is a good cobbler or a bad cobbler?
8.	Group (GR):	(mixed responses)
9.	T:	Yes or no?
10.	GR:	He's a good cobbler.
11.	T:	He is? How do you know?
12.	GR:	(Several students respond together)
13.	T:	Where does the poem say that he is good cobbler?

14. GR:	(Several students respond together)
15. T:	Sandra, read the part that tells us.
16. C:	(reads) "Ay tus suelas, zapa-zapa-zapatero remendon
	(Oh, your soles, cob-cob-cobbler mender
	¡Ay tus suelas, tipi-tape, duran menos que el carton!
	(Oh your soles, tipi-tape, they last less than the cardboard!)
17. GR:	Bad shoemaker.
18. T:	Why is he a bad shoemaker?
19. C:	"Duran menos que el carton." (They [soles] last less than the cardboard.)
20. T:	How long should the soles last?
21. C:	A little less time than the nails.
	(The teacher laughs at his response and then the lesson continues.)

The poem itself makes no direct reference to whether the cobbler is a good or bad shoemaker. This conclusion must be inferred from the information given in the poem. The teacher invites such a generalization in line 7. There are some differences of opinion among the group as to whether the cobbler is good (i.e., competent) or not (8, 10, 12). The teacher selects a student who has answered that the cobbler is not very good to specify which lines of the poem she has used to reach her conclusion (15). The girl does so (16), and the group confirms her opinion (17). The instructor then requests more information (18); a child quotes the specific part of the line (19) that tells the reader that the shoes do not last long. In this example, the teacher is less overt in her guidance of the children's actions, controlling alternatives through her choice of questions and the way she directs the children to find the relevant part of the text. We have, however, sometimes observed her being more direct in the use of text to mediate discussions, as she was in the middle group's activities. Consider the following brief example from a lesson in which the students were reading about a Native American group and their customs. In the portion of the transcript presented here, the teacher is asking questions regarding the story's content.

1. T: Who can . . . How can the Navajos be hurt?
2. C: The corn, rain and wind.
3. T: The corn, rain and wind, and what else? (She looks around the entire group.)
4. C: The sun.
5. T: The sun and what else?
6. C: (Inaudible response)
7. T: What do they [the book] say could also damage them? The what . . . What type of thoughts (she points to her head)?
8. C: Bad thoughts.
9. T: Very good, then can you make it into a complete sentence? You (points to a girl who answered previously)? Okay, read the question so you can remember how you are going to construct it.
10. C: (Hesitates in providing answer.) The Navajos can be hurt by the sun, the rain . . . (interruption, then the child continues) . . . and bad thoughts.
11. T: Very good. (The lesson continues.)

Note how the teacher, in requesting that the answer be given in a complete sentence (9), points out to the student that she can use the question in the text to help her organize her response. The result is an independent construction using the text as a tool of oral communication.

In the next example, a different student readily provides an answer by incorporating the question into his response:

1. Monica: (to Julio) What do they do with the hogan when a person dies?
2. Julio: When a person dies in the hogan, they burn the hogan.

In this case, the answer's construction is independent of teacher directions or the use of material aids. Note that the student responds in the form of a complete sentence. This is the same form that the teacher so frequently requires from the lower groups and occasionally from the high group. This student's adherence to the form without its being requested of him suggests that he now uses those communication activities previously provided by interaction with the teacher as a means of organizing his own responses.

Finally, consider book reports. This is the most advanced reading-related activity to be found in this classroom. The students must select a book of interest to them and, virtually without help from the teacher, read it, analyze its content, and write a report about it. In the process of writing these reports, the children practice reading and simultaneously display their mastery of all the skills observed in the three lesson environments. These activities culminate in the children's carrying out their reading behaviors independently with new materials and creating a new product (i.e., the book report) in the process (c.f. Wertsch, 1985). Again, the children successfully assume those aspects of the activities that were carried out by the teacher during the lesson.

To summarize: We have briefly sketched the nature of the three reading environments found in the Spanish classroom. We have shown that these environments are organized to provide time on learning tasks that familiarize the children with various aspects of the subject of reading. Our basic observations fit our idea of a well-functioning system: the children practice and learn specific behaviors which become increasingly complex and, through modifications in the teacher's role, independent of adult mediation and regulation, as we move from the lower to the higher ability groups. These differences in lessons represent the pregression of behaviors[5] reflecting the teacher's implicit "theory" of reading and reading acquisition.

The English Classroom

There was a strong correspondence between the memberships of the high groups in the two classrooms: the target children in the Spanish high group were also members of the English high group. However, some of the children in the Spanish middle group had been assigned to the English low group.

This section will make the following five points: (1) The English reading groups are also organized differently for each ability group but at a much lower level than the Spanish lessons. (2) The overriding orientation of the lessons in English is on the process of decoding, pronunciation and other forms related to the sounds of the second language; (3) This focus is based on the implicit theory that the children need to develop their pronunciation, and decoding skills before they can engage usefully in more complex reading tasks. (4) Having compared the educational activities in the two classrooms, we will conclude that (a) there is an underestimation of the children's level of reading skills in English, (b) that this misestimation arises from the confounding of phonetic errors and decoding errors, and (c) Furthermore, the resulting interaction limits the children's involvement in English to the lower ranges of their reading abilities (that is, to the lower end of their zones of proximal development).

The Low Group

The predominant activity for the low group in the English classroom was practicing isolated word sounds. In fact, all of the lessons were organized to teach phonically correct pronunciation. The following example illustrates one such activity. The teacher has written words on the board and is asking the students to identify and cross out the letters that correspond to the sounds he is making.

1. T: mmmuh . . . mmuh . . . Juan (calls on student to answer) . . . mmuh.
2. S: (student crosses out the correct letters)
3. T: All right, what's the letter?
4. S: "m"
5. T: All right, "m." Angelica, thhuh . . . thhuh . . .
6. S: thhuh (crosses out the correct letters)
7. T: All right, what are the letters?
8. S: thhuh.
9. T: No, what are the letters? Tha's the sound . . . "t . . ."
10. S: "t, n"
11. T: No, that's not an "n" . . . "t . . ."
12. S: "n . . ." (hesitates) "h"
13. T: "t," "h," all right. (lesson continues)

In addition to providing help with phonics, the teacher spent a great deal of time on decoding a text. We observed no reading comprehension exercises, such as those we saw these students receiving in Spanish.

The Middle Group

Pronunciation and decoding are also the primary activities for the middle group. What distinguishes this group is that the teacher also provides some help with the identification and construction of words, pluralization, and so on. But, like the lower group's lessons, there are no activities related to reading comprehension. (Recall that the Spanish middle group was organized to promote reading comprehension and to provide instruction in how to answer in ways that communicated the student's knowledge of the story's content.)

The High Group

The high group's lessons were also primarily devoted to decoding and oral language practice (word construction and identifying sounds). The lessons we observed contained a few reading activities designed to assess comprehension. In the next example, the teacher is reading passages and assessing whether the children understand them.

1. T: "Sue played on the playground after lunch." Where did she play?
2. S: (The students bid to answer.)
3. T: Julio
4. S: Playground
5. T: All right, on the playground. Who was it? Who was doing this?
6. S: Sue.
7. T: All right. When was it? When was it? Eduardo.
8. S: After lunch.
9. T: All right, after lunch. "Joan had dinner at night at her own house." When did she have dinner?
10. S: At night.
    (Lesson continues)

Note that this is a lower level of comprehension testing than was characteristic for the middle group in Spanish, although there is no linguistic constraint on the production of full sentences for these children.

It is clear that the children do not encounter "similar environments" when they shift from one language setting to another. In the English classroom, there is no demand for inferences or complete sentences; recall demands focus on smaller chunks and less distance in time. We never find correspondence in lesson tasks for the Spanish and English classes' high groups, although these children have demonstrated the ability to read with comprehension beyond that which they exhibit in the example above.

In sum, the organization of the reading environments in English is such that students are made to focus primarily on decoding skills, word sounds or lexical meaning. Practically absent are those key activities that promote reading comprehension and help the students learn to communicate their knowledge of content.

Discussion

A possible rationale for the low level of organization of lessons in English (one which was suggested by the English teacher himself) is that the children are weak in English and cannot engage in more advanced reading tasks. This "English deficiency" explanation makes sense, and initially we were inclined to accept it. As we gathered more information, however, we began to realize that the social organization of lessons in the English classroom is not solely a matter of the children's limitations in English. Remember that the children are not allowed to participate in the English classroom lessons until it has been determined (through testing and teacher observation) that they have sufficient fluency to benefit from English instruction. This fact, coupled with our observations of the children in various informal classroom situations, leads us to conclude that the children were much more fluent in English than they appeared to be during the videotaped reading lessons. We taped several occasions in which children interacted outside the general structure of the lessons (see Moll et al. 1980), and discovered that even children in the low groups were able to speak English in ways that were more sophisticated than those prompted by the lessons.

The analysis of the Spanish lessons clearly shows that most of the children, and especially those in the high group, had developed sophisticated reading skills in Spanish. The high group children also displayed good decoding skills in English. In this limited sense, at the very least, they demonstrated that they knew how to read. But if the children were relatively fluent in English—as they are—and possess good decoding skills—as they do— how was the difference in the level of performance between the two classrooms constructed? If most of the high group children could already decode in Spanish, why were the English lessons organized to place so much importance on phonics or accurate pronunciation?

A likely source of the problem is that in the English setting, pronunciation and decoding problems were being mistaken for one another. Teachers assume that decoding is a pre-requisite to comprehension; correct pronunciation is the most obvious index of decoding. Consequently, the teacher (who, after all, does not speak Spanish), organized the lessons to provide the children with the necessary practice in pronunciation, phonics, and other aspects of language learning, such as lexical meaning, in order to be able to "go on." His implicit theory seems to have been that correct pronunciation (i.e., decoding) must precede comprehension. To make an accurate differentiation between a child's inability to decode and incorrect pronunciation of English words, it would seem that the teacher must assess reading comprehension. But as our analysis indicates, activities permitting a display of reading comprehension rarely occurred in the English reading lessons.

Further information about the interactional sources of this mismatch between language sessions came from "viewing sessions" with the teachers. Because of their hectic schedules, these teachers had never observed their classrooms performing in one another's classrooms. When the Spanish teacher first saw the children participating in English, she exclaimed, "Those can't be my kids. Why are they doing such low-level work? They are much smarter than that." What she indicated, of course, was that the children's behaviors in the English lessons did not represent their reading skills as manifested in her own (Spanish) classroom.[6]

One interpretation of the difference between reading levels exhibited in the two classrooms would be to claim that reading skills do not transfer across language settings. But if adults do not totally lose ability when shifting, say, from English to Spanish, why should children who are able to read be afflicted by such lack of transfer? The problem cannot be rooted solely in the children's lack of language or reading skills in English. It seems rather to arise from the social organization of reading and speaking in these lessons. The lessons in English presuppose deficiency in both reading and oral competence; this assumption is reinforced by the children's pronunciation problems. Consequently, the teacher restricts the children to decoding or phonics work. This orientation of the zone of proximal development is below the children's reading ability level.

We began this research in order to better understand some of the complexities of implementing classroom lessons in a bilingual program. In this final section we will point out what we consider to be the most important results of the study, their possible implications for the practice of bilingual education, and the direction of our future work.

Our analysis of lessons across language and instructional settings indicated that the manifestation and complexity of reading behaviors within them is heavily influenced by the lessons' organization of instruction. This organization is itself heavily influenced by accepted organizational constraints and presuppositions about children's competence. When the students encountered roughly comparable organizations of instructional activities in these two language settings, their reading behaviors were very similar in both. However, the occurrence of such equivalent experiences in both language settings was infrequent. The organization of instruction associated with the more advanced Spanish classroom was generally absent from the English setting. This disparity in instructional organization made the children seem competent readers in Spanish but inadequate in English. This description of Spanish-English instruction in one bilingual setting raises a more general issue: the extent to which skills learned in Spanish may transfer to English depends on the degree of similarity in the organization of instruction found in the two classrooms. These results are consistent with a large and growing body of literature showing that learning is primarily situation specific; that generalizability to other situations depends on whether the environment is organized to provide similar features facilitating its applicability to a different setting (Laboratory of Comparative Human Cognition 1983).

These findings remind us of the warnings featured in cross-cultural literature regarding evaluations of performance in situations divorced from the everyday contexts in which people learn and regularly use their skills (e.g., Laboratory of Comparative Human Cognition 1979). At the very least, we must have multiple assessments of bilingual children which seriously take into account the influences of the situations in which these children's skills are evaluated (LaBelle, Moll and Weisner 1979; Moll 1978).

Our results also emphasize the need for careful study of the situation to which skills are supposed to transfer. An explicit purpose in most bilingual schooling is to stimulate the cross-lingual transfer of skills. It is expected that the students will apply in English the skills they learn in Spanish, thus accelerating their academic competence in English. Recent attention to this issue has focused on students' development of a minimal level of competence in Spanish before such transfers of skills to English may successfully occur (Cummins 1980). Without denying the importance of investigating such "threshold" levels of language development, it seems to us that the key to transfer of skills is the construction of lesson environments that are strategically linked to facilitate the generalization of behaviors from one situation to another. But how do we know when cross-lingual environments are sufficiently

similar or unnecessarily different? What are the salient
environmental features that may help us to use and extend
the resources each student brings to the classroom? A
theory as to how such environments may be created has
not generally been available to researchers in educational
psychology, because of our traditional emphasis on skills
as internal abilities.

The kind of detailed analysis of classroom behaviors
presented in this paper was only possible because we
directly examined the contexts where teaching/learning
takes place.[7] Doing so provided us with valuable insights
into the ways in which learning is mediated by adults in
the classroom and the sorts of concrete communication
activities that shape the ways children cope with their
various learning tasks. The Vygotskian perspective we
adopted helped us interpret the significance of the behaviors
we describe. These combined factors make this research
approach pedagogically optimistic—indicating that
children's development is accessible to adult guidance,
permitting us to specify how such guidance takes place
and suggesting relationships between learning environments
in English and Spanish that may be used to develop more
beneficial educational activities. This last is the goal of our
forthcoming work.

Before describing this work, however, we wish to make
clear some of the limitations of the present study. Our
concentration on the immediate contexts of learning, while
providing detailed understanding of the process of
instruction, may limit our perspective of the bilingual
program in its totality. Important out-of-classroom factors
which may greatly influence the classroom's structure, such
as administrative priorities, political realities, and parental
wishes, should not go unexamined. There is a need to
explore the impact of organizational, community, and
political constraints on what is going on in the classroom.
These additional factors would place the classroom in the
larger school and community contexts and help us
understand more fully its dynamics.

Similarly, there is a need to explore students' reading
activities outside the formal lessons studied here. Griffin
(1977), for example, has documented the extent to which
the teaching and learning of reading may occur as part

of other classroom events. In such cases, children use reading as a means to accomplish other ends—something that rarely occurs in formal lessons. This additional reading practice and experience may have—or could be organized to have—important implications concerning how and what is taught in formal reading lessons. The same argument may be made for exploring the functions of reading outside the classroom, and how these reading activities are culturally and socially organized in the children's community. Au (1979), for example, provides a good example of how information from children's activities in the community may be incorporated into lessons, critically affecting their educational impact. All of the above points need to be developed as part of future efforts.

Endnotes

1. Dr. Luis C. Moll, University of Arizona, Stephen Diaz, California State University, San Bernardino, Elette Estrada, University of Texas, Austin, and Lawrence M. Lopes, University of California

2. This does not mean that the Soviets reject "drill and practice." As early as 1939 Zaporozhets discussed the necessity for drill and practice as a means of consolidating ("operationalizing") important subskills. But the orientations of the activity cannot be at this level, or "rote" learning results (see Zaporozhets, 1980).

3. Also videotaped were English oral language development lessons.

4. The examples provided in this section have all been translated from Spanish and edited for brevity.

5. We should emphasize that these general "stages" of development of the lesson environments are not as clearly distinguishable as we have briefly described them and that there is a considerable overlap of "participation structures" between them. This is a point to which we will return later in the paper, since we think it may have important implications for the children's transfer of skills across contexts.

6. Initially the English-speaking teacher was unable to comment on or benefit from viewing the children in the Spanish setting. As soon as these lessons were translated, however, he made several suggestions about how his own lessons could be immediately modified to complement what was going on in the other classroom.

7. A total of 20 hours of videotaped data was collected during the months of March and June 1979. The goal in each case was to videotape the twelve target children at least twice in each type of lesson.

References

Au, K.
    1980   Participation Structures in a Reading Lesson with Hawaiian Children. Analysis of a Culturally Appropriate Instructional Event. Anthropology and Education Quarterly XI (2).
Carter, T., and R. Segura
    1979   Mexican-Americans in School: A Decade of Change. New York: College Entrance Examination Board.
Cole, M., J. Dore, W. Hall, and G. Dowley
    1978   Situation and Task in Children's Talk. Discourse Processes 1:119–176.
Cummins, J.
    1979   Linguistic Interdependence and the Educational Development of Bilingual Children. Review of Educational Research 49:222–251.
Dowley, McNamee, Gillian
    1979   The Social Interaction Origins of Narrative Skills. The Quarterly Newsletter of the Laboratory of Comparative Human Cognition 1(4):63–68.
Erickson, F., and G. Mohatt
    1980   Cultural Organization of Participant Structures in Two Classrooms of Indian Students. In Doing the Ethnography of Schooling. G.D. Spindler, ed.
Erickson, F., and J. Shultz
    1977   When Is a Context? Quarterly Newsletter of the Institute for Comparative Human Development 1(2):5–10.

Griffin, P.
1977 How and When does Reading Occur in the Classroom? Theory into Practice, December.
LaBelle, T.J., L.C. Moll, T. Weisner
1979 Context-Based Educational Evaluation: A Participant Research Strategy. Education Evaluation and Policy Analysis 1(3):85–93.
Laboratory of Comparative Human Cognition
1979 Cross-Cultural Psychology's Challenges to Our Ideas of Children and Development. American Psychologist 34(10).
Laboratory of Comparative Human Cognition
1983 Culture and Cognitive Development. *In* Mussen's Handbook of Child Psychology, Vol.1 History, Theory and Method. 4. W. Kessen, ed. New York: Wiley.
Leont'ev, A.
1973 Some Problems in Learning Russian as a Foreign Language (Essays on Psycholinguistics). Soviet Psychology 11(4), Summer.
Markova, A.
1978–79 The Teaching and Mastery of Language. Soviet Education, Vol. 21.
McDermott, R.P., and D. Roth
1979 The Social Organization of Behavior: Interactional Approaches. Annual Review of Anthropology 7:321–345.
Mehan, H.
1979 Learning Lessons. Cambridge, Massachusetts: Harvard University Press.
Moll, L.C.
1978 The Importance of the Social Situation in Assessing Bilingual Communicative Performance. Quarterly Newsletter of the Laboratory of Comparative Human Cognition 1(2).
Moll, L.C., E. Estrada, S.E. Diaz, and L. Lopes
1980 An Ethnography of a Bilingual Classroom. Final Report, National Institute of Education, Washington, D.C.
Shultz, J., S. Florio, and F. Erickson
1980 Where's the Floor?: Aspects of the Cultural Organization of Social Relationships in Communication at Home and at School. *In* Ethnography and Education: Children In and Out of School. P. Gilmore and A. Glatthorn, eds. Philadelphia: University of Pennsylvania Press.

366   CROSS-CULTURAL LITERACY

Siegler, R.R., and D.D. Richards
    1981   The Development of Intelligence. *In* Handbook of
            Human Intelligence. R. Sternberg, ed. Cambridge:
            Cambridge University Press.
Talyzina, N.F.
    1978   One of the Paths of Development of Soviet Learning
            Theory. Soviet Education 20(11).
Vygotsky, L.S.
    1978   Mind in Society. Cambridge, Mass.: Harvard
            University Press.
Watzlavick, P., J. Beavin, and D. Jackson
    1967   Pragmatics of Human Communication: A Study of
            Interactional Patterns, Pathologies and Paradoxes.
            New York: W.W. Norton and Co., Inc.
Wertsch, J.V.
    1979   A State of the Art Review of Soviet Research in
            Cognitive Psychology. Manuscript, Department of
            Linguistics, Northwestern University.
    1985   Vygotsky and the Social Formation of Mind. New
            York: Cambridge University Press.
Wertsch, J.V., ed.
    1981   The Concept of Activity in Soviet Psychology. White
            Plains, N.Y.: Sharpe.
Wood, D., J.S. Bruner, and G. Ross
    1976   The role of Tutoring in Problem-Solving. Journal of
            Child Psychology and Psychiatry, 17.
Zaporozhets, A.V.
    1980   Thought and Activity in Children. Soviet Psychology,
            18(2):9-23.

Communicative Competence in a Bilingual Early Childhood Classroom

Dinah Volk [1]

The Context

A four-year-old bilingual conversing with two friends as they sit around the art table in a bilingual Headstart classroom in New York City . . .

Transcript		Translation	
Nilda:	(to Patricia) Pero Kathy. Yo voy para casa de Kathy.	Nilda:	But Kathy. I'm gonna go to Kathy's house.
Nilda:	(to Kathy) **Right, Kathy? I'm going to your house?**	Nilda:	**Right, Kathy? I'm going to your house?**
Kathy:	(nods yes) You're gonna come next week.	Kathy:	You're gonna come next week.

Two four-year-old bilinguals conversing in the house corner of the same classroom . . .

Transcript		Translation	
Blanca:	(goes to house corner) **Ay Dios. ¡Mujer!** Yo no quiero . . .	Blanca:	**Oh goodness. Lady!** I don't want . . .
Nilda:	**Espérate. Déjame** . . .(runs behind counter, calls to Blanca) **Ven. Señora.**	Nilda:	**Wait. Let me . . . Come. Ma'am. Buy it from me**

367

(gestures to come) **Comprámela. Señora. Ven.** Dime—**Dame una medicina ¿ok Blanca?**	**Ma'am. Come.** Tell me—**Give me some medicine, ok Blanca?**
Blanca: **Pero . . .** Yo quiero una medicina para mi. (gestures to self)	Blanca: **But . . .** I want some medicine for me.
Nilda: **¿Para tu hermana?**	Nilda: **For your sister?**
Blanca: No, para mi.	Blanca: No, for me.
Nilda: (takes puzzle pieces to use for medicine for medicine) **Señora. Toma.** Me paga. **¡Págame! Este es mucho dinero que me tienes que pagar.**	Nilda: **Ma'am. Take it. Pay me. Pay me! You have to pay me a lot of money.**
Blanca: **Ay. Pero . . . no tengo dinerito, ¿ok?** (tries to take another piece from Nilda)	Blanca: **Oh no. But . . . I don't even have a little bit of money, ok?**

Those of us who study, teach, work, or live with bilingual children are often impressed with their communicative competence, their understanding of how to use language in socially appropriate ways, and their ability to do so. Many bilingual children display considerable skill in communicating in two languages in a variety of contexts with many different kinds of speech partners.

This study[2] was designed to increase our understanding of these competencies by providing a close look at the communicative competence of very young children who are becoming bilingual in the classroom. Its purpose was to describe, in depth, turn allocation in conversations with peers—one aspect of bilingual classroom language use and a critical conversational skill.[3] The study's findings revealed that the four-year-old participants were able to use turn allocators to create cohesive conversations with peers in both Spanish and in English. When they were using allocators, their language appropriately reflected important aspects of the bilingual classroom context.

Theoretical Considerations

As a study of communicative competence, this research was based on the assumption that children's language is best understood when studied as it is used in context. Language use in context was analyzed as a meaningful and rule-governed aspect of social behavior (Hymes 1971). Research has shown that, especially for children, context is intimately related to the meaning of what is said and heard (Cook-Gumperz 1981).

Conversations were studied as communicative events and, therefore, as systematically organized social encounters. When all participants in a conversation share an understanding of the event and its inherent obligations, they can then converse cooperatively (Sacks, Schegloff & Jefferson 1974; Schegloff 1972). Because of the need for such understanding and cooperative behavior, it is often difficult for very young children to master some aspects of conversations (Ervin-Tripp 1979; Umiker-Sebeok 1976).

Nevertheless, as demonstrated here, by four years of age children are competent in one of the most basic of these aspects, turn allocation: the use of communicative acts that obligate speakers to take turns. With the cooperative use of allocators such as those used and boldfaced in the examples above, children initiate and maintain conversations with others.

For example, in the conversation around the art table, Nilda first makes an assertion in Spanish to Patricia ("Yo voy para casa de Kathy.") that requires no response. She then switches to English to speak to Kathy, employing other-selecting allocators (**"Right, Kathy? I'm going to your house?"**) which require a response, and so place a conversational obligation on Kathy to take a turn. In the house corner conversation, Blanca frequently uses self-selecting allocators (**"ay Dios," "pero"**) to signal the beginning of her own turns and to create space for them in the flow of talk. The children's use of and response to these allocators in Spanish and English is one sign of the cooperative nature of their conversations.

It is important to note that much research on bilingual children's conversations provides a limited view of their competencies by focusing only on their use of English, the language they know least (Hatch 1978; Keller-Cohen and Dennis 1975; Peck 1978). Other research on bilingual children's language use has focused broadly on the use of two languages in context, on dominance, or on specific aspects of communicative competence such as code switching and coherence in discourse (Attinasi, Pedraza, Poplack and Pousada 1982; Genishi 1981; McClure 1981; Olmedo-Williams 1979; Solá 1983; Zentella 1981). Consequently, in order to provide a rich description of turn allocation—a little explored aspect of bilingual communicative competence—this research focused on the allocating forms used in two languages and the functions they served.[4] The researcher also explored the relation of turn allocation to speech partner's language dominance, to activity, to code switching, and to acknowledgment. This chapter reports the findings concerning allocation in relation to speech partner's language dominance and activity, two elements of the bilingual classroom context.

Participants and Setting

The participants in the study were Nilda, Blanca, Javier, and Pepe, all four-year-old children. Their ethnicity reflected the character of the neighborhood around the Headstart Center in New York City where the study was conducted: Nilda was Ecuadorian and Dominican, Blanca was Dominican, Javier was Puerto Rican, and Pepe was Peruvian. All four were native Spanish speakers who had entered the Center when they were three years old, with a minimal receptive knowledge of English. In the spring of their first school year, when most of the language use data was collected, all had turned four and were using both Spanish and English in the classroom. They were beginning to become bilingual.

The two teachers in the participants' classroom were

both bilingual: the head teacher was a native English speaker who spoke Spanish; her assistant was Dominican, a native Spanish speaker who spoke English. About a third of the children in the room were English monolingual Black Americans. Another third were Hispanic English dominant bilinguals. The rest were Hispanic Spanish dominant bilinguals like the participants.

As a matter of principle, the staff of the Headstart Center defined their program as bilingual and were committed to the development of children's learning in Spanish as they acquired English. Although English was the dominant and more prestigious language, Spanish was spoken throughout the school. In the classroom studied, there was no direct instruction in either language and the teachers tended to use more English as the year progressed. The organization of this classroom was open and child centered. During free playtime, children were able to select activities and speech partners. Other times of the day were more structured.

Methodology

The collection of language use data employed ethnographic techniques developed in previous research (Attinasi et al. 1981; Erickson, Cazden, Carrasco, and Maldonado-Guzmán 1980; Erickson and Shultz 1981). These techniques included a year of participant observation in the classroom, interviewing, and audio and videotaping. Field notes taken on patterns of social interaction and language use in the classroom were combined with transcripts of the immediate situation as shown on tape as well as with interviews of the teachers, school staff, and the children's parents at home and in the school to provide a rich context for the interpretation of the language use data.

Children's conversations as communicative events were identified first in the transcripts. Within the conversations, turn allocators as communicative acts were then found, and, finally, allocating episodes consisting of allocators and acknowledgements were noted (Erickson

1980). The linguistic form of each allocator was coded, as was the function. Thus identified, allocators were analysed in relation to aspects of the situational and conversational contexts. For each variable, the frequencies with which allocators were used in Spanish and English in the relevant categories were tabulated and percentages were calculated. Patterns in the use of allocators in relation to these variables were then described.

Results: Turn Allocation in the Classroom Context

Allocation and Speech Partner's Language Dominance

Like language use in general, language dominance has been shown to be context-specific (Pedraza and Pousada, in this volume). Consequently, just before the taping was begun, teachers, parents and researchers categorized all the children in the classroom into two groups—Spanish speakers and English speakers— depending on the language they spoke most often and apparently most competently in that Headstart classroom context. The Spanish speakers were all bilinguals who were dominant in Spanish and less proficient in English. The English speakers were divided into bilinguals who were English dominant, with limited proficiency in Spanish, and monolinguals who spoke only English. Nilda, Blanca, Javier, and Pepe were all classified as bilingual Spanish speakers.

The analysis of allocation in relation to speech partner's language dominance showed that the four children studied used 59% of their allocators when talking with Spanish speakers and 38% when talking with English speakers (see Table 1). Of those allocators to English speakers, 24% were used with English monolinguals and 14 percent were used with English dominant bilinguals. It is significant that the four children selected the language appropriate to the speech partner's dominance for 90% of all allocators used.

This sensitivity to an important part of the bilingual classroom context is demonstrated in the example at the beginning of the chapter. Nilda typically switches from her use of Spanish with Patricia, who is Spanish dominant, to English for a turn allocator addressed to Kathy, who is English monolingual. In this way, Nilda was able to converse with both friends while they were sitting around the art table painting together.

In addition to demonstrating a high degree of accuracy in accommodating their choice of allocating to their speech partner's language dominance by distinguishing between Spanish and English speakers, the four bilingual participants also distinguished between English speakers who were English monolingual and knew no Spanish and those who were English dominant and who knew some Spanish, if only receptively. Specifically, while the children used Spanish for only 3% of the allocators directed at English monolinguals, they used Spanish for 17% of those directed toward English dominant peers. English was used for only 6% of the allocators directed at Spanish dominant peers (see Table 1). The children apparently knew which English speakers were bilingual and which were not.

In the following example, Nilda demonstrates her understanding that Gaby, who is English dominant, understands Spanish, too. In other contexts she addresses him in English; but here, as he intrudes growling, on all fours, on a group of Spanish-speaking girls playing house, she uses Spanish for a turn allocating question. Nilda was never heard to use Spanish in the same circumstances with Kathy, an English monolingual.

Example 1

	Transcript		Translation
Blanca:	(grabs for Nilda, points to Gaby, wails)	Blanca:	
Nilda:	(to Blanca) Ese no es un monstruito. Ese es papi.	Nilda:	This isn't a little monster. This is daddy.
Nilda:	(to Gaby) **¿Verdad que tu eres el papá?**	Nilda:	**Right you're the dad?**
Gaby:	(nods yes) Woof.	Gaby:	Woof.

Table 1

Language of Allocators Used by Four Bilingual Participants with Speech Partners of Differing Language Dominance

Dominance of Speech Partner	Spanish speakers/ Spanish dominant				English speakers										Total				Matched allocators	
					Eng. dominant				Eng. monoling.				Speech partner unclear							% of all alloc.
	Sp.		Eng.		Sp.		Eng.		Sp.		Eng.				Sp.		Eng.			
Lang. used	f	%	f	%	f	%	f	%	f	%	f	%	f	%	f	%	f	%	f	%
Subtotal by language used	317	94	19	6	14	17	66	83	4	3	130	97			341	60	226	40	513	90
Total	336	59			80				134				17	3	567	100				

(brace grouping: 80 + 134 = 214, 38)

(Eng. monoling. subtotal: 134, 24)

The children also distinguished between English dominant peers and English monolinguals by using some different allocators in English with each, not simply by using more Spanish with those who were English dominant. That is, when speaking English to English dominant peers, they often used the same allocators that they used characteristically in Spanish with Spanish speakers. For example, the chidren tended to use exclamations functioning as attention directors (**"¡Ay!"**/**"Oh no!"**) and one-word questions employed as requests for information and clarification (**"¿Qué?"**/**"What?"**) more often with English dominants in English just as they did with Spanish dominants in Spanish. In contrast, when speaking English to the English monolinguals, the children tended to use different allocators more often: imperatives functioning as requests for action (**"Quítatelo."**/**"Take it off."**); deictics functioning as summonses (**"Aquí."**/**"Here."**); yes/no questions as requests for information (**"¿Eres mi amiga?"**/**"Are you my friend?"**) and tag questions as requests for acknowledgment (**"Soy la mamá, ¿ok?"**/**"I'm the mommy, ok?"**)

The accuracy with which the children matched their choice of allocating language, form, and function to the language dominance of their speech partner suggested that the analysis of the few nonmatches of language to dominance would be fruitful. These nonmatches were, thus, analyzed within the context of the surrounding conversations, taking into consideration the group around the participants, the topic, and the activity involved. In almost all of the instances analyzed, the nonmatch of allocator to dominance appeared to enhance the child's efforts at turn allocation. This was possible because most nonmatches (89%) were used with bilingual peers who could, at minimum, understand their nondominant language.

In half of the nonmatches (51%), participants used the language that was more appropriate to the group in which they and their speech partners were playing. In groups of mixed language dominance, the children accommodated to the monolinguals present or used the dominant language of the majority of peers in the group.

In Example 1, Nilda continues to use Spanish with Gaby, who is English dominant, since all the other members of the group are Spanish speakers.

In other instances, nonmatches occurred when children took on authority roles in dramatic play and wanted to emphasize their allocators (19%), or when they wanted to allocate in a way that was apparently too difficult for them in their second language (19%). In only a few instances of nonmatched allocating (11%) did participants use a language that the speech partner probably could not understand. In sum, these four-year-old bilinguals almost always made accurate assessments about the language dominance of their speech partners and, on the basis of those judgments, used allocators in two languages to successfully participate in peer conversations.

Allocation and Activity

For the purposes of the analysis, classroom activities for which language use data were collected were divided into seven categories: table/floor play; dramatic play; organizing dramatic play; lunch; toy/book allocation; clean-up, and other. All but lunch and clean-up occurred during free play time.

The findings show that the children's use of turn allocators during the activities was influenced in three ways. First, allocators were used more frequently in some activities than in others (see Table 2). For example, most allocators were used during table/floor play (30%) and during dramatic play (25%), both activities which required peer interaction and cooperation. Clean-up time, on the other hand, when children usually carried out tasks individually under a teacher's supervision, accounted for few of the allocators (1%).

Second, there were distinctions among the various activities in the allocating forms used and the functions they served. For example, while imperatives requesting action (**"Toma."**/**"Take it."**) were most frequent in all activities, yes/no questions requesting information (**"¿Quieres jugar?"**/**"Wanna play?"**) were the next most frequently used allocators during table/floor play, as

Table 2
Language of Allocators Used by Four Bilingual Participants During Different Activities

Activity	Table/floor play				Dramatic play				Organizing dram. play				Lunch				Toy/book allocation			
Lang. used	Sp.		Eng.		Sp.		Eng.		Sp.		Eng.		Sp.		Eng.		Sp.		Eng.	
	f	%	f	%	f	%	f	%	f	%	f	%	f	%	f	%	f	%	f	%
Subtotals by language	72	43	96	57	120	84	23	16	76	72	30	28	35	58	25	42	23	53	20	47
Totals	168		30		143		25		106		18		60		10		43		8	

Activity	Other				Unclear				Clean-up				Total			
Lang. used	Sp.		Eng.		Sp.		Eng.		Sp.		Eng.		Sp.		Eng.	
	f	%	f	%	f	%	f	%	f	%	f	%	f	%	f	%
Subtotals by language	9	28	23	72	6	67	3	33	0	0	6	100	341	60	226	40
Totals	32		6		9		2		6		1		567		100	

children sought and shared information necessary to their mutual play. In the example below, Pepe, Javier, Benny, and Rolando keep a color matching game going with requests for action in Spanish, since everyone in the group is dominant in that language. When Tommy, who is English dominant, approaches, Javier allocates to him in English, using a request for information to draw Tommy into the conversation and the game.

Example 2

	Transcript		Translation
Pepe:	**Coge el white, Benny.** (points to Benny)	Pepe:	**Pick up the white one, Benny.**
Javier:	**Coge este.** (pushes balloon across the table)	Javier:	**Pick up this one.**
Benny:	(picks up balloon)	Benny:	
Rolando:	**Toma.** (hands Tommy balloon) **Toma. Toma.**	Rolando:	**Take it. Take it. Take it.**
Tommy:	(takes balloon)	Tommy:	
Javier:	**Here Tommy.** (hands Tommy balloon) **Tommy. You know-bb- you wanna play?** (nods head)	Javier:	**Here Tommy. Tommy. You know-bb- you wanna play?**
Tommy:	Yeah.	Tommy:	Yeah.
Javier:	Ok. (rolls dice)	Javier:	Ok.

Similarly, during dramatic play, vocative/role titles functioning as summonses (**"Blanca,"** **"¡Señora!"**/ **"Blanca,"** **"Ma'am!"**) were the second most frequent allocator employed after imperatives, as children used names and roles, real and imaginary to draw others into their dramatic conversations. The second example at the beginning of this chapter illustrates the use of these allocators. When the children were organizing dramatic play, they frequently used tag questions requesting acknowledgement (**"Soy la mamá, ¿ok?"**/"I'm the

mommy, ok?") as they continually confirmed with each other the establishment of certain roles. When seated around the lunch table with a group of peers, the children frequently used appositional beginnings as self-selecting attention directors (**"Pero . . . pero . . ."**/**"But . . . but . . ."**) because of the need to compete for attention when they were attempting to begin their own turns. In all these ways, the characteristic interaction of each activity influenced the kinds of allocators used.

Third, the proportion of allocators used in Spanish and English varied by activity (see Table 2). For example, most of the allocators used during dramatic play (84%) and when organizing dramatic play (72%) were in Spanish. This apparently occurred because the girls, who spoke Spanish more often, frequently engaged in dramatic play, acting out home and family scenes in Spanish.

In contrast, over half the allocators used during table/ floor play (57%) and all of those used during clean-up time (100%) were in English. English was frequently used in table/floor play because the boys, who spoke it more often, played together around tables or in the block area on the floor much more often than the girls. During clean-up time, the use of English was related to the teachers' customary directions to the group in that language.

The results discussed here indicate that the relation of turn allocating to activity was complex, taking into account the communicative needs of speakers during each activity; the associations of one language or the other with specific activities in the classroom context; the speech partners' language dominance, and the language choices made by the participants themselves.

Discussion of Results

The literature on code switching has suggested several "rules" of bilingual discourse relevant to speech partner's language dominance (Genishi 1981; Zentella 1981). The primary rule is that bilinguals usually accommodate their language choice to the language dominance of the speech partner. The results of the present study confirm evidence in other research showing that this rule is part of the conversational competence of children as young as four years old (Genishi 1985).

It has also been hypothesized that there is a second rule that parallels the first: "When your listeners are of different linguistic abilities, favor the monolinguals . . ." (Genishi 1981). The findings here suggest still another rule: "When your listeners are of different linguistic abilities and none are monolingual, favor the dominance of most of the members of the group." This indicates that the influence of the group sometimes superseded the individual speech partner's in the participants' use of turn allocators.

The findings also suggest that, contrary to some of the evidence in the literature, these four-year-olds were able to do more than simply divide speech partners into two categories: English and Spanish speakers (McClure 1981). Like the older children described in other research, they not only distinguished between English and Spanish speakers but also between speech partners with varying degrees of competence in English and Spanish, some monolinguals and some bilinguals (Genishi 1981; McClure, Saville-Troike, and Fritz 1982). Most often they made and acted on these assessments appropriately when allocating, thereby making the maintenance of conversations more likely in this bilingual classroom context.

Of course, the children did not always accommodate the language of their allocators to their speech partner's language dominance. Of the nonmatches that occurred, a few could only be explained as unsuccessful attempts to communicate, since the participants used Spanish with English monolinguals. Other researchers have described the same "communicative tactic" of last resort among Spanish-speaking second graders in attempts to communicate with English-speaking peers (McClure et al. 1982).

Most of the nonmatches, however, occurred because the children distinguished between monolinguals and bilinguals. With bilinguals, English and Spanish dominant, the children used the nondominant language as another allocating resource; the nonmatch itself could convey a message.

In addition to speech partner's language dominance, the activities in which children engage have been shown to influence their language choice and the formal and/or functional aspects of any single language used (Carrasco, Vera, and Cazden 1981; Fillmore 1977; Mace-Matluck, Hoover, and Domínguez 1981; Tikunoff and Vásquez-Faría 1982). In previous studies researchers have primarily examined school-age children in classrooms or in experimental situations, and the activity categories researchers used have been based on those contexts. As a result, researchers have compared talk in structured and unstructured settings, in instructional and informal settings, and/or between children and adults. The results of the present study, however, suggest that within the context of what others have called "informal" or "unstructured" play among peers, there are both similarities and variations in the allocators used during the different activities. These children displayed overall competence in allocating, while they also showed that their repertoires varied across activities. They used allocators in appropriate and creative ways to initiate and maintain the peer conversations in which they participated during different activities. This finding confirms what other research has demonstrated: that beyond the scope of their structured interactions with adults, children's talk in classrooms is richer and more varied than most teachers imagine (Carrasco 1981; Carrasco et al. 1981; Fillmore 1977).

The Communicative Competence of Bilingual Four-year-olds: Implications for Research and Education

The turn-allocating language used by Nilda, Blanca, Javier, and Pepe in their classroom was highly varied and sensitive to context. The picture presented of their competencies here is a very different one from that conveyed by one-dimensional labels such as "Spanish dominant," "language deprived," or "limited English proficient" that are usually given to children such as the participants.

This picture of competence raises a number of issues and questions for both researchers and teachers.

First, the results show that the children were sensitive to two aspects of the classroom situation simultaneously; they could vary their allocating language in response to differing degrees of dominance, while making it appropriate to a diverse array of activities. Further research is needed to investigate how bilingual children acquire the ability to make their languages contextually appropriate. How early, where, and in what kinds of interactions are these aspects of communicative competence acquired? Few studies of the development of bilingual competence have focused on children like Nilda, Blanca, Javier, and Pepe who grow up in the rich environment of extended families within bilingual communities (Huerta-Macias 1983). In what ways are their experiences different from those of children raised almost exclusively by two parents who maintain a strict separation of the languages? Other studies have described several factors which may all be parts of such bilingual language socialization: direct instruction by family members in culturally appropriate ways of speaking (Eisenberg 1986), community norms of "respeto" that require accommodation to adults' language preferences (Attinasi et al. 1982; Zentella 1982), modelling by adults from which rules can be inferred (Zentella 1982). The processes through which very young children such as those studied here are socialized as bilinguals in family, peer, and community contexts have yet to be explored longitudinally.

Second, this description of the children's bilingual language competencies suggests that they possessed some conversational skills which are not in the repertoires of monolingual children. Because of their experience as speakers of a minority language, functioning in bilingual community and classroom contexts, these children were aware of speech partner's language dominance, an aspect of context not usually relevant to children who are monolingual speakers of a majority language. Further research might explore this aspect of competence in the same way that children's knowledge of the appropiate use of different registers has been studied. For teachers, this evidence of heightened awareness in social encounters leads to questions of how language development curricula can build on bilingual children's special communicative strengths. Are bilingual settings most conducive to the development of the competencies described here for both bilingual and monolingual children? What aspects of the early childhood curriculum can use and expand such competencies? As recent research has emphasized, educators can learn to identify the strengths and knowledge bilingual children bring to school and use them ". . . as legitimate and powerful resources for improving students' performance in schools . . ." (Díaz, Moll, and Mehan 1986:54).

Third, while these results show the breadth of the children's competence, they also raise the question of limitations. Although other research has suggested that it is difficult for children under six to simultaneously consider as many contextual variables as adults can, we do not fully understand the dimensions of this developmental constraint among young bilinguals (Genishi 1981). What is the relation of very young children's bilingualism, as well as their experience in varied contexts, to their ability to sort out the many contextual variables which may be relevant to language choice, form, and function in their conversations? How can this aspect of communicative competence be expanded by providing children with new experiences in the classroom?

Fourth, this research highlights the usefulness of ethnography to teachers and researchers. With practice, ethnographic techniques can be used to develop an understanding of both children's communicative competencies in the classroom and the relation of their competencies to others acquired and used in the broader community. Although the present study focused on the classroom, sufficient ethnographic data were collected in the Headstart Center as a whole, and from the children's parents at home, to suggest that the children's use of allocators was also influenced by aspects of the context beyond the immediate situation in which the conversations took place. For example, Javier often played with a group of English- and Spanish-dominant boys who usually spoke English together. While there were more English dominant children in the group and they therefore spoke English often, it is possible that there were also other influences on the boys' use of English in allocating.

As noted earlier, English was the more prestigious language in the Center, and both teachers in the classroom tended to use more English as the year progressed. It may be that this emphasis on English influenced the language choice—and hence the allocators—of Javier and his playmates. Why the group of boys was apparently more influenced in this way than the girls is an important question for future research on classroom language use. A possible explanation may be the children's participation in gender-related patterns of language use within their communities, a process described in other research (Attinasi et al. 1982; Solá 1985; Zentella 1982).

In summary, the analysis of turn allocating by these four children shows that, by four years of age, they were well integrated into a complex sociolinguistic system that included their experiences in the community and in their homes, their experiences at school, their bilingual language competencies, the peers with whom they played, the activities in which they engaged, and the processes of socialization within their communities. Both the Spanish and English allocators they used to signal the beginning of their own turns and to obligate others to respond reflected immediate aspects of the situation and the broader context too. Although these children were only four years old, they were already competent allocators and active conversationalists in a complex bilingual classroom context.

Endnotes

1. Dr. Dinah Volk is currently an Assistant Professor at Cleveland State University.
2. The author would like to thank Dr. Dabney Narváez and Dr. Marietta Saravia-Shore for their helpful comments during the preparation of this chapter.

The study from which the chapter was drawn was supported in part by grant #80:26 from the Research Foundation of the National Council of Teachers of English.

    3. This study was part of a joint research project developed with Dr. Dabney Narváez. The companion study (Narváez, 1984) focused on requestive language used by the same participants.

    4. Allocating forms studied:

self-selecting allocators	
exclamation	"¡Ay!"/"Oh no!"
appositional beginning	"Pero . . . pero . . ."
	"But . . . but . . ."
affirmative	"Sí..."/"Yes . . ."
other-selecting allocators	
vocative/role title	"¡Pepe!" "Señor"/
	¡Pepe!" "Sir."
deictic	"Aquí."/"Here."
imperative	"Quítatelo."/"Take it off."
assertion	"Está pisando en mi cartera."/You're standing on my purse."
wh-question	"¿Qué es eso?"/ "What's that?"
yes/no question/ intonation question	"¿Eres mi amiga?"/ "You my friend?"
one word question	"¿Qué?"/"What?"
partial repetition with	("Vamos pa' fuera.")
question information	"¿Pa' fuera?) ("Let's go out.") "Go out?"
tag question	"Es mio, ¿verdad?"/ "It's mine, right?
routine gambit	"¿Y tu sabes lo que hice?"/"And you know what I did?"
Allocating functions studied:	
self-selecting allocators	
attention director	"¡Ey! . . . ahora . . ."/ "Hey! . . . now . . ."
other selecting allocators	"Rolando. Mira."/
summons	"Rolando. Look.
request for action	"Dámelo."/Gimme it."

request for information	"¿Qué quieres?"/"What you want?"
request for clarification	("¿Viniste ayer?") "Qué?"/("You came yesterday?") "What?"
request for acknowledgment	"Soy la mamá, ¿ok?"/ "I'm the mommy, ok?"
request for elaboration	("¡Mami!") "¿Uh?"/ ("Mommy!") "Huh?"

References

Attinasi J., P. Pedraza, S. Poplack, and A. Pousada
  1982   Intergenerational Perspectives on Bilingualism: From
          Community to Classroom. (Final Report No. G-78-
          0091. Washington, D.C.: National Institute of
          Education.
Carrasco, R. L.
  1981   Expanded Awareness of Student Performance: A Case
          of Applied Ethnographic Monitoring in a Bilingual
          Classroom. In Culture and the Bilingual Classroom:
          Studies in Classroom Ethnography. H.J. Trueba, G.P.
          Guthrie & K.H. Au, eds. Rowley, Mass.: Newbury
          House.
Carrasco, R.L., A. Vera, and C.B. Cazden
  1981   Aspects of Bilingual Students' Communicative
          Competence in the Classroom. In Latino Language
          and Communicative Behavior: Advances in Discourse
          Processes Vol. 6. R.P. Durán, ed. Norwood, N.J.:
          Ablex.
Cook-Gumperz, J.
  1981   Persuasive Talk—The Social Organization of Children's
          Talk. In Ethnography and Language in Educational
          Settings. J.L. Green and C. Wallat, eds. Norwood,
          N.J.: Ablex.
Díaz, S., L.C. Moll, and H. Mehan
  1986   Sociocultural Resources: A Context Specific Approach.
          In Bilingual Education Office, Calif. State Dept. of
          Education, Sacramento, Beyond Language: Social and

Cultural Factors in Schooling Language Minority Students. Los Angeles, Calif.: Evaluation, Dissemination, and Assessment Center, California State University.

Eisenberg, A.
1986 Teasing: Verbal Play in Two Mexicano Homes. *In* Language Socialization Across Cultures. B.B. Schieffelin and E. Ochs, eds. Cambridge University Press.

Erickson, F.D., C.B. Cazden, R.L. Carrasco, and A.A. Maldonado-Guzmán
1980 Social and Cultural Organization of Interaction in Classrooms. (Second Year Progress Report No. G-0099). Washington, D.C.: National Institute of Education.

Erickson, F.D., and J. Shultz
1981 'When is a Context?: Some Issues and Methods in the Analysis of Social Competence. *In* Ethnography and Language in Educational Settings. J.L. Green and C. Wallat, eds. Norwood, N.J.: Ablex.

Ervin-Tripp, S.
1979 Children's Verbal Turn-Taking. *In* Developmental Pragmatics. E. Ochs & B.B. Schieffelin, eds. New York: Academic Press.

Fillmore, L.W.
1977 The Second Time Around: Cognitive and Social Strategies in Second Language Acquisition. Unpublished doctoral dissertation. Stanford University. DAI, 39, 6443A. University Microfilms No. 77-07085.

Genishi, C.
1981 Codeswitching in Chicano Six-year-olds. *In* Latino Language and Communicative Behavior: Advances in Discourse Processes. Vol. 6. R.P. Durán, ed. Norwood, N.J.: Ablex.

Genishi, C.
1985 Observing Communicative Performance in Young Children. *In* Observing the Language Learner, A. Jaggar and M.T. Smith-Burke, eds. Newark, Del.: International Reading Association.

Hatch, E.
1978 Discourse Analysis and Second Language Acquisition. *In* Second Language Acquisition: A Book of Readings. E. Hatch, ed. Rowley, Mass.: Newbury House.

Huerta-Macias, A.
  1983   Child Bilingualism: To Switch or Not To Switch? *In* Early Childhood Bilingual Education: A Hispanic Perspective. T.H. Escobedo, ed. New York: Teachers College Press.

Hymes, D.
  1971   On Linguistic Theory, Communicative Competence, and the Education of Disadvantaged Children. *In* Anthropological Perspectives on Education. M. Wax, S. Diamond & F.O. Gearing, eds. New York: Basic Books.

Keller-Cohen, D. and J. Dennis
  1975   The Acquisition of Conversational Competence. *In* Parasession on Functionalism. R.E. Grossman, L.J. San & T.J. Vance, eds. Chicago: Chicago Linguistic Society.

Mace-Matluck B., W.A. Hoover, and D. Domínguez
  1981   Variation in Language Use of Spanish-English Bilingual Children in Three Settings: Findings and Implications. Paper presented at the meeting of the American Educational Research Association, Los Angeles, California, April.

McClure, E.
  1981   Formal and Functional Aspects of the Code-Switched Discourse of Bilingual Children. *In* Latino Language and Communicative Behavior: Advances in Discourse Processes (Vol. 6). R.P. Durán, ed. Norwood, NJ: Ablex.

McClure, E., M. Saville-Troike, and M. Fritz
  1982   Children's Communicative Tactics Across Language Boundaries. Paper presented at the Chicago Linguistics Society, Chicago, April.

Narváez, D.H.
  1983   Making Requests: An Ethnographic Study of Communicative Competence in the Bilingual Early Childhood Classroom. Unpublished doctoral dissertation. New York University.

Olmedo-Williams, I.
  1979   Functions of Code-switching in a Spanish-English Bilingual Classroom. Paper presented at the First Delaware Symposium on Language Studies, Newark, Del., October.

Peck, S.
  1978   Child-child Discourse in Second Language Acquisition. *In* Second Language Acquisition: A Book of Readings. E. Hatch ed. Rowley, Mass.: Newbury House.

Pedraza, P., and A. Pousada
1987   Bilingualism In and Out of School: Ethnographic Perspectives on the Determination of Language 'Dominance.' In this volume.
Sacks, H., E.A. Schegloff, & G. Jefferson
1974   A Simplest Systematics for the Organization of Turn-taking in Conversations. Language 50:696–735.
Schegloff, E.A.
1972   Sequencing in Conversational Openings. *In* Directions in Sociolinguistics: The Ethnography of Communication. J.J. Gumperz & D. Hymes eds. New York: Holt, Rinehart & Winston.
Solá, Michèle
1984   Coherence, Contradiction and Resistance in Child Discourse. Paper presented at the meeting of the New York Child Language Group, New York, N.Y. May.
Tikunoff, W.J., and J.A. Vásquez-Faría
1982   Successful Instruction for Bilingual Schooling. Peabody Journal of Education 59:234–271.
Umiker-Sebeok, D.J.
1976   The Conversational Skills of Preschool Children. Unpublished doctoral dissertation. Indiana University. DAI, 37, 2161A. University Microfilms No. 76-21609.
Zentella, A.C.
1981   Tá bien, You could answer me en cualquier idioma: Puerto Rican Codeswitching in Bilingual Classrooms. *In* Latino Language and Communicative Behavior: Advances in Discourse Processes. R.P. Durán, ed. Vol. 6. Norwood, N.J.: Ablex.
Zentella, A.C.
1982   "Hablamos los dos: We Speak Both": Growing up Bilingual in El Barrio. Unpublished doctoral dissertation. University of Pennsylvania. DAI, 42, 3142A.

Language Use, Lesson Engagement, and Participation Structures: A Microethnographic Analysis of Two Language Arts Lessons in a Bilingual First-Grade Classroom

Robert L. Carrasco
Carmel T. Acosta
Sylvia de la Torre-Spencer[1]

Introduction

This classroom microethnography analyzes the language use and participation structures of a group of Spanish-dominant bilingual first-grade students, focusing on teachers and students' methods and strategies relative to communication and engagement in academic tasks. The students were observed and videotaped during two small-group language arts lessons, both structured around an instructional game: one group was led by a bilingual, bicultural Chicana teacher; the other by a monolingual English-speaking teacher. Four of the five students participated in both lessons, which took place on the same day and in the same classroom. This research was done in conjunction with the Harvard-Michigan State Bilingual Classroom Project, "Social and Cultural Organization of Interaction of Classrooms of Bilingual Students," funded by NIE and conducted by Erickson, Carrasco, [Maldonado-] Guzman, and Cazden.[2]

The underlying premise of the study is that teaching and learning are mutually influenced, so that, as in Erickson's (1980:3) analysis, a successful lesson is a cooperative accomplishment of both teacher and students:

> Cooperative social activity in the conduct of lesson discourse is fundamental to its organization and meaning. Some of this cooperation is found in the communication of referential content, some in the performance of communicative actions such as prodding, warning, requesting, and insisting. An additional aspect of social cooperation in lesson discourse—apparently in all discourse— is found in the use of verbal behavior to maintain coordination of everyone's participation in interaction as it is happening across moments of real time. Study of real time coordination of social action in and through communicative behavior is among the most recent areas of research of sociolinguistics. From this perspective, conversation is viewed as an intimate partnership. The partners seem to be relying on each other's knowledge of a signal system regulating their mutual participation.

These two videotaped language arts lessons have been used to study how students and teachers interactionally cooperate (or do not) in academic lesson engagement, and this process analyzed across moments of real time. The videotaped lessons are similar in class population, since four of five Spanish-dominant bilingual students are participants in both. They are also similar in structure: in both lessons instructional games are employed as vehicles for transmitting the academic subject matter as well as serving to keep the students engaged in the tasks. The lessons differ in that one is taught by a monolingual English-speaking teacher teaching English language arts, while the other is taught by a bilingual, bicultural Spanish and English-speaking teacher teaching Spanish language arts. Furthermore, it is important to mention that these two lessons took place on the same day and in the same classroom environment. These similarities and differences provide a contrastive view for the investigation of communicative activities in instructional contexts.

A general assumption underlying the rationale for bilingual education is that monolingual English-speaking teachers who work with Spanish-dominant bilingual children encounter difficulty in teaching academic content because of language and cultural differences. It is also assumed, on the other hand, that bilingual, bicultural teachers' use of the children's native language would facilitate the teaching of both academic and non-academic content. The contrast provided by the two lessons studied allows us to examine, in part, the quality of interaction in the teaching of bilingual students, a fundamental line of inquiry based on the assumption stated by the U.S. Commission on Civil Rights (1973:7):

> The heart of the educational process is in the interaction between teacher and student. It is through this interaction that the school system makes its major impact upon the child. The way the teacher interacts with the student is a major determinant of the quality of education the child receives.

The body of knowledge produced by educational research in the 1970's suggests that teachers should allocate more time to academic subjects and that students should be kept engaged in such tasks (Stallings, 1980). But this recommendation is not very helpful to teachers, particularly bilingual ones, unless more specific statements are made about how to use academic time, how to engage students, and in what types of academic activities they should be engaged. There is a need to go beyond the simplistic notions of academic learning time and engagement; we must (1) study the academic activities and strategies that teachers are presently using to keep their students engaged, (2) investigate if, in fact, the students and teachers are engaged and on task interactionally during these activities, and (3) explore the types of activities that are more appropriate and more conducive to learning the academic content in question.

Employing a comparative case study approach, we have begun to address this need by attempting to describe and understand the process of engagement in a bilingual, bicultural setting.

Some leading researchers in this area have observed that we still know very little about what happens inside the bilingual classroom (Cazden et al. 1980; Erickson et al. 1978). Most of the research available has not focused on the dynamics of the bilingual classroom, "even though the consensus of expert opinion is definitely that the school environment is of over-riding importance with respect to bilingual education outcomes" (Fishman 1977:32).

An ERIC search on studies of the social and cultural organization of interaction and teacher-student and peer interactions in bilingual classroom contexts reveal the lack of basic qualitative research in these settings. While there are a few on-going classroom ethnographic efforts at present, there are relatively few studies available that have focused on the dynamics of the bilingual classroom (e.g., Carrasco et al. 1981; Moll 1980). Fishman (1977:32) wrote that studies of bilingual classroom dynamics were "all little more than gleams in the eyes of a few researchers;" this is still true in 1981. It is no wonder that bilingual education is poorly understood. Erickson (1980), we believe, is right in stating that "we need stories" on bilingual classroom life if we are to begin to understand bilingual education. This is but one attempt to meet the need.

Methodology

Ethnography has been suggested as the appropriate approach in this endeavor (Erickson 1978; Mehan 1981), and a few researchers have begun doing ethnographic studies. Ethnography is an attempt to describe a particular culture to gain an understanding of it, a "process of constructing through direct personal observation of social behavior, a theory of the working of a particular culture in terms as close as possible to the way members of that culture view the universe and organize their behavior within it" (Bauman 1972:157). Ethnographic inquiry's initial orientation toward discovery rather than verification is especially appropriate here. (Moll 1980; Carrasco 1980; Erickson et al. 1981).

Microethnography is an attempt to describe a situation of relevance within a culture using a more focused approach. It is an investigation of the organizational structure of interaction, both verbal and nonverbal, in contexts that determine the social meaning of behavior from moment to moment. (For extensive definitions and discussions on the microethnographic process, see Erickson and Shultz 1977 and Trueba 1980.)[3] The basic unit of analysis involved is the speech community—in this case, the school class. Within the classroom, the various instructional and noninstructional situations of relevance to the teachers, students, and researchers are studied. These situations include the lesson process as well as lining up, getting ready, executing morning business, and the like. The intention of such study is to gain an understanding of the ways in which the social roles of teachers and children (i.e., participation structures) help to create the quality of interaction and instruction.

An Overview of the NIE Study

Erickson, Carrasco, Vera, and Cazden (1978) began the process of observing and videotaping two bilingual first-grade classrooms in the heart of the Chicano community in Chicago. There were six major periods of observation and taping: early in the months of September, October and December of 1978; a week at a time in the months of February and March; and two weeks in April and May of 1979. We collected data in various forms: (a) videotapes; (b) field notes; (c) teacher questionnaires; (d) informal and formal interviews of teachers; e) photographs of each participant, labelled with names and other data; (f) information on aides and student teachers; (g) notes on all individuals—including parents, other teachers, other students and the principal—who entered the classrooms; (h) information on each teacher's home, educational background, and personal history, and (i) information on each child's home background. During the analysis stage, we also collected information from the teachers as they viewed some videotaped segments with us.

We began this ethnographic study with a general question, "What happens in bilingual classrooms?" The specific questions imbedded in this question (see Erickson et al. 1978) made our units of analysis apparent: the classroom, the classroom event (e.g., math, reading, language arts), the sequential constituents within an event (e.g., getting ready, teacher-led whole group instruction, independent work using a follow-up sheet), and episodes of social interaction taking place during any of these larger units. Increasingly during the process of collecting data, our observations and videotaping became more specifically focused on these units of analysis, with a closer investigation of particular individuals across a range of event types in both classrooms. As a result, we have collected a videotape corpus of over 100 hours of classroom interaction, along with the other information mentioned above.

Data Reduction Process

In planning for the indexing of these classroom videotapes, we sought an indexing system appropriate to our research questions that would be consistent across all the tapes and across all the participant-observational field notes. Building on the procedures mentioned in Erickson and Shultz's (1977) "When Is a Context?" paper, Carrasco and [Maldonado-] Guzman (1979) developed a videotape indexing, coding, and analysis system (see p. 437 in this volume) which facilitated the retrieval of taped instances according to cross-classifications among activity type variables and individual student variables. This system also allowed retrieval of static information, such as field notes, qualitative descriptions, and speculations concerning each taped instance. The indexing process involved two stages: reviewing and cataloguing the contents of all the tapes and writing interpretive comments stimulated by this review. Before actually cataloguing the videotapes, a time-date generator was used to superimpose numbers over the original videotape footage to allow analytic review. The numbers show the elapse of time in hours, minutes, seconds, and tenths of seconds as well as the date on which the videotape was collected. In effect, a digital clock face was printed onto the videotape and was visible on the TV screen during playback. This provided time reference points for the videotape indexing system.

The first step in indexing the contents of the tapes was the identification of major classroom events or activities such as math or reading lessons. The next was the identification of constituent phases or sub-activities within an event—in a reading lesson, for instance, "getting ready," "lesson," "wind-up," and "seat work." Finally, the researchers identified particular sets of individuals participating in interactions—teacher-student, for example, or student-student—the language they were using, the topic of their talk (academic or non-academic), and the location of each interaction in the classroom. Using the time reference points together with these indexing retrieval categories, the complete corpus of tapes can be searched for all instances of particular interactional events of interest. (See the Appendix for coding/indexing categories.)

The tape index was prepared by Carrasco and Guzman. As they viewed the tapes, the researchers wrote brief descriptions of those occurances which seemed particularly interesting, sometimes adding interpretive comments or questions raised by what had been seen and heard. This material is analogous to the field notes of participant observers and contains, as do field notes, three different types of comments: descriptive, methodological, and theoretical. These review notes were filed and indexed together with the videotapes and the original field notes. This enabled us, for example, to scan the review notes and field notes before searching the videotapes themselves for instances to be played back for detailed analysis. The index to the review notes and field notes, then, is an index both to a synoptic description of an event and to the ideas and issues raised by reviewing it. The notes provide framing for the analysis of interactional scenes and events on the tapes. Moreover, actually writing out the review notes provides a way for the researchers to make explicit their initial impressions of the videotapes and recollections about the field site. Because the review notes are dated, they document the changes in the researchers' thinking during the course of their work. Thus, like field notes, the review notes serve as evidence for the evolution of inquiry during the project. This study is but one result of this evolution.

It was during the indexing process that we came across an event in which one of our focal students, Ernesto, seemed to behave qualitatively differently than he had in other contexts. We began to review the tape and quickly decided that, for a contrastive analysis, we should look for another similar situation in which Ernesto had participated. It so happened that on that same day of taping, we had not only captured Ernesto's behavior during another lesson but also the other children's in the first lesson. We transcribed both videotaped instances. While repeatedly viewing these tapes, we examined the corresponding transcriptions and field notes. We transcribed and analyzed the first lesson with prior knowledge of what would happen in the second. This process provided an immediate contrastive perspective on each event as we described it; we could quickly select similarities and differences across both instances.

Thus we continued the initial ethnographic approach of inquiry with which we began collecting data "in the field" in the analysis phases of the study. In a sense, we "brought the field with us," since what we had observed and documented in our field notes was also recorded on videotape and could be reviewed for further analysis. With repeated viewings of the videotapes, we were able to consider different interpretations as new insights into the classroom community emerged, allowing us to overcome some of the problems that reliance on written field notes alone would have created.

In the next sections of the paper, we will (1) describe the participants in each lesson, (2) describe their academic tasks, (3) describe and analyze the participants' communicative activities and adaptive strategies in each lesson, (4) provide a contrastive analysis of the two lessons, and (5) discuss some of the practical and policy implications of this work.

Description of Site and Participants

The students in the two language arts lessons are first graders in one of two bilingual classrooms studied by Erickson, Carrasco, Guzman, and Cazden (1980). The students are Chicanos who reside in the Pilsen Chicano community in Chicago, in which the elementary school is located. While the dominant language of the community is Spanish, English is also used, either interspersed with Spanish (code switching) or dominantly by the younger members of the community (upper grades and high school), according to Carrasco's field notes (1978).

In general, the Pilsen community is considered the center of the larger Chicano community in Chicago. It is also a "port of entry" for newly arriving Mexican immigrant families seeking work in the United States. The neighborhood can be characterized as a lower socio-economic area, and the school, which was built near the beginning of this century, exemplifies the surrounding social conditions.

The school has virtually no playground, so that the students must play in the streets and alleys during recess and lunchtime periods; old and extremely small mobile bungalow classrooms were placed in the former school playground to meet the ever-increasing bilingual population. Of approximately 55 classrooms, there are eight K–3 bilingual classrooms. The year before our investigation, the Title VII Bilingual Classrooms were housed in the bungalow section. Today, while the principal has attempted to physically integrate the bilingual program into the school building, most of the bilingual classrooms are still housed in the bungalows. In fact, a sign is still posted on the fence indicating the existence of the bilingual program. It is in this section of the school that the bilingual classroom under study here is located.

Spanish is the native language of the students in the two videotaped lessons. The language abilities of the students in both lessons were described in the written notes and other data collected by the field researchers. Ernesto is a Spanish-dominant boy with some functional use of English, while Ramiro is assessed as functional in both languages but stronger in Spanish. William is dominant in Spanish with very minimal skills in English; he had been in the United States for two months at the time of videotaping of both lessons (April 3, 1979). Sacramento and Alejandra, more recent arrivals from Mexico who had been here for about one week, do not seem to understand or speak English. Ernesto and Ramiro have both lived in the community before attending this school and have bilingual kindergarten experience here, which may help to further account for their knowledge of English.

The teacher in the first lesson, Lesson 1, English Language Arts Game, is a young monolingual Black student-teacher from a local university doing her required training for teacher certification in this classroom. It is important to mention that the bilingual (master) teacher deliberately chooses monolingual student-teachers because she wishes to give her students, who are primarily Spanish-dominant, experiences which force them to use English "to prepare them for real-life situations outside the classroom" (Carrasco, Teacher Interview, 1979).

The bilingual (master) teacher in Lesson 2, Spanish Language Arts Game, is Chicana, has been teaching primary grades at the school for five and one-half years, and speaks the language of the community, "Chicano Spanish" (Penalosa 1980). She is married, has three children, and lives in another low socioeconomic Chicano *barrio* in Chicago.

Lesson 1
English Language Arts Game

This nine-minute segment involves the four male students in an instructional game context with the monolingual English-speaking teacher (Tape 47, generated real time: 04:20–13:48 minutes, April 3, 1979).

A descriptive illustration of the physical structure of the classroom which is the setting for the lesson and its participants is shown in Figure 1 below. Included in this illustration is the vantage point or angle of the camera.

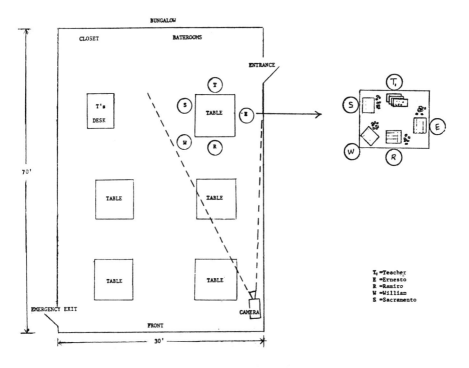

Figure 1

Classroom Floor Plan, Lesson 1

The Task

The purpose of the lesson is to teach skills in English sight word recognition and oral sentence production. The videotaped segment is structured around an instructional game, "English Word Lotto," a game like bingo in which each player or student is given a matrix board with various words and their related pictures imprinted in each of the matrix squares. Each of these picture/word squares has a matching flashcard. A stack of these cards is placed in the center of the table. The leader of the game, the teacher, randomly selects one card from the stack and announces the word in English (e.g., "the tub") while simultaneously showing the flashcard to the students. All of the students are required to repeat the word aloud. The players must then examine their individual boards and match the teacher's flashcard. The player who possesses and locates the picture/word must say so, using a complete sentence—for example, "I have the tub." Having stated the complete sentence, the student covers the corresponding picture/word on his playing board with a paper square. The winner of the game is determined by the first player to completely cover the board.

Description of the Lesson

This particular game begins with the teacher announcing the first flashcard, (1) "My head hurts." The students, with the exception of Sacramento, and teacher repeat this statement in a series of exchanges similar to second-language teaching strategies. It is important to emphasize here that this teacher neither speaks nor understands Spanish. She therefore seems to rely on a "learning by doing" approach in teaching the rules of the game. How the rules of the game are formulated and how knowledge is transmitted to the students by the teacher is our concern here.

Given that the teacher does not provide instructions as to how the game is played, we investigated how the rules are formulated "in the doing," as shown in Figure 2 below.

Figure 2

Rule Making

Rules	Speaking Turns	
Rule 1. The teacher introduces the word(s) which the students must repeat.	T to all	1. My head hurts.
	E to T	2. Ahhh! My hurts.
	T to all	3. My head hurts.
	R to T	4. My head hurts
	E to self	5. Boom dee deeboom, etc.
	W to T	6. My head hurts.
Rule 2. The students must scan their boards.	T to all	7. Who has it?
Rule 3. The students must make a complete sentence and cover the board square.	E to T	8. Ow! My head hurts
	T to W	9. My head hurts. Okay. Give it back. You cover it . . . cover it.
Rule 4. More than one player's board can have the same square.	R to E	10. My heart loves.
	T to all	11. My head hurts. Do you have this one?
	R to E	12. My heart loves.
	T to all	13. XXXXXXXXXX
	R to E	14. My moco loco.
	T to all	15. Does anybody have this one?

The first rule of the game requires the teacher to introduce the words, "My head hurts." The students must repeat them. No explanation is required since the children (with the exception of Sacramento) are responding appropriately.

Rule Two is that the students examine their boards to match the picture/word card. The teacher uses an explicit directive—(7) "Who has it?"—to get this rule across.

Rule Three requires the students to make a complete
sentence in English but only if the student locates the
corresponding picture/word on his board. William finds
it—(6) "My head hurts"—and the teacher acknowledges
him by an evaluative repeat—(9) "My head hurts. Okay."
But William violates the "unknown rules" by taking the
card from the teacher's hand, forcing her to further qualify
and clarify the rules; she directs him to "give it back," (9)
saying that he must "cover it" with a piece of square paper
available on the table. The teacher then provides variations
of the rules by informing the students that more than one
player may have the same square on their boards: (11)
"Do you have this one?" (15) "Does anybody have this
one?" (Rule 4).

The formulation of instructions does not end here.
It continues throughout the lesson as the teacher monitors
the children in action. If the rules are violated or if the
students do not respond appropriately, she provides explicit
rules in various directive forms, verbally and non-verbally.
If they follow the rules, she simply allows them to continue.
The following are some examples of explicit rules
interspersed throughout the lesson:

T to E	69.	Let me have this one. You cover it up with this (re: paper square).
T to W	77.	You have it. You have to tell me . . .
T to S	79.	Sacramento, can you say it?
T to R	144.	He has to tell me.
T to E	151.	Say it!
T to E	153.	What else?
T to all	157.	Anybody else?
T to S	160.	Do you get the picture?
T to E	161.	Put your . . . Put this over it (Verbal and non-verbal directives)
T to W	180.	Give it back.
T to W	218.	William, let me hear you say it.
T to S	289.	Let me hear you say it.
T to E	297.	You tell me.

While some of these statements by the teacher may
be in the form of questions, all seem to be directives for
teaching the students how to play the game. These verbal
directives generally co-occur with non-verbal ones, since

the teacher may be relying on other communicative means to try to relay the rules of the game. These include communication strategies very familiar in cross-cultural communication in which languages are not shared, such as pointing to things, modelling how to do something, and speaking slowly in English as if the listener understood English slowly (Hall 1959).

The monolingual teacher skillfully uses referential speech, communicating literal meaning, for rule-making but "social" speech to get feedback on the students' understanding of the rules:

T to S	158.	Did you get the picture? Do you get the picture?
W to T	159.	Ehh. No sabe /inglis/ (He doesn't understand English)
T to S	160.	Do you get the picture?

The teacher actually asks Sacramento, who neither speaks nor understands English, if he "understands" ("Did you get the picture?"). William attempts to use his minimal English to explain to her that Sacramento does not understand the language—(159) "Ehh. No sabe /inglis/." The teacher asks Sacramento a third time—(160) "Do you get the picture?"—and is satisfied with his very slight positive nod of the head, perhaps imitating the response she expects and expresses herself non-verbally, through her own nod, during her statement to him. This is an interesting but confusing moment. First, the expression the teacher uses is an idiomatic one—that is, social speech; secondly, this expression could also be taken literally, since the children could interpret it with reference to the game. They are using "pictures," and "getting the picture" is part of the game. But in the momentary context in which it is asked, it is clearly a question elicing the student's understanding of the rules. One wonders in what sense the student responds—the literal meaning, or the social one? Or could it be simply that Sacramento decides that the appropriate response is the positive up and down head-nod, prompted by the teacher's nod?

Nevertheless, it seems logical to make this statement to Sacramento. Throughout the game, the teacher gives him extra attention, because she knows that he doesn't speak English and perhaps because, up to this point, Sacramento has not been so active in the game as the others. This may explain why the teacher doesn't take William's advice. Of course, this is mere speculation.

Interactionally, the teacher and students seem to follow a discourse pattern similar to the one described by Mehan (1979) in teacher-led classroom lessons: teacher elicitation, student reply, and teacher evaluation. However, it seems to more closely resemble a modified version of the Mehan model used by Garcia and Carrasco (1981) in an analysis of bilingual mother-child discourse. In that study, in which they were teaching their children a second language, the mothers seemed to follow the Mehan pattern with a slight variation due to the subject matter being taught—language. In general, as shown in Figure 3 below, the teacher elicits the words by stating them; the child repeats the words, the teacher repeats the words as an evaluation and sometimes tags a praise after it, such as "Okay, very good."

In these interactions, the variations on the Mehan model are related to the subject content of the lesson— teaching English. In the interactions presented we see teacher "elicitations" in the form of English words, which the students are to repeat correctly. The students "respond" by repeating the words, and the teacher "evaluates" the students by repeating the words once more, sometimes followed by tag-on praise. Finally, a new set of words indicates the end of the topic and signals the beginning of a new one. But if the students' responses are incorrect, such as (90) "Hou'glass," the teacher recycles the words, an evaluation and eliciting strategy to get the students to respond again until all are correct. We can see the end of the cycle when the teacher ends her statement with a praise, e.g., (97) "Very good".

Figure 3

Teacher-Student Discourse Pattern, Lesson 1

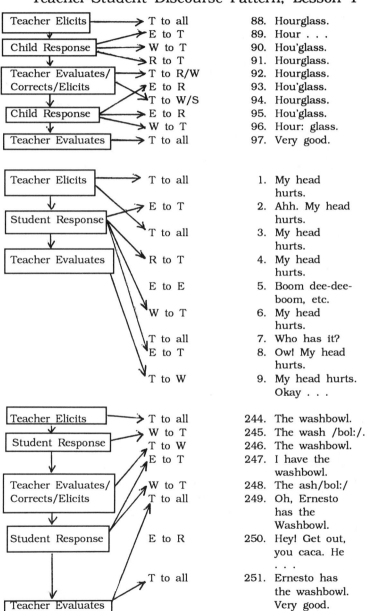

Teacher Elicits → T to all	88. Hourglass.
→ E to T	89. Hour . . .
Child Response → W to T	90. Hou'glass.
→ R to T	91. Hourglass.
Teacher Evaluates/ → T to R/W	92. Hourglass.
Corrects/Elicits → E to R	93. Hou'glass.
→ T to W/S	94. Hourglass.
Child Response → E to R	95. Hou'glass.
→ W to T	96. Hour: glass.
Teacher Evaluates → T to all	97. Very good.

Teacher Elicits → T to all	1. My head hurts.
	2. Ahh. My head hurts.
Student Response → E to T	3. My head hurts.
T to all	4. My head hurts.
Teacher Evaluates → R to T	5. Boom dee-dee-boom, etc.
E to E	6. My head hurts.
W to T	7. Who has it?
T to all	8. Ow! My head hurts.
E to T	9. My head hurts. Okay . . .
T to W	

Teacher Elicits → T to all	244. The washbowl.
→ W to T	245. The wash /bol:/.
Student Response T to W	246. The washbowl.
E to T	247. I have the washbowl.
Teacher Evaluates/ W to T	248. The ash/bol:/
Corrects/Elicits T to all	249. Oh, Ernesto has the Washbowl.
Student Response E to R	250. Hey! Get out, you caca. He . . .
T to all	251. Ernesto has the washbowl. Very good. The table.
Teacher Evaluates	

Review of the tape makes evident the presence of not only two languages (Spanish and English) but also two separate conversations involving two different topics. We saw the children speaking in Spanish with each other but not with the teacher; they used English when they interacted with the teacher. Repeated review of the tapes, with recourse to the transcriptions, clarified the two participation structures and two agendas. English was used for "academic talk," while Spanish was used for "social talk." When all the participants were interacting on the task at hand (learning and teaching English), English was the medium employed. And it was used for teaching the rules of the game, as well as for control. We called this "academic talk." "Social talk" was defined in this case not only by such student-generated off-task topics as mocos (mucus) but also by the exclusive use of Spanish among the students themselves.

Before further explication of academic and social talk, we will attempt a theoretical explanation of how both evolved in this lesson. In the beginning, as set forth in Figure 3 above, the teacher started with a three-syllable sentence: (1) *My head hurts*. The ensuing series of exchanges may be characterized rhythmically as a waltz, 1-2-3, 1-2-3, 1-2-3, etc.:

T to all	1.	My head hurts.		
E to T	2.		Ahh. My head hurts.	
T to all	3.			My head hurts.
R to T	4.			My head hurts.

Ramiro deviates from the topic with his statement to Ernesto, (10) "*My heart loves*," but this is also a three-beat/syllable statement, constructed so as to maintain the rhythm of the interaction. The teacher follows this statement with (11) "*My head hurts*," and Ramiro repeats, (12) "*My heart loves*." Ramiro's pronunciation of his statements may be characterized as exaggerated English, stressing and elongating "loves" verbally and acting it out non-verbally by putting his hands on his chest or heart as he makes the statement. Ernesto builds on Ramiro's statement by stating, (14) "My/mov;kov/. . . /Lov:kov/" which is rhythmically in tune with "My head hurts" and "My heart loves," and also in tune phonologically in English, although the statement is mostly in Spanish. The topic of mucus is born in this manner. This new off-task topic takes on a more refined form as the academic content changes. The teacher now begins teaching the words, "Alarm clock";

T to W	21.	Alarm clock
		1 2 3
W to T	22.	Alarm clock
		1 2 3
E to T	23.	. . . . . clock
		3
T to all	24.	Alarm clock
		1 2 3
W to T	25.	. . . . . clock
		3
E to R	26.	a mo: co
		1 2 3
W to T	27.	Alarm clock
		1 2 3
R to T	28.	Alarm clock
		1 2 3
E to R	29.	A ca: ca, mo: :co: :, caca, moco, Ha! Ha! Ha!
		1 2 3 1-2 3

Once again Ernesto has used the rhythmic beat of "alarm clock" to entrench this new topic with Ramiro, who is busy with the academic topic. But this time, Ernesto shifts from English phonology to Spanish in stating "moco" and "caca." Thus there seems to be a rythmic organization of speech within and across speaking turns. Erickson (in press) provides some basis for the investigation of such rhythmic behavior by participants in lessons. He states:

> . . . the regularly rhythmic timing and continuity of intonation in the answerer's speech are culturally conventional cues that "tell" us that what is being produced are items in a connected list. . . . (Erickson:9).

> Especially in lessons (both in English and in Spanish) it is important to be able to display speech rhythm because it is through rhythm as a contextualization cueing device that the alternation between successive slots in question-answer discourse routines is socially organized

so that each conversational partner can ask or
answer in the properly reciprocal time
(Erickson:11).

In this case, however, both Ernesto and Ramiro seem
to be using rhythmic timing to deviate from the academic
task to begin their own social topic. In a first-grade bilingual
classroom peer-tutoring situation, Carrasco (1980) showed
how a Spanish-dominant bilingual student successfully
penetrated a peer-tutoring dyad by rhythmically entering
interaction using the topic of the tutoring scene. Having
penetrated the situation, he used the academic topic as
a means for changing it to social talk. Miguel, the bilingual
first grader in that report, entered the scene by helping
the tutor, Veronica, formulate instructions to the tutee (as
if on cue). Miguel then built on the academic talk by
introducing a social topic in one sentence, saying to the
tutee: "No lo hagas de volada con tu novia" (Don't do it
[the work] fast with your girlfriend). These two topics were
addressed throughout the rest of the peer-tutoring process.
Like Miguel, Ernesto and Ramiro seem to be very skillful
in rhythmed academic talk, using the rhythmic behaviors
to create another topic.

Prior to the following (Figure 4) interaction, Ramiro
and Ernesto have been conversing in Spanish on the topic
of "mocos," involving William who once came to Ernesto's
rescue as Ramiro attempted to hit him. The teacher, not
privy to the student social talk, has continued with the
academic topic by introducing the new word, (111) "the
closet." In this interaction, we see the logic of the academic
and social talk carried out, each in its appropriately
established language—English for academic talk, and
Spanish for social talk.

Figure 4

Academic and Social Talk

ACADEMIC TALK			SOCIAL TALK
T to all	111.	The closet.	
			R to E 112. Ya no tengo mocos.
T to all	113.	The closet.	
T to all	114.	Who has the closet?	

T to all	114.	Who has the closet?		
E to T	115.	I have the closet.		
			R to E 116.	Ya no tengo mocos.
				Ya no tengo macos
W to T	117.	XXXXXXXXXX		
			E to R 118.	Si tiene moco.
				Poochy negro, mocos.
T to all	119.	Who has the closet?		
T to R	120.	Ramiro, did I hear you say it?		
			E to R	121. Poochy negro,
T to R	122.	Who has the closet?		
R to T	123.	I got it.		

Notice that while Ernesto is engaged in academic talk with the teacher (see turns 111, 113, 114, and 115), Ramiro tries to engage him in social talk (turns 112 and 116). As soon as Ernesto successfully accomplishes his academic task with the teacher, he responds accurately to Ramiro on the social topic (see turn 118). The teacher meanwhile takes Ramiro out of social talk and brings him into academic talk by asking him, (120) "Ramiro, did I hear you say it?" Now it is Ramiro who is involved with academics, while Ernesto is in a social mode. Ramiro is also successful in the academic context, stating (123) "I got it." All of the transcriptions of the lesson were broken down in the manner shown in Figure 4, and the discourse became logical for both agendas as a result.

In this lesson, we find examples of peer-tutoring that are opaque to the monolingual teacher. For example, William tries to help the teacher by informing her that Sacramento doesn't understand English. William also consistently tries to keep the game going by rebuking Ramiro and Ernesto for fooling around, but the teacher, not understanding his motive, reprimands him for speaking out of turn. Ramiro and Ernesto help each other in the task verbally in Spanish and, more often, non-verbally in locating the matching squares. But the teacher seems to. miss this as well. As the game progresses the students seem to lose interest in it, while Ernesto and the others became more involved with social talk. At one point the teacher asks Ernesto if he has the "table."

T to E	293.	The table, Ernesto.
E to T	294.	Table? I don't have /lito teyblz/
T to E	295.	You have the table.
E to T	296.	Le' me see
T to E	297.	You tell me.
E to T	298.	I have the table, hombre!
T to E	299.	Very good.

Ernesto's response, "I have the table, hombre!" is an indication that he is no longer involved in the lesson, that it's a bother. That statement may be interpreted as meaning, "All right, I'll play your game. I have the table; does that satisfy you?" Ernesto is clearly in a hurry to get this over and is not concerned with having the "table" on his board. Yet the teacher does not seem to pick up his social message. Eventually, he is ousted from the game for spitting on the floor, and the others also decide to stop playing.[4] They leave angrily, throwing the game boards all over the table, and the teacher calls them back one by one. Each slowly returns to the scene (except for Sacramento, who has remained at the table). The game gets underway once more, but this time the teacher has to leave the scene for a moment. During her absence, William and Ramiro decide to fill their boards and to arrange the flashcard stack in such a way that the game will end as soon as the teacher attempts to continue it. In other words, they cheat in her absence to get the game over with. It ends with William and Ramiro leaving the scene and Sacramento, realizing that he's the only one left at the table, leaving last.

In general, the lesson is characterized by miscommunication. The students are reprimanded for trying to help each other, and we find instances in which the teacher reprimands the wrong child when several are out of hand. The students fulfill what is expected of them during their individual turns in the game, but they don't fully cooperate when they are not involved. They seem to know how to come in and out of academic instruction at appropriate times, thus demonstrating their adaptive skills. They also seem to make use of the teacher's lack of Spanish to take partial control of the situation. Would these children have performed socially in similar ways if the teacher had been bilingual in Spanish and English? Would the presence of a bilingual teacher have made the engagement in the instructional task more cooperative in nature? For example, the students' attempts to help each other accomplish the tasks could have been taken into consideration as a strategy for providing a more cooperative engagement process for accomplishing the lesson.

Finally, the students seem to get away with introducing taboo words and topics in Spanish, a potentially powerful factor when magnified for an entire classroom in which the teacher does not understand Spanish. G. Alexander Moore, Jr.'s *Realities of the Urban Classroom* (1967) provides an example of what may happen in such a real situation. In his example, Gustavo, a Hispanic student in a regular classroom, skillfully upstages the monolingual English-speaking teacher. Moore uses this example to study the problem of what the children might be learning in classrooms, since they do not seem to be learning academics. The following was interpreted as a lesson in scene-stealing for Gustavo's peers in class:

> In spite of her affection for him, she had to work with his well defined campaign of classroom sabotage. Any weakness of hers could be the cause of his own little scene. Thus at one point she banned the use of a Spanish word that she had heard being bandied around the class by the Spanish-speaking youngsters. She was ignorant of the meaning of the word but "it sounded wrong" to her. Since the word was actually quite innocent, Gustavo seized this excellent opportunity to make a fool of her and sat in the back of the class steadily shouting the obnoxious word for ten minutes. This is only one of many such instances, but it illustrates how well the boy was able to upstage the teacher.

In both Moore's example and our own, it seems a teacher's lack of Spanish, which is spoken by all the children involved, seriously undermines her control over the situation.

Lesson 2
Spanish Language Arts Game

This eleven-minute segment involves the same four male students who participated in Lesson 1, with the addition of Alejandra and the bilingual, bicultural teacher. (Tape 44, generated real time: 00:44–11:42 minutes, April 3, 1979). The physical arrangement of the lesson and its participants and the angle of the video camera during taping are shown in Figures 5 and 6.

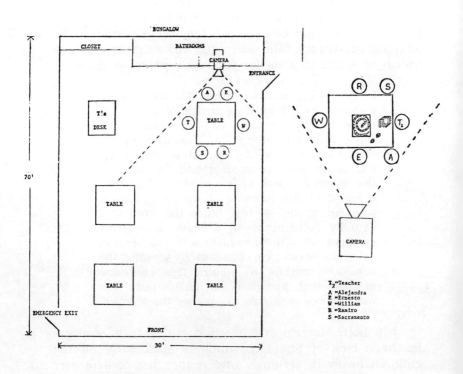

Figure 5

Classroom Floor Plan, Lesson 2

The Task

The purpose of the lesson is to teach both basic Spanish syllable sounds and sight word recognition skills in Spanish. The videotape segment is a Spanish language arts lesson, structured around an instructional game modelled on Monopoly: a large playing board is placed in the center of the table, and each player is required to move an individual marker along the sequence of squares on the board. The winner is the player who reaches the last square first. The dice featured in the game have imprinted on them, instead of the usual dots representing numbers, the vowels on one die and a set of consonants on the other. Thus, when a player rolls the dice, they form a basic Spanish syllable (e.g., C̲ E̲ = Ce). A stack of sight-word cards is placed upside-down o n the playing table. The players also have access to an answer picture/word chart, which matches the sight words with the picture or has the object itself, such as a ribbon, glued to the chart. Thus if, for example, the sight word is *perro* (dog), the player may check his answer by matching the sight word card with the dog on the picture/word chart.

To begin, a student takes the dice and tosses them. He must then arrange them in consonant-vowel sequence to form a syllable and must pronounce this syllable. Having successfully done so, he selects the top card from the sight word stack and must then pronounce this word before advancing on the board. A child who fails in the first part of the task cannot continue with his turn. The number of spaces the player can move for each turn is determined by the number indicated on the sight-word card.

Description of the Lesson

The game begins with the bilingual teacher providing a set of instructions in Spanish on how to play the game (the rules). She uses Sacramento as a model in explaining what each player must do in his or her turn. The interaction begins as follows:

T to S	1.	Okay. Ponle tu. Lo tiras, lo tiras. (Okay. Put it there. Throw it, throw it.)
E to self	2.	Wua-ca-la-ca, la-ca, wua-cha-la-ca (just sounds)
T to S	3.	Lo- ¿Que es? (/lo/ What is it?)
W to S	4.	Mo:::lo (/mo:::lo/)
T to S	5.	Lo- lo. Ahora tu agarras uno de estos, y si lo sabes, mueves cuatro. (/lo:::lo/. Now you get one of these [cards] and if you know it, you can move four [spaces].)
E to self	6.	Cha-ca-la-ca (sounds)
T to S	7.	¿Que es? (What is it?)
S to T	8.	Perro. (Dog.)
T to S	9.	Perro. Y si no lo sabes, aqui esta. (Dog. And if you don't know it [the word], here it is [the chart with the answers].)
E to self	10.	Tuk-tuk-tuk-tuk. (sounds)
T to S	11.	Pe:::Perro? Te dice que te tienes que mover, cuantos? (D:::Dog. It [the card] tells you, how many to move?)
E to self	12.	Tik-tik-tik-tik, wu-uu-lu-lu-lu-lu-la-la-la-la
W to T/S	13.	Uno, dos, tres, cuatro. (One, two, three, four.)
T to S	14.	Cuatro. Okay. ¿Que es el tuyo? (Four. Okay. Which one [marker, crayon] is yours?)
W to T/S	15.	El amarillo. (The yellow one.)
T to S/W	16.	¿El amarillo? Okay. (The yellow one? Okay.)
R to T	17.	El amarillo es mio, maestra. (The yellow one is mine, teacher)
T to self	18.	¡Oh!
W to T/S	19.	Yo te lo puedo menear. (I can move it for you.)
T to R	20.	¿Tu? . . . . . Oh . . . . . ¡Oh! ¡De veras! (You? . . . . . oh . . . . . Oh! That's right!)
R to T	21.	Est . . . el tiene el mio. (This one . . . he has mine.)
T to S	22.	Oh si . . . este va ser la tuya. (Oh, right . . . This one will be yours.)
T to S	23.	¿Mueves cuatro? ¿Donde esta el azul? (Move four spaces? Where is the blue one?)
W to self	24.	Uno, dos, tres, cuatro. (One, two, three, four. This is said as Sacramento moves his marker.)
S to T	25.	¿Cuatro? (Four?)

The teacher formulates the rules of the game orally to all participants and directs Sacramento as a model. In this beginning sequence, we quickly notice the interweaving of the teacher's formulation of rules with the student's mechanical concerns in playing the game. As the teacher explains the rules through Sacramento's actions, she asks him which marker is his (14). William informs her that it's the yellow one (15). But Ramiro corrects William, stating that the yellow one is his (17). The teacher acknowledges this and finds the blue one for Sacramento (23). This sequence demonstrates students' help in the formulation of instructions (13. "Uno, dos, tres, cuatro"), and in the mechanisms of moving pieces (19. "Yo te lo puedo menear") as well as peer-tutoring (4. "Mo::lo")—all contributions to the atmosphere of cooperation in which the instructional task is executed.

Reinforcement of the rules continues throughout the game, carried out not only by the teacher but also by the children, who are allowed to check one another's actions and moves. (This seems to keep them engaged even when it is not their turn.) So we quickly can see that the teacher is not the only social controller of the lesson—it is a shared endeavor. Let us review some examples of the teacher's continual monitoring of the rules:

T to A	44.	Agarre una tarjeta. Leame lo que es alli. (Go get a card. Read what it says.)
T to E	73.	Collecta mas ahora. (Collect more now.)
T to W	114.	¿Ahora? ¿Cuantos te dice? Cuatro. Muevele cuatro. (Now. How many does it tell you? Four. Move four.)
T to R	128.	Toma una de estas. (Take one of these.)
T to S	155.	. . . ahora tu escojes uno de estos. (. . . now you pick up one of these.)
T to A	223.	P:::ra. Okay. Cuatro. Tu le meneas cuatro. (D:::og. Okay. Four.)
T to E	245.	Okay. Toma una de estas. (Okay. Take one of these.)
T to W	264.	Ahora, toma una carta a ver si la puedes leer. (Now, take a card and see if you can read it.)
T to R	285.	Me . . . Okay. Agarre uno de estos. (Me . . . Okay. Take one of these.)
T to S	311.	Mo. Ahora con este. (/Mo/. Now with this one.)
T to S	321.	Okay. ¿Cuantas veces tienes que mover? (Okay. How many times must you move?)
T to A	369.	¿Cuantas veces te vas a mover? (How many times are you going to move?)

In the teacher's decontextualized statements above, we can begin to see the range of ways she uses language for reaching the same ends. For example, sentences 44, 73, 128, 155, 245, 264, 285 and 311 are all directions asking individual children to choose a card from the stack.

But as mentioned earlier, the students also monitor the rules, even when it is not their turn.

E to A	46.	Se pone /po/. (You put . . . [you say] /po/.)
W to A	60.	Puedes mover cuatro. (You can move four.)
R to T	67.	Ahora yo sigo, Maestra. (It's now my turn, teacher.)
W to all	89.	One, two . . . (Code-switch; but monitoring Ernesto's move.)
W to E	94.	Cuatro. (Four—monitoring Ernesto's last move.)
W to T	117.	¿Se pone esta carta abajo? (Do we put this card under the stack?)
W to R	134.	Beautiful! (Code-switch: in reference to Ramiro's move.)
W to E	156.	Alli empiezas. (You begin there.)
R to W	160.	No, aqui. (No, here.)
W to R	161.	Este es la mia, y este la tuya. (This is mine and this one is yours.)
W to T	190.	Aca esta. (Here it is.)
W to E	207.	No comiences. ¡Mira! ¡Ernesto! ¡No empieces! (Don't start. Look! Ernesto! Don't start! In reference to Ernesto getting out of hand and disrupting the game.)
R to E	232.	Tu::::::tu, Ernesto. (You::::::you, Ernesto—it's your turn.)
A to T	235.	Hice algo mal. (I did something wrong.)
W to T	246.	Esa, esa, esa . . . (That one, that one, that one . . .)
W to E	290.	Hay empiezas tu. (You begin there.)
W to R	318.	Empiezas tu. (You begin, or it's your turn.)
A to T	325.	No lo movieron asi, Maestra. (They didn't move it that way, teacher.)
R to T	328.	Estaba asi. (It was like that.)
W to S	339.	Aca. (Put it here.)
R to T	340.	Hay esta. (There it is.)

But these students are not only reinforcing the rules; they are also monitoring the game to keep it going. Students and teacher act in concert to succeed in the academic task—even though helping another student may cause the benefactor to lose the game, which is a competitive one. This altruism is illustrated by the following statements:

E to A	46.	Se pone /po/. (You put, or you say /po/—Ernesto helps Alejandra to understand the process.)
W to A	56.	. . . to . . . pito (/to/ . . . horn—William helps the teacher and Alejandra decipher and sound out

		the sight word on the card.)
T to E	64.	El colorado. Ponlo alli para ella, Ernesto. (The red one. Put it over there for her, Ernesto—this is a case where the teacher asks a student to help Alejandra in the task.)
E to W	109.	Moño. (Ribbon—Ernesto helps William sound out the word on the card with the teacher.)
W to T	123.	Mimo. (/mimo/—William helps Ramiro with the syllable /mi/.)
E to T	271.	Todos. (All—Ernesto helps William sound out / todos/.)
E to T	312.	Ma::ma (Ma::ma—Ernesto helps Sacramento with the syllable.)

These peer-tutoring statements are inserted in the teacher-player discourse, as the teacher allows the students to join in the teaching and learning process—not an unusual case in this classroom. In two other contexts, small group reading lessons, we have seen the teacher and students (Ernesto and William included) help another student who is reading aloud, thus sharing the teaching and learning process. And in this scene, the teacher not only allows all those involved to practice peer-tutoring in the fulfillment of the academic task but also in the formulation and regulation of the rules of the game.

The lesson discourse pattern the teacher and students follow here, as in Lesson 1, resembles the Mehan (1979) model of teacher elicitation, student reply, teacher evaluation, with some variations. First of all, the elicitation is inherent in the game itself—that is, the teacher elicits by directing the student to roll the dice. The student responds, and the teacher evaluates. Also, the teacher often recycles the words, the child responds again; the teacher evaluates by repeating the words and adding to them a tag-on statement, such as "Ahora," "Okay," or "Muy bien." There are many examples of this pattern. We present but a few here in Figure 6.

Figure 6

Teacher-Student Discourse Pattern, Lesson 2

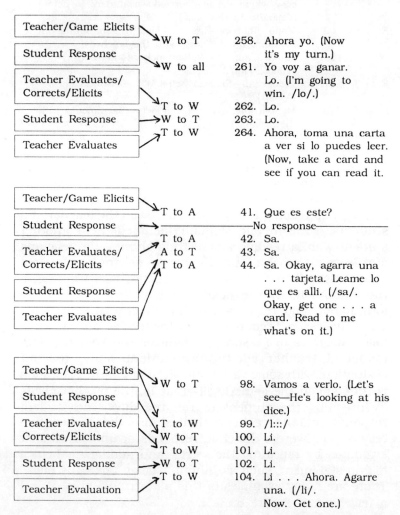

Teacher/Game Elicits	↘W to T	258. Ahora yo. (Now it's my turn.)
Student Response	↘W to all	261. Yo voy a ganar. Lo. (I'm going to win. /lo/.)
Teacher Evaluates/ Corrects/Elicits	↘T to W	262. Lo.
Student Response	→W to T	263. Lo.
Teacher Evaluates	↗T to W	264. Ahora, toma una carta a ver si lo puedes leer. (Now, take a card and see if you can read it.
Teacher/Game Elicits	↘T to A	41. Que es este?
Student Response	→ ——No response——	
Teacher Evaluates/ Corrects/Elicits	↗T to A, A to T, ↗T to A	42. Sa. / 43. Sa. / 44. Sa. Okay, agarra una . . . tarjeta. Leame lo que es alli. (/sa/. Okay, get one . . . a card. Read to me what's on it.)
Student Response		
Teacher Evaluates		
Teacher/Game Elicits	↘W to T	98. Vamos a verlo. (Let's see—He's looking at his dice.)
Student Response	↘	
Teacher Evaluates/ Corrects/Elicits	↘T to W, W to T, T to W	99. /l:::/ / 100. Li. / 101. Li.
Student Response	→W to T	102. Li.
Teacher Evaluation	↗T to W	104. Li . . . Ahora. Agarre una. (/li/. Now. Get one.)

This pattern is evident throughout the lesson. Many of the participants talk while the teacher is working with one individual, and their contributions may usurp her role in the lesson discourse pattern. In other words, once again more than one teacher is manifest in this discourse. Let's take a closer look at a representative example of this phenomenon:

T to W	99.	/l:::/
W to T	100.	Li.
T to W	101.	Li.
W to T	102.	Li.
E to T	103.	Li.
T to W	104.	Li . . . Ahora agarre una. (Now, get one.)
W to T	105.	Li, li. (He gets a card.)
W to T	106.	Corvata. (Tie.)
T to W	107.	Mo:::
W to T	108.	Mo . . . mo.
E to W	109.	Moño. (Bow)
W to T	110.	Mono. Moño. (Monkey. Bow.)
T to W	111.	Moño. (Bow.)
E to all	112.	No sabia. (He didn't know.)

In this example, the teacher assists William with the initial sound of the syllable on the dice (99). William responds (100); the teacher repeats the syllable, reinforcing his correct pronunciation (101). William responds again (102), and Ernesto mimics him (103). The teacher repeats the syllable again and instructs William to pick up the card (104). After having reviewed the sight word card, William answers incorrectly (106): "Corvata." The teacher gives him a clue to the correct answer by slowly pronouncing the first syllable of the word (107). The child mimics her clue (108): "/mo:: mo::/." Then Ernesto helps him by completing the word (109): "Mono." William repeats the word (110): "Mono. Moño." He says it correctly on the second try. (Mono without the tilde over the "n" means "monkey"; with the tilde it means "bow," as in "bow tie.") The teacher verifies William's and Ernesto's correct pronunciation of the word by repetition and praise (116): "Muy bien."

Not only is Ernesto helping William succeed in the academic task here, but he may also be learning the academic content task in the process. In many classrooms, if an individual student is taking a turn—in a reading lesson, for example—the teacher may not allow the other students in the group to interfere, interrupt, or help. And the teacher may initiate or reinforce this turn-talking rule by reprimanding students for attempting to do so. But in this case the teacher does allow the students to insert their statements and even acknowledges their contribution (116). "Muy bien"), establishing a shared instructional process as well as a shared learning process.

Our analysis of the talk in this lesson showed that almost all social talk among students, and between the teacher and students, was directly related to the lesson. Social talk among students mostly involved their relative position in the game:

R to A	32.	No va sab:::er. (She's not going to know the answer.)
W to all	79.	No sabe, no saca, hee, hee, hee. (He doesn't know)
W to E	120.	Ya voy ganando, y Ernesto, mira donde voy. Imaginate. (I'm winning, and Ernesto, look here where I'm at. Can you imagine?)
R to E	259.	Err:::nesto /ts/. Tu estas ganando. (Ernesto. You're winning.)
R to W	308.	Sacramento . . . Sacramento va a ganar todo. (Sacramento . . . Sacramento is going to win it all.)

One student, Ernesto, attempted to deviate from the lesson, but his attempts were short-circuited by his peers:

a)	W to E	202.	¡Ay! Vas a empezar, tu. Como un baby. (Ay! Now you're going to start. Just like a baby.)
b)	E to W	206.	Booda-booda-boodoo-boo-doo. (Noises that interrupt.)
	W to E	207.	No comiences. ¡Mira! ¡Ernesto! No empieces. (Don't start. Look! Ernesto, don't start.)
c)	E to self	230.	Poo, poo, poo. (Disrupting noises.)
	T to E	231.	Okay, Ernesto. (Teacher calls Ernesto for his turn—not to reprimand.)
			But Ernesto doesn't respond.
	R to E	232.	Tu:::::::::u, Ernesto:::::: (You:::::::::u, Ernesto::::::—meaning, Hey it's YOUR turn.)

It seems that the students were holding each other accountable as to the appropriate behavior in this context. In *Interaction Ritual* (1967), Goffman explains the obligations of participants involved in a conversational encounter.

> When individuals are in one another's immediate presence, a multitude of words, gestures, acts,

and minor events become available, whether desired or not, through which one who is present can intentionally or unintentionally symbolize his character and his attitudes. In our society a system of etiquette obtains that enjoins the individual to handle these expressive events fittingly, projecting through them a proper image of himself, an appropriate respect for the others present, and a suitable regard for the setting. When the individual intentionally or unintentionally breaks a rule of etiquette, others present may mobilize themselves to restore the ceremonial order, somewhat as they do when other types of social order are transgressed (Goffman 1967:114).

In our example, we see William helping to maintain the social order of the lesson as Ernesto attempts to break away. Perhaps because the teacher allows the students to help, tutor, talk to, and reprimand their peers—in effect, to co-teach—the resulting participation structure allows her, in turn, to spend more time teaching and less time reprimanding to maintain the social order of the lesson. We therefore hypothesize that this type of participation structure, which allows the bilingual students to participate in the teaching and learning process, fosters their active engagement in all aspects of the lesson.

One element in this participation structure is the role of the game itself, which may be characterized as "competitive," since all participants are competing to win and there is only one winner possible. But because the bilingual students help each other in accomplishing their turn in the game and therefore to advancing toward winning, we can also characterize the game situation as cooperative. It is interesting to note, in relation to this lesson, that some studies suggest Chicano students' learning styles are cooperative in nature (e.g., Ramírez and Castañeda 1974).

In general, the lesson seems to flow very smoothly and cooperatively. It is particularly interesting that the language use of all the participants (including the teacher) seems to match the general language use of the community surrounding the school. The community language, while mostly Spanish, is interspersed with English words and sentences inserted into the conversation. Such code-switching occurs at various points in the lesson, and both teacher and students seem very comfortable with it. Erickson (in press) comments:

> Classroom lessons as task environments can be seen to require complementary patterns of conversational inference by teachers and students. They must be able to "read" in reciprocal and complementary ways the cues organizing conversational partnership from moment to moment. They must be able to "read" the social meaning of talk and its referential meaning as well. To the extent that the talk in the lessons concerns subject matter, successful participation in the lesson involves knowledge of the subject matter information and the logic of its organization as well as knowledge of discourse and its social meaning.

Clearly, the ability to "read" one another in classroom lessons requires "shared cultural knowledge," including language, among all participants. If code-switching is part of that shared knowledge, it is one of many cultural aspects necessary in order to "read" one another in conversational partnership. In this case, both teacher and students seem to be in tune with the cultural norms of the community, allowing cooperative participation in the lesson.

Constrastive Analysis and Theoretical Issues

Our analysis of each lesson has in effect already provided a contrastive view of both. In this section, we discuss those salient issues which further ground our educational theories and contribute to our hypotheses.

One obvious difference between the two lessons lies

in the "participation structures" or patterns of social roles or norms which shape their appropriate enactment. Since participation structures consist of what people do, when they do it, and where they do it (Erickson and Shultz 1977), each person in these lessons has an appropriate role. But participation structures in classroom lessons have another dimension: the "academic task structure," which Erickson (in press) defines as a pattern of constraints created by the internal logic of sequencing in the subject matter content of the lesson. Successful participants must understand the lesson's academic task structure as well as its social participation structure.

In each of our two lessons, the academic task structure is defined not only by what the teacher plans to accomplish in the lesson but also by the nature of the instructional game used. In the first lesson, one would expect participants to be quite involved interactionally since (1) all students had to look at the teacher's flashcard each time to determine whether they had the matching picture or word on their charts, and (2) it was possible that more than one student could have a match. But in fact, the students participated in the lesson only when they had to. In contrast, the second lesson's instructional game required individual turn-taking, so that less interactional involvement was expected. Nevertheless, our transcripts reveal that almost all of the utterances in Lesson 2 were topically on task.

There are several possible explanations for this outcome. First of all, in Lesson 1 the teacher's lack of Spanish seemed to be a factor in the lesson's participation structure. The students participated appropriately with her in English (on-task), but they also participated among themselves inappropriately, using their own language for social purposes (off-task). In contrast, participants in Lesson 2 shared the same language, and the students seemed to be cooperatively engaged with the teacher in accomplishing her goals. Sacramento, who was very inactive in Lesson 1, was very active in Lesson 2. In Lesson 1 he responded only when directly requested to do so by the teacher; whereas in Lesson 2 he interacted independently, socially as well as academically.

In both lessons, the participants seemed to understand the academic task structure but differed in their understanding of the social participation structures. In Lesson 1, neither teacher nor students seemed to adequately comprehend the lesson's social participation structure. The students produced their own social participation structure, using their own language. This excluded the teacher, who nevertheless successfully fulfilled the academic task structure. In Lesson 2, both teacher and students seemed to understand the social as well as the academic structure; this is evident in the nature of the interactions, which were both socially and academically on task.

There are other factors which may help to explain these two different participation structures. For example, in Lesson 1, the teacher's style may be characterized as teacher-centered. She adhered to her academic goals despite the students' off-task social conversation in Spanish. She often attempted to bring the children into the lesson, not only by controlling the social order but also by monitoring the rules of the game and the progress of individual students. She did not acknowledge students' attempts to help each other, and to help her communicate.

In contrast, the teacher's style in Lesson 2 may be characterized as child-centered. This implies that the teacher had some knowledge of the students' social and cultural norms of interaction. She allowed students to help each other, for example, during one another's turns, to help clarify the rules of the game and to praise each other as they succeeded in their turns (W to R 133 "Beautiful!"). All of these student actions are factors in a more cooperative participation structure.

The student and teacher behaviors in Lesson 2 which seem to contribute to the enactment of an appropriate participation structure are not idiosyncratic to this lesson. In fact the behavior of her students and the teacher's style are the results of her own conscious philosophy of teaching. In an informal interview the day before the taping of these two lessons (Carrasco-Teacher interview 1979), she expressed this philosophy, revealing her knowledge of her students' social and cultural relationships and styles, and explained how she used this knowledge to develop strategies for teaching them. We provide a few transcriptions of that interview with some interpretations and clarifications.

Carrasco asked the bilingual teacher how she made her students work in class.

> I'm going to tell you it has nothing to do with education. I adopt them. Maybe it sounds weird. I am very personal with them. I adopt them completely. When one [child] isn't achieving, it's not like a reflection on the teacher. It's a reflection on the parent [myself]. I see my own child there. And I want them to hold their own when they go to the next class. And they won't be afraid of the teacher or of anybody.

When asked if she thought she was culturally in tune with her students, she replied, "I wasn't really aware of it." She explained that she uses her

> intuition as a parent because I'm a mother first. I relate to them as [if] they were my children. And I even give them cascarones [gentle taps on the head]. I want them to learn so bad that sometimes I'll sit with them and I'll say, ¡Te voy a rascar. Te voy a dar unas nalgadas!' [I'm going to scratch you. I'm going to spank your bottom.] At the moment I have to say it to them. And they understand it.

Without being prompted, the teacher explained the contrast between herself and Anglo teachers.

> There's no home visitation. They don't give out their [telephone] numbers, like I do. I get a call in the morning, evening, night. Every note I give out I write my [home telephone] number. They can call me anytime. I'm open to them [parents]. Parents can call me anytime. I'll even go to their house. And cuando [when] I talk with another parent [I talk] not exactly as a teacher but as a parent, 'cause I'm a parent too. I see myself as a parent first and a teacher second.

The interviewer asked a question concerning her classroom organization:

> I can't do it the way it says in the book. I tried.
> My structure is structured with the child in mind.
> I structure my structure around them so that it
> will fit them. And they feel comfortable, and yet
> it's a very trying structure. . . . and it takes a
> lot out of me.

Throughout the interview the teacher displayed her understanding of her students' learning styles and explained how she used this knowledge in developing teaching strategies.

> My opinion is that they [bilingual students] have
> to talk to each other. That's part of their cognitive
> style.
> They have to talk to each other. Camaraderie is
> important to them.
> They ask one another, ¿"Esto quiere decir esto
> y otro?" [Does this mean this or that?] Another
> child replies, "Si" [yes]. Then they have something
> to transfer. They help each other.
> They're all abogados [lawyers] in my classroom.
> They're all lawyers. When they discuss [with us],
> they'll make a deal with me. Which I don't mind.
> "Si quieres hacer esto, que vas hacer por mi?"
> [If you want to do this, what are you going to
> do for me?] I do that all the time. I think it's
> very cultural [to bargain with them]. You rub my
> back and I'll rub yours. That kind of thing.

Near the end of the interview, the researcher asked about an incident that had happened that day in her classroom. The students were getting too noisy for her and running around the room. The observer (Carrasco) was astounded by the way the teacher stopped this; the students froze and instantly cooperated. All she did was go to the front of the room and place her right hand on the side of her head, and look as if she were in extreme pain, "Como un dolor de cabeza" (like a headache).

> That's very typical mother. Mother goes like this
> [hand on head], then the kid knows, "Hey man,
> Mom's had it."

We can see in this revealing interview that the bilingual teacher incorporates her teaching philosophy in her lesson, Lesson 2. But it is also representative of a pattern in the teaching philosophies of at least three other bilingual bicultural teachers: that "they adopt their students," [5] and that they are "parents" when the children are in their classrooms as well as outside them. Given the prevalence of the "extended family" among Hispanics, it may be that the teacher is perceived as part of the cultural family.

This interview and the analysis of her lesson also suggest that besides relying on her intuitions as a Chicano mother, this teacher also draws upon her understanding of her students' cultural and social roles and relationships to develop culturally relevant teaching strategies, such as allowing bargaining, peer tutoring, and student talk.

This study provides the basis for the further investigation of participation structures in bilingual settings, leading us to propose that appropriate lesson participation structures are best constructed when all the participants and, specifically the teacher, are attuned to the social and cultural norms of the bilingual students and their community. If they are not so attuned, Au (1980) warns us of the possible consequences:

> Inappropriate contexts (participation structures) for learning may contribute to the poor academic performance of minority children by functioning to decrease the amount of context (number of propositions or idea units) that will be present in a lesson. It may be the case that minority children receive less academic material than mainstream children throughout their school careers (Au 1980:92).

Finally, our concern is with bilingual education and with bilingual children and their teachers. Our analysis of the lessons is not intended in any way to judge teacher performance. Instead, our aim has been to discover, describe, and analyze potentially important factors operating in the bilingual lesson which may help improve pedagogical practice. Methodologically, the contrast provided by Lesson 1 has aided in our identification of important tacit and perhaps cultural behaviors in Lesson 2, which may otherwise have been ignored.

Discussion

We set out in this paper to investigate the nature of teacher and student engagement in lessons through a study of the participants' language use in these contexts. This has been an effort to provide "real stories" about the dynamics of bilingual classrooms which we hope will serve as bases for more informed policy decisions as well as revealing the need for training, retraining, and hiring more bilingual teachers.

The Spanish-speaking population is the United States' fastest-growing minority and is projected to be its largest by the year 1985. According to *The New York Times* (January 7, 1981) ". . . in strong contrast to the rest of the community, more than half of them [Hispanics] are under 18 years old" and ". . . are increasing in the classrooms particularly at the elementary school level." This young population needs services in tune with its members' cultural norms if they are to play a significant role in this country's future. Already Hispanics are being heard in politics through their votes, and this will continue. However, we must begin now to increase the number of bilingual teachers if we are to preserve cultures and languages which we consider valuable assets for this country.

In considering the need for more bilingual teachers, we must also confront the reality that there are "bilingual teachers" who are not bicultural and that there are even monolingual English-speaking teachers teaching non-English-dominant students in multilingual, multicultural classrooms today. We see the need to continue training all these teachers in two cooperating educational institutions: in academia and in the schools and their communities.

At the college and university level, it is not enough to teach potential teachers theories, methods, and philosophies and to provide student-teacher experiences. What is needed is training which will prepare teachers to investigate the social and cultural norms of their communities. Potential teachers should be trained in community research, so that they are able to explore local language use, social organization, and economic reality. This knowledge should lead to teaching strategies that are more congruent with the community's cultural norms. Such fieldwork could be included as part of the student-teacher requirement. It is highly unlikely that student-teachers will be assigned to the schools in which they have received teaching experience. However, if colleges and universities provide skills for investigating any community for the purpose of "practicing" to develop relevant teaching strategies, teachers may be able to use their skills in the communities in which they will actually work.

However, the community must also play a role in the relevant education of its children. Schools might offer teachers time, financial support, and opportunity to carry out such a community investigation before and during teaching in the classroom. Thus the school would share in the responsibility of meeting its community's needs and desires. Since this country encompasses so many regional, economic, social and cultural differences, all school settings could benefit from such an educational approach.

As to the cost-effectiveness of such a proposal, it is possible to take advantage of the few bicultural-bilingual teachers already in service as valuable resources for the training of their colleagues and potential teachers. It is more than likely that these teachers have knowledge of their own culture and the norms of the communities in which they teach. In our study, for example, the bilingual-bicultural teacher described the various teaching strategies she had developed on the basis of her knowledge of that community's social and cultural norms and even used this knowledge to develop for herself a culturally relevant philosophy of teaching. We need to tap such sources of practitioner knowledge.

The present study also leads us to recommend further research on the teaching and learning process in bilingual settings. Many investigations have concentrated on bilingual achievement testing and scores to promote, justify, and preserve bilingual education. But there are many problems in measuring bilingual student achievement outcomes. Few researchers are concentrating on the ways bilingual teachers teach bilingual children. There is a need to make explicit the strategies for the teaching of bilingual students and their development. In our collaborative work with the teachers in the Chicago study, we were able to elicit from each teacher her own philosophy of teaching as well as the various strategies she employed. The bilingual teacher in this study said in an interview (Carrasco 1979), "I knew all the time what I was doing in the classroom. But I never had a way of explaining it, nor did I think that anyone would listen. Now I have a way of explaining what I do."

Finally, and directly related to this issue, there is a practical need to describe and justify relevant teaching strategies and styles. Our bilingual teacher, for example, was being evaluated by the principal on one of the days we were observing her classroom. He saw what he called a noisy, unstructured, and uncontrolled classroom. In the teacher's eyes, this was her philosophy put into practice, but at that time she was neither able to explain nor defend it.

We, as teachers and researchers, have first to learn more about our communities and our students, and we already have ways of obtaining this knowledge. Then we must learn to put this knowledge into practice to provide a more culturally relevant education as well as to develop culturally appropriate and effective educational strategies and techniques.

Endnotes

1. Dr. Robert L. Carrasco, Carmel T. Acosta, and Sylvia de la Torre-Spencer, Harvard University.

2. I have analyzed these lessons and four others in much more detail in my dissertation, "Collective Engagement in the 'Segundo Hogar' A Microethnography of Engagement in a First Grade Classroom," 1989, Harvard University.

3. The Trueba paper referred to is in this volume.

4. The tape segment under study ends at this point. Because Ernesto is ousted from the game, the context changes, and so we provide a general account of what happened afterward.

5. The teacher in Carrasco's (1981) study, "Expanded Awareness of Student Performance" and two other bilingual-bicultural teachers in the Chicago school site each independently shared the same view of their role as teachers: they were parents. All three of these bilingual-bicultural teachers were women; one wonders if male Hispanic teachers share the same philosophy.

References

Au, K.H.
  1980   Participation Structures in a Reading Lesson with Hawaiian Children: Analysis of a Culturally Appropriate Instructional Event. Anthropology and Education Quarterly 11(2).

Bauman, R.
  1972   An Ethnographic Framework for the Investigation of Communicative Behavior. *In* Language and Cultural Diversity in American Education. R.D. Abrahams and C. Troike, eds. Englewood Cliffs, N.J.: Prentice-Hall.

Carrasco, R.L., A. Vera, and C.B. Cazden.
  1981   Aspects of Bilingual Students' Communicative Competence in the Classroom: A Case Study. *In* Latino Language and Communicative Behavior. Discourse processes: Advances in Research and Theory, Vol. 4. R. Duran, ed. Norwood, N.J.: Ablex Pub.

Carrasco, R.L.
1978–1979 Chicago field notes of two bilingual classrooms.
1979 Teacher interview.
1980 Ethnography and Bilingual education. A colloquium presented at Arizona State University, College of Education. December.
1981 Expanded Awareness of Student Performance: A Case Study in Applied Ethnographic Monitoring in a Bilingual Classroom. In Culture and the Bilingual Classroom. H.L. Trueba, G.P. Guthrie, K.H. Au, eds. Rowley, Mass.: Newbury House.
1984 Collective Engagement in the Segundo Hogar. A Microethnography of Engagement in a Bilingual First Grade Classroom. Unpublished doctoral dissertation, Harvard University.

Cazden, C.B., R.L. Carrasco, A.A. Maldonado-Guzman, and F.D. Erickson
1980 The Contribution of Ethnographic Research to Bicultural Bilingual Education. In Current Issues in Bilingual Education. Georgetown University Roundtable on Language and Linguistics. J.E. Alatis, ed. Washington, D.C.: Georgetown University Press: Pp. 64–80.

Erickson, F.D.
1978 The Politics of Speaking. Bilingual Education Paper Series 1(6). Los Angeles, Calif.: National Dissemination and Assessment Center, California State University.
1980 Classroom Discourse as Improvisation: Relationships Between Academic Task Structure and Social Participation Structure in Lessons. A manuscript in preparation for publication. Institute for Research on Teaching, Michigan State University.
1980 Participation Structures as Learning Environments. A paper presented at the American Anthropological Association's Annual Meeting, in a Symposium, The Anthropology of Learning, Washington, D.C. December.

Erickson, F.D., R.L. Carrasco, A. Vera, and C.B. Cazden.
1978 The Social and Cultural Organization of Interaction of Classrooms of Bilingual Students. A Proposal to NIE from Harvard Graduate School of Education. NIE-G-78-0099.

Erickson, F.D., and J. Shultz
1977 When Is a Context? Quarterly Newsletter of the Laboratory for Comparative Human Develpment 1(2). December.

Garcia, E., and R.L. Carrasco
1981   An Analysis of Mother-child Discourse. *In* Latino Language and Communicative Behavior. Discourse Processes: Advances in Research and Theory, (4). Norwood, N.J.
Fishman, J.
1977   The Social Science Perspective. *In* Bilingual Education: Cultural Perspectives: Social Science. Arlington, Va.: Center for Applied Linguisitics. Pp. 1–49.

Goffman, E.
1967   Interaction Ritual. Garden City, N.Y.: Doubleday.
Hall, E.T.
1959   The Silent Language. New York: Doubleday.
Mehan, H.
1979   Learning Lessons. Cambridge, Mass. Harvard University Press.
1981   Ethnography for the Study of Bilingual Education. *In* H.T. Trueba, G.P. Guthrie, K.H. Au, eds., Culture and the Bilingual Classroom. Rowley, Mass.: Newbury House.
Moore, G.A., Jr.
1967   Realities of the Urban Classroom. Garden City, N.Y.: Doubleday.
Moll, Luis, E. Estrada, E. Diaz, and L.M. Lopes.
1980   The Organization of Bilingual Lessons: Implications for Schooling. In the Quarterly Newsletter of the Laboratory of Comparative Human Cognition 2(3). July. [See Moll et al. in this volume.]
Penalosa, F.
1980   Chicano Sociolinguistics: A Brief Introduction. Rowley, Mass.: Newbury House.
Ramirez, M., and A. Castaneda
1974   Cultural Democracy, Bicognitive Development and Education. New York: Academic Press.
Stallings, Jane
1980   Allocated Academic Learning Time Revisited, or Beyond Time on Task. *In* Educational Researcher (American Educational Research Association). 9(11). December.
Trueba, H.T., and P.G. Wright.
1980   Meta-analysis of Microethnographies: Their Meaning and Potential for Multicultural Education Practice and Policy. Presented at the 79th Annual Meeting of

the American Anthropological Association and CAE, Washington, D.C. December. [Rpt. in this volume.]

U.S. Commission on Civil Rights Report

1973   Teacher and Students. Report V: Mexican American Education Study, Differences in Teacher Interaction with Mexican American and Anglo Students. Washington, D.C.: U.S. Government Printing Office. March.

Appendix: Carrasco/Guzman Macro and Micro Level Coding System for Videotapes

Method for Reducing Videotaped Data Into Units of Analysis

The coding sheets represent the horizontal indexing or breaking-down-of videotapes-system used by Erickson and Shultz (1977). We further developed that system into a computerized retreival system simply by shifting the horizontal line system into symbolic yet understandable functions to accommodate a large *corpus* of videotapes.

For example, *Level #1, Marco Context Coding*, refers to the first level of tape breakdown. In this case, since we are interested in lessons, the first level will identify the duration of the lesson (e.g., math).

E.G. |——————————— MATH ———————————|
3:10   15:00

Level #2, Macro-Subcontext Coding, refers to the second level of videotape breakdown. This section breaks down the taped lesson into its constituent parts (e.g., the "*opening,*" *formal reading,* and *Culmunation.*)

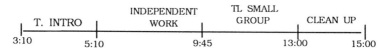

| | T. INTRO | | INDEPENDENT WORK | | TL SMALL GROUP | | CLEAN UP | |
3:10   5:10   9:45   13:00   15:00

Level #3, Micro Level Coding of Interactions, refers to the smaller units of analysis, the interactions themselves. This will be as far as we will attempt at this point. As we get further into this system, more variables may be added.

(Note: please note that each coding sheet has "Other Data" sections. This is for the addition of more data variables if needed.)

03:10   05:10   09:45   13:00   15:00

E.G. Each of these points represents an interaction of some sort. This case may be: Juan interacting with Maria, S-S instruction during independent Math work, duration: 06:00–06:45, etc.

Transcription Symbol Key

Symbol			Example from Transcription
:	=	Elongated sound production	Tu::: (You:::)
/ /	=	Phonetic notation brackets	/moukou/
	=	One utterance immediately follows another without pause.	The tub. Tub. I gat th' tub.
	=	Overlapping utterances said simultaneously	My hand hurts. My hand hurts.
/	=	Pause; // = longer pause	Ernesto// Ernesto.
xxx	=	inaudible or unable to transcribe	

How we numbered the transcription: By turn. Therefore, two or three statements in any participant's turn was given a number.

T to R   192.   No, you don't have the buffet.
                   You don't have the buffet. He has it.

T = Teacher	W = William	E = Ernesto
R = Ramiro	A = Alejandra	S = Sacremento

T to R = Teacher speaking to Ramiro
E to W = Ernest speaking to William

The international phonetic alphabet (consonants) was used. Listed below are the phonetic notations used for vowel sounds in English and Spanish.

ey = (Table)	I = (bit)	ʌ = (mud)	a = (mama)
ay = (cry)	ɔ = (bought)	ð = (butter)	e = (menos)
oʋ = (road)	æ = (bat)	3 = (bird)	i = si
ε = (bet)	ə = (unable)	ʋ = (book)	o = (loco)
			u = (tu)

CARRASCO/GUZMAN
BCIP CODING AND ANALYSIS SYSTEM
9-22-79

MACRO CONTEXT CODING: LEVEL #1

Classroom teacher: _____

Date of taping: __Month____ Day____ Year____

Event: _____

Actual Time of Day: _____

Event Duration:
  Start Tape # _____
  Start Time _____

  Stop Tape # _____
  Stop Time _____

Predominant event language: Spanish   English
Field notes availability (list by corresponding number)

Other Tapes with same event: _____

Other data: _____
_____
_____

Total # of Constituents: _____
Total # of Interactions: _____

QUALITATIVE COMMENTS

Evaluative Comments:

Particular Salient Examples:

Questions and Speculations:

Coding and Comments by: _____   Date: _____

(Use a separate sheet for more comments).

CARRASCO/GUZMAN
BCIP CODING AND ANALYSIS SYSTEM
9-22-79

MACRO SUBCONTEXT CODING: LEVEL #2
EVENT:

Constituent (

Name: _____ FORM (circle one)

Duration:

Start Tape # _____	TEWG		
Start Time _____	TESG		
	TW		
Stop Tape # _____	ACADEMIC:	Yes	No
Stop Time _____	CODESWITCH	Yes	No

Constituent (

Name: _____ FORM (circle one)

Duration:

Start Tape # _____	TEWG		
Start Time _____	TESG		
	TW		
Stop Tape # _____	ACADEMIC:	Yes	No
Stop Time _____	CODESWITCH	Yes	No

Constituent (

Name: _____ FORM (circle one)

Duration:

Start Tape # _____	TEWG		
Start Time _____	TESG		
	TW		
Stop Tape # _____	ACADEMIC:	Yes	No
Stop Time _____	CODESWITCH	Yes	No

QUALITATIVE COMMENTS

Narrative Description of Constituents:

Questions and Speculations:

Coding and Comments by: _____ Date: _____
(Use a separate sheet for more comments)

CARRASCO/GUZMAN
BCIP CODING AND ANALYSIS SYSTEM
9-22-79

MICRO CODING OF INTERACTIONS: LEVEL #3
EVENT: _____ CONSTITUENT: _____

INTERACTION( )
INSTANCE DURATION:
Start Tape # _____   PREDOMINANT LANGUAGE:
Start Time _____   Spanish _____
                             English _____
Stop Tape # _____   CODESWITCH: Yes _____   No
Stop Time _____   POLYCHRONIC: Yes _____   No
SHOT: (circle one)   Dyad   Triad   Small Grp   Whole Grp
PARTICIPATING TEACHER/AIDE NAME: _____
(Only if T or A is interacting in this instance)
Initiator: _____

MAIN PARTICIPANTS: STUDENTS
Student ( )
Focal: YES   NO
Bilingual Status: _____
Student ( )
Focal: YES   NO
Bilingual Status: _____
TYPE OF INTERACTION
SSI
SSN   T   NT

TSI
TSN   T   NT

INSERTED PARTICIPANTS: STUDENTS
Student ( )
FOCAL: YES   NO
Bilingual Status: _____
Student ( )
FOCAL: YES   NO
Bilingual Status: _____
TYPE OF INTERACTION
SSI
SSN   T   NT

TSI
TSN   T   NT

LOCATION OF INTERACTION WITHIN CLASSROOM (Circle one)
1. Floor Assembly Area   4. Back Work Table.
2. Child's Desk   5. Front Blackboard
3. Distar Table or Area   6. Other _____
OTHER: _____

QUALITATIVE COMMENTS

Narrative Description of Interaction:

Questions and Speculations:

Coding and Comments by: _____   Date: _____
(Use a separate sheet for more comments)

TIME MARKER	SPEAKER		Transcript	Notes
9:22	E to all	176.	My hand huurt. [hurtu-hurtu	
	T to S	177.	O.K. You have it too.	
	R to E	178.	Tu va' a hacer uno	You're going to do one.
	E to self	179.	[Ooow-ooow-ooow	
	T to W	180.	Give it back.	
	R to E	181.	[Ah, tu va'a hacer una mirala [ay a mi no :::: :: ::::a mi.	
	T to S	182.	[My: hand: hurt [My hand hurts	You're going to do one,
	S to T	183.	My head	Look it, Oh and for me
	T to S	184.	O.K.	no, for me . . .
	R to T	185.	My hand hurts.	
	W to T	186.	Mira teacher	Look, teacher
	T to all	187.	The buffet.	
	E to T	188.	I got the buffet.	
	T to E	189.	He has the buffet. . . . Anybody else have the buffet?	
	R to T	190.	I got the buffet	
	E to R	191.	I got the buffe-	
	T to R	192.	No, you don't have the buffet. He's has it	
	E to R	193.	You don't have the buffet. He's has it [/hʌ?/|	
	R to E	194.	[Yeah.	
	E to R	195.	*That's not buffet*	
	T to outsider from Classrm	196.	You take a look, can you look there?	
	T to all	197.	O.K. you look there.	
	W to T	198.	Sundial.	
	T to W	199.	dial	
	T to all.	201.	Who has the sundial?	
	E to T	202.	I have [I have the sundial	
	T to S	203.	I have the sundial	
	E to T	204.	I have the sun/dayal/	

Look.

TIME MARKER	SPEAKER		
	T to R	205.	Can I hear you say it?
	E to R	206.	/tʌtʌtʌ.../
10:17	R to W	207.	Mira
	S to T	208.	[-- have ⊤ the ⊤ sundia
	R to T	209.	[xxxx [xxxx [xxxxx xxx
	T to S	210.	Look it teacher!
	R to T	211.	Very good.
	R to T	212.	He /westədə/ me ::::::
	T to W	213.	William, let me hear you say it.
	T to W	214.	William [...........
	W to activity	215.	(is looking away from T)
	T to W	216.	William
	W to activity	217.	....
	T to W	218.	William. You need to tell me.
	W to T	219.	Yeah xxxxxxxx
	T to W	220.	I have /ə/sundial
	W to T	221.	I have the xxxx
10:37	E to self	222.	cooo
	T to W	223.	I have the sundial
	E to T	224.	/se:ndayll/ I have the sundəəl
	T to all	225.	Firecrackers.
	R to T	226.	[I has a fire/kræku
	E to T	227.	[I have a firecracker.
	T to R	228.	Very good. You have some too.
	R to T	229.	/kræku/
	W to T	230.	Yeah.
	R to T	231	I have the /fayʊkræk:z/
	T to R	232.	Crackers, very good
	E to self	233.	Boo-doo, boo-doo, boo-doo, boo-doo
	R to T	234.	[Crackers
	T to all.	235.	The steps
	R to T	236.	Who has the [steps
	T to all	237.	[Who has the steps.

Theoretical and Methodological Issues in the Ethnographic Study of Teachers' Differential Treatment of Children in Bilingual Bicultural Classrooms

Abdil Abel Maldonado-Guzman[1]

Preface

We are saddened by the loss of Abdil Abel Maldonado-Guzman, a reflective scholar, committed teacher, engaged musician, and delightful person. This chapter has not been updated but remains essentially as he wrote it in 1980 in the tradition of the use of the ethnographic present.

Introduction

This paper[2] raises issues and offers preliminary theories and analyses which have grown out of my current research on teachers' differential treatment of children in two first-grade Chicano bilingual-bicultural classrooms in Chicago. This work is part of a major study, "The Social and Cultural Organization of Interaction in Two Chicano Bilingual Classrooms: A Two Year Study," funded by the National Institute of Education. The other investigators of the project, which is based at Harvard University and Michigan State University, are Robert L. Carrasco, Frederick Erickson, and Courtney Cazden. Other data presented here were derived from the Puerto Rican-San Juan Ethnographic Project at the University of Massachusetts, Harbor Campus,

445

to which I am a consultant. The principal investigators of that project are German Diaz and Lucia David.

The categories of differential treatment that I report here are working ones; new categories, and even additional hypotheses, may emerge from further data analysis.

General Theoretical and Methodological Issues

There are many dimensions involved in differential treatment of children in the classroom, some within and others outside of the awareness of the interactors. Such treatment may, in other words, be so much a part of everyday behavior that it is tacit, or unconscious (Erickson 1973). Or it may, at an opposite pole, represent the kind of carefully planned conscious behavior which Goffman (1974) calls "strategic." For instance, researchers have noted the tendency among teachers to interact more frequently with students who facilitate the teaching task by being "good learners." Too often, students who display the most "talent" in the classroom receive encouragement at the expense of "less talented" students who may need such encouragement much more.

This paper attempts to demonstrate some of the dimensions of differential treatment and to show how these may be rooted in one or more of five aspects of the experiential histories of individuals and groups.

The first of these aspects is ethnocentrism, the belief that the cultural behaviorial ways of one's own ethnic group are better than those of other groups. Ethnocentric behavior reflects personal socio-cultural experience within an ethnic group or sub-group which supports this behavior. It is expressed at both the conscious and unconscious levels of behavior.

The second is orthodoxy, or adherence to what is perceived as the accepted and customary or traditional beliefs and behaviors while other behaviors and beliefs are considered illegitimate. Like ethnocentrism, orthodoxy is expressed at both conscious and unconscious behavioral levels. It can be related to cultural or social experience but can also be idiosyncratic or esoteric.

The third aspect is motive, or intent, which here refers to that which a group or individual wants to obtain from other groups or individuals. This paper will focus upon those objectives, needs, and desires which are consciously recognized. Such motives may produce strategic and even manipulatory behavior in an interaction. The fourth aspect is attraction. This involves the preferences, likes, and dislikes of a group or individual. This dimension may be either tacit or overt in an interaction.

Philosophy or ideology is the fifth aspect, defined as the articulated organization of thoughts and knowledge about the world, the immediate environment, and human processes. Through philosophy and ideology, people analyze and evaluate phenomena and behavior as well as create a basis for their own behavior. A philosophy may be ethnocentric or orthodox and can affect the operation of motive and attraction. In other words, this fifth aspect may influence the manifestation of all the other aspects in any interaction, e.g., degree of tolerance or intolerance, fairness or unfairness, and so forth.

Although the five aspects outlined are not mutually exclusive, this taxonomy can be very useful in the analysis of the nature of interactions that involve differential treatment. Social, political, and economic theorists and researchers of ethnic and race relations suggesting associations between these aspects of discriminatory and differential treatment include Barth (1969), Blalock (1967), Brewer and Campbell (1976), Schermerhorn (1970) and Wilson (1973). These categories may also provide a useful means of relating differential treatment at the face-to-face interactional level—that is, the micro context—to larger social and cultural phenomena, or the macro context.

So far, most educational researchers of differential treatment have not attempted to construct social or cultural theoretical postulates about the origins of the phenomenon. Educational research has instead been focused on identifying differential treatment at the micro level of the classroom. Teachers and students have been studied apart from the society and community which they experience daily outside the classroom; teachers' expectations have served as the major criteria for the existence of differential treatment. In these "self-fulfilling prophecy studies," teachers' expectations have been correlated to such aspects as sex, socio-economic status, expectancy of achievement, the subject matter involved, and pupils' ethnic and racial identity. The variables employed have been objectively defined: social class, for instance, by parents' jobs or income; racial or ethnic identity as defined by skin color, surname, or group ascription. These studies have suggested that teachers' behavior toward students, the attention they pay to them, and the opportunities provided for students' engagement in the teaching-learning process are largely affected by the teachers' expectations and perceptions. Analysis of the issue has been left at the individual or idiosyncratic level; that is, it has employed primarily individual, idiosyncratic definitions and conceptions of expectations and perceptions rather than socio-cultural ones.

In this regard, I would agree with Carew and Lightfoot (1980:7), who say that such research "exaggerates the teacher as the dominant, overpowering, even malicious figure of the classroom." Furthermore, such research does not consider tacit or customary behaviors which are performed out of the awareness of teachers and which may be rooted in social experience. Teachers have been seen as primary reinforcers of such social processes as class stratification, which is not a process carried out solely by teachers. It is perhaps more accurate to understand the teacher as the unconscious vehicle for the preservation of racial, ethnic, or social class distinctions, resulting from his or her own socialization into a stratified and/or highly ethnocentric group or society (Memmi 1970; Freire 1968). If "discriminatory" differential treatment takes place in the classroom, it is supported not only by the teacher but also by the whole educational system and society. Given this social reality, the importance of the five aspects of experiential history of groups and individuals becomes clear.

The shortcomings of educational research on differential treatment may reflect the absence of social and cultural theory in the analysis of classroom interaction.

Another possible cause is the use of questionnaires, tests, observation scales, and other instruments which identify surface variables but cannot tap more dynamic but tacit realms. The lack of comparative studies—to contrast the ways in which Anglo teachers interact with Hispanic children as opposed to Anglo children, for example—is another problem. Finally, there is a need to focus on natural interactions to expose the tacit realms of differential treatment and to clarify the overt ones. Ethnographic methods of research in the study of classroom interaction have much to offer in this respect. Some ethnographies which have focused on the social and cultural organization of classrooms deal with the issue of teachers' differential treatment of children (Carrasco 1978; McDermott; and McDermott and Gospodinoff 1980). However, the need exists to emphasize this as a focal issue, central to ethnographic studies of the classroom.

Teachers' differential treatment of children may occur in any type of classroom. Nevertheless, classrooms reflecting sharp ethnic or racial distinctions (bilingual, bicultural and multiracial), class differences, or differences in academic performance may display some kinds of differential treatment more overtly than more homogeneous classrooms. Specifically, one could expect that ethnocentrism, orthodoxy, attractions and preferences, ideologies and intent would be more easily recognizable in bilingual-bicultural classrooms. This expectation is based upon the work of those theorists and researchers who hold that the more diverse the group examined, the more evident differential treatment and discriminatory practices will be along cultural, racial and linguistic boundaries (Barth 1969; Blalock 1967; Schermerhorn 1978; van den Berghe 1967).

The condition of being culturally different in a social setting in which different ethnic groups are ascribed varying degrees of power and prestige may encourage either one's ethnocentrism and cultural orthodoxy, on the one hand, as a means of preserving and defending what one's individual and social life has been, or one's assimiliation, on the other, as a way of surviving within a social group in which one's social history is considered negatively.

Nevertheless, when there are clear intents that require negotiations among diverse members of a group, mutual understanding and adjustment can also occur (Barth 1969). Specifically, in bilingual-bicultural classrooms, despite the power of the teacher and the educational system to decide which cultural practices will officially prevail and which will be suppressed, it is dialectically impossible that some kinds of mutual adjustment between those with different cultural behaviors will not occur. Teaching and learning imply the use of a pedagogy that is not only a priori but that also develops in the making, in constant interaction, on a dynamic basis, as experience stimulates its creation. Therefore, both teachers and students must try to develop ways of communicating with one another that respect each other's realities, and in this process affect the modality which differential treament takes in the classroom setting. In this way, pedagogical intent affects orthodox and ethnocentric behaviors in bilingual-bicultural settings. It is important, then, to try to understand the interaction between ethnocentrism, orthodoxy, intent, preferences and attractions, and ideologies and philosophies in classroom interaction.

The magnitude of the importance that ethnocentrism and orthodoxy, for instance, may have on teachers' differential treatment of students in the classroom, is revealed in the following excerpts from a discussion with six Puerto Rican participants in a teacher's exchange program sponsored by the University of Massachusetts, Harbor Campus. These teachers had come to work in Boston for one year, while their colleagues from Boston went to Puerto Rico to teach. This discussion was recorded with the teachers' permission.

Teacher #2:

> One arrives with 10 years of teaching experience, brings all the materials considered to be necessary from Puerto Rico, expects to know what to do right away, expects that the students know Spanish and the basic elements of Spanish literature, but finds that nothing can be done.

The students are at a very low level. I have to teach sixth grade skills to 11th and 12th grade students.

These students know neither English nor Spanish. They say "mah mejol" (better) instead of "mejor," "emprestame" instead of "prestame" (lend me) and "jallal" instead of "hallar" (to find).[3]

Here, students don't know anything. A 12th grade student who is close to graduating had never analyzed a short story the way we do it in Puerto Rico. Here, nobody analyzes anyway. You can call the procedure that American teachers use "the one to ten procedure." This means, they give a mimeographed paper to the students with ten questions and tell them: "Here, answer this!" The student doesn't know how to think, to discuss or to argue. The student doesn't know what lies behind a sentence in a short story. The student doesn't know how to answer, because in this educational system the important thing is to keep the student silent and quiet with games and punishments.

A student here treated me with lack of respect. He dared to talk back to me when I scolded him. I told him to leave the room, and again, he talked back to me. I told him: "Look, you better shut off, because I'll shut your mouth off myself!"

Those exercises, hobbies and crosswords are shameful! When a student doesn't have anything to do the teachers tell him: "Here, do this!" How is it possible? I have come to the conclusion that a 12th grade in Puerto Rico is equivalent to a first year of college in Boston.

My students like my new method. I forgot about mimeographed papers and told them: "Here, everybody brings a notebook!" If a student comes into the classroom without a notebook, I say: "Hey, where are you going? Listen, go back! You don't come into this classroom without a notebook!"

The procedure that I follow in the Spanish class is that the student has to talk . . . Well, a Spanish class is one of the most beautiful classes.

I have the case of a boy who just arrived
from Puerto Rico. And I have never seen a sadder
little face than the face of this creature[4] I feel
sad because of that little face. And I get close
to him, and he tells me: "Ay teacher, here is not
the same, I can't get used to it."

Teacher #3:

Well, I have the flip side of the coin. I have Richard
Gines, a fourteen-year-old boy who is about six
feet tall. When this "apparatus" comes into my
classroom, I say to myself: "My God!, where is
this coming from?" And two weeks went by, and
this boy has become contaminated with the bad
habits of the students of Boston. In only two
weeks that boy who came from the countryside
of Puerto Rico has changed!

The next statement by one of these teachers shows
the importance of ideological stands or philosophies in
teachers' differential treatment of students.

Teacher #3:

I have my Ramon Figueroa. He is a "000" case
because the social environment has pushed him
to be "000." He never feels that he belongs to
the group; nor can he do satisfactory work. I
have to give him special attention. He is in the
grade he is—third grade—because he has been
unstable. . . . The system has pushed him to
be a slow learner, retarded, because his family
is always moving. . . . In this sense he has been
very unfortunate. Ramon mentions the problem
of the climate and the language, and I understand
him.

The above excerpts, besides providing teachers'
perceptions and opinions, also make reference to specific
teachers' actions or behavior as responses to student
behavior and perceived conditions. Their statements
indicate that these teachers tend to be supportive and

understanding of newly arrived Puerto Rican migrant students. But they also suggest (specifically teachers #2 and #3) that students who do not conform to their views and ideals may be in a difficult situation—at least, their behavior will be sanctioned. Students who do not represent the essence of the Puerto Rican culture and experience as the teachers themselves have lived it and who therefore do not display in the classroom the student model to which these teachers are accustomed, will probably be sanctioned or censored. That is, students who represent what in the teachers' view is American education, or possibly Puerto Rican American, and who also do not speak either standard English or standard Spanish, will be censored and an attempt may be made to uproot them from their everyday cultural context. These teachers may try to impose a new history upon the children's actual history, in effect denying the legitimacy of these children's life experiences in Boston.

It is important to mention here that the teachers involved in this discussion are Puerto Rican, educated there and trained in the Puerto Rican modalities of teaching and learning. They come from a centralized educational system which prescribes what students at different grade levels will study and what abilities are expected to be developed among them. Every student in every public school on the Island, except for those in special needs programs, is given the same educational curriculum or agenda. The children to whom the teachers refer are also Hispanic, and mainly Puerto Rican. Most of them were born or have been raised in the United States and have studied here. Thus, these children are immersed in the practices and modes of a different educational system, which is not highly regarded by these ethnocentric and pedagogically orthodox teachers. Despite having cultural roots similar to their students', the specific cultural reality of these teachers differs from that of children who have lived in Hispanic communities in the United States. This is a clear situation of ethnic borders within a major group. These teachers view only newly arrived children or children who display the same cultural behavior as themselves with empathy and sympathy.

The economic competition and cultural incongruence reflected here between Puerto Ricans from the Island and Puerto Ricans born on the United States mainland has not been examined in most research on these groups, although the Puerto Rican community is generally aware of it. Puerto Rican return migrant children—both those born on the mainland and those born in Puerto Rico but raised on the mainland—suffer from intolerance and rejection by teachers and students when they return to schools in Puerto Rico. In this case, ethnocentrism seems to be related to economic class and the degree of mainland acculturation. The majority of the Puerto Ricans who have migrated to the mainland have been peasants from the countryside and people from the slums, whose cultural expression and language are regarded as inferior by the upper classes. Puerto Ricans from the Island commonly complain of the fact that returnees speak in old-fashioned ways and listen to peasant music. Similar intolerance and competition for economic opportunities is experienced by Chicanos returning to Mexico. Again, though many Chicanos discuss such issues privately, the topic is avoided by Mexican officials, community leaders, and both Mexican and Chicano researchers.

Why this silence? Many times, in defense of bilingual education for Hispanics, one argues for the employment of Hispanic teachers with the expectation that they will be more sympathetic to and understanding of, for example, Chicano or Puerto Rican children than an Anglo teacher would be. However, qualifications should be made. Although Hispanic teachers often support Puerto Rican mainland or Chicano culture, the foregoing discussion with Puerto Rican teachers shows that this is not always true. Hispanic teachers who have not lived the reality of Hispanic children on the United States mainland may be just as threatening to the culture and history of these children and to their knowledge and survival skills as any highly ethnocentric and orthodox teacher from a radically different culture might be. This threat would be strongest during the period when the teacher has not learned about the social and living situation of the students or has not yet confronted similar realities. Any teacher's increasing experience in the new situation might lead to changes in perception; in many cases, however, the differences are strengthened and misunderstanding prevails. On the other hand, a need remains to complement the children's Puerto Rican mainland or Chicano realities with Puerto Rican or Mexican culture in a conscientious educational program. It is possible to clarify the original Latin American linguistic and cultural matrix while supporting the mainland Puerto Rican or Chicano culture. Such strategies are very much needed when the mainstream culture threatens to erase the imprint of "barrio" life, as well as the attachment to a mother culture.

Issues in the Study of Differential Treatment of Children in Two Bilingual Classrooms

My focus on teachers' differential treatment of children in two bilingual classrooms came as a result of viewing, coding, and analyzing videotapes during my participation in the Bilingual Classrooms Interaction Project. It was clear that some children were receiving "preferential treatment" over others, suggesting that in the daily educational work some students were likely to benefit more than others. But how does the process of preferential treatment take place? And why do some teachers prefer some students over others?

Some children were very persistent in trying to elicit attention and preference from their teachers. They constantly behaved according to the teachers' wishes and were enforcers and guardians of the organizational structure that their teachers had instituted in the classrooms. These children seemed to play "classroom politics." In each of the classrooms there were, interestingly, one boy and one girl who performed these roles.

Children in general tended to value the teacher's recognition of their work and behavior a great deal. In one classroom I saw two boys jumping together, hugging each other and doing a "give-me-five" exchange as an expression of satisfaction and happiness after having been chosen "capitanes" (helpers) by their teacher. In that case, the task was to distribute papers to other children. Their behavior demonstrated a spirit of competition for leadership which may sometimes have positive implications for learning, although careful consideration should be given to the possible negative implications of competitive practices in the classroom.

Some children in the two classrooms that were studied constantly struggled for attention from the teacher by performing prestigious behaviors; they seemed "tacitly" or clearly to know that the teacher had a concept of the "ideal student." They may have learned this by interpreting teachers' behavior and their verbal messages as to what was expected from students. Children who were good competitors and/or leaders were the most likely to try to get attention from the teacher and to be appointed to perform prestigious or status-bearing roles and tasks in the classroom. On the other hand, in both classrooms there were students who did not compete for status-bearing roles. Their behavior did not seem to demonstrate interest in their being named "capitanes" or special helpers. The skills needed to strive for status-bearing assignments may not have been part of their experiential history or may not have been fostered by the social conditions of their lives. Possibly their personality characteristics did not permit these children to try to be competitors; they might not have possessed the skills and traits that make some children attractive to teachers. For whatever reason, they were not able to "get the floor."

Teachers praise those children who do everything within the accepted and institutionalized "legal limits" of the classroom structure, while constantly reprimanding those whose behavior is not compatible with the classroom social structure. Also, children who display knowledge in ways expected in the classroom are praised, but children who display streetwise behavior, communicating the essence of the barrio, are reprimanded. Only when these streetwise children are able to adjust their conduct in ways the teacher finds appropriate is such street knowledge and behavior permitted. For instance, in one of the classrooms a child rapidly echoed the words his teacher read; in the eyes and ears of this teacher he knew how to read, and the teacher praised him. But not all the children were competent in using their previous or current out-of-the-classroom knowledge to manipulate classroom realities. Those students who could not harmonize their co-existing and often conflicting spheres of knowledge therefore received more reprimands than praise. Or they simply remained silent. However, in these classrooms the children who were silent tended to receive little attention. Although their teachers sometimes tried to include them in the on-going active classroom interaction, outspoken and active children captured much of the teachers' attention. Thus the problem of borders existing within a culture may be one of differing exposure to the "new" culture as it is for the Puerto Rican teachers vis-a-vis the Puerto Rican mainland children or one of different social contexts within the original culture as it is for the Chicano teachers and Mexican children. The apparent incongruence in the second case between the formal rules and behavior of the school and the informal rules and behavior of the community may, however, be influenced by Anglo culture, since both Chicano teachers involved had been educated in Anglo universities. Social class may also be a variable here. But whether or not miscommunication is indeed ethnocentric, orthodoxy does seem to play a role.

The process of coding events and interactions (see Appendix to Carrasco et al. chapter for Carrasco/Guzman Coding System) revealed differential treatment which was not associated primarily with teachers' ethnocentrism, orthodoxy, or preferences but rather with their classroom procedures and structure and their pedagogical objectives. Different students, and even the entire group, were instructed in different ways during different lessons. It was apparent that differential treatment could no longer be defined as solely preferential, therefore the concept of such treatment as a response to perceived group and individual needs began to develop. This new dimension, identified by placing and interpreting interactions within definite contexts (Erickson and Shultz 1977), implies that pedagogic philosophies and teaching objectives should be considered in the study of differential treatment in order to be fair to the teacher's efforts.

In the coding process, academic events were divided into their various constituent parts, allowing the researcher to analyze the structure of a lesson or event and to see patterns of organization, enactment of rules, and participation structures in the classroom.

Thus new interpretations of previously observed behavior emerged. For example, during some constitutent parts of the lessons there was almost no teacher/student or student/student verbal interaction. If a student, even one of those the teacher apparently preferred, tried to start an interaction, some type of reprimand was the likely response. However, during other constituent parts such interactions abounded, and children were permitted to initiate them freely. Focusing on this dimension of context constituents led to the concept of procedural treatment, that is, differential treatment which is influenced by rules and social structure in the classroom.

To summarize, by following a research focus through different contexts, three different dimensions of differential treatment were identified. First, at the level of teacher-student interaction—the micro contextual level—preferential treatment occurred, independent of contexts and sub-contexts. It is important to clarify, however, that at this level the interaction was not always independent from context, especially in very formal contexts in which students at least seemed to be treated equally. Aside from these specific formal contexts, however, the teachers gave more attention to some students than to others, expressed more warmth, or *cariño*, toward them, and seemed closer to them than to others. At the level of context constituents, that is, the macro sub-context, procedural differential treatment appeared. And at the macro, or lesson level, differential treatment occurred as the result of teacher's perceived and students' verbally expressed academic needs. This treatment, involving, for example, frequent math-related interactions between teachers and particular students throughout the academic year, is needs-related differential treatment.

Other research, in which analysis has been based on participant non-ethnographic observation scales, tests, and questionnaires (Rist 1970; Carew and Lightfoot 1980; Rosenthal and Jacobson 1968), has not identified all three of these dimensions of differential treatment. And even these three do not constitute an exhaustive taxonomy of differential treatment. Nonetheless, it may be hypothesized that these categories of differential treatment are rooted in the five major aspects or attributes of group and individual experiential history defined at the beginning of this paper. Preferential treatment may be based on ethnocentrism, orthodoxy, and personal attraction. Procedural and needs-based differential treatment might relate to educational philosophies and pedagogical motives. It is also possible that each of these categories of differential treatment is influenced by all five factors, even though one could identify the most significant source(s) in each case through overt verbal expressions and recurrent behavior.

An Interpretive Example of Differential Treatment in Two Videotaped Lessons in a Bilingual Classroom

Through videotape viewing and interpretation, several major indicators were identified as means of studying differential treatment of children. These indicators may be considered "grounded": they were not preconceived, but rather emerged from the data (Glaser and Strauss 1979). Three major categorical levels were identified:

1. Level of Analytic Indicators: Teacher's attention, or engaged time with children:
- Time duration of engagement with individual children or small groups of children;
- Number of interactions with particular children or small groups of children and proportion of this number in relation to other individual children, and/or small groups;
- Teacher's response or readiness to respond to individual children or small groups who attempt to get teacher's attention.

   2. Level of Analytic Indicators: Teacher's
      expressive style while interacting with
      particular children or small groups of children:
   • Endearment phrases and gestures;
   • Praises and/or reprimands (positive or negative
     sanctions);
   • Proximity, or physical distance;
   • Language matching (style and level of
     abstraction—attempt at better communication
     with individual children and groups);
   • Revealing knowledge of particular children;
   • Other recurrent language patterns and
     expressions (e.g., messages that may indicate
     bias towards individual children and particular
     groups).
   3. Special Tasks Assigned to Individual Children:
   • Tasks that may involve prestige, or conversely,
     no prestige at all;
   • Tasks that may involve stereotyping.

   In order to provide a more reliable interpretation of
the quality of differential treatment, two types of
questionnaires were developed. The first one was aimed
at obtaining information about the teachers' perception of
each individual student—the appraisal they had made of
the student's behavior, skills, and physical appearance.
The second elicited information concerning the teachers'
educational philosophies, their conceptions of the ideal
student, their perceptions of their own roles and of the
students' roles, and their opinions as to the ways individual
and group differences should be addressed in the classroom.
Some of the issues raised in this questionnaire also
appeared in taped interviews with the teachers. These
audiotapes, as well as portions of the videotapes, were
analyzed for messages and expressive styles. Additional
data were garnered from videotape viewing and discussion
sessions with the teachers.
   The research process may be clarified by a brief
description of two lessons, Math and Language Arts, in
one of the classrooms. Figure 1 illustrates how the coding
system and the identified indicators were applied to analyze

the teachers' differential treatment of children in these lessons. The Math lesson is 56:48 minutes long, while the Language Arts lesson is 47:34. Here both lessons have seven different constituents (see Figure 1). Certain constituents—lesson introduction, group formation, letter introduction and board instructions—are shorter than those which require students to practice at the board or at their desks; consequently, these feature few or no interactions. Those interactions which are found in the introductory constituents of the academic events occur between the teacher and the whole class or between the teacher and small groups of students. These interactions—group formation, lesson introduction, board instructions, letter introduction, and letter recognition—are either to enforce order and structure or to illustrate and clarify the lesson or exercise that is to follow. The introductory constituents do not usually involve interactions between the teacher and individual students.

On the other hand, one-to-one teacher-student interactions are frequent during board exercises and individual desk work. During introductory constituents, all students receive reprimands if they do not conform to the order of the lesson. Usually the teacher initiates the interactions rather than the students. Preferential treatment is not as evident here as it is during periods of board or desk exercises, although this does not mean that it does not exist. Actually, expressions of preferential treatment can be seen along sex dimensions during these introductory constituents. In this classroom there is a distinct division in the seating patterns of boys and girls: boys sit to the left of the teacher, and girls to the right. The teacher's gaze and postural shifts are directed more often toward the boys' side during the introductory constituents of both lessons. Procedural differential treatment is common during these constituents, however, on the basis of being in order or out of order.

During the Math lesson, there are fourteen children in the classroom: six girls and eight boys. Even though the majority of students are boys, the majority of individual interactions occurring during this lesson (26) are with girls (19). These take place during board exercises and individual desk work. Interpreted in terms of quality, which is basically instructional, this imbalance in frequency of interactions suggests that the teacher believes girls need more help in Math than boys do—an indication of social stereotyping which is borne out by informal talks with both teachers. Moreover, given the average time girls spend at the board doing the exercises or in obtaining help from the teacher, it seems they indicate that they need or believe they need extra help in Math. In other videotaped Math lessons in this classroom, the teacher appoints boys to go to help girls at the board.

Similarly, when desk work begins in this Math lesson (37:13 date-generated time), the teacher first asks the boys, who are sitting close together, if they have understood the instructions; they respond affirmatively. The teacher then asks the same question of the girls, most of whom answer negatively. The teacher then tells them to try to do the work and says that she will help them later. Among all the girls who need help, one is particularly given attention during board and individual desk work. It so happens that the teacher has referred to this girl in a questionnaire, saying, "I wish I had one thousand Saluds in the classroom."[5] During individual work the teacher devotes the most time to this girl and kisses and hugs her three times. There is also a special boy who receives a lot of attention, including a hug and a kiss, during this constituent. The teacher regards this boy as the most brilliant child in the classroom, rating him "high plus." In lessons recorded in other videotapes, he is constantly appointed as a tutor to help other children. The girl who receives the most attention is rated "high." She is regarded as "silent, well-behaved and charming."

During Language Arts there are 22 children in the classroom, fourteen boys and eight girls, which is the regular size of the class.[6] In this lesson, the boys are the clear and immediate focus of attention. Here again, the boys are seated on one side and the girls on the other. There is more frequent interaction with boys, and during individual work periods interactions with boys are longer. Girls remain almost silent until the board work constituent when the teacher asks them to go to the blackboard to

Figure 1

Teachers' Individual Treatment of Children in Two Lessons:
Math and Language Arts

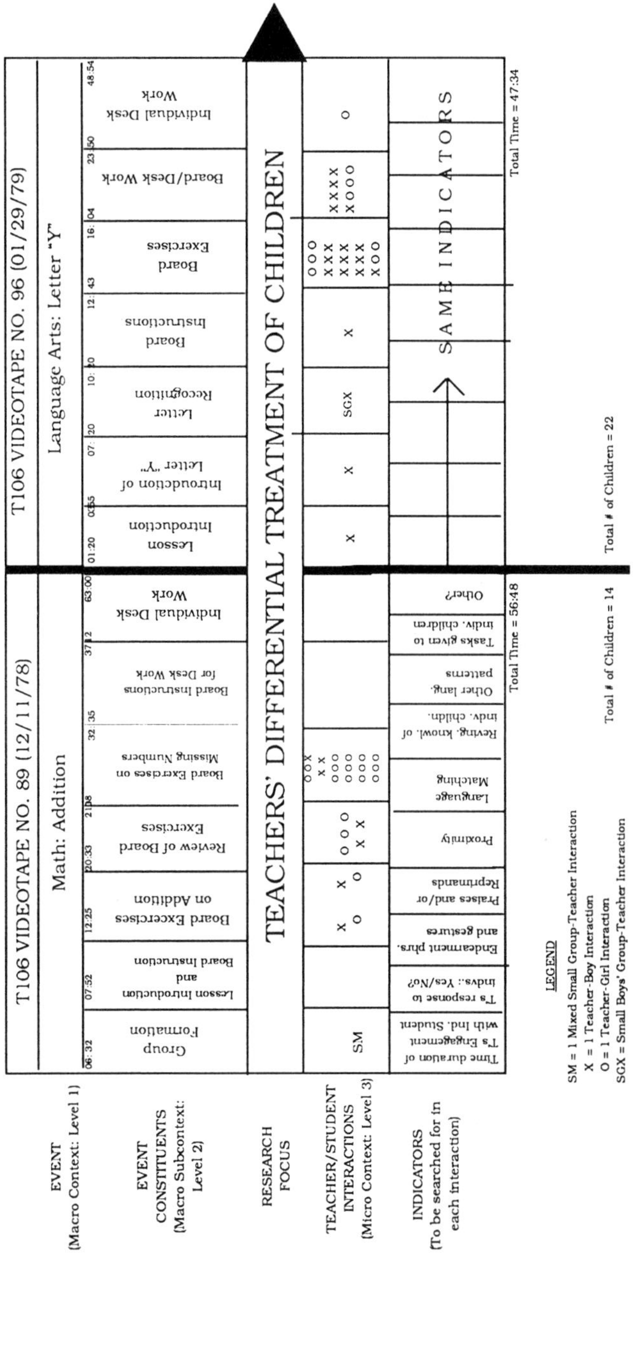

EVENT [Macro Context: Level 1]	T106 VIDEOTAPE NO. 89 (12/11/78) Math: Addition	T106 VIDEOTAPE NO. 96 (01/29/79) Language Arts: Letter "Y"

TEACHERS' DIFFERENTIAL TREATMENT OF CHILDREN

SAME INDICATORS

LEGEND

SM = 1 Mixed Small Group-Teacher Interaction
X = 1 Teacher-Boy Interaction
O = 1 Teacher-Girl Interaction
SGX = Small Boys' Group-Teacher Interaction

practice writing the letter "Y." Besides interacting more frequently with boys during this lesson, the teacher gives them the first turn at the blackboard.

During board work done during constituents five and six (Figure 1), the teacher divides the class into three groups which take turns going to the blackboard. Of the first group, the teacher asks seven boys and three girls to do the board work. It is interesting that when the teacher asks boys to take their turns, meanwhile dividing the blackboard into portions with chalk lines, she repeats their names rapidly and spontaneously, without having to turn toward them to decide which will be given a turn. However, before selecting the three girls to take their turn, the teacher carefully looks at them. While the boys are at the board, the teacher closely monitors their work. She helps them, even guiding their hands, without making evaluative comments about their work. But when she helps one girl, the teacher says, "Slowly, slowly, don't get nervous," even though the girl does not seem to be acting differently from the boys. She later uses the same verbal expression while helping another girl to write the letter "Y." The teacher makes no such statement, however, addressing the boys during these exercises.

The second group sent to the board is composed entirely of boys. The teacher asks them to write at the right side of the blackboard, and she herself erases that side when they have finished. When it is the girls' turn to practice, however, she asks one of them, who is seated on the floor among the waiting group of girls, to erase that portion of the board where they will practice. Similarly, during a previous constituent devoted to board instructions, the teacher asked a girl to pick up the letter set the teacher had left on the floor. It seems that some gender stereotyping is involved in the teacher's delegation of work in the classroom, asking girls to perform tasks similar to those which women (or Hispanic women) are "supposed to do" in the home. Boys, however, are not asked to perform this kind of task.

The last group to be sent to the board consists entirely of those girls who have not yet practiced.

The sex-linked differential treatment reflected in these two lessons raises the following questions:

- Does the differential attention correspond to the traditional and widely held notion that girls do better in Language Arts and boys in Math and that girls therefore need less help in Language Arts while boys need less help in Math?
- Does the differential treatment respond to a special attraction that the teacher has to boys, as opposed to girls?

Here the teacher's use of endearing terms in addressing boys and girls may be relevant. The most common terms are "pa," "ma," "mami," and "papi," generally used among Hispanics by husband and wife to address one another or by parents to address their children. In addition, they are conventional and not necessarily endearing terms to call one's parents. There are twice as many boys as girls in this classroom, so it should be expected that "papi" be used more frequently than "mami." However, girls receive proportionally far fewer endearments than boys. During Math, the teacher uses "papi" or "pa" seven times in addressing boys, but "ma" only once in addressing a girl. During the Language Arts lesson, the teacher uses "papi" or "pa" nine times while using "mami" and "ma" twice. Also, in both lessons, boys are given a turn to work at the board or at their desks before girls.

The differential treatment of children according to gender raises a third question involving culture in these classrooms in which both teachers and students are Chicano:

Is the greater amount of attention paid to boys and the greater number of turns at board and desk given to them, a reflection of social and cultural practices rooted in the home, the community, and the society at large?

To address this question, the researcher must go beyond the context of the classroom to social, community, and cultural contexts. This teacher did not offer any specific comments about differential treatment according to sex in the classroom. When asked why boys and girls sat clustered in different sides of the classroom, she did not seem to have noticed this differentiation. Furthermore, she said that the children had automatically assumed that seating pattern when they came to her classroom for the first time. They were used to it, possibly as a result of the experience they had had in the kindergarten bilingual classroom with another teacher, a Mexican. This teacher denied that she was fostering the division, possibly because this is part of her tacit behavior. However, when the children are lining up to leave the room, at lunchtime, or at the end of the day, she places them in two lines—the boys on one side, the girls on the other. Actually, the Mexican kindergarten teacher and the other Chicano teacher who participated in this study do exactly the same thing. A comparison with Anglo teachers, which will be a next step in the Bilingual Classroom Interaction Project, may provide more reliable information about the social and cultural nature of gender differentiation in the classroom.

During the two lessons studied, there are children who receive less individual attention than the others. Two of these students, a boy and a girl, are very much liked by the teacher, who assesses them as brilliant. This suggests that the brightest children, even if preferred, do not necessarily get attention, especially if the teacher has a clear conception of individual and group needs. Possibly, in the teacher's mind, these children do not need as much attention as others do. During these lessons, these two kids try to initiate interactions with the teacher. They go after her to show her their work, seeking her approval, but she pays them minimal attention. On the other hand, children who do need attention and help and try to get it might not receive any at all if the teacher is not especially attracted to them. One child tries twice during the Math lesson to have the teacher review his work: she does not respond to him. In other videotapes, this boy is constantly "invisible." In a videotape viewing session with this teacher, she could not readily remember his name. The questionnaires indicate that the teacher appears to have less information about this child than she has about the average student.

During the Math lesson, there is another child who tries unsuccessfully to get the teacher's attention. However, the teacher feels especially attracted to this boy because he looks like an *indito*, or "little Indian." She also feels compassion for this child because he is poor, and always wears the same clothes to school. The teacher says that sometimes he does not smell good; still she kisses and hugs him. During the present Math lesson, however, she gives him minimal time. She classifies this boy as a low academic performer; during other events, especially Language Arts, she may spend a disproportionate amount of time helping him. She does not do so during this Math lesson because he seems to be doing fine. At least, this is what her verbal message suggests.

Final Comments

The above analysis reveals five different dimensions of differential treatment: (1) sex; (2) attractiveness; (3) academic performance; (4) need for help, and (5) deportment. These dimensions may be related to the aspects of human experience already identified as possible sources of behavioral differentiation: motives or intent, attraction,[7] orthodoxy, and philosophy or ideology. One might hypothesize, for example, that:

- The teacher is more attracted toward boys than girls, and toward high achievers more than low achievers overall. (Attraction)
- At the conscious level, the teacher seems to believe that all children should have equal opportunity to learn; consequently, when some students need more attention than others, she provides it as a way of levelling the opportunities. (Philosophy or ideology)
- During some events, when the objective is academic and order is considered necessary for its fulfillment, students who are out of order receive sanctions, regardless of who they are, and students who behave in an orderly manner are acknowledged. (Motives or intent; orthodoxy as to how things should be done could be reflected, too.)

- Some behaviors considered inappropriate to
  the environment of the classroom such as like
  talking loudly, chewing gum, etc., are not
  permitted there even when they do not disturb
  the order and flow of the class. (Orthodoxy)
- There are characteristics other than gender
  and high academic achievement that attract
  the teacher to a child such as poverty or
  physical appearance. (Attraction)

In the examples provided in the research exercise,
the teacher displays no behavior that could be clearly
described as ethnocentric. It so happens that children and
teacher are Chicano and that, ideologically, the teacher is
interested in the preservation of Chicano culture and
Mexican cultural ways. An interesting idiosyncracy noticed
in other videotapes is that the teacher recognizes that her
Spanish is not as "standard or appropriate" as that spoken
by many of the children, especially those who are Spanish-
dominant, because she has become interested in being
proficient only as an adult. She constantly asks children
to correct and help her with Spanish. This teacher often
incorporates in her lessons—whenever it seems relevant
and congruent to do so—the experiences some of the
children have had in Mexico and the experience of their
everyday lives as members of the Chicano community.
Thus a great deal of the children's cultural behavior is
acknowledged in the classroom. This seems to differ from
the Puerto Rican teachers portrayed earlier in this chapter.
The qualitative difference lies in the fact that this teacher
is Chicano and has experienced the same social conditions
and culture that her students have; also, she has taught
in this community for a number of years. A newly arrived
Mexican teacher, on the other hand, might be as
ethnocentric as the Puerto Rican teachers were.

In order to assess ethnocentrism in differential
treatment, it is necessary to do comparative studies
involving a variety of ethnic experiences undergone within
and outside a given major ethnic group. One way to do
this would be to study a multiethnic classroom in which
children and teacher are radically different or have had

different social experiences despite belonging to the same major ethnic group. Within these settings, however, it would be desirable to include children who share the teacher's ethnicity (Erickson 1975). Such a comparative study, involving these same two classrooms which feature Chicano teachers and bilingual Chicano students as well as classrooms having bilingual Anglo teachers and bilingual Chicano children, has been funded by the Ford Foundation; the co-investigators are Robert L. Carrasco and myself.

The clear separation of sexes and differential treatment according to sex seen in the settings dicussed may also be related to orthodox lifestyles which are part of the socio-cultural experience of the children, as well as of the teacher. Also, such separation and differential treatment according to sex is not specific to Chicano culture, but is fostered by the mainstream culture as well. The phenomenon cannot be called ethnocentric; there is no evidence concerning the differences between the separation by gender portrayed in this classroom from, for instance, that occuring in Anglo classrooms.

Other practices that might be described as orthodox take place in this classroom, but are not reflected in the examples above. These have to do with the perception of appropriate behavior in school, and in the community. Some behaviors appropriate to the community and home— talking loudly, for instance, or hand-playing—will never be accepted in school, despite the teacher's familiarity with them, and possibly her own participation in them, outside school. Some behaviors may not be permitted in the classroom because they are linked to a specific class or group, despite cultural commonalities. The teacher observed often displayed behaviors and attitudes that indicated social class orthodoxy: strict rules of formality, for example, sometimes to the extreme of total inflexibility; very different from the degree of formality expressed in poor Chicano communities, but typical of the Hispanic upper classes. This strictness, even if idiosyncratic—since, in this case, the teacher was raised in a very disciplined Mennonite family—would still be an orthodox manifestation of behavior.

In conclusion, at least three theoretical and

methodological considerations should be taken into account in studying teachers' differential treatment of children in bilingual bicultural classrooms, as well as other kinds of classrooms and settings:

- Socio-cultural dimensions are present in the manifestation of differential treatment and are not simply idiosyncratic as self-fulfilling prophecy and educational psychological research suggest. For Merton (1949) and Parsons (1951), every type of behavior displayed in the classroom is a reflection of the culture and society in which the actors live. In contrast to this social determinism, individual determinism proposes that teacher behavior occurs without any influence from socio-cultural structure. An integrated theoretical approach to research on teachers' differential treatment of children would consider the individual as part of a dynamic relationship with the surrounding socio-cultural reality and would address the nature of this relationship.

- Differential treatment is not a uni-dimensional phenomenon that can be exhaustively studied using the traditional criterion of teachers' expectations, although traditional methods have been useful in establishing its existence. Many dynamic forces, both social and individual, underlie differential treatment; new methods could uncover the natural manifestation of the dynamic forces involved. The integration of different sources of data, including long periods of observation at different points in time, could be very useful in providing information on these dynamics accounting for historical changes. Ethnography has a great deal to offer here.

- Ethnocentric differential treatment can occur within a major cultural group. Geographical diversity as well as differing degrees of assimilation and acculturation among members of a major cultural group in another socio-cultural environment may account for this type of differential treatment. This applies to the Puerto Rican teachers reported in this article and the Puerto Rican mainland children they teach. Other types of differential treatment might also be manifested within a major cultural group. For instance, differential treatment based on religious orthodoxy, social class orthodoxy, or any other type of orthodoxy may lead to miscommunication and the establishment of borders within a cultural group. All three of these aspects are important not only to research but to the design and operation of bilingual bicultural educational programs.

Endnotes

1. At the time of writing, Dr. Abdil Abel Maldonado-Guzman was Assistant Professor, Graduate School of Education, Pennsylvania State University.

2. This paper was presented at the 79th Annual Meeting of the American Anthropological Association, Symposium on Policy Implications of Ethnographic Research in Bilingual Education, Council of Anthropology and Education, December 3–7, 1980.

3. These examples reveal the conflict between "standard prestigious" forms of Spanish and the "non-standard, peasant lower class forms" (Labov, 1972).

4. "Criatura" in Spanish involves a lot of compassion.

5. "Salud" is the name of this girl.

6. The other lesson was videotaped a month before, in December 1978, when many of the children were absent because of a snowstorm in Chicago. The present lesson was videotaped in January 1979.

7. Attractive here includes physical appearance but also general objective and subjective characteristics, other than gender, that make a child attractive to the teacher.

References

Adams, R.. and B. Biddle
1970   Realities of Teaching: Explorations with Videotape. New York: Holt, Rinehart and Winston.

Adelman, C., and R. Walker
1972   Classrooms: A Grounded Theory. Centre for Applied Research in Education, University of East Anglia, England (Mimeograph).

Allington, Richard
In   Teacher Interruption Behaviors During Primary Grade Oral Reading. To appear in the Journal of Educational Psychology.

Barth, F.
1969   Ethnic Groups and Boundaries. Boston: Little, Brown and Co.

Billington, R.A.
1966   The Historian's Contribution to Anglo-American Misunderstanding: Report of a Committee on National Bias in Anglo-American History Textbooks. London: Routledge and Kegan Paul.

Blalack, Hubert M., Jr.
1967   Toward a Theory of Minority Group Relations. New York: John Wiley and Sons.

Brewer, Marilyn B., and Donald T. Campbell
1976   Ethnocentrism and Intergroup Attitudes. New York: John Wiley and Sons.

Carew, J.V., and S. Lawrence-Lightfoot
1979   Beyond Bias: Perspectives on Classrooms. Cambridge, Mass.: Harvard University Press.

Carrasco, R.
1978   Expanded Awareness of Student Performance: A Case Study in Applied Ethnographic Monitoring in a Bilingual Classroom. Qualifying Paper, Harvard Graduate School of Education.

Case, C.
1977   Culture, The Human Plan: Essays in the Anthropological Interpretation of Human Behavior. Washington, D.C.: University Press of America.

Cazden, C.
1978   Ethnography and Education: Children In and Out of School. Paper presented at a conference sponsored by Research for Better Schools and the Graduate School of Education, University of Pennsylvania.

Cazden, D., R. Carrasco, A.A. Maldonado-Guzman, and F. Erickson
   1980   The Contribution of Ethnographic Research to Bicultural Bilingual Education. In the 31st Annual Georgetown University Roundtable on Language and Linguistics: Current Issues in Bilingual Education.
Cazden, C., V. John, and D. Hynes, eds.
   1972   Functions of Language in the Classroom. New York: Teachers College Press.
Cazden, C., and E. Leggett
   1978   Culturally Responsive Education A Discussion of Lau Remedies II, ISSN 0161-3707, Dept. of Health, Education and Welfare, Office of Education 2(2).
Dumont, R.V.
   1972   Learning English and How to be Silent: Studies in Sioux and Cherokee Classrooms. In Functions of Language in the Classroom. Cazden, C., V. John, and D. Hymes, eds. New York: Teachers College Press.
Dweck, Carol S., et al.
   1978   Sex Differences in Learned Helplessness: the Contingencies of Evaluative Feedback in the Classroom. Developmental Psychology 14:268–276.
Dweck, Carol S., et al.
   1980   Sex Differences in Learned Helplessness: An Experimental and Naturalistic Study of Failure Generalization and its Mediators. Journal of Personality and Social Psychology 3:441–452.
Eder, Donna
   1979   The Impact of Management and Turn-Allocation Activites on Student Performance. Sociolinguistic Working Paper #65. Austin, Tex.: Southwest Educational Development Laboratory.
Eder, Donna
   n.d.   The Social Context of Learning: A Micro Analysis of Ability Grouping. Indiana University (Mimeograph).
Erickson, F.
   1973   What Makes School Ethnography 'Ethnographic'? Council on Anthropology and Education Newsletter 4(2).
   1975   Gatekeeping and the Melting Pot: Interaction in Counseling Encounters. Harvard Educational Review 45:44–70.
   1977   Some Approaches to Inquiry in School-Community Ethnography. Anthropology and Education Quarterly 8(2).

Erickson, F., C. Cazden, R. Carrasco, and A. Maldonado-Guzman
1980   Social and Cultural Organization in Classrooms of Bilingual Children, Second Year Progress Report to NIE G-0099.

Erickson, F., et al.
1978   Social and Cultural Organization of Interaction in Classrooms of Bilingual Children: A Two Year Project (1978–1980). Proposal to NIE 1978.

Erickson, F. and G. Mohatt
1980   Cultural Organization of Participant Structures in Two Classrooms of Indian Students. In Doing the Ethnography of Schooling. G.D. Spindler, ed.

Erickson, F., and J. Shultz
1977   When Is a Context? Quarterly Newsletter of the Institute for Comparative Human Development: The Rockefeller University. 1(2).

Freire, P.
1968   Pedagogy of the Oppressed. New York: Herder and Herder.
1971   La Educación como practica de la libertad (Education as a Practice of Freedom). Mexico, D.F.: Siglo Veintiuno Editores S.A. (Spanish version.)

Giles, H., and B. Saint James, eds.
1979   Language and Ethnic Relations. Oxford: Pergamon Press.

Glaser, B.G., and A.L. Strauss
1979   The Discovery of Grounded Theory: Strategies for Qualitative Research. New York: Aldine Publishing Co.

Goffman, E.
1959   The Presentation of Self in Everyday Life. New York: Anchor Books.
1974   Strategic Interaction. Philadelphia: University of Pennsylvania Press.

Good, T.
1970   Which Pupils Do Teachers Call On? Elementary School Journal Pp.190–198.

Good, T., and J. Brophy
1971   Analyzing Classroom Interaction: A More Powerful Alternative, Educational Technology Vol. 11:36–41.

Johnson, P.
1977   A Bilingual Teacher Is Not Enough. Integrated Education 15(3).

Kranz, P., W. Weber, and K. Fishell
  1970   The Relationship Between Teacher Perception of
         Pupils and Teacher Behavior toward Those Pupils.
         Paper presented at the Annual Meeting of the
         American Educational Research Association.
Kranz, P., and A. Tyo
  1973   Do Teachers' Perceptions of Pupils Affect Their
         Behavior toward These Pupils? Unpublished
         manuscript, Millersville State College.
Labov, William
  1972   Sociolinguistic Patterns. Philadelphia: University of
         Pennsylvania Press.
  1972   Language in the Inner City. Philadelphia: University
         of Pennsylvania Press.
Leacock, E.B.
  1969   Teaching and Learning in City Schools. New York:
         Basic Books.
  1977   Race and the "We-They Dichotomy" in Culture,
         Anthropology and Education Quarterly 8(2).
Lightfoot, S.
  1972   An Ethnographic Study of the Status Structure of
         the Classroom. Unpublished doctoral dissertation.
         Harvard Graduate School of Education.
Longstreet, V.S.
  1978   Aspects of Ethnicity: Understanding Differences in
         Pluralistic Classrooms. New York: Teachers College
         Press.
Maldonado-Guzman, A.A.
  1978   The Role of Student Oral Participation in Teacher's
         Attention: An Ethnographic Study of A Community
         College English as a Second Language Classroom.
         Unpublished paper, Harvard University.
  1980   A Multidimensional Ethnographic Framework for
         Studying Classroom Organization and Interaction.
         Qualifying Paper, Harvard University.
  1978   A Rationale for Studying Ethnic Relations in the
         Classroom. Unpublished paper. Harvard Graduate
         School of Education.
McDermott, R.P.
  1976   Kids Make Sense: An Ethnographic Account of the
         Interactional Management of Success and Failure in
         a First-Grade Classroom. Unpublished doctoral
         dissertation, Stanford University.
  1977   Social Relations as Contexts for Learning. Harvard
         Educational Review 47(2).

McDermott, R.P., and K. Gospodinoff
    1980   Social Contexts for Ethnic Borders and School Failure.
            In Nonverbal Behavior. A.A. Wolfgang, ed. Toronto:
            Ontario Institute for the Study of Education.
Memmi, A.
    1970   The Colonizer and the Colonized. Boston: Beacon
            Press.
Merton, R.K.
    1949   (1968) Social Theory and Social Structure. New York:
            The Free Press.
Moll, Luis, Elette Estrada, Esteban Diaz, and Lawrence Lopes
    (Draft) The Organization of Bilingual Learning Environments:
            Implications for Schooling. [See Moll et al. in this
            volume.]
Parsons, T.
    1951   The Social System. New York: The Free Press.
Power, C.
    1971   The Effects of Communication Patterns on Student
            Sociometric Status, Attitudes and Achievement in
            Science. Unpublished doctoral dissertation, University
            of Queensland, Australia.
Rist, R.C.
    1970   Student Social Class and Teacher Expectations: The
            Self-fulfilling Prophecy in Ghetto Education. Harvard
            Educational Review 40(3).
    1978   The Invisible Children. Cambridge, Mass.: Harvard
            University Press.
Rosenthal, R.
    1974   On the Social Psychology of the Self-fulfilling
            Prophecy: Further Evidence for Pygmalion Effects and
            Their Mediating Mechanisms. New York: An MSS
            Modular Publication.
Schermerborn, R.A.
    1978   Comparative Ethnic Relations: A Framework for
            Theory and Research. Chicago: University of Chicago
            Press.
van den Berghe, Pierre L.
    1967   Race and Racism: A Comparative Perspective. New
            York: Wiley.

Stories of Hope in the Midst of Despair: Culturally Responsive Education for Latino Students in an Alternative High School in New York City[1]

Maria E. Torres-Guzman[2]

Striving to reach the human potential within ourselves and creating spaces for others to do so, in any field, is not an easy task. Our entire lives are dedicated to this goal and we are in a constant state of "becoming." Teachers who can claim to achieve a small step in this direction, while within the broader societal context may merely have accomplished but a small victory, can, in my estimation, be declared heroes and heroines because they have made a difference in the lives of children. As a researcher I have witnessed how meaningful what teachers do can be in the lives of children. I firmly believe that each of the small victories (or major accomplishments, depending on how you want to look at it) deserves recognition and acknowledgement. As I tell the stories of two teachers struggling to give hope and provide the conditions for the growth and empowerment of a group of Latino youth, I intend to impress upon you my admiration for their work. Through the telling of the teachers' stories, I will point out how the kind of successes the students experience make a difference, independent of what grades they receive or what their test scores may look like. Furthermore, I will argue that these school events are the kind that need to occur nation-wide in order to prevent the high drop-out rates and failures that Latino youth face today.

Background

The setting is an alternative high school funded by the Office of Educational Services of the Board of Education of the City of New York and housed in a community-based organization in one of the poorest *barrios* in the City. About two years ago, shortly after the school was established, the opportunity arose to work in a research collaborative with the alternative high school. The collaborative was designed as a staff development/research project and as an ethnographic study of the school and its community. An explicit understanding of the collaborative was that what was learned would be used for the purpose of social change within the school, the organization, and the community.[3] By the very nature of the collaborative, the research was participatory.[4]

Empowerment[5] emerged as a key concept during the early stages of the dialogue that was established with the teaching staff. The term was used frequently by the two teachers described within. In the discussions about how to set up their classrooms, how to deliver the content of their classes, what they envisioned the outcomes to be, and how they differed in teaching styles, the concept of empowerment was central. For example, the teachers would ask, how does the structuring of my classroom empower students? Soon the members of the collaborative realized that the term was used loosely to mean many things and moved to explicit conversation about its definition. When the teachers were asked to define empowerment, there were as many definitions as there were teachers.[6] The definitions ranged from making sure that the students were well prepared academically, to creating a context for validating individuals so that some day they would believe in themselves, to engaging students in activism, collectivity, and community development.

The teachers' concern with the definition and implementation of empowerment was in line with what was institutionally expected of them. "Youth growth and empowerment" was an organizational motto and the school had been conceptualized in this framework. In light of the organizational mission, when the teachers found themselves grappling with what empowerment meant and looked like in their classrooms and in the school, they turned to the organization for help and clarification. However, a clear definition of what was meant by empowerment in educational processes was new to all involved. The organization had a history of participation in community struggles for empowerment and had developed a perspective of what it meant, but they could not give the teachers the guidance they needed.

The research-collaborative became the vehicle for probing and discovering "empowerment" in the school context. The premise of the collaborative was that by teachers reflecting on their practice, a shared understanding of what empowerment meant and looked like could be arrived at. Various examples of classroom and organizational behavior that could be characterized as empowering were observed and discussed.

I will now turn to two examples. The 'student experience approach' is an example of how the teacher organizes a lesson that validates students as learners; it changes the power relationships between teachers and students whereby student experience is given primacy (McLaren, 1989). The second example, which will follow, is of an integrated environmental science curriculum where the teacher plays the role of moral and social agent as he involves students in cleaning up a chemical storage lot in the neighborhood.

Cognitive Empowerment via the Student Experience Approach

It was a language arts lesson in the month of November. Written on the chalkboard was the following vocabulary list:

racism
discrimination
segregation
integration
emancipation
ghetto
freedom
etc.

The students had brought in dictionary definitions of the vocabulary they were to deal with in the lesson. After providing the dictionary definition, the teacher began to elicit from students' examples in their own lives that would help explain the concepts.

> T: Now, think about the images you see in your
>   minds when you hear the word: segregation.
>   How would you tell someone who did not
>   know this word what it describes?

The responses included an example of Hasidim girls who were segregated in an afterschool program in a local school. Other examples of racism, discrimination, and ghetto led to a discussion about the conditions of the Latino community in their neighborhood. After this exchange, the teacher asked them to read the text.

During a discussion about the school among the researchers, this lesson was framed according to assumptions held about what lessons should look like; the assertion made was that the school focused on social rather than academic goals.

Evidence from previous observations was marshalled to substantiate this statement. One of the observers[7] described how some students had been very articulate on issues of Puerto Rican liberation during a visit to the United Nations. Other observers gave classroom examples. One of the examples was a world history lesson that had been observed by the entire research team. The teacher had made some assumptions about the connections between the conditions of the community and the Iran-Contra events. The facts were elicited from students through questions, but the analysis was provided by the teacher. Since the types of questions asked were framed by the assumptions made by the teacher, the questions were labelled as "leading" and the lesson as "distorted." In final instance, the political philosophy of the school was perceived as guiding what occurred in the history as well as English lessons. Thus, the vocabulary on the board were viewed as "politically loaded terms."

What disconfirming evidence did the observers find?

One of the observers went to the subsequent lesson of this language arts class. In her words, she wanted to see where the discussion would go and what was next; the observer wanted to find out how traditional or different the lesson would look like. On top of the teacher's desk the observer found *Steps in Composition* (Second edition). She browsed through it and found a section on civil rights with the suggested vocabulary list that had been written on the board in the previous lesson. The question then became, "What happened in this lesson and why did the observers conclude that there was something unique about it if the vocabulary had been suggested by the text?"

New perspectives emerged when the researchers realized what was different. While the text included the vocabulary list, the suggested order of instruction differed from what had been observed in the lesson. Usually, the reading of the selection comes first, followed by the identification of vocabulary words. The follow-up activities frequently include discussions connecting the concepts studied with student experiences. The teacher did the reverse. The students' experiences were connected with the vocabulary first. This was followed by reading a selection on the topic. Why was this change significant?

The teacher had used an approach that differed from the process structured by the text. When the teacher was asked why she changed the process provided by the text she responded:

> Because these are words and terms they live with. So they can relate it to their own lives, and get all that out, . . . and then they can concentrate . . . they have more knowledge about these terms than someone [else] . . . using the same book.

The use of the terms in this lesson was not resulting directly from a need to follow a political philosophy, but the need to cover the material provided in a fairly traditional textbook. Learning in this lesson was organized, consciously or unconsciously, as an act of validation. It challenged the process structured into the text, which implicitly defined the text as authority and by acknowledging personal experience as knowledge, the role of the teacher as expert was also being challenged.

By using the students' experiences first, the teacher elicited an affective as well as a cognitive response to the topic at hand. By acknowledging that the students "knew" something about the topic, the process became validating; it tapped into the students' cultural knowledge. The passage on civil rights in the text could subsequently be read from the standpoint of the student as "authority." The interaction of the student with the text could thus be transformed to a critical one; the "reading" of the text would be screened by the "truths" established collectively by teacher and students through the discussion. When a teacher promotes the text as authority, not only is the topic distanced, it may also be unrecognizable and alien to the young reader.

The emergent assertion focused on the pedagogical process and the issue of empowerment. The teacher incorporated instructional methods that promoted empowerment of students as learners, that gave them the confidence to draw from, and build on, their own experiences and, thus, become active learners. I refer to this first example as cognitive empowerment because students were enabled and validated as active participants in their learning. The elaboration of concepts were first embedded within the experience known to the students and the positioning of the learner in relation to the text is that of a critical thinker. This is an example of the primacy of student voice, where the stories not only counted because they were personally meaningful to the student, but where the stories became part of negotiating meaning, placing them in a broader world and understanding the significance of their lived experiences within a broader context.

This example served to make visible to the teachers and researchers how classroom experiences could be organized to "empower" students as learners. When the teacher was asked to make a presentation on what empowerment of Latino youth meant in the school, she used this and other similar examples to make the point that teachers have the power to turn despair into hope within the classroom walls and make a difference in the lives of our youth.

Leadership for Community Development as Empowerment

The second example is based on the environmental science curriculum developed by one of the teachers who focused on developing a pedagogical approach that would incorporate the process of action-reflection-action. The environmental science project proved to be the most integrated and fully developed curriculum of the school during the 1987–88 academic year. It is an example of building leadership for community development.

Early in the fall the class had a series of field experiences. They took a walk through the neighborhood of Williamsburg; they visited Radiac, a waste storage facility for toxic and radioactive waste in the neighborhood; and Prospect Park, a nearby preserved natural environment. Because of the menace to the environmental health of the community, Radiac, was conceived of as the target of the class' investigations. Students with photographic skills, or developing these skills, found a role during these field trips as visual recorders. The rights of individuals and communities to healthy environments were discussed as they analyzed and contrasted the environments observed. The role of citizens/community involvement to ensure a voice in the decisions and actions affecting their livelihood were also discussed.

During the first stages of the environmental science curriculum the Toxic Avengers, as the youth involved in the project soon came to be known, were engaged in observations, analyses, and reading and writing about what they saw in the different environments and what the photographs revealed. A lot four blocks away from the school, which was used by an adhesive factory to store barrels of residue, became their first target for investigation. For a few days the Toxic Avengers visited the lot and took photographs of barrels with hazardous alert labels. At various times the barrels were counted to determine the traffic flow in and out of the lot. On one occasion, the students played football on the street and the ball "accidentally" flew onto the premises. A faintly disguised excuse was, thus, established to trespass on private property and continue the count. The number of barrels kept in the lot began to decrease; the number went from 200 barrels to 30.

Shortly after the counting began, liquid from the drums spilled onto the street and streamed into the gutters. One of the students, protected by surgical plastic gloves, took some samples that were later analyzed by a chemical lab. Then one of the Toxic Avengers was "bullied" by one of the men at the lot. But shortly after, the lot was cleaned up and a high sheet metal fence topped with barbed wire was put up which obstructed any further observations and brought the counting to an end. While cautiously refraining from claiming a causal relationship, the teacher and the students felt that the "snooping" might well have been a factor in the clean up of the lot; they felt victorious.

In the classroom, meanwhile, the students learned about cell structures, chromosomes, mutants, chemicals, toxicity, and so forth. They began to distinguish different categories of hazardous materials and the specific effects these could have on an individual's health as well as on the environment. Their experience with the lot helped them to learn about government structures and lines of authority. They found out who was who; they determined their audience, the appropriate officials to write to. Trying to determine what message they wanted to convey and how to write it led the students to learn about zoning laws and about the Environmental Protection Agency. When the lab analysis of the substance taken from the street gutters showed the presence of a hazardous and toxic substance, they identified it chemically and discussed its implications for the Williamsburg community. Although they never found a need to send the letter, they collectively wrote a letter to the fire chief, making the writing process as well as the value of writing part of what they were learning.

Using a cooperative learning approach, the students also prepared for their mid-term, an oral presentation to their classmates about what they had learned. The mid-term became a tool for reflection on the significance of the events as well as an opportunity for expanded instruction and learning. In the development of the mid-term the students were asked to disentangle government, legal, science, and health considerations, recount the events that occurred chronologically, and reflect upon the organizing process. The students were able to communicate what they perceived to be the victory of the chemical storage lot to TV reporters, to fellow students, to the community-based organization's staff and teachers, and to the research team members. The culmination of rehearsals, videotape analysis, and preparation of charts, photos, transparencies, maps, and slides was a presentation at a conference of the Citizen's Committee of New York.

Reflecting on the chemical storage lot experience, the students wrestled with various principles: that knowledge is power, that learning is necessary in order to exercise and ensure the individual's and the community's right to a healthy environment, and that social responsibility for community development is a process that warrants pulling together all the resources, information, and talents of the members of a group. The environmental project also provided the teacher and the students with meaningful structures for learning social studies and science concepts, and generated great enthusiasm among some of the best as well as some of the more difficult and resistant students.

The experience embodied the empowerment of students both as individual learners and as participants involved in collective action. As members of a larger community where playgrounds and residential homes exist side by side with the hazardous environment created by the storage lot and Radiac, the Toxic Avengers were engaged in community empowerment. According to a study by the United Church of Christ, a higher proportion of active toxic waste dumps can be found in minority communities, thwarting severely these communities' right to a healthy environment. The study linked the incidences of violations of environmental protection laws to the broader societal structural disempowerment these communities face and the silence surrounding the tolerance of such violations to the perpetuation of the status quo. They coined the relationship "environmental racism." The students began to make similar connections through the environmental science curriculum.

The environmental curriculum embodied many valuable features of a critical pedagogy.[8] Students were not passive recipients of knowledge but active creators of knowledge. The teacher created a learning environment in which the students assumed the posture of active co-participants in the process of learning/teaching. The openness of the curriculum fostered imagination, creativity, and rigor (Brimfield, 1988). The educational experiences were meaningful. The nature of the task was sufficiently complex so as to call for collectivity and mutual caring as the students engaged in each step of the process. The students' actions were embedded in the passion, morality, and caring they felt for what happened to their family and friends in the community. The processes of experiential and abstract learning were facilitated by the integration of classroom learning and community action. The learner had to apply what was learned in the classroom to what happened in the community, and their community action informed and gave meaning to the classroom learning.

This working together encompassed what Noddings (1984) calls pedagogical caring. Both teacher and students existed in what she calls "a state of connectedness that was built on mutual respect." It was through continuous dialogue on a one-to-one basis as well as in small and large groups that they integrated the various pieces of knowledge and created a cohesive structure. The students assumed the role of teacher; they made presentations to fellow students, to the organization's staff, and to the public-at-large. In so doing, they gained insight into the process of teaching and the responsibilities of both information-givers and information-receivers. The mid-term was the pivotal point in which the integration of knowledge was facilitated by the teacher, thus creating the conditions for stretching the students' world beyond their actual experience. It permitted the students to distance themselves sufficiently so as to gain understanding of the political, social, and scientific complexity of the work they were engaged in. And it was through cooperative endeavor that the multiple talents of students were acknowledged and validated. They were faced with the need to rely on each other's strengths: some contributed with photography, some with writing, and others were most comfortable in storytelling.

The future of this curriculum is connected to the community organizing around Radiac. Thus, the teacher and the Toxic Avengers continue to engage in this work beyond the academic year. In February 1989, the Toxic Avengers received a New Yorkers for New York Award from the Citizen's Committee in the presence of the New York City Chancellor and Mayor at a formal reception at the Waldorf. They have also been asked to spearhead a national movement to set up Toxic Avenger Clubs throughout the United States.

These are only two of the examples of what the alternative school looked like. I tried to select examples that would help us examine the process of teaching/learning and student/teacher interaction rather than focus on who the actors were. The story of the Toxic Avengers is the more dramatic of the two and may go beyond what some teachers can do, but the more subtle examples, the 'student experience approach,' is potentially more powerful because of its feasibility and generalizability to other settings. As for the alternative school, I cannot make sweeping claims. There were many occasions in which the positive interactions described above were far from being the norm. But, overall, the school was a positive experience for the youngsters involved as the examples tried to illustrate.

My stories are full of hope. They are intentionally presented this way because they represent vivid attempts at turning around, in a very localized way, the world of schooling as experienced by today's Latino youth. But I would like to suggest that these stories are embedded in very grave ones at the local level as well as in a broader sense. The story of the public schools today is a sad one because the deplorable conditions of our society—the weakening of the economic system, the growing military tensions, the threat of nuclear war, and the despair that all these realities bring—are in many ways recreated systematically in the student teacher/interactions in our schools. The changing demographics in our society are also changing the "complexion," literal and symbolic, of our schools. And our schools are not equipped to understand how to educate a culturally diverse youth population that finds itself in the midst of social change and must be educated for participation in social change. Unlike many public school situations, an explicit goal of the organization housing the alternative school is to promote youth growth and empowerment in the context of community development. The rhetoric of social change surrounds the school. But similar to the situation of teachers in the regular public schools, the teachers in this alternative school did not receive the organizational support that was necessary to implement social change as the teachers had envisioned it to be. The teachers, thus, lived with social, organizational, and personal constraints that limited the development of their potential, and ultimately, that of the students they taught. It is in this gloomy context that the upbeat stories gain significance. Within difficult conditions, the teachers in the stories strove to learn from their own lives and from how they constructed reality with their students in the school. The urgency of the students' needs and the teachers' commitment to make this world a better one gave way to insights into the educational process and to glimpses of hope for a brighter future.

The message of the stories is not complex: incorporating student experiences as a way of giving primacy to students' voice changes the relationships of power and collaboration in the classroom. Learning can become meaningful and purposeful for the individual and can create spaces for exploring what the relationship of the individual is within the broader social context. This type of learning can turn the schooling experience around for some. It is worth our pursuit.

Endnotes

1. This chapter was presented at the Tenth Anniversary Colloquium of the College Board's Council on Academic Affairs on May 4–5, 1989 in New York, New York.

2. Dr. Maria E. Torres-Guzman is an Assistant Professor and the Director of the Program in Bilingual/Bicultural Education at Teachers College, Columbia University and was the Principal Investigator of the Alternative High School Staff Development/ Research Collaborative.

3. The design of the collaborative was based on my experience as a researcher in the Teacher Development and Organizational Change Project of the Institute of Research on Teaching at Michigan State University which has been reported in Campbell (1988).

4. It would be erroneous to think that the participation of all those involved—researchers, teachers, and the community-based organization's staff—was of the same nature or the same intensity. Initially, the roles each group played were very much within tradition, i.e., researcher with knowledge and teacher expecting to receive evaluative feedback. Gradually, we moved into a relationship of mutuality and reciprocity, particularly as the teachers began to tell their own stories.

5. The term empowerment is widely used to mean many things. The concept is central to this paper; it was a local term used to characterize the relationship between the adults and the youth in the school and organization. The specific meaning of empowerment as negotiated by the adults and youth in this context is the focus of the paper.

6. The school had three teachers and close to thirty-five students on the roster.

7. The research team consisted of the principal investigator, a senior researcher, a research assistant, a parent researcher, and 6 doctoral students from the Program in Bilingual/Bicultural Education at Teachers College.

8. See McLaren (1989) for an introduction to critical pedagogy.

References Cited

Brimfield, R. M. B.
    1988   Imagination, Rigor, and Caring: One framework for Educational Reform. Journal of Curriculum and Supervision. 3:253–262.

Campbell, D.
    1988   Collaboration and Contradictions in a Research and Staff Development Project, Teachers College Record. 90:99–121.

McLaren, P.
    1989   Life in Schools. New York: Longman Inc.

Noddings, N.
    1984   Caring. Berkeley: University of California Press.

Implications for Policy and Practice

Marietta Saravia-Shore and Steven F. Arvizu[1]

Policy implications and the challenges for educational practice suggested by the ethnographies in this volume will be explored in this chapter. Some of the critical policy issues which are informed by the ethnographic research presented above include controversy over language policy and "curricula of inclusion," the need for schools to respond to change, competition among advocates for equity and quality education, the struggle for reform in the educational arena, public debate over "cultural literacy" within general education, and dialogue concerning alternative futures.

Multilingualism and Cross-Cultural Literacy as Policy

The cross-cultural approach and the ethnographic research on the schooling of ethnolinguistic minority students presented within this book have multiple policy implications. Education for multilingualism and cross-cultural literacy are major policy issues in education in the United States.

Many people still question the need for bilingual education despite the recognition a decade ago by the 1980 President's Commission on Foreign Languages and International Studies of the need for Americans with second language and cross-cultural communication skills to conduct international business, national defense, and

diplomacy. The Commission deplored the scandalous
ignorance of foreign languages by U.S. citizens and
recommended greater development of bilingual and cross-
cultural skills. Ignoring these needs, organized groups such
as English Only and teachers' unions have disseminated
paid advertisements and newsletters against bilingual
education, gaining increasing support through state
referendums. Comprised primarily of monolingual English
speakers, English Only represents the fear expressed by
some members of the majority culture of the economic
implications of immigration and the changing demographics
of the United States. English Plus, an organization which
advocates English as well as a second language, represents
an alternative to English Only.

Few critics of bilingual education recognize that the
goals of foreign or modern language education, second
language education, and bilingual education are compatible.
All three are educational processes that develop second
language skills and cross-cultural competencies among
American students.

How do bilingual education and foreign language
programs differ? Minority language students in bilingual
education programs bring a language other than English
to school. Their development of skills in both English and
the home ("foreign") language is the goal of bilingual
education. (Many programs, however, are bilingual in name
only and drop the student's home language after it has
served as a bridge to English.) By contrast, the students
who study "foreign" languages are for the most part English
monolinguals. Typically, foreign language education begins
at the secondary level, while bilingual education more often
starts at the elementary level. Exceptions to this distinction
are the foreign language programs for "gifted" monolingual
English students, which begin at the elementary level.
Perhaps one of the most interesting contradictions in the
public's perception of second language learning is that the
study of a foreign language is viewed as enrichment for
English monolingual students. Yet minority language
students who speak that same foreign language and learn
English as a second language are viewed as needing
"remedial" education. Such contradictions are part of the

sociopolitical context of the bilingual education programs which are analyzed by the researchers who contributed to this volume.

Furthermore, legislative battles and policy discussions have not been well grounded in empirical research recognizing the diversity among bilingual programs. As can be seen in the variations among bilingual programs reported in the ethnographic research in this book, programs differ markedly in their characteristics and structure. Yet inferences drawn from a program at one site have been generalized invalidly to different programs and contexts.

The most comprehensive, longitudinal study of bilingual education programs, which began in 1983, was released by the U.S. Department of Education in February 1991. The "Longitudinal Study of Structured English Immersion Strategy, Early Exit and Late-Exit Children" could not directly compare the late-exit programs, which have at least 40% of instruction in the native language (often Spanish) to English immersion programs. However, the study

> contains substantial evidence indicating the superiority of programs that make extensive use of the students' native language. The study also found that the level of parent involvement in helping their children with homework and the level of parent satisfaction with their children's educational program was directly associated with the extent of native language instruction (Lyons 1991:11).

Program effectiveness was defined as the extent to which limited English proficient students caught up with monolingual English speaking peers through growth in English language and reading as well as mathematics. An important result of the study (Ramirez 1991:22) is that limited English proficient students can be provided with a substantial extent of primary (native) language instruction (at or more than 40 percent) without impeding their acquisition of English language and reading skills. Of even greater import, the rate of growth for late-exit students was accelerating as grade level increased while the rate of growth of students in the other two programs that used more English was slowing down as grade level increased.

The treatment of culture in the education of language minority students is a policy issue which has proven increasingly controversial during each of the cycles of Congressional reauthorization in the history of the Bilingual Education Act (Title VII of the Elementary and Secondary Education Act). Supporters of bilingual education want recognition and use of the knowledge of students' cultural backgrounds in the teaching/learning process as a significant feature of any program. Critics going back to Epstein (1977) allude to the fear of separatism and cultural nationalism in the bilingual education movement, conveyed by such phrases as "affirmative ethnicity" and "destructive divisiveness."

Several alternatives exist in the formulation of policy and legislation relating culture to bilingual education. One alternative is reflected in previous reauthorization legislation, which includes references to "a primary means by which a child learns is through the use of such child's native language and cultural heritage." Here culture is considered in relation to overall background and community environment, which must be understood in order to motivate learners. Implicit is the notion that students who learn English will become mainstreamed into schools and U.S. society; yet the cultural aspect of adjusting to American life is left unclear. This ambiguity with regard to culture allows contradictory interpretations of bilingual education activity as both assimilationist and separatist. The current legislation has, however, permitted local schools to experiment with culturally relevant learning strategies, some of which have been evaluated positively in terms of student achievement.

Another policy alternative would be to use a clear cross-cultural approach. The major benefit of such an approach would be the clarification of federal policy concerning the development and operation of bilingual and culturally relevant programs. This would facilitate federal response to national problems in education such as integration of newcomer groups and assurance of equity of opportunity, support for innovation and development that cannot occur at the state or local level, and assistance in the linguistic preparation for international commerce, national defense, and national unity.

The teaching of cultural values is the primary responsibility of the family unit and community reference group. Local school districts and states are responsible for curriculum decisions affecting their own populations. The federal government becomes involved at the point of addressing educational issues across a diverse citizenry, for learners who are of national concern because of their refugee status, their migration and mobility across local district and state lines, or because their civil rights are in question, as, for example, whenever there are linguistic and cultural barriers to educational opportunity.

A cross-cultural policy would allow for local autonomy and decentralized decision-making in curriculum matters. It would also provide a clear message of leadership to practitioners in bilingual education and other federally supported programs regarding the goal of "mainstreaming" students without destroying their linguistic linkage to their home, family, and cultural heritage. Most importantly, bilingual, cross-cultural education would serve to overcome factionalism and divisiveness. On implementing such programs, conflict resolution training could become a basic skill for practitioners and students to further the goal of inter-ethnic harmony and national unity.

Culture and learning are intimately related, with or without a clear federal policy; but a cross-cultural policy would link every group into a whole, thus addressing major articulated concerns.

Responding to Change

Educational institutions will be struggling with change and dealing with diversity over the next several decades, according to demographic projections. First, birthrate and immigration patterns are changing the demographics of our country, particularly our public schools. Census projections are that middle American enrollments will decline and minority enrollments will increase. By the year

2000, one in three Americans will be members of minority groups (Hodgkinson 1985). Minority workers will increasingly become the support base of those on social security, as social security/ retirement systems respond to the shifts in demographics and the aging of our society (Hays-Bautista et al. 1989). Second, our society will need to respond to changing world situations in which economic competition and political/diplomatic relations will depend on the capacity of our people to communicate and function in more multilingual and cross-cultural settings and situations. Third, our own citizenry and those of other countries in Eastern Europe, Latin America, the Middle East and East Asia will develop greater interest in one another through televised current events, increased awareness of economic interdependence, tourism, thoughtful analysis, and small group exchanges. We will also see more corporations and leaders from the private sector becoming involved in educational change given the realization that the workforce needs of the future demand a more educated citizenry, competent in English and second languages, as well as cross-cultural understanding (California Roundtable Report 1988).

We can look at the ways that two of the many state education departments, New York and California, are responding to change. The New York State Board of Regents revised their policy on bilingual education in 1989 with the recognition that the opportunity to acquire a second language would be an enrichment for all the students of New York State. They established the study of one unit of a foreign language as a requirement for high school graduation. The New York State Education Department, through its Division of Bilingual Education, was also a pioneer in financially supporting "two-way" bilingual programs since 1984. These programs are reciprocal in that English monolingual students learn a second language while language minority students learn English and develop their home language. Thus, all the students in the program have an opportunity to learn a second language not only from their teachers, but from other students who speak the language. Foreign language educators use this model as well calling it "dual immersion" or "two-way immersion" programs.

A "Curriculum of Inclusion" was proposed in 1990 by the New York State Commissioner of Education, Thomas Sobol, that *The New York Times* called "the most extensive attempt in any state to revise the curriculum to give greater weight to nonwhite, non-Western contributions to American culture" (February 6, 1990). The proposal, to revise curricula in history and social studies to reflect "greater appreciation of the country's ethnic, cultural and linguisitic differences," generated much controvery and debate.[2]

In Sobol's statement concerning the curriculum of inclusion, he gave the New York State Regents' rationale for their proposed curriculum review and revision.

> In today's world and tomorrow's, our ability to compete economically depends in part on educating well all of our children, whatever their background. Our success also depends on our ability to understand other cultures and societies. If we wish to communicate effectively—as we must—with the majority of the world's peoples who are not white and English-speaking, we must know more about how they see the world, how they make sense of experience, why they behave as they do.
>
> We cannot understand our complex society without understanding the history and culture of its major ethnic and cultural components. We face a paradox: only through understanding our diverse roots and branches can we fully comprehend the whole. Only by accommodating our differences can we become one society. Only by exploring our human variations can we apprehend our common humanity (Sobol 1990:2).

An anthropological, cross-cultural approach in the curriculas as outlined below would enhance such efforts.

New York City has responded to the demographic diversity among its student population, 80% of whom are racial, ethnic, and linguistic minority students, by restructuring its former Office of Bilingual Education as a Division of Multilingual, Multicultural Education in 1989. The same year, the late City Schools Chancellor Richard Green initiated competitive funding for district programs of multicultural education and submitted a policy statement on Multicultural Education and Promotion of Positive Intergroup Relations which was approved by the city's Board of Education. Building on that policy, the current chancellor, Joseph Fernandez, has instituted "An Action Plan for Multicultural Education" (1991).

California has experienced similar developments that demonstrate considerable dialogue regarding language and culture in education. Even though California voters approved an English-only initiative for the state, the California legislature has fully supported international studies and global education legislation. The legislation includes a network of resource centers to assist schools in the reform of curricula and training and development of educators. The global education movement can facilitate knowledge about the world as well as knowledge about the ethnic minority and newly arriving groups to this country which would assist in inter-cultural understanding. The California State Board of Education has adopted new state frameworks for history and social science, language arts, foreign languages and ESL, all of which propose interactive pedagogy and relevant content and proficiency goals for California students. Similarly, the California Roundtable, an influential group of business and educational leaders, has advocated educational reform including English and second language acquisition for all California students and effectiveness in educating citizens for a more global and diverse future.

Two major events at Stanford University provide further examples of California's struggle with diversity: reform of the general education core involving Western Civilization and the Report of the University Committee on Minority Issues. The curriculum reform debate culminated in an integration of a cross-cultural perspective into the Western Civilization core, with content and perspectives added from minority, female, and comparative cultural views. The Minority Issues Report called for building a multiracial, multicultural university community advocating interactive pluralism, defining a new vision for the university where all ethnic groups can engage their differences in a process of mutual enrichment and respect for their similarities as well as their differences. The goal adopted by the University, and proposed as a new mission through the Report is the building of a pluralistic community and the preparation of students for effective leadership in a multicultural society (Stanford University, March 1989).

Implications for Educational Practice

While agreeing on the need for reform of education, although most reports advocate excellence, only a few advocate equity, and even fewer address the relationship between both issues. Since education is perceived as a major mechanism for opportunity in our society, advocates of increasing and improving learning opportunities for the undereducated underclass seek tools for improving services, changing organizations, and building and evaluating model programs. Those concerned with equity and excellence are bound by a common problem—how to deal with diversity?

Accreditation agencies are already pressuring universities and public schools to respond to diversity in their curricular offerings and programs. Clear, explicit strategies which do not favor one group at the expense of others will be needed to negotiate tension and channel innovative energy into plans for action through which people can work together. Advocates of underrepresented groups and protected classes of people will need to expand their concerns across groups and form coalitions to become powerful enough to change their environments. Race, ethnicity, gender, class, and special needs will all have to be considered as interactive variables in the equation of educating historically undereducated populations. Identity, inter- and intra-group cohesiveness and individual and group empowerment are issues needing careful consideration. Strategies for dealing with diversity that facilitate such developments and which create healthy educational environments will be needed.

Teacher Education

Teacher education institutions face the issues of the preparation of teachers who will be teaching ethnic and language minority students who have become the majority in most large urban districts. The diversity of learning styles, expectations, values and patterns of interaction in any classroom with multiethnic students is one of the major issues to be addressed. Alternatives to the teacher-centered social organization of the classroom are becoming increasingly attractive since such models are more responsive to differing learning styles by allowing for a range of participation structures as well as active participatory learning by more of the students. Such alternatives as cooperative learning, learning centers that include manipulatives and offer choices of modes of learning, peer learning or cross-age peer tutoring, which often are more compatible with the socialization patterns of the home, are being tried in the classroom. These alternative social organizations of learning, however, require different models of teacher education.

Because cooperative learning is not prevalent in the schools, most teachers have not participated in this mode of learning and may be hesitant to implement such a change unless they experience the benefits of the approach themselves. Therefore pre-service development in teacher education institutions and in-service development in school districts need to provide the experiences of these alternative modes of learning.

Some of the alternative models of professional development include teaming teachers to develop interdisciplinry curricula, instituting circles of support in which teachers each research an alternative and return to share it with their peers and asking teachers to watch themselves interacting with their students in videotapes so that they observe themselves and identify the range of learning styles in their classrooms. The social organization of cooperative learning in courses for the professional development of teachers has been found to draw out more sharing of experiences and resources among teachers.

Ethnographic Tools. Teacher education can also be

enhanced by including courses in which teachers learn to use the tools of ethnographic participant observation and interviewing and collection of oral histories to learn more about the cultures of the parents of students in their classes.[3]

Through cross-cultural comparison, teachers can identify more explicitly aspects of their culture. In a Multicultural Education course taught by Saravia-Shore teachers were asked to write their recollections of what remained significant to them from their childhood, then to share their reflections with one another. Greater understanding of similarities and differences was drawn from the teachers themselves. The bringing to awareness of that which is taken for granted is one of the more unsettling and also enriching aspects of cross-cultural literacy.

Today we can "travel" to other countries via films and television, particularly films directed by members of other cultures that portray interaction in those cultures. In graduate teacher preparation courses, teachers have become more aware of such differences through analyzing filmed interactions. Segments of a video have been replayed, to compare differences in patterns of interaction among Blacks and Whites in Paris and New York, for example, interactions with an African-American jazz musician portrayed by a French director with a cast of French and American actors in the the film *'Round Midnight.*

An important tool for understanding other cultures is provided by Lakoff and Johnson (1980) in their book, *Metaphors We Live By.* Metaphors tend to be pervasive, and it is exciting for teachers and their students to become aware of how much of our language is metaphorical and how our metaphors provide us with cultural lenses through which we view the world and which shape our behavior. Metaphors are also systematic and, through cross-cultural comparison, can tell us what a culture emphasizes. For example, time, which is duration, flow, and process is transformed in the United States into a valuable commodity; "time is money" and we "buy time," try not to "waste it," try to "budget" and "invest" and "save" it. But can we really save it, bank it and draw it out later when we might want to live on "borrowed" time? Metaphors, by taking the part for the whole, or the whole for the part, can hide as much as they explain; thus both literary and visual metaphors are key to understanding what cultures, our own as well as others, emphasize and obscure.

Curriculum Development

In developing curricula that infuse cross-cultural literacy across the grades, the structure of the curriculum can also be reviewed as it relates to the norms of American society with its emphasis on analysis rather than synthesis. The fragmentation of the curriculum into separate subjects is particularly difficult for younger students of a different culture. The alternatives of interdisciplinary, holistic curricula, core curricula with a theme to which the various disciplines and skills can be related, often make sense of specific subject areas by relating them to a whole or to a common context. For example, a core curriculum theme such as "architecture across cultures"[4] can integrate geometry, art, science and social studies. By doing cross-cultural comparisons of architecture in different ecologies, students can learn the concept of adaptation to different ecologies through the types of dwellings that humans have constructed in each, thus integrating science and social studies. Further, if students learn that one purpose of geometry is for planning buildings and architectural complexes, the study of two-dimensional geometry makes sense. Instead of studying geometrical theorems in a vacuum, students see a context to which they apply. One math educator has questioned why the study of two-dimensional plane geometry precedes three-dimensional geometry. Students are surrounded by three-dimensional forms in their everyday life and can abstract the two-dimensional shapes from them. Particularly for students learning a second language, context-embedded subjects organized thematically tend to be more comprehensible.

Regional Approaches in the Curricula. As part of an effort to contextualize learning about cultures, teachers can use a regional approach. One objection to studying cultures has been that since there are so many, some will be emphasized and others will be neglected. A regional approach enables a class to learn about several cultures related geographically by locating them physically within their continent and grouping them within a region. Rather than studying only Puerto Rico, for example, the unit might be the Hispanic Caribbean islands and also study Cuba and the Dominican Republic. Students can explore the similarities that cultural groups share by being located on islands in the same temperature zone, having a similar ecology to draw upon, sharing a language and some of their history, and by being proximate and in contact. Differences can be acknowledged while the reasons for similarities can be identified.

Social History as a Curriculum Framework. So far the New York State Curriculum of Inclusion has generated more debate than curricula, yet some school systems within New York have developed model curricula that fit within that framework. In 1990, the New York City Public Schools released *Grade 7 The United States and New York State History: A Multicultural Perspective* that incorporates the perspectives of the different groups that formed the United States. The curricula

> traces the human experience in the United States from earliest times to the present, tying major political, economic, and social trends in United States history to parallel trends and timeframes in New York State history. References are also made to Canada and Mexico, where relevant to the history of the United States. (1990:vii).

The curriculum includes original or translated documents from twelve Native American cultures throughout the Americas; the Spanish, Norse, Chinese and British explorers; the Dutch, British and Spanish colonists; an African account of the Middle Passage and an African-American's experience of slavery and resistance. Through the incorporation of social history as an organizing framework, the inclusion of the voices of often-neglected sectors of the population, women, and ethnic minorities, the curriculum has become more inclusive.

The response to the use of social history in the 1990 PBS series on the Civil War, which brought out the viewpoints of "ordinary" men and women from the North and the South, both White and Black, showed the power of this approach to capture the imagination of the public.

Entry points in the curriculum for students to learn to hear and take alternative perspectives need to be appropriate to the student age group. Asking students what they would like to know about children in other cultures as well as what they know and can share is one starting point that draws from the "everyday life of ordinary people."

Literature, the Arts, and Museum Resources. Reading translations of literature from other cultures has long been a way of empathetically standing in the shoes of someone in another time or culture. Autobiographies, poems, fables, folktales, novels, and dramas introduce us to the similarities and differences among people in the same culture as well as among cultures. Through foreign language and bilingual classes, it is possible to expand cross-cultural awareness through literature in the original language. Taking stories from oral histories and having students rewrite them to present them as plays for younger students provides another way for students to empathize with someone of another culture and grapple with values, either actively by taking their role or through observing the performance of their peers.

As noted above, understanding the meaning of verbal and visual metaphors is a path toward deeper understanding of other cultures. Visual metaphors often provide an organizing base through which other aspects of the culture can be better understood. For example the circle divided into quadrants of the Mescalero Apache illustrated below is a visual base metaphor for a space time continuum identifying at the same time the four cardinal directions, the four seasons, and the daily path of the sun from East to West. Life is conceived of as cyclical, as the seasons recur cyclically. Given this base metaphor, students can understand relationships among aspects of the culture, that there are four ages of man, four days of a female initiation rite, ritual clothing is divided into four quadrants, and the lodge is built following the path

Mescalero Apache Base Metaphor

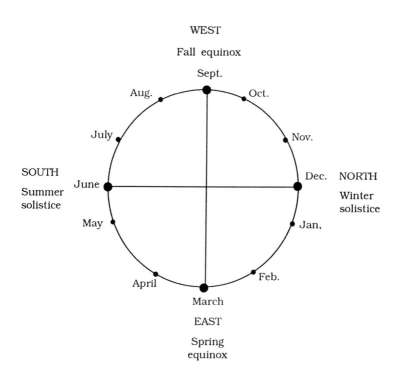

WEST

Fall equinox

Sept.

of the sun beginning with four postholes placed in the four cardinal directions.[5]

Visual symbols found in the visual and performing arts provide windows and doors opening to other cultures and other time periods. Direct encounters with the paintings and sculpture of other cultures allow students to see how people present themselves, their view of who they are and where they are in relation to other people, nature, technology, and the spiritual. Students can see for themselves that which is most important to another culture—and often the attitudes and feelings about an event that is presented.

Howard Gardner (1985) has suggested that the "introduction and mastering of symbolic systems . . . might even be regarded as the principal mission of modern educational systems" (1985:302). Cross-cultural literacy enhances the learning of symbol systems since students develop metacognitive skills in doing cross-cultural comparisons of visual and number systems. It may not be important for students to learn the Maya number system to use it in a practical way. But it is important for them to understand that there is more than one way to efficiently calculate, that numbers are part of a system, and that humans in many societies have developed number systems which show the brilliance of human minds.

In his seminal work on multiple intelligences, Gardner (1985) opened up the field of intelligence that had been narrowly defined as, "that which intelligence tests measure," (the linguistic and logical-mathematical intelligences) to seven distinct intelligences, including mastery of visual and musical symbol systems. Broadening the modes of schooling to include work and play with visual symbols reaches students with varying learning styles while it also enhances students' understanding of systems. Children can make sense of their world by drawing and representing through visual symbols the relationships between themselves and others and the world they experience.

Listening to the music and seeing the dances of a cultural group are ways students can directly encounter other cultures that engage more of the senses. Alan Lomax, an anthropologist and ethnomusicologist, brought the music of several African-American groups to a PBS series on the cultures that have created blues, cajun music, and jazz. Through listening, hanging out, interviewing, and asking some of the elders to share their history, both oral histories and memorabilia—where they live and how they celebrate and what they remember—Lomax brought social history to life in their own voices and music.

To develop respect for other ways of life it is helpful for students to see films, videos, or museum exhibits that show the total context of a culture—the human-made environment: dwellings, clothing, the extent of technology and the ecology: the natural resources, the physical environment, and the animals. To follow a day in the life of a child in another culture through a film or video is to see the multiple encounters between children and adults in that society. There may be children within the classroom, or in neighboring classrooms, or in the community, who can be resources for the questions students have after viewing a film. Pairs and small groups can research remaining questions in the library and write and share their findings.

Schools can also create museums within their school that provide historical depth to a culture, showing change over time. In a room about the size of a library, P.S. 123 in District 5, Manhattan, has created a museum called Harlem U.S.A. that celebrates the Harlem Renaissance. Enriched by donations from the staff and visitors, the museum has a parlor from the 1920's and different learning centers that focus on African-American authors, the Apollo theatre, photographs, tools and household articles from that era, *Life* and *Sepia* magazines, sports memorabilia, the front page of Marcus Garvey's newspaper, and photographs and clothing. The objects can be touched and poetry can be read aloud. The museum has the stuff to evoke creative writing and further research.

Introducing students to cross-cultural comparison in the classroom is not easy. By acknowledging that there are ways other than our own that are valid—maybe even better in certain contexts—we are allowing students to become more critical thinkers, to evaluate, to deal with ambiguity, and to identify the criteria on which they make

decisions. But isn't that one of the goals of our educational
system?

Alternative Futures

The dialogue for the future will face some compelling
issues. The current discourse on diversity will need to
work through competition and cooperation issues with
diverse populations. There will be tension and struggle
over control and creativity in education. Tools for
understanding between peoples will be required for survival.
The quality of role models and cross-cultural leadership
will affect the quality of relationships among peoples.
Learning how to celebrate uniqueness and commonalities
in the world will become a major arena in developing a
cross-cultural perspective. Individuals and groups will face
many challenges and choices in the future.

An important issue for the future will be the need
to face the insecurities of individuals and groups threatened
by multilingualism and multiculturalism. Most English Only
proponents are monolinguals; many who react negatively
to immigrant populations do so from the fear of competition
for employment; one minority group competes with another
minority group over short-term resources; some school
personnel resist change because the new tradition
challenges the old traditions. Dealing with diversity in the
schools through an anthropological approach of cross-
cultural literacy requires an investment in developing new
curricula, designing staff development programs, building
bridges between schools and communities, and a shift to
a more pro-active, humanistic goal for everyone.

Endnotes

1. Dr. Marietta Saravia-Shore, Director, Cross Cultural Literacy Center, Institute for Urban and Minority Education, Teachers College, Columbia University and Dr. Steven F. Arvizu, Dean, Graduate Studies and Research, California State University at Bakersfield.

2. A subsequent commissioned report by the New York State Social Studies Review and Development Committee, "One Nation, Many Peoples: A Declaration of Cultural Interdependence," in June, 1991, was approved by the New York State Regents.

3. See "Demystifying the Concept of Culture: Methodological Tools and Techniques," Monographs I and II by Margaret A. Gibson and Steven F. Arvizu, November 1978, Cross-Cultural Resource Center, Department of Anthropology, California State University, Sacramento.

4. Architecture Across Cultures: *An Interdisciplinary Cross-Cultural Curriculum.* Marietta Saravia-Shore. 1989. Cross-cultural Literacy Center, Institute for Urban and Minority Education. Teachers College, Columbia University.

5. Claire R. Ferrer and Bernard Second, Living the Sky, Aspects of Mescalero Ethnoastronomy, in *Archaeoastronomy in the Americas,* Ray A. Williamson, ed. Los Altos, Calif.: Ballena Press, 1981.

References

California Roundtable on Educational Opportunity
    1982   Statement on Competencies in English and Mathematics. Annual Report, The Academic Senates for the California Community Colleges, the California State University and the University of California.
Epstein, Noel
    1977   Language, Ethnicity and the Schools: Policy Alternatives for Bilingual Bicultural Education. Washington, D.C.: Institute for Educational Leadership, George Washington University.

Gardner, Howard
  1985   Frames of Mind: The Theory of Multiple Intelligences. New York: Basic Books.
Hayes-Bautista, David, Werner Schink and Jorge Chapa
  1988   The Burden of Support: Young Latinos in an Aging Society. Stanford: Stanford University Press.
Lakoff, George, and Mark Johnson
  1980   Metaphors We Live By. Chicago: University of Chicago Press.
Lyons, James J.
  1991   The View from Washington. NABE News. Washington, D.C.: National Association for Bilingual Education 14(5):1, 10–11, 16.
Ramirez, David
  1991   Study Finds Native Language Instruction Is a Plus. NABE News. Washington, D.C.: National Association for Bilingual Education 14(5):1, 20–22.
Sobol, Thomas
  1990   Memo from New York State Commissioner of Education re "A Curriculum of Inclusion." Albany: New York State Education Department. February 22.
Stanford University
  1989   Report of the University Committee on Minority Issues. Stanford: Stanford University.

CONTRIBUTORS

DR. STEVEN F. ARVIZU is Dean of Graduate Studies and Research and Professor of Anthropology at California State University, Bakersfield (CSUB), and a Scholar at the Tomas Rivera Center at the Claremont School. Dr. Arvizu has worked for several decades in program development, research, teaching, and administration related to cross-cultural education and community development. He directed the Mexican American Education Project and the Cross Cultural Resource Center at California State University, Sacramento, and the Career Beginnings Project for dropout prevention at CSUB. He was president of the Council on Anthropology and Education in 1980 and served on the CAE Executive Board and Committees for over a decade.

Dr. Arvizu spent many years working in the American Flag Territories in the Pacific through the Cross Cultural Resource Center, offering training, technical assistance, research and advocacy in the development of indigenously controlled education programs. The work at CCRC involved more than 60 different language and cultural communities. He co-directed, with Dr. Hernández-Chavez, a two-year NIE-supported research project entitled the Bilingual Education Community Study.

DR. ROBERTO LUIS CARRASCO (Ed.D. Harvard University) is Assistant Professor of Secondary Education at Arizona State University. His research interests are centered upon the ethnography of communication, particularly in school contexts. For the last five years he has focused on teachers' language use in bilingual classrooms.

More recently, his interests have expanded to include (1) second-language acquisition by non-native bilingual teachers and the re-acquisition of their native language by Chicano bilingual teachers, (2) language attrition of both native and second languages, and (3) the effects of metalinguistic, metacognitive, and metacultural knowledge on the acquisition of Spanish. In pursuit of these interests, Dr. Carrasco co-directed a three-year Title VII Bilingual Teacher Training and Research Project in which graduate student bilingual teachers were trained in classroom ethnographic research methods. These techniques enabled them to conduct their own observations and collect ethnographic data, to analyze their findings and writ up the results. This training and research project resulted in the development of a course and a book entitled *Spanish for the Bilingual Teacher* (Carrasco and Riegelhaupt, in press).

For the last three years, Dr. Carrasco has directed a five-week Summer Language and Culture Immersion Program in Guanajuato, Mexico, tailored specifically for pre- and in-service bilingual teachers. After many years of research and teaching, he and his colleague, Dr. Florence Riegelhaupt, have developed and approach to language and culture learning which they have termed META. META emphasizes the real-life experience of individuals during immersion and develops in them an awareness of personal growth in Spanish and a sensitivity toward the Mexican culture.

Dr. Carrasco is presently on academic leave from Arizona State University, researching the acquisition of language and culture by teachers during immersion and the effects of immersion in their teaching.

DR. JUDITH T. GUSKIN is President of Vision Quest Productions, based in Los Angeles. She has independently produced, directed, and written numerous documentaries, some aired on PBS. She was a founder and administrator of the Peace Corps and VISTA. At the time of writing, she was Adjunct Associate Professor of Anthropology, University of Wisconsin, Parkside, and one of four senior researchers on the Bilingual Education Community Study. Her publications include *Desegregation and Hispanic Students: A Community Perspective* (1980) and *Desegregation in Los Angeles* (1979).

Dr. Grace Pung Guthrie is a Project Director at the Far West Laboratory for Educational Research and Development in San Francisco. She is the author of the multilevel ethnography, *A School Divided: An Ethnography of Bilingual Education in a Chinese Community* (Lawrence Erlbaum Associates, 1985), and *Principles for Successful Multicultural Education* (University of the Pacific, 1991). She is also a co-editor of *Culture and the Bilingual Classroom: Studies in Classroom Ethnography* (Newbury House, 1981). She has also published numerous technical reports and actively engaged in disseminating research and evaluation findings on students-at-risk issues through speeches and workshops to practitioners. Dr. Guthrie holds a Ph.D. in educational psychology from the University of Illinois at Urbana-Champaign.

Dr. Eduardo Herández-Chávez is Assistant Professor of Linguistics, Department of Linguistics, University of Mexico, Albuquerque. He is a native of Nebraska, where he grew up as a farm worker in the sugar beet fields. He attended the University of Nebraska and received his B.A. in Spanish and Latin in 1956. Subsequently, he taught languages in California high schools for several years before entering graduate school at the University of California, Berkeley. In 1976, he obtained his Ph.D. in Linguistics with specializations in language acquisition and bilingualism.

Professor Hernández served as Director of the Chicano Studies Program at Berkeley between 1969 and 1971. He also taught linguistics at Stanford University for a number of years and was a Fulbright Lecturer at the Universidad de Santiago de Compostela. Professor Hernández is Director of the Instituto de Lengua y Cultura, an association of Chicano scholars engaged in collaborative research and community activities in language, arts, literature, and education.

Professor Hernández has written extensively in the areas of sociolinguistics, bilingualism, and education. His book of readings *El Lenguaje de los Chicanos*, and his work on code switching with John Gumperz have stimulated a great deal of scholarship in these areas.

Dr. Cathie Jordan is Research Anthropologist and head of the Anthropology Unit of the Kamehemeha Educational Research Institute in Honolulu. Before joining K.E.R.I. she worked for five years as a member of the Hawaiian Community Research Project, the first systematic study of modern Hawaiian culture, and co-authored a book based on that work. Her publications include *Culture, Behavior and Education: A Study of Hawaiian Americans* (1974), "Culture and Education" in *Perspectives in Cross-Cultural Psychology* (1979) and "The Selection of Culturally Compatible Classroom Practices" in *Educational Perspectives* (1981).

Dr. Abdil Abel Maldonado-Guzman was Assistant Professor at the Graduate School of Education of Pennsylvania State University, University Park, Philadelphia. He received his B.A. from the University of Puerto Rico in the fields of Anthropology, Sociology, and Geography. He earned a Master's degree in Geography and Anthropology from the University of Chicago and a second Master's and a Doctoral degree from Harvard University.

Dr. Herminio Martínez is Associate Dean of the School of Education and Educational Services at Baruch College of the City University of New York. He is also the Principal Investigator of the Multicultural Education Center. Prior to joining Baruch College, he was Director of the Division for Training, Evaluation and Social Services, Institute for Urban and Minority Education, Teachers College, Columbia University.

    Dr. Martínez has been a consultant in the field of cross-cultural education, program evaluation, testing, and educational policy to universities, government agencies, and professional organizations. He serves on numerous advisory boards and committees of civic and public institutions. He has taught courses in cross-cultural education, research and testing, urban education, second language instruction, and adult education at several institutions in the metropolitan area.

VERNAY MITCHELL, a Ph.D. candidate in anthropology at Teachers College, Columbia University, is a Research Associate at the International Center for Collaboration and Conflict Resolution, New York, and a consultant for the Academy for Educational Development, New York. She taught at the College of New Rochelle, New York, and Rutgers University, Newark, New Jersey, and has taught and written curriculum in public schools in New York and Massachusetts. A study of the British primary school system, on site in London and Birmingham, England, in 1978, whetted her interest in international studies. She is a 1985-86 Fulbright Scholar and lists her major areas of interest as anthropology and education, medical anthropology, and African development. Her work in qualitative research and program evaluation includes several studies conducted in Togo, West Africa, and consultant positions in various institutions and organizations such as Governor Cuomo's Task Force on Bias-Related Violence, the Center for Policy Research, Bellevue Hospital, the National Center for Research in Vocational Education and the National Centers for Disease Control. Her 1990 work, *Curriculum and Instruction to Reduce Racial Conflict*, was published by the ERIC Clearinghouse on Urban Education.

DR. LUIS C. MOLL is Associate Professor, College of Education, University of Arizona. Born in Santurce, Puerto Rico, he was awarded a Ph.D. in Educational Psychology/Early Childhood Development (1978) from the University of California, Los Angeles. He worked from 1979 to 1986 as a Research Psychologist at the Laboratory of Comparative Human Cognition, University of California, San Diego.

He has lectured at the Institute of Psychology, Moscow, USSR, at the Department of Psychology, Universidad Autónoma de Madrid, Spain, and the Department of Education, University of Puerto Rico. He served as Associate Editor, *American Educational Research Journal* (1985–1988), is Co-Editor, *The Quarterly Newsletter of the Laboratory of Comparative Human Cognition* (1983–present), and is Editor of *Vygotsky and Education*

(Cambridge Press, 1990), and of a forthcoming book (with S. Diaz), *Bilingualism, Literacy and Instructional Change: A Sociocultual Approach to Educational Research* (Ablex Corporation). His most recent research includes the study of Latino households' uses of knowledge and its implications for classrooms practice, and an analysis of biliteracy development in classroom contexts.

Since 1975 PEDRO PEDRAZA, JR. has held the position of Director of Research for the Language Policy Task Force of the Centro de Estudios Puertorriqueños, City University of New York. In this position he has participated in the conceptualization, planning, organizing, implementing, and publishing of results of three major research projects on language in the Puerto Rican community, including *Intergenerational Perspectives on Bilingualism: From Community to Classroom.* He has authored several articles and working papers and made numerous presentations to educators, researchers, and community members.

Pedro Pedraza, Jr. was born and raised in New York City. He graduated with a B.A. in Sociology from Occidental College, Los Angeles, and is presently engaged in completing his Ph.D. dissertation, "Ethnographic Observations of Language Use in El Barrio," at Columbia University. His area of specialization is the sociology of language. At present he resides in East Harlem with his two children.

DR. ALICIA POUSADA is currently Associate Professor at the Universidad de Puerto Rico, Hato Rey. She was born in Mt. Kisco, New York. She received her undergraduate degree in Languages and Literature at Hunter College in New York City, and her Master's degree and Ph.D. in Educational Linguistics at the Graduate School of Education of the University of Pennsylvania.

Dr. Pousada was a member of the Language Policy Task Force of the Centro de Estudios Puertorriquenos, Hunter College, City University of New York, from 1978 to 1985, where she was involved in planning and carrying out sociolinguistic research on the use of language in *El Barrio*, East Harlem. She is the author of several articles and reviews, as well as co-author of two major reports to the National Institute of Education entitled *Intergenerational Perspectives on Bilingualism: From Community to Classroom*, and *Speech and Ways of Speaking in a Bilingual Puerto Rican Community*.

DR. MARIETTA SARAVIA-SHORE, an educational anthropologist, is Associate Director of the Institute for Urban and Minority Education (IUME) and Director of the Cross-Cultural Literacy Center at Teachers College, Columbia University. Concern for interdisciplinary curricula led her to design *Modules for Teacher Trainers Implementing Multicultural Social Studies* (1976) and *Systems for Learning and Assessment of Bilingual Cross-Cultural Social Studies* (1977). In 1977 she initiated the course, Multicultural Education at Hunter College, CUNY Graduate School of Education. She earned a Columbia University Ph.D. in Anthropology and Education in 1986. Interest in the arts as processes for cross-cultural understanding prompted post-doctoral study in the program in Arts and Education at Teachers College and an invitation to teach the course, The Arts and American Education, for Teachers College at Simul University in Tokyo.

DR. MARIA E. TORRES-GUZMAN (Ph.D., Stanford University) is an Assistant Professor of Bilingual Education and Director of the Program in Bilingual/Bicultural Education at Teachers College, Columbia University. Her research interests include parental and community involvement in education, classroom ethnography, and the relationship between language, culture, and instruction. She has co-authored (with Bertha Perez) a book entitled *Learning in Two Worlds: An Integrated Spanish/English Biliteracy Approach* published by Longman.

DR. HENRY T. TRUEBA is a Professor in the Division of Education at the University of California, Davis. He is current editor of *Anthropology and Education Quarterly*. Dr. Trueba has a Ph.D. in social anthropology and has been involved in bilingual education research since 1969. For six years, he organized and directed one of the first doctoral programs with a concentration in bilingual education, at the

University of Illinois. He has contributed to more than sixty publications concerning the education of linguistic minority students, bilingual education, and the social context of instruction. Two of his well-known texts are *Bilingual Multicultural Education and the Professional: From Theory to Practice* (with C. Barnett-Mizrahi) and *Culture and the Bilingual Classroom: Studies in Classroom Ethnography* (with G. Guthrie and K. Au).

DR. DINAH VOLK is an Assistant Professor in the Early Childhood Education Program, Specialized Instructional Programs, Cleveland State University. She worked at the Institute for Urban and Minority Education, Teachers College, Columbia University, as a Coordinator of the Computer C.H.I.P.S. project, a computer training project for high school ESL teachers. Previously, she was Senior Project Associate with the Cross-Cultural Demonstration Project, in which she helped develop a bilingual, multicultural approach to elementary curriculum and to train parents and teachers in its implementation. Dr. Volk has taught at the early childhood level in monolingual and bilingual classrooms and at the graduate level in a teacher training program in bilingual education. She received her M.S. in Education from Bank Street College and her Ph.D. in Bilingual Education from New York University.

DR. ANA CELIA ZENTELLA is currently an Associate Professor at Hunter College of the City University of New York (CUNY) as well as the Graduate Center of CUNY. She received a Ph.D. in Educational Linguistics from the University of Pennsylvania. Her dissertation won First Place in the Outstanding Dissertations Competition sponsored by the National Advisory Council on Bilingual Education, 1982. Her research interest in Spanish-English code switching has led to studies of this phenomenon in East Harlem and Philadelphia, bilingual classrooms in the Bronx and high schools in Puerto Rico. Articles by Dr. Zentella include "Language Variety among Puerto Ricans," in *Language in the USA*, edited by Charles Ferguson and Shirley Brice Heath, Cambridge University Press, 1981, and "Spanish and English in Contact in the United States: The Puerto Rican Experience," in *WORD*, Vol. 33, Nos. 1–2, April–August 1982.

Index